KOREAN AMERICAN WOMEN

KOREAN AMERICAN WOMEN

From Tradition to Modern Feminism

Edited by
Young I. Song
and Ailee Moon

PRAEGER

Westport, Connecticut
London

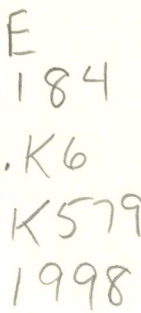

Library of Congress Cataloging-in-Publication Data

Korean American women : from tradition to modern feminism / edited by
   Young I. Song and Ailee Moon.
        p.   cm.
     Includes bibliographical references and index.
     ISBN 0–275–95977–5 (alk. paper)
        1. Korean American women—Social conditions.   I. Song, Young
   I. (Young In)   II. Moon, Ailee.
   E184.K6K579   1998
   305.42—DC21   97–26184

British Library Cataloguing in Publication Data is available.

Copyright © 1998 by Young I. Song and Ailee Moon

Library of Congress Catalog Card Number: 97–26184
ISBN: 0–275–95977–5

First published in 1998

Praeger Publishers, 88 Post Road West, Westport, CT 06881
An imprint of Greenwood Publishing Group, Inc.

Printed in the United States of America

The paper used in this book complies with the
Permanent Paper Standard issued by the National
Information Standards Organization (Z39.48–1984).

10 9 8 7 6 5 4 3 2 1

To our mothers,
Chong Ok Won and Ok Soo Kim,

with love and appreciation

Contents

Preface

From a widespread invisibility in history, literature, and feminist inquiries, minority women have recently been sought out to express themselves in feminist platforms. To some minority women, such as Korean American women, both the previous neglect and the recent tokenism of minority women result from a reluctance to deal seriously with the uniquely oppressed women's experiences along with the other minority women in the world.

To address issues related to Korean American women, the contributors to this book employ diverse approaches and perspectives. They do not describe feminist issues in similar voices. Whereas some suggest that progress is already under way, others focus on the history, culture, and ritual of Korean Americans and their political, social, and economic status in contemporary American society in an attempt to understand more clearly both how the Korean American community has been structured in the past, and what changes might be possible and desirable for the future of feminism. Everyone challenges the traditional Korean gender role differentiation and male dominance while maintaining strong attachment and commitment to Korean culture. The conflict, confusion, and tension between these two perspectives and struggles provide the framework for this anthology.

This collection is primarily the work of researchers who have lived and worked in the related areas for many years. Their contributions attest to the fact that feminist perspectives adapted and applied to Korean American communities are in the making. This book is not primarily one about the position of Korean American women across the United States. Rather this is an analysis of the debates between feminists and the voices of other Korean women in different situations. This book proposes the three strands of the debate that form the basis of an analysis of the arguments made by Korean feminists. It is the exploration within Western feminism concerning its direction and relevance to global feminism inclusive of Korean American feminism. Also, this book is the recognition of Korean feminists' concern regarding Euro-ethnocentrism and its ignorance of the specific experiences of minority women including Korean American women. Finally, this book debates between the non-feminist Korean population and feminists over whether feminism is a luxury or reality and whether feminism is a remedy of many past social ills or just another social experiment.

The authors of this anthology attempt to analyze beyond the triple oppression of gender, race, and status that defines Korean American women. It seems to be that gender, race, and status effects cannot be separated when explaining the lives of Korean American women. Some contributors have noted that the general invisibility of Korean American women has several related causes. The Korean culture has been able to ignore them because Korean women have not, until very recently, been a part of the power structure in Korean communities throughout the United States. The situation is not far different from the long-standing ignorance of white women's opinions, experiences, and talents. The difference is that white feminist women have also participated in ignoring ethnic and racial minority women, including Korean American women.

In the context of prevalent racial prejudice in the United States, we need to recognize the claim of minority women, such as Korean American women, for equal access to various social, economic, and political opportunities, support, and rewards as compared to white American women. The point is that the Korean feminist struggle has a specific ethnic, as well as gender relation, context. Some barriers to equal participation more directly affect the members of an excluded minority group. Korean American women, for example, confront all the ambivalence and complexities that present themselves to any potential participant in a movement for feminist social change. They are increasingly revealing ambivalent responses to this strong and enduring image of Korean American women. In reality, the strong image of Korean American women is in the face of oppression and overwork. The strength of Korean American women is a response to gender and racial oppression. This points to the significance of culture-based analyses in explaining the differential impact of institutional sexism, and of economic and political power.

Discussion in this anthology suggests that, on the whole, Korean American women live with the double barrier of gender and race, that occasionally Korean men are in a better position than white women within their respective communities. Given these two factors, it is by no means certain that the position of Korean American women can be better explained by racism than sexism. Gender, to some extent, creates a different quality and amount of social status, economic security, and political power. In this regard, many Korean American women claim that sexism is more important than racism in defining their situation. They further argue that sexism also has structural correlates to the limits in access to resources, more undesirable treatment toward women of color, and cultural stereotypes of Korean American women, all of which have contributed to maintaining and perpetuating their lower status in the American society.

While numerous factors differentially determine the experiences and lives of minority women in the United States, it is important to understand the preferences of Korean American women as well as the barriers to choices and opportunities they face in the context of cultural, social, economic, and political structures. Furthermore, many Korean American women may agree that one of the most serious barriers to Korean American feminism comes from the majority of Korean American men as well as from some women. Considering that Korean Americans have suffered from restricted access to power and resources in mainstream white society, it is ironic that Korean American men are even more reluctant than white men to accept the feminist anti-discriminatory ideas of equality, justice, and freedom for all men and women.

Though feminism in Korea has often been criticized as anti-traditionalism or extremism, Korean American feminism has seldom been studied. This book is one of the early contributions to a wider inquiry that, we hope, will expand exponentially in future.

Before closing, we want to acknowledge the unknown readers of this book to whom we wish increased knowledge to foster understanding of sexism to help promote feminism in the future.

We would also like to extend our thanks to each of the authors without whose contributions this book would not exist. And then our most hearty thanks goes to Nellie Byun, Sunja Kim, and Kristine Kim for their ceaseless dedication to help in many ways, any time, to prepare the manuscript.

Young I. Song
Ailee Moon
Danville, California

part one

INTRODUCTION: FROM TRADITION TO MODERN FEMINISM

The three chapters in Part One of this book provide the essential materials for understanding the theoretical and historical background of Korean traditionalism, Confucianism, and modern feminism.

In the first chapter, "A Woman-Centered Perspective on Korean American Women Today," Young I. Song begins with an observation that "Korean people tend to define women as wives, mothers, caregivers, or just simply as 'girls,' always with regard to their sexual behavior, rather than to their individuality as persons," and provides an overview of the five stages women experience as they strive toward full realization of a woman-centered perspective. By explaining what constitutes a woman-centered perspective and relating its significance and relevance to various aspects of Korean American women's lives, she clarifies the myths and realities of such a perspective.

In "A Critical Feminist Inquiry in a Multicultural Context," Sung Sil Lee Sohng investigates a culturally sensitive feminist framework to better understand women's experiences in their diversity and complexity, beginning with Korean American women's values and experience. She offers an insightful discussion of the extent to which mainstream feminist thinking has expanded to include perspectives and values of minority women, the problems and promises of reconciling the two perspectives into an integrated feminist framework, and how this expanded feminist framework can be applied to critical feminist inquiry, linking feminism and multiculturalism.

Korean American immigrant women continuously find themselves in a bind between traditional Confucianism and the prevailing social behavior in American society, according to El-Hannah Kim in "The Social Reality of Korean American

Women: Toward Crashing with the Confucian Ideology." Confucianism has not only been a great influence on Korean society but is inseparable from traditional Korean culture—it still is an integral part of mainstream Korean family and social life. El-Hannah Kim critically examines the role of this male-centered philosophy and its ill effects on the social conditions of Korean American women, and concludes that this Confucian model should not be practiced as a social necessity but only by choice.

1

A Women-Centered Perspective on Korean American Women Today

Young I. Song

> The way we conceptualize and define our problems has everything to do with the solutions we seek.
>
> —Morell (1981)

WHAT IS A WOMEN-CENTERED PERSPECTIVE?

A woman-centered perspective is presently in the process of formulation. The basic claim of this approach is that gender exerts a profound influence on all spheres of human experience, to an extent that has been insufficiently acknowledged and understood. Rethinking and redefining the problems of women, many Korean women have consciously set out on a radically divergent course in their search for solutions. The woman-centered perspective they seek to establish is about reframing gender and its relevance in the lives of Korean women and men.

Gender is a total experience for women. Korean people tend to define women as wives, mothers, caregivers, or just simply as "girls," always with regard to their sexual behavior rather than to their individuality as persons. The primary intention of a woman-centered perspective is to make women visible first and foremost as individual human beings. This requires a restructuring of thought and values. Women must become valued in and for themselves.

Making women visible also will require a greater understanding of the conflicts women experience, and of the demands placed upon them. This greater understanding of women will not be achieved without challenging currently held ideas about all aspects of society and the problems encountered in daily living by Korean women and men.

A woman-centered perspective proceeds from a basis of social equality, which cannot be achieved without the substantial modification of social dynamics that presently allow for, indeed foster, domination and control of some classes of people by others. But, rather than simply viewing individual men as the "enemy," a woman-centered approach defines the social institution of patriarchy, in all its forms, as the problem. Woman-centered approaches have provided varying interpretations of patriarchy, but the fundamental concept is that of a male-dominated social system characterized by hierarchical, dominant-subservient relationships between men and women.

Some theorists, dating from Plato, have maintained that patriarchy is the oldest form of the family. However, a line of thought originated in the nineteenth century by such sociologists and anthropologists as Benston (1969) and Engels (1972), and continued today by many contemporary woman-centered theorists, holds that patriarchy arose only after the demise of an original human family structure that was matrilocal and matriarchal in nature (Banks, 1981). Marxist and socialist feminists concur with this view. They believe that patriarchal structures as they exist today evolved as a consequence of the development of private property and, subsequently, capitalist economies. This perspective applied to Korean women at home and abroad offers suggestions on how societies motivated by values of conquest, competition, and acquisitiveness can engender life conditions that may predispose both men and women to toxic and addictive gender identities (Schmitt, 1987).

This chapter examines a range of stages women experience as they strive toward full realization of a woman-centered perspective. Although Korean women are the specific focus of this chapter, it should be apparent that a woman-centered approach is relevant to the widest range of cultural concerns. An explanation of what constitutes a woman-centered analysis follows.

Within patriarchal capitalist societies the dynamics of control and acquisition are paramount cultural forces that affect not only the workings of the economic system but also relationships between the sexes. Control by virtue of ownership becomes a generally recognized measure of personal status and worth. Hence, people are motivated to acquire something outside of themselves to provide them a sense of personal worth and importance. Yet, occupational segregation and sociocultural disadvantages have historically relegated women and ethnic minorities in the United States to social positions from which they could not easily gain access to the means for acquiring status and worth as measured by capitalist culture. Hence, an inherent frustration is engendered within capitalist patriarchy as individuals are taught to seek but are not able to acquire that which provides legitimacy and status.

Psychologically, over time, that frustration can produce feelings of inferiority and powerlessness. In turn, the impulse to deny these self-negating emotions can lead individuals to seek methods of numbing or supplanting their perceptions of themselves as powerless and worthless, through various addictive behaviors. During the initial stage, women accept traditional definitions of their proper social roles and potential as women. Women in this predawn state of cultural awareness adopt selective perception and/or denial to ward off cognitively dissonant information and experiences about their place in society. Their system of values is externally imposed by the male-dominated culture.

Who depends on who—women on men, or vice versa—is a question of judgment, relevant to understanding the paradoxes and contradictions in the lives of Korean women. The closer the dependency between men and women, the more likely women are to be abused. It is illogical for women to look to the men with whom they live for protection, because these are the men most likely to physically and sexually abuse them. But this painful reality is denied and carefully hidden.

Other dynamics associated with the predawn stage include being focused on ends rather than on means. In other words, women come to the self-defeating perception that no matter what they attempt to accomplish, or how they go about attaining their goals, they are bound to lose. This sets up a psychology of defeat, that only strengthens the hold of male domination and control. This dynamic ultimately can engender feelings of isolation, anomie, and despair on the part of women. It also precludes the promotion of affirmative values such as collective well-being.

Conformity is also a characteristic of patriarchal capitalism, which promulgates social control and the imposition of power over others. Hence, one's personal experience or philosophy is unimportant; what is rewarded is that which conforms to existing beliefs and norms.

During the second developmental stage of feminist consciousness, women experience events that cause them to begin questioning their assumptions. They become increasingly aware that things are not right with the world, yet they have difficulty in identifying the source of discordance. The dominant feeling they have is one of having been tricked or fooled, but by forces or agents yet unnamed.

Anger is necessary to propel the developments of women into the next stage. Indeed, the expression of anger is a primary goal during this stage, as is active involvement in some form of feminism. The experiences of women during this stage often involve much bitterness, and a conviction that men are the enemy. While anger is necessary and important, it may lead to inappropriate and ineffective actions, and to the submergence of personal values, priorities, and beliefs in order to fit into a new value system. Eventually, a woman-centered perspective must move on to an acceptance of a fragile internal balance between the external world and the self, to a transcendent triumph over anxiety and fear.

Many who would not in any clear way have identified themselves with the women's movement nevertheless have accepted that in many areas their case was substantiated and that change must come. What could not be achieved for the women of one generation is a goal for the next, and as research exposes area after area of inequality, education programs begin the desocialization of sex roles. Everything, from early reading schemes to sexual behavior, from career advice to ideas of parenthood, comes under scrutiny. We must strive to avoid handing down misleading stereotypes about the capabilities, appropriate education, and moral obligations of the different sexes.

We are therefore now seeing the quiet revolution of the fourth stage as offensive material is weeded out and replaced, but one more far-reaching than anything that took place in the heady days of discovery and consciousness-raising. It is in the middle of this quiet revolution when most women are called upon to make some response in their own lives to the ideas of the woman-centered approach, that many become confused. With traditional values still apparently upheld, but shifting beneath them, they are unable to say where they stand. Among these are single women, those married and with children, those contemplating marriage, those with adult families, those committed to a career, and those in student circles. The presentation and existence of alternative views and positions of women and their experiences come as the first crucial step in the emergence of a non-sexist, women-centered perspective. But even for women who want nothing more than to meet the demands of conscious choices, the struggle to achieve and maintain a "socially and culturally correct life" is made particularly difficult by the social context in which many women, and especially Korean women, lead their daily lives. Women in this fourth emergence stage have begun to forge their awareness of personal alternatives and their responsibility to make choices, but they may not yet see how they can make contributions to change society.

While viewing patriarchal relations, rather than individual men, as the prime target for change, women must acknowledge the importance of the class dimension of women's oppression. During this final psychosocial stage in establishing a woman-centered perspective, women also see where they stand in relation to other women moving through their own experiences of the first, second, third, and fourth stages. Solidification of a woman's sense of self is achieved, including a recognition of her personal needs and priorities and of her commitment to work for social change in ways appropriate for woman as individuals. The final stage of the woman-centered perspective is the end result of an internalization process experienced from the first to fourth state through taking part in actions necessary for social change.

Validating a woman-centered social approach also means claiming the right to define one's own direction and reality or indications of success rather than conforming to conventional criteria or norms. Finally, to see the personal as political means that experiences in one's personal life can be seen as the individualized outcome of societal inequalities. Additionally, this perspective means that the values and beliefs one holds, the goals one sets and the way one pursues one's life can be considered political statements. Utilizing a woman-centered perspective does not simply amount to a recipe of "add women and stir." Rather, it is a philosophy based on values of individual worth, an inherent connectedness to others, concern with collective well-being as well as a perspective that living is an ongoing process. Having provided a framework for understanding a woman-centered approach analysis, it is now appropriate to define what is meant by being women.

In fact no society ever returns to a former state. Discussion of the woman-centered approach to social thought is the antithesis of a patriarchal perspective. It is a "liberation" philosophy promoting nurturance of the self as well as concern with collective well-being. It is concerned with ending domination and resisting compression, so as to provide equality of opportunity regardless of one's demographic background. Values consonant with a woman-centered approach include working collaboratively, collectively, and cooperatively; valuing personal experiences; encouraging growth and development; caring for others; building supportive relationships as well as believing in the interconnectedness of people and events.

Although there have been many different definitions of woman-centered approaches to social theory, there are several premises common among them that have relevance to defining a woman-centered perspective. Those principles include eliminating false dichotomies and artificial separations; reconciling power; valuing process as equally important to product; validating renaming; and believing that the personal is political (Van Den Bergh & Cooper, 1986).

Eliminating false dichotomies is a reaction to patriarchal dynamics based on a "divide and conquer" model. In a woman-centered approach view, interconnectedness and relatedness are valued. For example, health has conventionally been separated into discrete entities (i.e., mental, physical, and spiritual). Woman-centered approach perspectives on health see one's well-being as the interrelatedness between those domains, whereby disease in one component engenders disease in all others. Reconceptualizing power is a central concern within the woman-centered approach analysis, as an alternative to the patriarchal notion of power as an energy of influence and responsibility that one uses in order to gain access to rights, resources, and opportunities. Valuing process equally to product means that the way in which one pursues a goal is an important as that goal's outcome. Competition and conquest are reinforced when only the ends are rewarded and the means to those ends are ignored (Van Den Bergh & Cooper, 1986).

The woman-centered approach is a response to structural questions which will not go away. There is widespread injustice to women in Korean society. The same issue crops up in family life, education, the law, the Church, and marriage; women are not respected as men's equals. They are frequently used and abused. Many women in fact experience not only frustration and discrimination but also real oppression at the hands of some men.

One could argue that the woman-centered approach in fact exacerbates the issue and makes women worse off. It is better to allow and encourage society to develop in such a way that justice will surface and the position of women will improve. I believe that, like most laissez-faire responses, this is unrealistic. To start with, "creating the right climate" is a very active endeavor. But the situation is that the problems are getting worse. In some areas, women are now shown less respect and concern, and differences between the sexes are more emphatic than they were some years ago. This is symptomatic of a widespread social deterioration.

Another approach is to say that these problems can be met on an individual level. Marriage guidance counselors should be available to help a woman with a "husband problem." School teachers should keep an eye open for early male chauvinism in the classroom. Women should not work for bosses who do not treat them with respect. More women ought to stand for Parliament to strengthen the female presence there. Yet, although these measures might tackle immediate issues, the problem is clearly much bigger than this since the patriarchal emphasis of our society means that the unjust ways many men behave toward women is legitimated in legal economic structures. It is embedded in attitudes and stereotypes. Frequently, women who object to all of this are pilloried; their womanliness is challenged because they will not have it defined for them by a male-dominated culture. An individual response then can only work away at small areas. The problem is also an overall structural one, and as such needs a coherent structural response.

One crucial feature of the stance we are adopting here is that a woman-centered approach is committed not just to the liberation of women, but to the liberation of men also. What is more, this liberation is not only from class oppression and work alienation, but also from the very slavery that a corrupted, male-dominated culture has produced. Cultural stereotypes have prevented men, too, from knowing real freedom. Many Korean men throughout Korea and the United States still think it unmanly to weep, to show remorse, to express emotion in a way that will be noticed. So many Korean men feel the need to distance themselves as far as possible from their feelings. In our rationalistic, cerebral age a display of feelings is either theatrical, indulgent, or indicates that a person is out of control. The only feelings men are allowed to exhibit are ones of anger, irritation or impatience.

It is not surprising then that embedded in many marital problems is a husband's inability to show affection and share himself in a deep and personal way. He may also see his marriage as secondary to work or leisure, and not be accustomed to investing time and energy in it. Women, socialized since childhood into making friendships and frequently meeting other women on a more familiar and personal level, often find marriage dissatisfying because the relationship stays superficial, and basic needs of companionship, warmth, sharing, and affection are not met. Although many men feel they show their affection through sex, women who are wanting an intimate relationship of a broader and deeper kind see sexual affection on its own as shallow. But it is not only with women that men are crippled by the stereotypes that have been developed in them.

Relationships between men often deteriorate into competitiveness and assertion where pride dominates, and no one dares to admit being wrong or making a mistake. Patriarchal values of dominance and power-seeking have their grips on men, whether at work, driving a car, or in the home, and enslave them as much as women. The growth of men's groups where men can relax together and try to verbalize their feelings of frustration, happiness, sorrow, or being let down testifies how many men themselves are concerned enough to escape from the rigid male roles prescribed. The difficulty some of them experience initially in such groups betrays the tenacity with which these attitudes are held.

A woman-centered approach is not, therefore, wanting any power struggle with men. That would be entirely foreign to their agenda. Nor are they wanting to construct an all-female reality that washes out its involvement with the other sex. The message they bring is a message of liberation, and it is for men also. So what, more comprehensively, does this liberation, mean? It does not mean freedom to do what one wants, or even independence from the other sex. For-given men and women are free to pursue gentleness, patience, peace, and self-control in their relationships with one another.

Injustice to women is not rooted in one sphere but is present in every aspect of life. A woman-centered perspective must therefore initiate research and direction for change in each sphere. In the areas of literature and education, concerns very different from those in marriage or work bring a different set of issues to consideration. Useful research could be done into teaching methods, into school curricula, and into school reading materials which would begin to redress the assumption of male supremacy. The way we are taught and the assumptions we hold about how we learn constitute a very important field for woman-centered investigatory approaches, and should be of fundamental emphasis in our agenda. Non-sexist resocialization will be something deeper and something which will be essentially critical of the assumptions of the day, however much they may be part of our Korean culture.

REFERENCES

Banks, Olive. (1981). *Faces of Feminism.* New York: Oxford University Press.

Benston, Margaret. (1969). "The Political Economy of Women's Liberation." *Monthly Review,* 21(4), September, pp. 13-27.

Engels, Friedrich. (1972). *The Origin of the Family, Private Property, and the State.* New York: International Publishers.

Morell, Carolyn. (1981). "Weaving a Feminist Social Work Practice: The Experience of Women Focus." *Focus on Women: Journal of Addictions and Health,* 2(1), Spring, pp. 38-47.

Schmitt, Richard. (1987). *Introduction to Marx and Engels.* Boulder, CO: Westview Press.

Van Den Bergh, N., & L. Cooper. (1986). *Feminist Visions for Social Work.* Silver Spring, MD: NASW.

2

A Critical Feminist Inquiry in a Multicultural Context

Sung Sil Lee Sohng

Feminism as ideology advocates that women should have political, economic, and social rights equal to those of men. The feminist movement since the 1960s in the United States has been involved in a number of issues to help women: equal pay for work of equal worth, revision of Social Security and pension plans to make them fair to women, more support for quality of life issues such as child care, health care, and education, and a number of other issues. Minority women share many of the same feminist goals and are increasingly aware that their constricted job opportunities and lower pay reflect gender discrimination as much as race discrimination. Despite these commonalities, however, women of color are likely to interpret their experiences within a framework different from that of mainstream feminists and to assign different priorities to feminist goals.

Are the values of the feminist movement compatible with Korean American values? Should we choose, or at least prioritize, between our Korean identity on one hand and our belief in equality for women on the other hand? Can we be an integral part of the Korean American community and an integral part of the feminist movement? Do we have a unique contribution to make to the feminist movement because of our ethnic values and experiences?

This chapter aims to explore these enduring tensions and points of difference in orientation and priorities among Korean American women and other women of color in the United States. This chapter is based on two basic premises articulated by Lavender (1986): (1) that females are entitled to equality with males, and that barriers that limit the opportunity for this equality should be removed; and (2) that people of color are entitled to be equal partners in American society without having to give up all of their identity, and that barriers that limit the opportunity for this equality should be removed. As Staples (1973), an African American feminist, states, it is not a question of whether it is black liberation or women's liberation that black women need, but rather that she needs both. Feminists must recognize the valid diversity of ethnic values and identities, and minority communities must recognize the valid concerns of feminists.

This chapter is concerned with a broad conceptual framework to integrate these concerns into feminist theory and inquiry. Starting from a Korean American woman's values and experience as a point of departure, attention is primarily given to the development of a culturally sensitive feminist framework to better understand women's experiences in their diversity and complexity. Three major themes are of special interest in shaping the discussion: (1) the extent to which mainstream feminist thinking and the feminist movement have expanded to include perspectives and values of minority women, and the extent to which women of color have contributed to feminist goals; (2) the problems and promises of reconciling the two perspectives into an integrated feminist framework, derived from the interweaving concepts of gender, race, and class; and (3) how this expanded feminist framework can be applied to critical feminist inquiry, particularly with women of color, linking feminism and multiculturalism. It is hoped that this new feminist scholarship can build new alliances with women of color in furthering a more equitable feminist value system.

WOMEN AND OPPRESSION

Feminist science questions philosophical and political traditions, and aims to change cultural values and attitudes and their ideological and institutional manifestations. Feminist theories arose out of a growing recognition that women's lives, their history, their struggles, and their ideas were absent altogether from established science (Ardener, 1975; Eichler, 1987; Harding, 1986; Oakley, 1981). As Smith (1978) describes: "It means that our experience has not been represented in the making of our culture . . . the concerns, interests, experiences forming 'our' culture are those of men in positions of dominance whose perspectives are built on the silence of women" (p. 282). The lack of knowledge about women's lives, past and present, needs to be remedied by new observations, new sources, and first-hand experiences of women themselves. In the course of making the invisible visible, feminist scholars and activists assert that knowledge building should be characterized by female-centered thinking, action, and experience.

A defining assumption in this female-centered framework is the proposition that "all women" share, by virtue of being women, a common experience of oppression (Friedan, 1973; Oakley, 1972; Rich, 1976). These common experiences derive, not from supposed biological facts, but from "socially established" gender relations. Gender relations are characterized by patriarchy in which the role divisions between gender groups grant fewer duties and more benefits to men than women. As Millett (1970) observes, the sexual division of labor doesn't stop at the bedroom or kitchen door, it radiates powerful influences on all aspects of social life: "Our society, like all other historical civilizations, is a patriarchy. The fact is evident at once if one recalls that the military, industry, technology, universities, science, political office, and finance—in short, every avenue of power within the society, including the coercive force of the police, is in male hands" (p. 25).

Furthermore, feminists contend that the differences between men and women's appointed activities generate different presuppositions about who they are and what their attitudes and behaviors will be. These assumptions then affect all their activities. Using these points of departure, feminists challenge the assumptions that some kinds of jobs are "naturally" suited to men and others to women, arguing that these "womanly" traits were part of the social transformation of the bourgeois home and workplace (Pateman, 1988; Weedon, 1987).

A central theme running through various theoretical perspectives in feminism is that gender relations are the primary structuring principle in social life and extend into the formulation of self images, social attitudes, academic attitudes and practices, and concepts and definitions of reality.

Unraveling of "Common" Oppression

While these analyses of women's oppression teach many important truths, the assumed unity under the proposition, "woman is oppressed" has a number of extremely problematic aspects, both theoretical and political. Are all women oppressed to the same degree and in the same way? Who or what oppresses them? Where does this oppressive power come from?

A patriarchal and sexist framework does not explain women's lives in all their diversity and complexity of social reality. Millions of American women share not only the problems of their sex but also those of being African, Native, Puerto Rican, Mexican, or Asian American, and in most cases of being poor. The exploitation of the labor of people of color, for example, has shaped the lives of the women in these groups. First, the constricted options for racial ethnic men meant their families incurred a lower standard of living than white families and varied from dominant patriarchal forms. Second, the economic situation of racial ethnic people forced women into the labor market, where at the same time they were limited by their color to the least desirable and remunerative jobs.

Korean American women like many other women of color have been partners in bread-winning activities ever since moving to the United States. Often, they work more hours than men and in more adverse conditions while the traditional division of labor persists (Bonacich, Hossain & Park, 1987). Yet, they are hesitant at viewing their men as necessarily the oppressors, since both they and their men suffer from a variety of social and economic inequalities. Rather, they tend to feel sympathy for their husbands and other men who live in similar circumstances. Their oppressors often have been women as well as other men.

By claiming gender as the central determinant of oppression and social change, mainstream feminist scholarship and the women's movement largely ignore racial, ethnic, and class dynamics that cause women of color, among others, to endure different oppressions. They underestimate the extent to which the gender experience of a working-class woman, for example, is different from the gender experience of an upper-class woman. Similarly, a Korean American woman has both racial and gender experiences that differ substantially from those of a white woman. In spite of their passivity in public, social, and occupational worlds, Korean and Asian women have fulfilled and established a strong and stable role in their culture.

Yet, all these differences are obscured by the monist framework, overlooking the diversity of values and the extent to which concepts such as family and motherhood are valued differently. As Stanley and Wise (1983) point out, the "woman" used in feminist writings actually reflected the experiences and analyses of white, middle-class, heterosexual, First World women only. This gender-focused, middle-class approach characterizes to a large extent the policy and issue orientations of the contemporary feminist movement in the United States.

A Silenced Feminist Standpoint

At the outset of the women's liberation movement, African American feminists and woman of color were reluctant to form enduring links with white feminists groups because they saw the narrow base of the feminist movement. Sidel (1978) notes that working-class women criticized the women's movement for being too individualistic and for putting too much emphasis on personal fulfillment relative to family and communal commitments. Black feminists and minority women criticized that the white feminist leaders ignored racism as a central factor in American life for communities of color. In the eyes of women of color, white women share the privileges of white males' dominant status, so that for women of color to focus on sexual discrimination would be to belittle the crucial nature of racial discrimination. La Rue (1970) forcefully expresses this point of view:

The American white woman has had a better opportunity to live a free and fulfilling life, both mentally and physically, than any other group in the United States. The surge of "common oppression" rhetoric and propaganda may lure the unsuspecting into an intellectual alliance with the goals of women's liberation, but it is not a wise alliance. It is not that women ought not to be liberated from the shackles of their present unfulfillment, but the depth, the extent, the intensity, the suffering and depravity of the real oppression blacks have experienced can only be minimized in an alliance with women who heretofore suffered little more than boredom, genteel repression, and dishpan hands. (p. 36)

African American women's experiences highlight the tension experienced by many minority women. Speaking for Mexican Americans, Chavez (1972) says, "In contrast to some of the white women of the Liberation Movement, Mexican American women want unity with their men. . . . We must rely on each other to fight the injustices of the society which is oppressing our entire ethnic group" (p. 82).

For Korean American women, there is a general response to the feminist movement that is similar to that of African and Mexican Americans. They are not likely to divorce themselves from their cultural heritage or be alienated from their men. Korean cultural heritage values strong family ties and respect for the family as an institution. Native American women, Thornton (1977) notes, could not identify with the women's movement of this time period because of its emphasis on the secularized American values of individualism and materialism. For most Native Americans, various familial, religious, economic, and political institutions are closely related and fused with each other. Even though oppressed by poverty and limited to unskilled jobs, Comer (1970) notes that Native American women have much influence in the home and in some tribal affairs. "Our feminism," Lichtenstein (1983) states, "comes from a sense of real importance, of knowing you are a very intimate and strong part of the community, the social structure, and the family" (p. 92). The enemy is not their men, but the inequalities structured by the government agencies and the larger society. Often, the absence of women of color from the organized feminist movement has mistakenly been attributed to a lack of feminist consciousness. In actuality, Davis (1981) argues, past feminist refusal to draw attention to and attack racial hierarchies have excluded black women and women of color from the mainstream women's movement. In spite of the debates over the relative importance of the two identities, the rise of feminism undoubtedly caused women of color to take a closer look at their men. For example, Asian women's identity has undergone change in recent decades. Their participation in the labor force and emphasis on education for males and females in Asian American communities led to a new identity for Asian American women (Amerasia, 1977). In the mid-1970s, they became more aware of the interests of the feminist movement. "Instead of alienating our men from ourselves," Payton-Miyazaki (1971) argues, "we can free them from our traditional expectations of them to achieve, to earn a living, and to succeed in an already sick society" (p. 18). Asian women can allow more room for Asian men to feel and choose what they want for themselves. At the same time, she calls for cooperation with Western women to help fulfill the sisterhood of all women.

Native American women have been in the forefront of a quiet revolution among women in a world more often associated with poverty and despair than with success. The return of young, educated Naranjo women from white society back to their ancestral pueblos represents a significant trend. Lichtenstein (1983) notes that they not only make art but raise their children and participate in traditional ceremonies. They are proof that strong family and community roles are compatible with careers and financial independence.

To formulate a workable feminist theory, we must incorporate the insights of feminism into a broader conceptual framework which retains the integrity of the gender focus while equally highlighting the impact of ethnic and racial diversity and class differentiation in the multicultural environment of our society.

THE INTERLOCKING NATURE OF OPPRESSION

Rejecting the "common identity of women" thesis, minority feminists theorize a feminist discourse grounded in the relationship between the social and individual and the interlocking nature of race, gender, and class oppression (Almquist, 1989; Beale, 1970; Davis, 1981; Dill, 1983; Higginbotham, 1983; hooks, 1984, 1989; Lewis, 1977; Lorde, 1984; Murray, 1970; Steady, 1981). Almquist (1989) writes:

While there are many forces that divide, individual women do not and cannot compartmentalize their lives. . . . They are not members of minorities first and women second. Nor are they women first and members of minorities second. They are individuals who have incorporated a whole constellation of roles, characteristics, and experiences into their self-concepts. (p. 439)

In real life, people aren't gender-affected in one part of their lives and racially affected in another. Instead they simultaneously participate in ideological, economic, and social systems. At a particular time gender may have more influence on molding a person's consciousness and behavior than class, or vice versa. But these influences must co-exist. Only by examining the total context within which women of color live can one unravel the relationship of the factors impinging on their lives.

Speaking for African American women, Dill (1983) and others point out that the choice between identifying as black or female is a product of "either/or" dualistic thinking that suppresses alternative views. Such dualistic thinking invariably leads to a myopic, one-dimensional viewpoint. The continued importance of class, patriarchal or racial divisions perpetuates choices both within women's consciousness and within the concrete realities of women's daily lives. Such dichotomous oppositional thinking is what Collins (1991) calls "a philosophical linchpin" in systems of race, class, and gender oppression because it fails to recognize the connections among the dualities and undermines solidarity among them.

In analyzing conflicting feminist positions and political strategies, Scott (1988) suggests that the critical feminist position must always involve the systematic criticism of the operations of categorical difference, the exposure of the kinds of exclusions and inclusions and its attendant hierarchies, and a refusal of their ultimate "truth." However, she states, this refusal should not be in the name of an equality that rests on differences.

The presence of women of color in the feminist movement has influenced the movement to embrace a diverse set of goals and a diverse set of supporters. This creative tension and the problems of integrating conflicting values may lead to instability, disorganization, and internal argument in the growing stages. But, in the process, Lavender (1986) argues, the base can be expanded, allies can be gained, and long-range strength can be gained.

INCORPORATING A MULTICULTURAL PERSPECTIVE INTO FEMINIST RESEARCH

Seeking to understand an interconnected reality as a conceptual framework for feminist scholarship, feminist researchers are challenged by a number of issues and questions around what specific groups of women and men do, why, with what resources, and within what cultural, political, economic, and familial contexts. How do we choose what is most appropriate for our own contexts? How do we recognize and use notions of gender difference and yet make arguments for equality? In raising these questions, many minority feminists criticize a number of problematic issues in the current state of feminist research. First, they note the neglect and exclusions of their histories and life situations in much of feminist research. Although feminist research on women in the last two decades has produced many useful theoretical and empirical studies, too often the emergent body of knowledge excludes women of color and working-class women (Zinn et al., 1986). As Scott (1982) points out, "From reading the literature, one might easily develop the impression that black women have never played any role in this society" (p. 85). Similarly, when white feminists produce generalizations about "women," women of color routinely ask, "Which women do you mean?"

We cannot develop theories of gender oppression if we do not incorporate the experiences of a large segment of women. Refocusing our attention to the major omissions and distortions concerning women of color could influence feminist scholarship to a great extent as it leads to reflection on racist and ethnocentric notions in one's own terms of reference, concepts, and themes. It is in the spirit of this quest that ethnic women's studies take their significance.

A second issue is the inadequacy of using old racial paradigms to deal with a new, multicultural reality. Pioneers in ethnic studies criticized the prevailing racial paradigm based on the assimilation-acculturation theory. They argue that the theory focuses on adaptation of the minority group toward the dominant society. Researchers working from this framework stress "cultural factors" (e.g., language and customs) in the ethnic community hindering this adaptation, while downplaying "institutional barriers" (e.g., institutional racism) in the dominant society. This paradigm also sees assimilation-acculturation as basically a one-way process; the minority group is influenced by the dominant society, but not vice versa. The theory ignores the important ways that "minorities" impact the "majority." But more importantly the theory completely misses significant changes that are occurring in American society of the 1990s, namely, the redefinition of American identity as "minorities" become the new majority. In this transformation, distinct new cultures are emerging—Native American, African America, Asian American cultures, and so on. Yet, most mainstream writers and researchers continue to approach communities of color from old systems of thinking.

If communities of color do not want to consent to our own scientific omission and distortion, then we must have a basis upon which we can stand, from which we can be sure of reality, and from which we can judge theories opposed to our own experience. It is in this sense that the study of women of color in their multicultural contexts takes on its theoretical and political significance.

CRITICAL FEMINIST INQUIRY: TOWARD A NEW VALUE SYSTEM

The foregoing discussions on feminist theory and the feminist movement point to a growing awareness that there are different dispositions toward the world. The coming of age of multiculturalism and the coming of age of women are occurring in the United States today. Women of color can act as catalysts for a merger of the two movements and build a natural alliance by joining these forces. A large group of women of color, mostly uninvolved in the current feminist movement, can be the major source of new support in the coming years.

The argumentation, debate, and cross-fertilization concerning tensions and conflicts among diverse feminist goals and supporters have a complementary quality, which makes for a more serious debate about feminism and the feminist movement. From this understanding, I outline a critical feminist inquiry, linking critical feminist scholarship with multiculturalism. The proposed framework is only a road map. It is intended to set out a direction and point to a destination, but the journey itself has only begun, and much of the landscape through which we will travel is still to be discovered.

Four dimensions frame the critical feminist inquiry. First, drawing upon insights from the feminist critique of science, the critical stance incorporates history as an integral part of the study methodology. I use the notion of history not as a chronology of events or in mere deference to context. History is, as Popkewitz (1990) conceptualizes, "to acknowledge the present as a heritage not only of physical goods but also of social forms and knowledge" (p. 50). For example, research which only documents differences between the sexes or races offers no understanding of why those differences exist or how such differences may be attenuated. A critical inquiry would present minority women's behavior with attention to the opportunity structures shaping their lives. Women's perceptions of their choices and their places in society become a critical part of the relationship between the working of oppression and minority women's actions. This approach involves more than just a different point of view upon which to base a historical account. This approach examines the historical genesis of a social system and shows how oppressive structures have emerged. As a result of a new perspective gained from such analyses, feminist scholarship reappraises minority women's issues, reduces the distortion and fragmentation of knowledge about their experience, and reconstructs their history.

Closely related to the historically grounded analyses is the use of feminist insights for the processes of social change. The construction of more appropriate social conditions involves making history fragile (Popkewitz, 1990). Human possibility, as feminism believes, occurs through understanding that gender norms and their attendant social regulations are formed through struggle rather than given as an inevitable and unalterable present. This critical inquiry confronts prevailing social practices by being continually skeptical of stereotypes, taken-for-granted patterns, and public rhetoric in our daily lives. In this context, Callaway (1981) conceptualizes feminist inquiry as "revision, an act of entering an old text from a new critical direction, thus bringing out what is not yet visible, a new ordering of human relation" (p. 457). In this process, the inquiry can provide a source of social consciousness.

Third, the critical stance has a cultural dimension. Ethnic cultural heritage—folklore, popular knowledge, or popular wisdom—is not usually codified but is the practical, vital, and empowering knowledge that has allowed minority woman to survive, interpret, create, produce, and work. Such knowledge remains outside the formal scientific structure and is constantly being devalued and suppressed by the dominant science. An emerging interest in ethnic cultures, a distinct sense of peoplehood, means of survival, and the role of creative expressions in sustaining minority women's self-valuation are important dimensions in countering the devaluation of their histories and life situations by the dominant society. Recent studies on minority mothers as mediators between the competing offerings of an oppressive dominant culture and a nurturing Asian American value system provide another example. Gee (1971) notes that "in America quietness and modesty tend to be equated with weakness, but with Japanese women quietness and modesty are sure signs of strength" (p. 15). Kitagawa (1967) notes that when the Japanese Americans were forcibly interned in camps in the United States during World War II, the women dealt with the ordeal much better than the men.

Exploring cultural influence and multiple values in women's reality can help us understand diverse relationships between women's ethnic heritage, their consciousness of oppression, and the actions they take in dealing with oppressive structures. Therefore, an analytical model exploring the relationship between oppression, consciousness, and activism requires attention to cultural heritage and its impact on women's self-definition and self-valuation.

Fourth, a claim of value-free research would be especially inappropriate in a critical inquiry whose purpose is to analyze links between economic, political, and cultural factors, and gain insight into the dynamic relationships between groups of women. A starting point for a critical inquiry recognizes alternative concepts themselves as political claims instead of granting them privileged status as universal truths. For the critical feminist researcher, knowledge is not just about finding out about the world but it is about changing it. It is important, therefore, that critical feminist research engages praxis. Praxis means practical reflective activity; it is what changes the world. So the subjects of any feminist inquiry are analyzed in terms of their potential for developing action. Knowledge does not reside in a cupboard or on a bookshelf. Knowledge exists in our everyday lives. We live out knowledge and constantly transform it through what we do, as much as it informs what we do. For critical feminist research this means that an analysis of oppressive social structures is in itself a political act. Knowledge cannot be shelved, it becomes part of our life, and informs our actions which engage these structures. The activity of engagement is at the root of further development. Critical feminist research is thus intrinsically praxiological.

In conclusion, the emergent feminism is a new challenge to domination, to end all forms of oppression. Feminism is thus opening the way to move beyond simple pressure for women's inclusion in the world. The critical feminist inquiry outlined above is one explicit attempt to get closer to a truth that is freer from the distortions of present racist, sexist, and elitist scholarship, and to move toward a new level of sensitivity, understanding, and equality for all.

REFERENCES

Almquist, E. M. (1989). "The Experiences of Minority Women in the United States: Intersections of Race, Gender, and Class." In J. Freeman, ed., *Women: A Feminist Perspective*. Mountain View, CA: Mayfield, pp. 414-445.

Amerasia. (1977). *Selected Statistics on the Status of Asian American Women*, 4(1).

Ardener, E. (1975). *Perceiving Women*. London: Dent.

Beale, F. (1970)."Double Jeopardy: To Be Black and Female." In Toni Cade, ed., *The Black Woman*. New York: Signet, pp. 90-110.

Bonacich, E., M. Hossain, & J. Park. (1987). "Korean Immigrant Working Women in the Early 1980's." In Eui-Young Yu & Earl H. Phillips, eds., *Korean Women in Transition*. Los Angeles: Center for Korean American and Korean Studies, California State University, pp. 219-247.

Callaway, H. (1981). "Women's Perspectives: Research as Revision." In P. Reason and J. Rowan, eds., *Human Inquiry*. New York: Wiley, pp. 457-471.

Chavez, Jennie V. (1972)."Women of the Mexican American Movement." *Mademoiselle*, April, 82.

Collins, P. H. (1991)."Learning from the Outsider Within: The Sociological Significance of Black Feminist Thought." In M. Fonow & J. Cook, eds., *Beyond Methodology*. Bloomington: Indiana University Press, pp. 35-59.

Comer, Nancy. (1970)."Hokahe!" *Mademoiselle*, October, 158-159, 195-198.

Davis, A. (1981). *Women, Race, and Class*. New York: Random House.

Dill, B. (1983)."Race, Class, and Gender: Prospects for an All-Inclusive Sisterhood." *Feminist Studies*, 9: 131-150.

Eichler, M. (1987)."The Relationship between Sexist, Non-Sexist and Woman-centered and Feminist Research in the Social Sciences." In G. Nemiroff, ed., *Women and Men: Interdisciplinary Readings on Gender*. Montreal: Fitzhenry & Whitside, pp. 21-53.

Friedan, B. (1973). *The Feminine Mystique.* New York: W. W. Norton.

Gee, Emma. (1971). "Isseis: The First Women." In Emma Gee & Jeanne Quan, eds., *Asian Women.* Berkeley: University of California Press.

Harding, S. (1986). *The Science Question in Feminism.* Ithaca, NY: Cornell University Press.

Higginbotham, E. (1983). "Laid Bare by the System: Work and Survival for Black and Hispanic Women." In J. Kritzman, ed., *Class, Race and Sex: The Dynamics of Control,* pp. 200-215. Boston: G. K. Hall.

hooks, bell. (1984). *From Margin to Center.* Boston: South End Press.

_____. (1989). *Talking Back: Thinking Feminist, Thinking Black.* London: Sheba Feminist Publishers.

Kitagawa, Daisuke. (1967). *Issei and Nisei: The Internment Years.* New York: Seabury Press.

La Rue, Linda. (1970). "The Black Movement and Women's Liberation." *The Black Scholar,* May, 36-42.

Lavender, Abraham D. (1986). *Ethnic Women and Feminist Values: Toward a New Value System.* New York: University Press of America.

Lewis, D. (1977). "A Response to Inequality: Black Women, Racism and Sexism." *Signs,* 3, 339-361

Lichtenstein, Grace. (1983). "Three Generations of Naranjo Women." *Ms.,* April, 59-60, 192.

Lorde, A. (1984). *Sister Outside.* Trumansburg, NY: Crossing Press.

Millett, K. (1970). *Sexual Politics.* Garden City, NY: Doubleday.

Murray, P. (1970). "The Liberation of Black Women." In Mary Lou Thompson, ed., *Voices of the New Feminism.* Boston: Beacon Press, pp. 87-102.

Oakley, A. (1972). *Sex, Gender and Society.* London: Maurice Temple Smith.

_____. (1981). "Interviewing Women: A Contradiction in Terms." In H. Roberts, ed., *Doing Feminist Research.* Boston: Routledge & Kegan Paul, pp. 30-61.

Pateman, C. (1988). *The Sexual Contract.* Stanford, CA: Stanford University Press.

Payton-Miyazaki, Yuriko. (1971). "Three Steps Behind and Three Steps Ahead." In Emma Gee & Jeanne Quan, eds., *Asian Women.* Berkeley: University of California Press.

Popkewitz, T. S. (1990). "Whose Future? Whose Past? Notes on Critical Theory and Methodology." In Egon Guba, ed., *The Paradigm Dialog.* Newbury Park, CA: Sage, pp. 46-66.

Rich, A. (1976). *Of Woman Born.* New York: W. W. Norton.

Scott, Joan. (1988). "Deconstructing Equality-versus-Difference: Or, the Use of Post-structuralist Theory for Feminism." *Feminist Studies,* 14(1): 33-50.

Scott, Patricia. (1982). "Debunking Sapphire: Toward a Non-racist and Non-sexist Social Science." In Gloria Hull, Patricia Scott, & Barbara Smith, eds., *But Some of Us Are Brave.* Old Westbury, NY: Feminist Press.

Sidel, Ruth. (1978). *Urban Survival.* Boston: Beacon Press.

Smith, Dorothy. (1978). "A Peculiar Eclipsing: Women's Exclusion from Man's Culture." *Women's Studies International Quarterly,* 1 (4): 281-295.

Stanley, L., & S. Wise. (1983). *Breaking Out: Feminist Consciousness and Feminist Research.* London: Routledge & Kegan Paul.

Staples, Robert. (1973). *The Black Women in America.* Chicago: Nelson Hall.

Steady, F. (1981). "The Black Woman Cross-Culturally: An Overview." In F. Steady, ed., *The Black Woman Cross-Culturally.* Cambridge, MA: Schenkman.

Thornton, Russell. (1977). "American Indian Studies as an Academic Discipline." *The Journal of Ethnic Studies,* 5(3), Fall, 1-15.

Weedon, C. (1987). *Feminist Practice and Poststructuralist Theory.* Oxford: Basil Blackwell.

Zinn, M., L. Cannon, E. Higginbotham, & B. Dill. (1986)."The Cost of Exclusionary Practices in Women's Studies." *Signs: Journal of Women and Culture in Society*, 11(2): 290-303.

3

The Social Reality of Korean American Women: Toward Crashing with the Confucian Ideology[1]

El-Hannah Kim

INTRODUCTION

The cultural heritage and traditional values of Korea have been derived and evolved from various sources such as Shamanism, Buddhism, Taoism, Confucianism, Kyung Chun Sa Sang, Sill Hak Sa Sang, and so forth. Confucianism has, however, been the mainstream of Korean culture and tradition for over five hundred years characterizing Koreanism and producing the Hyun Mo Yang Cho ideal for setting the image and social roles of Korean women. It has been deeply embodied for so long in Korean cultural tradition, political behavior, family institution, and educational system that the Korean people have all become "Confucian-minded." It has been the fundamental and major source from which Korean society has drawn the principal guidelines for social relations and social conduct. Koreans still strongly believe in Confucian values, behave, think and feel in Confucian ways, despite the fact that Koreans, particularly Korean Americans and specifically Korean American women, have experienced new social realities and such social changes as modern socialization, westernization, Christianization, industrialization, and immigration to the American socio-cultural setting.

The major premises for this chapter are (1) Korean American women struggle with conflicting pressures between two forces—to preserve Korean cultural heritage and traditional values on one hand, and to adapt to social changes for survival and mastery of a new socio-cultural environment on the other; (2) Korean American women experience discrepancies and incompatibility between traditional Korean women's roles defined by Hyun Mo Yang Cho ideals and desirable women's images demanded by the social reality of contemporary society; (3) Korean American women encounter a social reality posing direct pressures on immediate conditions for developing a new self-image for the ideal Korean American woman; and (4) Korean American women realize that the self-image and social roles of the Hyun Mo Yang Cho ideal are inadequate in the changed socio-cultural environment of American society and inconsistent with the principles of the women's human rights movement. Thus this chapter attempts to critically examine Hyun Mo Yang Cho idealism by presenting an overview of

Confucian ideals that have nurtured Korean sexism. The chapter is, however, ultimately concerned with the newly emerging ideals and images of Korean American women.

CRITICAL INTERPRETATION OF CONFUCIUS'S BELIEFS

Confucius (551–479 B.C.), the Chinese sage who originated Confucianism both as a religion and a socio-political philosophy, established an ethical and moral system to govern all social relations in family, community, and society. He believed that the graded social relation is an ideal approach to the harmony and order of human society. He identified many hierarchical social relationships such as father and son, husband and wife, older brother or sister and younger brother or sister, older and younger people, man and woman, master and servant, ruler and subject, and the like. He taught his followers that becoming a good father, son, wife, mother, brother, sister is the initial and essential step toward becoming a true human being and consequently toward becoming a good citizen and building a moral society (Yutang, 1938). Such hierarchical social relations and feudal approaches to an ideal society reflect fundamental values that are subject to criticism and challenge from egalitarian and democratic idealists. Confucian culture therefore has been one of the major causes for the Korean women's human rights movement since the 1970s (Lee & Kim, 1978).

The Confucian definition of a true human being and of his theoretical context of humanities were mainly based on ascribed social roles such as father, mother, wife, son, brother and so on. He deemphasized such values as the individual's efforts for self-fulfillment toward divine perfection, excellent performance of attained social roles for societal needs, and searching for an ultimate truth through metaphysical experiences. Thus, his conception of a man did not fully reflect a total person involved in various domains of life beyond the family context. For example, a Confucian woman is born to be a woman, not a human, to become a mother, wife, and daughter only, not an educator, philosopher, businessperson, government official, or the like. She is also born to be of submissive social status in the Confucian social order.

Confucian orientation with male preference and male centrism may be significantly related to the background of Confucius's birth and childhood. His father, 70 years old, and his mother, 18 years old, gave him birth through their extramarital union solely for the purpose of having a son. His father already had ten children—all, except one, a crippled son, were girls—before Confucius's birth (Chai & Choi, 1965). He was virtually the only son to his mother, who became a widow when she was only 21 and Confucius was 3. He himself had only one son and his son also had only one son. Confucius's negative perception and discriminating attitude about women may have contributed to the development of Confucian sexism. He treated women in friendly ways, but more as pets and not as equal human beings. He believed that women were inherently inferior to men and incompetent to perform nondomestic activities (Dawson, 1942).

He presented a noble reason for ritual values, especially for ancestor worship, and formulated a logical rationale for the positive impact of ritual activities on personal cultivation and social order (Yutang, 1938). Nevertheless, his ritual-loving character may be significantly related to his personal experiences pertaining to the loss of his own father during his early childhood, and his search for the whereabouts of his father's tomb because his mother kept it a secret (Yutang, 1938). In particular, he devoted himself to a three-year mourning period over his mother's death and restrained himself from all sensual activities during that time (Chai & Choi, 1965). Raised by his widowed mother, Confucius, as her only son, may be expected to have had a deep emotional attachment to her. He had a natural motivation and socially acceptable purpose for practicing this three-year-long mourning period of devotion and ritual. Such traditional discipline is thought to have been beneficial to Confucius and his followers. However, it implies that the longer the period of devotional mourning and the more complete the form of ritual ceremonies, the harder and heavier they imposed service roles on their women. Women were not given the opportunity for instrumental roles in ritual life.

It may be significant to note that his aristocratic lifestyle was so extreme and his aesthetic taste was so fastidious that he did not take food, dress, and mat unless they were in perfect and fresh condition. They may be the major reason why his wife ran away and eventually divorced him. His son, his grandson, and his disciples of consecutive successive generations were all divorced. Even Mencius was separated (Yutang, 1938). Confucius's 14-year-long life of traveling, visiting feudal lords and seeking jobs may reveal clues leading one to suspect that his life was unstable, and to question the stability of his family life and his wife's marital life (Chai & Choi, 1965).

Confucius's family roots in the ruling class, his strong elitism, aristocratism, and feudal belief have all been incorporated into Confucianism. Thus, Confucian ideology may represent idealism for the ruling class but not for grassroots society. He identified intellectual people with the moral upper class and therefore legitimized the influence of the ruling upper class on the other people (Yutang, 1938). His assumption was that the educated person as a moral man must realize his responsibility and duties over his inferiors in Confucian hierarchy, and inferiors must submit to such moral authority. Confucius himself admitted that there were very few, if any, except the Yu-Soon Moral Kings Era, who demonstrated the ideals of such moral authority (Yutang, 1938).

His emphasis on educational values regarding personal and moral cultivation and his moral-ethical approach to social orderings remained only as Confucian ideology of "false-consciousness" (in Karl Marx's term), since there has been a growing discrepancy between such ideas and the reality-stimulated educational needs for social mobility rather than for personal growth, and they strengthened the male authority of dictatorial behavior over all social relations. Thus, the social status of women became a double minority—sexually and socially—in Confucian society. Although Confucius was in a true sense an anarchist who disapproved of strong governments for law enforcement or rigorous coercion, his doctrines contributed to establishing strong governments of totalitarian states (Yutang, 1938). He did not give much thought to human dynamics and their impact on people with low status in the social hierarchy. His perspective on human dynamics was within the context of a static rather than changing society. A growing gap exists between his socio-political ideology and the reality of social changes in today's society.

CONFUCIANISM OF KOREAN SOCIETY

Confucianism is one of China's philosophies that has exercised a powerful influence for the past 2500 years. It has been a live force shaping thoughts and behaviors not only for people in China, but also for China's neighbors, particularly Korea. It has influenced the marriage institution, family structure, political culture, educational system, and other social relations. It has been strongly perpetuated in all domains of Korean life as the mainstream of Korean culture, particularly since the Yi dynasty government (1392–1910) adopted it as a state religion. Among many results of its impact on Korean society are the development of kinship-based community and social relations, indoctrination of strong familism and patriarchal family systems, institutionalization of Confucian sexism, the so-called Hyun Mo Yang Cho ideal and Nam Jon Yu Bi virtue, and the promotion of educational competition for social mobility.

Kinship-Based Community and Social Relations

The adoption of the Confucian social system has meant growth for Korean family structure in size. The Korean royal government granted official kin-names and land to families to encourage them to grow in number and settle in granted lands. The similar kin-name families provoked the consanguineous marriage in order to expand their lands as well as their socio-economic powers. These many different kin-name families constituted kinship-based communities and competed with each other in the struggle toward a central power monopoly. Thus, Confucian influence on Korean society contributed to societal disintegration, although it produced a monolithic culture and a homogeneous mentality (Kim, 1949; Kang, 1971).

Each kinship-based community developed a kinship-oriented social relationship. All individual members of the community are related to each other within the kin-family framework and thus are identified as uncle, aunt, and so on, instead of as Mr., or Mrs., or Miss in the individual framework. It is therefore a Korean custom that a friend calls my father as his father, and a neighbor calls any elderly person on the street as grandmother or grandfather. An individual's name and particularly first-name calling are not practiced in traditional Korean society.

Giving a name to an individual at birth means designation or assigning a social rank in the kinship-oriented social structure. The name indicates the birthplace (Bon Kwan), birth order of the family members (Hang Ryul), and birth status (Sung). The social rank of the name defines location in the kinship community and prescribes conduct in social relations with other people (Kim, 1949). Korean women were even excluded from being granted names of their own as they were confined to domestic life. They were simply called so-and-so's mother, or so-and-so's wife, or inside-person (An Sa Ram), house-person (Jib Sa Ram), or otherwise, after the name of the resident house (e.g., Sa Im Dang Kim Ci) if she was from a Confucian Yang Ban family (Chai, 1983).

Confucian Familism and Patriarchal Family

The Confucian political culture strengthened the Korean family system by legitimizing male authority and institutionalizing a patriarchal family structure. The Confucian emphasis on the importance of family life for personal cultivation and social ordering nurtured the growth of stronger familism, particularly preserving such values as family ties, filial piety, family discipline through submission, obedience, sacrifice and loyalty to the patriarchal authority. Thus, members of the family placed first priority on family interests rather than personal needs. Although Confucian humanism says that "I" exists within "We," the individual "I" as a woman in the Confucian family reality has been denied by demanding of her a lifetime of submission and sacrifice. Since the individual's reputation is directly related to a family background, all family members undertake to strive for family background, all family members undertake to strive for family reputation and power. An individual's worth and dignity are measured on the basis of family success, rather than on individual difference or accomplishment. This contributed to the development of shifting one's social status. Marrying into an influential kin-name family means security, reputation, and success for a Korean women (Kim, 1949). Therefore the woman is willing to submit to male authority and the patriarchal family system. She surrenders herself as man's property. Marriage for Confucian Korean women is therefore a transfer from the father's territory and protection to that of another male; it is the terminal station of her own life rather than the commencement of self development.

Hyun Mo Yang Cho Ideal and Nam Jon Yu Bi Virtue

Monopolistic Confucian traditions of male centrism developed in such humanitarian and discriminatory doctrines as Hyun Mo Yang Cho, which was the ideal image of a Korean woman in her limited roles as a submissive wife and a sacrificial mother. The Nam Jon Yu Bi belief originated from the Confucian concept of a woman's inherent inferiority and incompetence, and the confinement of the woman to lifetime sacrificial service roles. Thus, the Confucian male-centered and patriarchal family contributed to the socialization of woman as dependent on father before marriage, on husband after marriage, and on son after husband's death (so-called Sam Jong Ji Do). Her incompetences were further nurtured through such life experiences and led to the loss of her own rights for decision-making, or practice of her own freedom and independent judgment without permission from male authority (Lee & Kim, 1978).

Hyun Mo Yang Cho is a typical image of traditional sex-role stereotyping that is restricted to the domestic world. The marital life cycle for the woman is fixed with lifetime commitment to lengthy childbearing and childrearing, without her own life, own identity, own voice, and the experience of her human rights and freedom.

Confucian Aims of Korean Education

The Confucian civil examination and Confucian school system during the Yi dynasty increased the Confucian population and the Yang Ban ruling class. Admission to Confucian schools meant becoming a Confucianist, and Confucian conversion was the prerequisite to qualify for the Yang Ban class (Kang, 1971). The Korean educational system has since served as a legitimate means for social mobility to shift social status rather than for personal cultivation to improve moral character. One's social status and reputation were significantly based on one's educational background in terms of the years of training and the reputation of the school. As Korean society grew stronger, educational values and heated educational competition increased, producing many successful individuals but failing to achieve social harmony in successful group life.

Confucian culture discriminated against Korean women in the equal distribution of educational opportunities until the adoption of a modern educational system by the new Korean government was established in 1948. Although the adoption of a modern educational system opened wide the educational opportunities for Korean women, women's college education serves Korean women to prepare them for marriage or to increase marital power in general. Korean women including college graduates are, for the most part, choosing marriage for their terminal station in the pursuance of life goals rather than new departures for self-enrichment through both marital and other social life experiences. Marriage and career pursuits are thus becoming a matter of choice for Korean women as either/or rather than attempting both. Marital status poses a handicap for further educational opportunities and work experiences, rather than being an asset for social credibility or self-fulfilling activities. Many female college graduates in Korean society thus remain unemployed or, if not, are mostly employed in fields or at jobs irrelevant to their educational backgrounds and areas of interest.

The Charter of Korean National Education states that Korean education aims at preserving Confucian culture on one hand and implanting Western philosophies such as democracy on the other (Ministry of Culture and Information, 1982). It conveys that Korean education is devoted to such mutually exclusive ideologies as non-egalitarian Confucianism and egalitarian democracy. Korean schools continue to stress the importance of Confucian values such as familism, filial piety, obedience, traditional values, conformity, loyalty, collectivity, and nationalism. Confucian political culture still dictates curriculum contents, instructional modes, student culture, and hierarchical relations between teacher and student. The practice of male authority is persistently reinforced and Hyun Mo Yang Cho idealism is indoctrinated through educational goals, instructional patterns, textbooks, extracurricular activities, and the like (Son, 1978).

Such Confucian-influenced education may discourage students from developing personal reasoning and critical thinking skills, objective attitudes, and innovative changes; and it may desensitize them with regard to individuality, human diversity, universalism, internationalism, horizontal social relationships, future-oriented perspectives, and so forth. Coeducational schools are not yet a common practice, as the Confucian sexist culture has been in favor of sexual segregation in the school system. The ideal product of segregation in the school system may therefore be identified as the "most average man" because the ideal product is the one who conforms best to the societal norm; the norm may be defined as average behavior or standardized behavior of the society. The Confucian educational system does not encourage the production of "the best person," that is, an individual who realizes the best of his/her potential through self-fulfillment toward divine perfection.

THE SOCIAL REALITY OF KOREAN AMERICAN WOMEN

Korean American women encounter a social reality that is greatly different from the Confucian society of Hyun Mo Yang Cho as discussed in the previous chapter. Peter Berger defines social reality as a social construct, including social structure and social systems, institutionalization and socialization, social roles and life situation as taken-for-granted (Berger & Luckman, 1967). On the other hand, George Mead (1984) explains that self-consciousness or the self-product is the result of the incorporation of the given socio-cultural setting. It is thus significantly related to social reality as "a relational reality." These two theo-retical references confirm that the changed Korean American woman's social reality directly corresponds to the changing of her social roles and self-images; the Hyun Mo Yang Cho ideal of the Confucian society is therefore not necessarily true for the Korean American woman in American society. The changed or new social reality embodies the significant implication that the Korean American woman may experience direct pressures and immediate conditions demanding different molds of ideal self-products.

The social reality of Korean American women may be described as a social construct that refers to ubiquitous experiences with social changes that involved: (1) demographic reality; (2) industrialization; and (3) the feminists' movement; the other, "the particular" social construct that refers to unique experiences with immigrant life in the American socio-cultural setting. Korean American women's immigration experiences are, as revealed through several studies on Korean Americans, characterized as an unique pattern of their adjustment to such dualistic social conditions as: (1) ethnic identity with both Koreanism and Americanism; (2) a social system of both Korean ethnic community and American majority society; (3) a lifestyle of both traditional and contemporary modes; and (4) ideological orientation with both persistent Confucianism and predominant Christianity (Hurh, 1977; Kim, K., 1972; Boo, 1982).

Such universal and particular characteristics of social construction constitute the social reality of Korean American women and serve as the major impetus for affecting their Confucian mentality, shaping new forms of self-consciousness, and encouraging the emergence of nontraditional self-products. New self-products that are adequate to the changed social reality and consistent with the principles of human rights are necessary to Korean American women not only for their survival and mastery of the changed socio-cultural environment, but also for their self-realization and self-fulfillment.

The Universal Social Construction Serving as External Forces Changing Women's Social Roles and Images

Demographic Reality Changing Women's Marital Life Cycle

Both American and Korean statistics show that traditional patterns are undergoing change: first, the compression of childbearing years coupled with lengthened life; and second, the expansion of women's labor market forces combined with family responsibility. Longer life spans and shortened childbearing years contribute to increasing women's leisure time and the growth of flexibility in their marital life cycles. Such demographic reality and the socio-economic reality of more demand for women's paid work participation have complemented each other. They have contributed to the institutionalization of the small, nuclear family structure as well. Thus growing numbers of women are no longer confined to the world of home but are encouraged to participate in the world of work. More and more women have become free from lifetime service roles, and more and more become familiar with the practice of instrumental roles outside of the domestic boundary. They have become flexible enough find and enjoy more leisure time for their own life enrichment.

Industrialization and Emerging New Social Status for the Working Woman

Unlike the traditional housewife, who performs unpaid domestic work, the working woman (working mother) has emerged as a new symbol capable of changing social status for women. Industrial society has reinforced the work ethic as a powerful social norm, and women's work experiences have returned practical rewards such as economic freedom, opportunity for individual expression, a sense of self-worth and deserved self-esteem, and accessibility to the world beyond the domestic boundary. Particularly, paid work implies income, power, and privilege in the highly developed industrial societies and it commonly reflects educational background, competencies, self-discipline, success in competition, productivity and the like. Thus, more and more women develop their desires for higher and longer educational opportunities and their ambitions for better and more diversified work experiences. On the other hand, industrialized society has developed the perception of housewife status as a self-worthless, alienated social role, with low self-esteem, incompetence, and disorientation from the future.

The complex and changing social system, as a result of industrialization along with the creation of a variety of occupational fields and diversification of labor, demands specialized expertise, explosion of knowledge, and so on, all of which have stimulated women to meet the challenge for more education and nontraditional work. Industrialization developed societal institutions and strengthened the role of educational institutions to take over the major responsibilities of children's education from the mother's bosom and knees. Such division of work at the societal level has developed a variety of educational institutions (e.g., public and private schools, day-care centers, nursery schools, learning centers, and so on) that share in the mother's role pertaining to the educational and recreational needs of children. Joint responsibilities for childrearing have broadened the mother's nontraditional social relations and social roles beyond domestic boundaries (Giele, 1975).

In addition, industrial society has recognized specialization and expertise as valuable assets and authorized persons with such assets to exercise professional authority over all domains of social life. Particularly, the development of social welfare institutions has received public sanction to professionally intervene in family and marital life through social service agencies, welfare programs, and social work intervention. In other words, family and marital life has been exposed to such outsiders as family service experts, legal advisors, marriage counselors, domestic violence protection centers, home-maker services, paid baby-sitters, and so forth. The traditional family concealed family affairs and marital problems within its boundaries. This confined the wife to the most private zone of her husband's life. However, families in industrial societies no longer strictly remain in private zones but rather function as units between the private and public zones. Such joint involvement in the traditionally private zone has sensitized women to acknowledge their unmet needs within their social conditions. This has led to new desires on the part of women to perform new roles between the social zones (Romanyskin, 1971).

Women's extended social life has coincided with expanded leisure time, since technological advancement revolutionized the traditional patterns of housework and domestic management. Modernization and automatization for efficiency in the domestic system, including electronic household utilities, modern housing structure, instant food products, and the like, have all contributed to reducing women's work at home and in the kitchen. In addition, the joint responsibility of husband and wife over household chores and child-rearing has become common practice. More men have come to accept ideologically (if not behaviorally) the joint responsibility to share housework and child care with women. Thus, women have been freed from prolonged domestic engagement and have become more and more flexible with regard to leisure time and doing their own things (Toffler, 1970).

The Feminist Movement and the Struggle for Women's Better Self-Images and Improvement of Women's Social Status

Today, such words as feminist, women's rights movement, women's liberation, and the Equal Rights Amendment (ERA) are familiar not only to women but also to men, particularly those in American society. There are two aspects of women-related issues and movements. First, there is the struggle of women to discover their own identities and to shape better self-images. Women exist in this world and in this time but have lost their own identities and voices. Particularly, the Korean woman has traditionally lived with secondary identity (e.g., so-and-so's mother or so-and-so's wife) and concerned only with her husband's purpose and her family's interests. The culture—whether it be Eastern or Western—has not permitted women to accept or gratify their basic needs as human beings and to grow and fulfill their potentialities beyond sexual roles (Friedan, 1973).

Second, there is an effort to engage in the re-examination of the role of women in all spheres of life, and the relationship of men and women in all spheres of life, and the relationship of men and women in all social, political, economic, and cultural institutions. This effort is primarily aimed at the eradication of sex discrimination through attempting legislative, economic, and educational reforms. These efforts hold self-evident truths such as "all men and women are created equal: that among their rights are life, liberty and pursuit of happiness" (excerpt from the Declaration of Sentiments of the 1848 Seneca Falls Woman's Rights Convention).

Korean women's human rights movements have been growing firmer and more active, particularly since the 1970s. The Declaration made by the Organization for the Korean Family Law Reform for Korean Women (Bum Yu Sung Ga Jok Bup Gai Jung Chock Jin Hoe), with support from sixty other Korean women's organizations, in 1973, articulates the social and legal status of Korean women today and accuses the Confucian cultural structure and traditions that have the major responsibility for Korean sexism and sex discrimination under the law (Lee & Kim, 1978). It cries out that Korean women are the victims of the Confucian social system that has denied them their basic needs as human beings, has deprived them of the opportunity to realize their potentialities, and has restricted their efforts to become free and complete persons.

As the women's rights movement has grown stronger and more widespread, an increasing number of women in both Korean and American societies have experienced awakened self-awareness and increased consciousness of the need for self-realization and self-fulfillment. More and more women are becoming independent, productive, competent, human beings who are struggling to mold self-images with deserved self-esteem and human dignity and worth (Giele, 1975).

The Particular Social Construction Serving as Internal Forces Changing Korean American Women's Self-Consciousness and Mentality

According to survey findings that the author conducted for the study of the Korean American's consciousness structure in 1982, Korean Americans have changed since their immigration, and the present status of their consciousness and mentality shows tendencies such as: (1) a more positive attitude toward Americanization with continuing pride in Korean ethnicity; (2) no longer sojourner mentality but still strong attachment to Koreanism; (3) a greater sense of commitment to the American society, but prevailing feelings of alienation; (4) adaptation to the contemporary lifestyle, but maintenance of traditional behaviors; (5) stronger ties with ethnic social relations, but social distance from American social systems; (6) liberalized paternal roles but strong conservative beliefs in women's sex roles; and (7) a predominant Christian influence over individual Korean American's life; but persistent Confucian dominance over Korean ethnic community life (Boo, 1982).

The survey results confirm that Korean American women are no longer in the same social reality as Hyun Mo Yang Cho Korean women, because the Korean American women's consciousness and mentality are the products of dualistic social environments such as the Korean ethnic community and the American majority society. The dualistic features of their social reality and their relational reality have implications for Korean American women who are identified with double minority status both as ethnic and sexual minorities. They are overburdened with double social roles both in the traditional life at home and the ethnic community, and in the contemporary life at work and in American society; confused between the two mutually exclusive orientations of Confucianism and Christianity; and in conflict between two pressures—to preserve traditional values and cultural heritage on one hand and to change the traditional behaviors and adapt to the new social reality on the other. These implications convey that Korean American women must necessarily mold new self-products that will be nontraditional but adequate and desirable for a changed social reality.

NOTE

1. From Minza Kim Boo (now El-Hannah Kim), *The Social Reality of the Korean-American Women: Toward Crashing with the Confucian Ideology.* Ed. Inn Sook Lee. Publication Series No. 5. Reprinted with permission of the Association of Korean Christian Scholars in North America.

REFERENCES

Berger, Peter, & Thomas Luckman. (1967). *The Social Construction of Reality: A Treatise in the Sociology of Knowledge.* New York: Doubleday.

Boo, Minza Kim. (1982). "The Self-Consciousness of the Korean-American Women." *Sae Gae Shin Bo Weekly Newspaper,* New York, January-March, 12 series.

Chai, Chiu, & Winberg Choi, eds. (1965). *The Sacred Books of Confucius.* New York: University Books, pp. 18-21.

Chai, Jae-suck. (1983). *The Social Characters of Korean People.* Seoul: Gae Moon Sa, pp. 27-42.

Dawson, Miles Menender. (1942). *The Basic Teachings of Confucianism.* New York: The New Home Library.

Friedan, Betty. (1973). *The Feminine Mystique.* New York: Dell.

Giele, Janet Zollinger. (1975). *Women and the Future: Changing Sex Roles in Modern America.* New York: Free Press, pp. 160-178.

Hurh, Won Mo. (1977). *Comparative Study of Korean Immigrants in the United States: A Typological Approach.* San Francisco: R and E Research Associates.

Kang, Hyo-sok. (1971). *The Making of Confucian Society in Tokugawa Japan and Yi Korea: A Comparative Analysis of the Behavior Patterns in Accepting the Foreign Ideology, Neo-Confucianism.* Washington, DC: American University, pp. 102-107, 177.

Kim, Kwang Chung. (1972). "An Exploratory Study of the Koreans in the United States: A Research Proposal." An unpublished working paper.

Kim, Tu-hon. (1949). *A Study of the Korean Family System.* Seoul: Uryu Mun Hwa Sa, pp. 128-130.

Lee, Hyo-Jai, & Kim Ju-Sook. (1978). *The Status of Korean Women.* Seoul: Ewha Woman's University Press, pp. 195-240.

Mead, George. (1984). *Mind, Self, and Society.* Chicago: University of Chicago Press, pp. 164-194.

Ministry of Culture and Information, Republic of Korea. (1982). *Facts about Korea.* Seoul, Korea: Korean Information Service, p. 21.

Romanyskin, John. (1971). *Social Welfare: Charity to Justice.* New York: Random House.

Son, Dug-Soo. (1978). "The Status of Korean Women from the Perspective of the Women's Emancipation Movement." In Harold H. Sun Woo & Dong Soo Kim (eds.), *Korean Women in a Struggle for Humanization.* Korean Christian Scholars Publication, no. 3 (Spring), pp. 11-37.

Toffler, Alvin. (1970). *Future Shock.* New York: Random House.

Yutang, Lin. (1938). *The Wisdom of Confucius.* New York: Modern Library, pp. 13-22.

A PROFILE OF KOREAN WOMEN AND MEN IN THE UNITED STATES

The chapters that follow in Part Two focus on the demographic and socioeconomic characteristics of Korean American women and men and their settlement patterns during the last three decades.

Korean Americans constitute one of the fastest growing ethnic groups in the United States. Based on the 1990 census data, Ailee Moon, in "Demographic and Socioeconomic Characteristics of Korean American Women and Men," portrays Korean American women and men in light of their immigration, demographic, and socioeconomic characteristics, such as age, year of immigration, language use, region of residence, education, occupation, and income. She also compares Korean American women's demographic and socioeconomic characteristics with those of men and two other reference populations, Asian Pacific Islanders and all American women and men.

Although Korean American immigration history covers a period of nearly one hundred years, the Korean American community before 1965 was almost negligible in terms of its population size. It was the 1965 Immigration and Naturalization Act that contributed to the large influx of Korean immigrants to the United States. In "Demographic Characteristics and Trends of Post-1965 Korean Immigrant Women and Men," Pyong Gap Min and Young I. Song provide an overview of the post-1965 Korean immigration, including immigration motives, characteristics, and settlement patterns.

Many Korean American women do not hold traditional Korean values concerning marriage, sex roles, living arrangements, and the importance of inheriting the family line, according to survey findings presented in "Attitudes Toward Ethnic Identity, Marriage, and Familial Life among Women of Korean Descent in the United States, Japan, and Korea" by Ailee Moon. Comparison of the women of Korean descent in the three countries also reveals more similarities than differences in their attitudes toward traditional Korean values and norms. The findings provide empirical evidence for considerable change in the women's value systems concerning their roles in the family and society and suggest further deviation from traditional values and ways of life in the future for the majority of women of Korean descent in the three countries.

4

Demographic and Socioeconomic Characteristics of Korean American Women and Men

Ailee Moon

GROWTH AND GENERAL CHARACTERISTICS OF THE KOREAN AMERICAN POPULATION

Korean Americans constitute one of the fastest growing ethnic groups in the United States. The 1990 census counted 798,849 Korean Americans, an increase of 125.3% over the 1980 count of 354,593. While Korean Americans make up only 0.32% of the total U.S. population, they represent the fifth largest group among Asian Pacific Islanders (APIs), or 12.0% of the total 7,273,662 in 1990.

Nativity, Immigration, and Language

The growth of the Korean American population in the past two decades has been attributed primarily to immigration. Table 4.1 presents selected demographic and socioeconomic characteristics of Korean Americans, APIs, and the total U.S. population. Almost 73% of Korean Americans were born outside the United States, compared to 63% of all APIs and 8% of the entire U.S. population. Furthermore, among those foreign born, over 56% of Korean Americans and 58% of all APIs came to the United States in the 1980s, and only 23% and 24% of them, respectively, before 1975.

One consequence of the relatively short immigration history of Korean Americans is difficulty with the English language. Of the 727,164 Korean Americans 5 years old and above in 1990, 52% did not speak English "very well," and 35% were linguistically isolated. These figures were considerably higher than for all APIs (38% and 24%, respectively). In fact, the overwhelming majority of Korean Americans, 82%, spoke other than English (mostly Korean) at home, compared to 73% for APIs and 14% for the total population.

Age, Sex, and Region of Residence

As Table 4.1 reveals, Korean Americans' median age of 29.1 in 1990 was younger than the national median of 32.9 and the API median age of 29.8. In addition, persons 65 years old or more composed only 4.4% of the Korean

Table 4.1
Selected Demographic and Socioeconomic Characteristics of Korean Americans,
Asian Pacific Islanders, and the Entire U.S. Population, 1990

CHARACTERISTICS	U.S.	API	KOREAN
Total persons	248,709,873	7,273,662	798,949
Nativity & Year of Entry (%)			
Foreign born	7.9	63.1	72.7
Year of entry			
1980–1990	43.8	57.5	56.4
1975–1979	13.9	18.7	21.1
before 1975	42.2	23.8	22.5
Language (%)			
Persons 5 years & older who			
speak a language other than			
English at home	13.8	73.3	81.6
Speak API language at home	1.9	63.3	80.8
Do not speak English very			
well	6.1	38.4	51.6
Linguistically isolated			
household[a]	3.1	24.2	35.1
Age & Sex			
Median age	32.9	29.8	29.1
Under 5 years old (%)	7.4	8.1	8.8
18 years old & over (%)	74.4	71.4	69.1
65 years old & over (%)	12.6	6.2	4.4
Males per 100 females	95.1	95.8	79.5
Region (%)			
Northeast	20.4	18.4	22.8
Midwest	24.0	10.6	13.7
South	34.4	15.4	19.2
West	21.2	55.7	44.4
State (%)			
California	11.9	39.1	32.5
Illinois	4.6	3.9	5.2
New York	7.2	9.5	12.0
New Jersey	3.1	3.7	4.8
Types of Family			
Total numbers	64,517,947	1,559,043	161,645
Married-couple			
families (%)	78.6	81.2	83.4
Female householder, no			
husband present (%)	16.5	12.2	11.6
Male householder, no			
female present (%)	4.9	6.6	5.1
Persons per family	3.2	3.8	3.6

(continued)

Table 4.1 (continued)

CHARACTERISTICS	U.S.	API	KOREAN
Educational Attainment (Persons 25 years old & over) (%)			
High school graduate or higher	75.2	77.5	80.2
Bachelor's degree or higher	20.3	36.6	34.5
Labor Force Participation (Persons 16 years old & over) (%)			
In labor force	65.3	67.5	63.3
Unemployed	6.3	5.3	5.2
Occupation (Employed persons 16 years old & over) (%)			
Managerial & professional specialty	26.4	30.6	25.5
Technical, sales, & admin. support	31.7	33.2	37.1
Farming, forestry, & fishing	2.5	1.7	0.7
Precision production, craft, & repair	11.3	8.0	8.9
Operators, fabricators, & laborers	14.9	12.1	12.8
Income In 1989 ($)			
Per capita	14,143	13,683	11,177
Median household	30,056	36,784	30,184
Median family	35,225	40,360	33,909
1989 Income Below Poverty Level (%)			
Families in poverty	10.0	11.6	14.7
Persons in poverty	13.1	14.1	13.7

[a] Linguistically isolated refers to a person in a household in which no one 14 years old or over speaks only English and no one who speaks a language other than English speaks English "very well."

Note: Data for total persons, age, sex, and type of family are based on 100% tabulations. Remaining data are based on sample tabulations.

Source: U.S. Department of Commerce, Bureau of the Census, 1990a, 1990b, 1993, 1994.

American population, but 6.2% of APIs and 12.6% of the entire U.S. population. The ratio of males and females is also remarkable: only 80 males per 100 females versus 95 and 96 for the total population and all APIs, respectively. In 1990, 44% of Korean Americans lived in the west, 23% in the northeast, 19% in the south, and 14% in the midwest. While the proportion living in the west was more than double that of 21% for the total population, their concentration in the region was less phenomenal than that of 56% for the APIs. More specifically, 55% of Korean Americans lived in four states: California (33%), New York (12%), Illinois (5%), and New Jersey (5%).

Types of Family and Educational Attainment

The average Korean American family had 3.6 persons in 1990, larger than the average of 3.2 for all U.S. families, but smaller than the 3.8 for all APIs. The proportion of Korean American families headed by a husband and wife was 83%, higher than both the national figure of 79% and APIs of 81%. Similarly, the proportion of families headed by females with no husband present, 11.6%, was significantly lower than the national average of 16.5%, but only slightly lower than the API of 12.2%.

The average educational level of Korean Americans is relatively high. In 1990, 80% of those 25 years old and above were at least high school graduates, compared to 78% for all APIs and 75% for the total population. Approximately 35% held a bachelor's or higher degree by 1990, significantly higher than the 20% for the total population but slightly lower than the 37% for all APIs.

Economic Activities, Income, and Poverty

Approximately 63% of all Korean Americans 16 years old and over were in the labor force in 1990, less than the 68% of APIs and 65% of the total population. However, despite their lower labor force participation rate, Korean Americans' 5.2% unemployment rate was lower than the national 6.3%. This suggests that compared with APIs and the total population, a higher proportion of Korean Americans 16 years old and over chose not to participate in the labor force. Furthermore, Korean Americans were more likely to be employed in technical, sales, and administrative support jobs (37%) than APIs (33%) and the total population (32%). An additional 26% of those employed held managerial and professional jobs, compared with 31% of APIs and 26% of the total population.

Korean Americans had a lower median income than both reference groups. In 1989, their per capita income was $11,177 compared with the national $14,143 and API $13,638. Similarly, their median family income of $33,909 was considerably lower than the $35,225 for all U.S. and $40,360 for all API families. In the same year, almost 15% of Korean American families lived in poverty, a rate considerably higher than the 10% for all American and 12% for all API families.

However, the number of poor individuals, rather than families, revealed no significant difference among the three groups, although the poverty rate of Korean Americans, 13.7%, was still higher than the national rate of 13.1%. This suggests that the poverty problem of Korean Americans is more concentrated in families than it is for APIs and the total population.

DEMOGRAPHIC AND SOCIOECONOMIC CHARACTERISTICS OF KOREAN AMERICAN WOMEN AND MEN

This section compares Korean American women's demographic and socioeconomic characteristics with those of men and the other two reference populations. Table 4.2 presents age distribution, marital status, U.S. citizenship, education, percent in labor force, type of employment, occupation, and income of Korean American, API, and all American women and men.

Demographic Characteristics

As mentioned earlier, the gender distribution for Korean Americans is far more skewed than for API and the overall U.S. population. In 1990, women accounted for almost 57% of Korean Americans, compared to 51% of APIs and nationally. Furthermore, women in all three populations were older than their male counterparts: the median age was 30.3 and 26.9 years old for Korean American women and men, respectively, 30.7 and 28.7 for APIs, and 34.1 and 31.7 for the U.S. population. Women being older and a higher proportion of all three populations is partially attributable to their longer life expectancy. As Table 4.2 portrays, persons 65 years and older constituted 4.9% and 3.6% of Korean American women and men, respectively, 6.7% and 5.7% of APIs, and 14.7% and 10.4% nationally. In addition, a greater percentage of Korean American women, almost 65%, were between 18 to 64, compared to 61.3% of Korean American men. This reverses the national percentages of 61% and 63%. The younger population under 18, however, accounted for a higher percentage of men than women for all three populations.

A considerably lower percentage of Korean American women, 46.5%, were currently married than of API and U.S. women (58.7% and 52.4%, respectively), while the percentage never married, 43.1%, was significantly higher than the 27.6% of API and 23.4% of U.S. women. While this is perhaps due to the imbalance of gender ratio in the Korean American population, the percentage of Korean American men never married, 53.8%, was almost 11% higher than for women, and substantially higher than the 38.2% of API and 30.7% of the U.S. male populations. In fact, for all three populations, the percentage of men never married was considerably higher than that of women.

The majority of the foreign-born U.S. population in 1990, including APIs and Korean Americans, were not American citizens. Approximately 43% of foreign-born Korean American women and a lower 37% of men had obtained citizenship, similar to the national figures of 42% and 38%.

Socioeconomic Characteristics

Table 4.2 clearly indicates that while Korean American men in general enjoyed higher levels of formal education than API and U.S. males, Korean American women had less education than API women, yet more than the U.S. women overall. The disparity between Korean American women and men in their educational attainment is remarkably large, and in fact, the largest among the three populations. For example, the percentage of Korean American women 25 years and older with a bachelor's or higher degree in 1990, 25.5%, was about half the 47.4% for Korean American men. The percentages compare with 32% and 45.5% of API women and men, and 17.6% and 23.3% nationally.

Similarly, of those 16 years old and over, the percentage of Korean American women in the labor force, 55.5%, was lower than the 60.2% of API and 56.8% of U.S. females. The figure was also significantly lower than the 73.8% of Korean American men in the labor force. As to type of employment, the percentages of Korean women and men self-employed, 16% and 26.2%, respectively, were about three times greater than for API (6.3% and 9.0%) and nationally (5.1% and 8.5%). Consequently, those whose employment characterized

Table 4.2
Selected Demographic and Socioeconomic Characteristics of Korean American,
Asian Pacific Islander, and all American Women and Men, 1990

CHARACTERISTICS	U.S.		API		KOREAN	
	Women	Men	Women	Men	Women	Men
Sex (%)						
Persons	51.3	48.7	51.1	48.9	56.7	43.3
Age						
Under 18 (%)	24.3	26.9	27.5	29.9	30.4	35.1
18–64 (%)	61.0	62.8	65.8	64.4	64.7	61.3
65 & older (%)	14.7	10.4	6.7	5.7	4.9	3.6
Median age	34.1	31.7	30.7	28.7	30.3	26.9
Marital Status						
(Persons 15 years & over) (%)						
Now married	52.4	57.3	58.7	56.1	46.5	43.3
Divorced	9.5	7.4	4.7	3.1	3.9	1.6
Separated	2.6	2.0	1.8	1.3	1.2	0.8
Never married	23.4	30.7	27.6	38.2	43.1	53.8
Widowed	12.0	2.5	7.2	1.3	5.3	0.5
U.S. Citizen						
(Foreign-born only) (%)						
Yes	42.4	38.5	41.1	40.4	43.1	37.4
No	57.6	61.5	58.9	59.6	56.9	62.6
Education						
(Persons 25 years old & over) (%)						
Less than 8 years	10.1	10.4	18.0	10.8	13.9	4.9
9–12 years	14.8	13.9	10.8	8.4	12.3	5.7
High school diploma	32.1	27.5	19.2	14.1	29.0	19.2
Some college	25.1	24.7	20.0	21.2	19.3	22.8
Bachelor's degree	11.9	14.4	22.4	23.3	19.6	26.2
Higher degree	5.7	8.9	9.6	22.2	5.9	21.2
In Labor Force (%)	56.8	74.4	60.2	75.6	55.5	73.8
Type Of Employment						
(Employed persons 16 years & over) (%)						
Private & salary workers	76.8	78.0	80.2	78.4	66.4	56.7
Local gov't workers	8.7	5.8	4.7	3.4	7.8	1.8
State gov't workers	5.7	3.8	4.3	4.9	2.5	3.5
Federal gov't workers	3.1	3.6	3.4	3.7	3.7	3.9
Self-employed	5.1	8.5	6.3	9.0	16.0	26.2
Unpaid family worker	0.6	0.3	1.2	0.6	3.6	2.5

(continued)

Table 4.2 (continued)

CHARACTERISTICS	U.S.		API		KOREAN	
	Women	Men	Women	Men	Women	Men
Occupation						
Managerial & professional	27.8	25.2	27.5	34.7	20.3	30.8
Technical, sales, & administrative	43.6	21.7	37.5	28.0	38.7	34.8
Service	16.9	10.2	17.3	12.9	20.6	9.2
Farming, forestry, & fishing	0.8	3.8	0.5	1.1	0.4	0.9
Production, crafts, & repairs	2.3	18.9	4.8	10.7	5.8	12.6
Operators, laborers, & fabricators	8.5	20.3	12.5	12.5	14.2	11.7
Income in 1989						
Full-time workers (%)	9.5	7.4	4.7	3.1	3.9	1.6
Median income ($)	10, 371	20,409	11,986	19,396	10,570	18,101
Median income of full-time workers ($)	19,570	29,237	21,335	30,075	18,760	28,256

Note: Data for total persons, age, sex and type of family are based on 100% tabulations. Remaining data are based on sample tabulations.

Source: See Table 4.1.

them as unpaid family workers were a higher percentage of Korean American women and men in the labor force, 3.6% and 2.5%, compared to 1.2% and 0.6% for APIs and 0.6% and 0.3% nationally. For all three populations, the percentage of women self-employed was considerably lower than for men, while a higher percentage of women than men in the labor force were unpaid family workers.

Table 4.2 also reveals that the percentage of Korean American women who held managerial or professional positions, 20.3%, was substantially lower than the 30.8% of Korean American men, 27.5% of API women, and 27.8% of U.S. women in the labor force. In contrast, a higher percentage of Korean American women, or 20.6%, were working in service, compared to 9.2% of Korean American men, 17.3% of API women, and 16.9% of U.S. women. Similarly, the percentage of Korean American women who worked in operations, labor, or fabrication (14.2%) was higher than the 11.7% of Korean American men, 12.5% of API women, and 8.5% of U.S. females.

Finally, the income differential between working women and men was substantial for all three populations. In 1989, women earned little more than half the median income of men. At the same time, of those 15 years and older, the percentage of women who worked full-time was considerably lower than that of men for all three groups. While about half of Korean American men worked full-time, far fewer, 38.2%, of women did. The latter was also lower than the 40.6% for API women, but higher than the national figure of 33.9%. It must be noted that even when only full-time workers' incomes were counted, the income disparity between women and men remained large for all three populations. The median income of full-time working Korean American women, $18,760, was about 66% of the $28,256 for Korean American men. Also, it was lower than the median income of API and all U.S. full-time working women ($21,335 and $19,570, respectively).

REFERENCES

U.S. Department of Commerce, Bureau of the Census. (1994). Characteristics of the Asian and Pacific Islander Population in the United States. 1990 Census of Population and Housing Subject Summary Table File (SSTF) 5.
____. (1993). *We the Americans . . . Asians*. Table 3, 8-9.
____. (1990a). *Census of Population: General Characteristics*.
____. (1990b). *Social and Economic Characteristics*.

5

Demographic Characteristics and Trends of Post-1965 Korean Immigrant Women and Men

Pyong Gap Min and Young I. Song

Korean communities in the United States are rapidly growing. Undoubtedly, Korean women play important roles in the life of Korean immigrants through which women have influenced the Korean community. Because the history of the United States is based upon the hardships and accomplishments of people who have immigrated here for political, religious, and economic reasons, immigration affects all of us.

A minority group is one that is socially, politically, and economically subordinate; its members are excluded from various opportunities, which limits their freedom of choice and self-development. They tend to have lower self-esteem and often become the objects of contempt, ridicule, and violence; generally, they are socially isolated.

In terms of this definition, Korean immigrant women are a minority group within another minority group in the United States. The lives of Korean immigrant women in the United States are an extension of thousands of years of battering, which is compounded by the problems and frustration caused by cultural conflict. Although these immigrant families came to the United Sates to better their lives, not many were ready to confront life in the Unites States, particularly with regard to cultural differences. Regardless of each Korean's motivation for immigration to the United States, there are drastic differences between the lives of Korean and American families, differences that often cause misunderstanding and frustration when two cultures come into contact with one another. Korean immigrant society at the present time is undergoing a stage of transition in which Korean traditional social structures and norms are breaking down and have not yet been replaced by clearly discernible Western norms. Thus, Korean immigrant women and men are subjected to various factors that determine how they are to behave and feel both before and after transplantation into a new culture. Subsequently, Korean American women are influenced either negatively by cultural conflict or positively during the process of cultural adjustment. Until a few decades ago, the number of Korean immigrants to the United States was negligible.

The United States is a country of immigration. This indicates that the United States consists of different immigrant groups from all over the world.

Since different ethnic groups have moved to the United States in different periods, it may be very difficult to make a generalization of immigration patterns. However, most immigration historians seem to agree that there have been three major turning points in U.S. immigration history. The first major turning point came in 1880. It is a well known fact that a large influx of Catholic and Jewish immigrants from eastern and southern European countries began with the year of 1880, whereas almost all immigrants before that year came from northwestern Protestant countries. The second major turning point came when a very conservative immigration act was passed in 1924 to curb the massive immigration from non-Protestant countries. The 1924 immigration act, commonly known as the National Origins Quota System, justified discrimination in immigration based on national origin. Thus it severely curtailed immigration from eastern and southern European countries and completely abolished immigration from Asian countries.

The last major turning point came in 1965 when a very liberal immigration act was passed, replacing the old conservative one. The Immigration and Naturalization Act of 1965 opened the door for immigration to all countries by abolishing discrimination based on national origin. More significant for Asian immigration is that the new immigration law abolished Asiatic Exclusion, which had eliminated Asians from quota immigration for nearly forty years. As a result, the new immigration law has encouraged immigration from non-European countries, particularly from Asian countries. European immigrants constituted approximately 80% of total immigrants in 1960 and eight of the ten largest source countries were European countries (Arnold et al., 1987). The pattern reversed after 1965. For example, in 1984, immigrants from European countries made up only 18% of total U.S. immigrants and all ten major source countries were non-European countries (Arnold et al., 1987). The number of immigrants from Asian countries has achieved dramatic gains since the enactment of the new immigration law. The proportion of Asian immigrants increased from 9% in 1960 to 25% in 1970 and 44% in 1980 (U.S. Immigration and Naturalization Service 1960, 1970, 1980). Asian countries sent 40-47% of the total U.S. immigrants in the 1980s.

The passage of the Immigration and Naturalization Act of 1965 has probably had the most significant effect on the Korean American community. Although the immigration of Koreans to the United States is a century old, the Korean American community before 1965 was insignificant in terms of population size. Allowing for a large error margin in the 1970 census estimation (69,130), the Korean population in 1970 may have been less than 100,000. However, as will be shown later in this chapter, some 700,000 Koreans have immigrated since 1970. Thus, the current Korean community in the United States is largely the by-product of the liberalization of immigration law in 1965.

This chapter intends to provide an overview of the post-1965 Korean immigrant women and men based on data issued by the Immigration and Naturalization Service and the U.S. Bureau of the Census. It will focus on trends in patterns of Korean immigration over the past 25 years, characteristics of the new immigrants and their trends.

THE RADICAL GROWTH OF KOREAN IMMIGRATION

Annual Korean immigrants numbered a few thousand in the early 1960s. The annual number of Korean immigrants gradually increased in the later 1960s and the early 1970s. It reached the 30,000 mark in 1976 and maintained an annual immigration flow of over 30,000 in the 1980s. A total of 600,000 Koreans immigrated to the United States between 1965 and 1989. Korean immigrants accounted for 6-8% of total immigrants to the United States over the last fifteen years. Korea has been the third largest source country of U.S. immigrants during recent years, following Mexico and the Philippines.

The Korean American community has consequently witnessed a radical population growth. The 1990 census estimated the Korean population to be close to 800,000. It seems to be an underestimation. Considering Korean students, visitors, and illegal residents, the Korean population may have been close to one million as of December 1990. The Korean American population has experienced a ten-fold growth since 1970. Although all major Asian ethnic groups experienced a high rate of population growth in the 1980s, the Korean group, along with Indian and Vietnamese ethnic groups, achieved a radical population growth. Although the 1990 census estimated the Japanese and Indian American populations, respectively, slightly larger than the Korean American population, in actuality, Korean Americans may have outnumbered either Japanese or Indian Americans, since the Korean American population included more illegals and recent immigrants who may not have been included in the census tabulation. One million Koreans in the United States make up 22% of approximately 4.5 million overseas Koreans. They are the second largest overseas Korean group, next to the over two million Koreans in China.

FACTORS BEHIND MASS IMMIGRATION

Economic Opportunity

A majority of recent Korean immigrants have come to the United States not so much for survival itself, but rather to elevate or to improve their opportunities. In contrast to their motives for immigration, however, many Korean immigrants in the United States, upon arrival, experience a great deal of difficulty. Each member of the Korean immigrant family faces serious problems. Moreover, the women seem to encounter more hardships than any of the other family members. Although there are several clear factors that have motivated mass immigration, recent Korean immigrants, like other Asian immigrants, with the exception of Indochinese refugees, are largely economic immigrants. That is, the prospect of a higher standard of living in the United States has motivated most Asian immigrants to choose a trans-Pacific migration. This is illustrated by the fact that recently fewer than 5,000 people have annually emigrated from Japan, where standard of living is as high as or even higher than that of the United States. Recent Korean immigrants, particularly those who came to the United States in the 1970s, decided on a U.S.-bound migration largely because of their expectation for a higher standard of living (Hurh et al., 1979). This view gains support from the fact that the United States maintained a standard of living approximately ten times as high as that of South Korea in 1975.

Structural Linkages between the United States and South Korea

However, as international migration is determined by a combination of factors, the movement of Koreans to the United States cannot be completely explained by economic motivation alone. If the gap in the standard of living between the host country and the source country is the only determinant of international migration, why has India, with a lower standard of living than South Korea, sent a smaller number of immigrants to the United States than has South Korea? As indicated by several other scholars (I. Kim, 1987; Light & Bonacich, 1988), the close military, political, and economic connections between the United States and South Korea have also contributed to a large influx of Korean immigrants to the United States.

Although we recognize the structural linkages between the United States and South Korea as an important factor for the massive migration of the post-1965 Korean immigrants, we consider certain structural explanations, which do not pay attention to the decisions of immigrants themselves at all, not very useful. For example, using the world capitalist system perspective Bonacich argues that the strategy to develop cheap labor mainly to serve the interests of U.S. corporations led to dislocations in South Korea, which resulted in pressure on individuals and families to relocate (Bonacich, 1988; Light & Bonacich, 1988). Thus Bonacich's interpretation suggests that recent Korean immigrants are mainly those who have been dislocated by the U.S. military and economic involvement in South Korea. As argued elsewhere (Min, 1989b, 1989c), whether the military and economic connection between the United States and South Korea has resulted in a one-sided exploitation of Korea by the United States is a complicated issue that cannot be resolved by empirical data. What is clear, however, is that most recent Korean immigrants are not, as suggested by Bonacich, victims of this exploitation. It is well documented that the new Korean immigrants, especially those admitted to the United States in the 1970s, represented the upper-middle- and middle-class segments of the Korean population. They were generally the more successful people in their homeland, and they were able to come to the United States mainly because of their advantages in resources for immigration such as education, money, and knowledge.

To explain the motives of the post-1965 Asian immigrants, Portes & Rumbaut (1990) suggest that those groups most exposed to the contradictions between reality and the attraction of modern life are most likely to choose immigration. We believe their argument is very useful for understanding the motives of many Korean middle-class immigrants. Koreans, particularly middle-class Koreans, have been well exposed to American life through the presence of U.S. servicemen and the American mass media, including the *American Forces in Korea Networks* (*AFKN*), since the Korean War. Many Koreans chose immigration in the early 1970s because of the exposure to American life. In this sense, the U.S. military and economic involvement in South Korea is important for the mass exodus of Koreans to the United States, mainly because of its cultural influence on the aspiration of middle-class Koreans for a higher standard of living.

The U.S. military presence in South Korea has had a direct influence of the international movement of Koreans to the United States in that a large number of Korean women have immigrated to the United States as wives of U.S. servicemen since the end of the Korean War. As will be shown later in this chapter, the number of Korean women admitted to the United States through interracial marriage has increased since the early 1970s. The interracial marriages between Korean women and U.S. servicemen have had far more significant effects on the influx of Koreans to the United States than the number of those intermarriages indicates, since most interracially married Korean women have invited their relatives to this country. The U.S. military presence in other Asian countries such as Japan, the Philippines, and Vietnam has also contributed to the Asian-U.S. international migration.

Opportunity for Children's Education

Koreans put emphasis on the value of education, and consideration of a better educational opportunity has been another important factor for the mass migration of Koreans to the United States during recent years. "A better educational opportunity for children's education" is found to be one of the frequently cited reasons for immigration next to "a better economic opportunity" (Hurh et al., 1979; Min, 1983). Moreover, most Koreans who came as alien students for further study have changed their status to permanent residents (Fawcett & Carino, 1987). In the 1960s and the 1970s the Korean government discouraged Korean students from going abroad for further study through the national qualification examination. However, the Korean government loosened its tight restriction on Koreans' studying abroad by abolishing the qualification examination in 1979. It restored the qualification examination in 1985. The Korean government adopted the most liberal policy in 1988 by abolishing the qualification examination again and allowing even high school graduates to go abroad for further study. As a result, the number of Korean students abroad has significantly increased since 1988.

Political Unrest and Fear of Another War

Between 1961 and 1986 South Korea was ruled by two military governments, first led by Park Chung Hee and then, after the assassination of Park in 1979, led by Chun Doo-Hwan. Two military governments ruthlessly oppressed opposition parties, radical students, and other intellectuals to continue their illegitimate rule. Many intellectuals came to the United States in the 1970s and the early 1980s to escape oppression and political persecution. Many Korean students who had completed higher education in the United States did not go back to Korea because of political problems. Although the Korean War came to a formal end in 1953, military conflicts between North and South Korea continued until recently. The possibility of another war in Korea and quasi-war conditions also pushed many Koreans to the United States (I. Kim, 1981).

Improvements in South Korea and Moderation of Immigration

The economic, political, and social conditions in South Korea have recently improved. First of all, South Korea has made a great improvement in economic conditions over the last ten years or so. For example, Koreans experienced a growth in per capita income from $843 in 1977 to $2,199 in 1987 (Korean National Bureau of Statistics 1984, p. 451; 1988, p. 467). Many middle-class householders in Seoul and large cities have their own cars. Moreover, social and political insecurity, which pushed many Koreans to the United States, has been substantially reduced recently. South Korea had a popular presidential election at the end of 1987, putting an end to the 16-year-old military dictatorship. Although the Roh Tae-Woo government still involves many undemocratic elements, it is a great improvement over the two previous military governments. Militarily, the unification of Germany in 1990 and the breakdown of communist governments in eastern European countries during recent years, which climaxed with the collapse of the Soviet Union, have helped to reduce tensions in the Korean peninsula. North and South Korean governments have taken some positive measures to reduce tensions and establish communications since 1990. The North and South Korean governments have just reached an agreement to eliminate nuclear weapons from the Korean peninsula, thus substantially reducing the chance for a nuclear war in Korea.

The significant improvements in economic, social, political, and military conditions in Korea during recent years have mitigated the influx of Koreans to the United States. As shown in Table 5.1, the number of U.S.-bound Korean immigrants has slightly decreased since 1988. Consideration of several factors leads us to speculate that it will be further reduced to below 30,000 in the 1990s. It is important to note two new developments in this connection. The *New York Times* and other major U.S. media have criticized South Korea for never stopping sending orphans to the United States in spite of a great improvement in her standard of living. Under the pressure of U.S. media criticisms, the South Korean government is beginning to take some measures to discourage sending Korean orphans to the United States for adoption, and thus the immigration of Korean adopted children is expected to be drastically reduced in the future. Withdrawal of U.S. military forces from South Korea seems impending, as North and South Korean governments have significantly improved dialogues to reduce tensions. And the absence of U.S. military servicemen in South Korea will put an end to immigration of Korean women to the United States through intermarriage.

DEMOGRAPHIC CHARACTERISTICS OF POST-1965 KOREAN WOMEN AND MEN

Korean immigrants, like immigrants from other countries, do not represent the general population in Korea. They are a select group in terms of their demographic, socio-economic, and religious characteristics. This section will analyze the characteristics of recent Korean immigrants, with special attention to changes in their characteristics over time.

Demographic Characteristics

Table 5.1 shows the sex composition of Korean immigrants admitted to the United States between 1965 and 1989. Female immigrants outnumbered male immigrants in all the years, although the sex imbalance in favor of female immigrants has been substantially moderated during recent years. This trend makes a good contrast with the earlier Korean immigrants at the turn of the century,

Table 5.1
Sex and Age Distribution of Korean Immigrants, 1965–1989

Year	Sex	<10	10–19	20–29	30–39	40–49	50–59	60+	Total
1965	Male	9.6	2.6	2.3	3.3	0.4	0.2	0.2	18.6
	Female	15.8	6.5	45.7	11.9	0.6	0.3	0.6	81.4
1966	Male	6.5	3.2	4.2	8.3	1.1	0.3	0.3	23.9
	Female	14.3	5.8	39.6	14.0	0.9	0.7	0.8	76.1
1967	Male	6.9	3.4	4.9	13.0	2.0	0.3	0.3	30.8
	Female	11.0	6.5	33.5	14.9	1.6	0.9	0.8	69.2
1968	Male	7.1	3.7	5.9	10.2	1.7	0.5	0.1	29.2
	Female	12.6	5.9	35.6	13.0	1.7	1.2	0.8	71.8
1969	Male	7.8	3.2	6.4	10.8	1.9	0.5	0.4	31.0
	Female	11.7	5.9	35.3	12.6	1.8	1.0	0.9	69.0
1970	Male	7.9	4.1	7.5	10.0	2.0	0.8	0.3	32.6
	Female	11.8	6.0	33.2	12.4	2.1	1.1	0.8	67.4
1971	Male	8.7	4.2	6.9	12.8	2.1	0.7	0.5	35.9
	Female	12.3	6.0	29.2	12.8	2.1	0.9	0.8	64.1
1972	Male	9.4	4.9	7.4	12.2	2.8	0.9	0.6	38.2
	Female	13.7	6.4	25.1	11.7	2.5	1.3	1.1	61.5
1973	Male	11.1	5.9	7.1	9.7	3.0	1.0	0.7	38.5
	Female	14.7	7.7	22.3	10.4	2.8	1.0	1.7	61.5
1974	Male	11.6	6.9	6.6	9.4	3.6	1.1	0.7	39.9
	Female	14.1	8.2	21.3	10.6	3.1	1.4	1.4	60.1
1975	Male	12.9	8.0	7.4	8.2	3.4	1.1	0.8	41.8
	Female	15.9	8.8	18.2	9.4	3.0	1.4	1.5	58.2
1976	Male	13.0	6.6	7.2	7.0	3.0	1.1	0.9	38.8
	Female	16.1	8.3	22.1	8.4	2.9	1.7	1.7	61.2
1977	Male	11.7	6.9	7.7	6.9	3.3	1.4	1.3	39.2
	Female	15.4	8.4	21.1	8.3	3.1	1.9	2.5	60.2
1978	Male	10.5	6.4	6.9	7.6	3.8	1.7	1.7	38.6
	Female	14.1	8.1	20.8	8.6	3.7	2.6	3.5	61.4
1979	Male	9.5	7.5	7.6	6.7	3.6	1.9	2.2	39.0
	Female	11.8	7.8	21.8	8.3	2.8	3.4	4.1	61.0
1980[a]	Male	20.7	15.2	29.3	15.0	7.8	5.3	6.7	100.0
1981[a]	Female	17.9	14.3	30.8	14.4	7.6	6.7	8.3	100.0
1982	Male	14.7		11.4	5.5	3.5	2.2	3.0	40.3
	Female	18.0		19.7	6.8	4.0	4.7	5.6	59.7
1983	Male	17.0		10.1	6.1	4.1	2.1	2.5	41.9
	Female	21.0		18.1	7.2	4.3	3.6	3.9	58.1
1984	Male	17.8		9.4	5.9	4.0	2.0	2.6	41.7
	Female	21.8		17.3	7.2	4.2	3.8	4.0	58.3
1985	Male	18.2		9.4	6.0	3.8	2.0	2.7	42.0
	Female	20.7		16.9	7.6	4.1	4.0	4.7	58.0
1986	Male	18.2		8.7	6.4	3.7	2.3	3.2	42.5
	Female	20.8		15.5	7.4	3.9	4.7	5.2	57.5
1987	Male	18.2		8.9	6.3	3.8	2.3	3.2	42.7
	Female	20.2		15.9	7.5	4.2	4.5	4.9	57.3

(continued)

Table 5.1 (continued)

Year	Sex	<10	10–19	20–29	30–39	40–49	50–59	60+	Total
1988	Male	18.5		7.2	7.0	4.7	2.8	3.0	43.2
	Female	19.5		14.5	8.3	5.2	4.6	4.8	56.8
1989	Male	17.0		8.0	7.6	5.2	3.6	3.2	44.6
	Female	16.2		15.2	9.1	5.5	4.5	4.8	55.4

[a]Immigration data for 1980 and 1981 were not tabulated by sex.

Note: Age distributions from 1982 and on combine those under age 10 with the age group 10–19.

Source: Adjusted from Annual Reports by Immigration and Naturalization Service,1965–1989.

who consisted mainly of young men (Choy, 1979, p. 77).

The numerical dominance of female immigrants over male immigrants can be explained by three major factors. First, as previously noted, a large number of Korean women have married U.S. servicemen and subsequently immigrated to the United States.

Table 5.1 indicates that the sex imbalance is most severe in the 20–29 age category. This is so because most Korean women married to servicemen are in this age category. Second, a large number of Korean children have been adopted by U.S. citizens, who tend to prefer girls over boys. Most adopted children are under the age of 10, and the table shows that there is a greater sex imbalance in the age category of under 10 than for total Korean immigrants. Third, a large number of Korean nurses immigrated to the United States in the 1970s as medical professionals and most of them were in the age category of 20-29. The sex imbalance for the age group of 20–29 is less conspicuous in the 1980s than in the 1970s, because the immigration of Korean nurses virtually came to an end in the 1980s (see the next section).

Table 5.1 further shows the age composition of Korean immigrants admitted between 1965 and 1989. The category of 20–29 is the largest age group. In addition to immigrants in general who are in this age category, two special groups, Korean women married to U.S. servicemen and Korean nurses, are greatly overrepresented in this age category. That explains why Koreans in their twenties constitute the largest age group. Children under 10 constitute the second largest age group, which is due to the fact that many Korean children under 10 have been adopted by U.S. citizens. Those in the age category of 30–39 also constitute a fairly large proportion of Korean immigrants, ranging from 15% to 25%. This means that the new Korean immigrants consist largely of young, economically active people.

As shown in Table 5.1, the proportion of older Korean immigrants has gradually increased over the years. Korean immigrants 50 and over constituted less than 5% of the Korean immigrants admitted up to 1975. But the proportion increased to over 10% in 1979 and maintained at approximately 15% in the late 1980s. This increase in the proportion of Korean elderly immigrants in the 1980s was due to the fact that more and more Korean immigrants who had come in the 1970s were able to bring their elderly parents through naturalization. As previously noted in Table 5.1, the number of Korean immigrants naturalized greatly increased in the late 1970s. Most naturalized Koreans seem to have changed their legal status to naturalized citizens mainly because of the benefit of inviting their family members, including elderly parents, for permanent residence in the United States. In addition to the increase in the number of elderly Korean immigrants, many Korean immigrants who came in their late forties and early fifties are reaching retirement ages. Accordingly, the elderly population in the Korean community is currently rapidly expanding.

Middle-Class and Urban Background

Another significant effect of the 1965 Immigration and Naturalization Act on immigration patterns is a significant change in the socioeconomic background of immigrants. While the earlier immigrants consisted largely of farmers and unskilled workers, the post-1965 immigrants, with the exception of some Hispanic groups, were mainly recruited from the urban middle-class strata of each source country. Recent Asian immigrants in particular represent high levels of socioeconomic background. Of the 1970–1980 Asian adult immigrants (25 years old and over), 37.4% completed four years of college in comparison to 22.2% of all new immigrants admitted during the given period and 16.2% of the U.S. total.

Recent Korean immigrants, like other Asian immigrants, generally represent the middle-class strata of the Korean population. The 1980 census indicates that 32% of Korean immigrants 25 years old and over had completed four years of college. Indian and Filipino immigrants surpass Korean immigrants in the rate of college graduates. However, a much smaller proportion of the U.S. total population than of Korean immigrants completed four years of college. Moreover, recent Korean immigrants surpass the general population in Korea in educational level. The 1980 Korean census indicates that only 7.8% of Korean adults completed four years of college (Korean National Bureau of Statistics, 1983, pp. 120-121).

The high educational levels of Korean immigrants are suggestive of their high pre-immigrant occupational background. U.S. census data do not provide information on pre-immigrant occupations of recent immigrants. However, several case studies shed light on the professional and white-collar background of recent Korean immigrants. For example, nearly 50% of the Korean respondents in Chicago indicated professional, administrative, managerial, and technical occupations as their pre-immigrant occupations, and only 7% were found to have been engaged in blue-collar occupations in Korea (Hurh & Kim, 1988). The 1986 Los Angeles data also show a similarly high pre-immigrant occupational background (Min, 1989a). As shown in Table 5.2, 54% of the respondents who worked in Korea at the time of immigration held occupations classifiable as professional, administrative, executive, and managerial occupations, and only 4% were engaged in blue-collar occupations.

Another important set of findings reflected in Table 5.2 is the large proportion of Korean immigrants who have business experience in Korea. Twenty-five percent of male respondents who worked in Korea at the time of immigration were engaged in one or another kind of business. Including those who held managerial positions, close to 40% of Korean male immigrants held occupations relating to business transaction in one way or another. Although most Korean immigrant entrepreneurs were not engaged in Korea in the same type of business they operate in the United States, a significant proportion of them were exposed to the business environment in Korea. This pre-immigrant occupational background of Korean immigrants partly explains a higher self-employment rate of Korean immigrants than other Asian immigrant groups (Min, 1986-1987).

Recent Asian immigrants are characterized by their pre-immigrant urban background, which makes a good contrast with the earlier peasant immigrants (B. Kim, 1978). This urban background is probably most conspicuous for Korean immigrants. Approximately 1800 of the 1986 Korean prospective immigrants were interviewed at the U.S. Consulate in Seoul at the time of the visa interview. More than half the respondents in this pre-departure survey reported to be residents of Seoul at the time of interview, although only one-fourth of Koreans lived in the capital city (Park et al., 1990, p. 31). The survey showed that more than three-fourths of the respondents lived in the five largest cities in Korea at the time of interview. Although many of the residents in Seoul and other large Korean cities are migrants from rural areas, before their departure for the United States they became familiar with urban life styles, which have many similarities to life styles in large U.S. cities. Thus, the interurban migration of Koreans to U.S. cities could reduce the sense of crisis, isolation, and alienation experienced by the earlier white immigrants from southern and eastern European countries (Thomas & Znaniecki, 1927).

Table 5.2
Korean Immigrants' Pre-Immigrant Occupations by Sex

	Male		Female		Total	
	N	%	N	%	N	%
Professional	81	28.7	32	41.6	113	31.5
Executive &						
administrative	29	10.3	7	9.1	36	10.0
Managerial	37	13.1	6	7.8	43	12.0
Proprietors	69	24.5	9	11.7	78	21.7
Technical	14	5.0	4	5.2	18	5.0
Sales & clerical	11	3.9	12	15.6	23	6.4
Blue-collar	13	4.6	2	2.6	15	4.2
Military service &						
others	28	9.9	5	6.5	33	9.2
Total employed	282	100.0	77	100.0	359	100.0
Employed	282	76.8	77	43.2	359	65.8
Not employed	4	1.1	53	29.8	57	10.5
Students	81	22.1	48	27.0	129	23.7
Total	367	100.0	178	100.0	545	100.0

Note: Total employed takes into account all of those listed in the Employed category.

Source: Min (1989a).

Changes in Immigration Motives and Demographic Backgrounds

The 1965 Immigration and Naturalization Act admits aliens as legal immigrants using three criteria: (1) having a relative in the United States (immigration based on family unification); (2) possession of an occupational skill needed in the United States (occupational immigration); and (3) vulnerability to political persecution (refugee immigration). Few Koreans have immigrated to the United States as political refugees, since refugee immigration has usually been awarded to aliens in Communist countries. Thus, almost all Korean immigrants have come to the United States by virtue of their relationship to those already settled here or occupational skills in demand in the U.S. labor market.

In the early 1970s a large proportion of Korean immigrants were admitted through occupational preference categories, which include primary occupational immigrants and their family members. For example, 45% of Korean immigrants in 1972 were admitted under occupational preference categories. A substantial proportion of the Korean occupational immigrants were medical professionals, consisting of nurses, physicians, surgeons, and pharmacists. However, as the unemployment rate rose in the United States with the economic recession in the late 1970s, the U.S. Congress passed the Eilberg Act and the Health Professional Assistance Act in 1976 in order to discourage the immigration of alien professionals (Youchum & Agarwal, 1988). The Eilberg Act required the alien professional to gain a job offer from a United States employer to be admitted as a legal immigrant. The Health Professions Act stated that alien physicians and surgeons are inadmissible unless they pass the National Board of Medical Examiners Examination. The enforcement of the two acts since 1977 has resulted in a drastic reduction in the immigration of professionals, particularly those in medical professions (Youchum & Agarwal, 1988). It has inflicted a terrible blow particularly to Korean professionals, who have more difficulty in passing the qualification examination in English due to their serious language barriers than other alien professionals. Consequently, Korean occupational immigration has significantly declined since the late 1970s. Korean occupational immigrants have accounted for less than 10% of total Korean immigrants since 1979.

This change in Korean immigrants' entry mechanisms involved a change in their socioeconomic characteristics. Recently arrived relative immigrants received lower levels of education and held lower levels of occupations in Korea than those occupational immigrants in the 1970s. This change in social background is well reflected in the 1986 Los Angeles data. The data indicate that 67% of the respondents who immigrated in 1977 and earlier completed college, in comparison to 53% of those who immigrated after that period (Min, 1989a). This difference in socioeconomic status between the early 1970s occupational immigrants and recent relative immigrants was found in other studies of Korean immigrants and other Asian immigrant groups (Curino et al., 1990; Hurh & Kim, 1988; Park et al., 1990). Since more recent immigrants have acquired lower levels of education than earlier occupational immigrants, the overall educational level of Korean immigrants in the 1990 census is likely to be lower than that reflected in the 1980 census.

The Significant Influence of Christianity

Recent Korean immigrants are also a select group in terms of their heavy Christian background. Although only a little more than 20% of people are affiliated with Christian churches in Korea (Korea National Bureau of Statistics,

1987), the majority of Korean immigrants are found to have had Christian background in Korea. For example, in a survey of the 1986 cohort of Korean immigrants conducted in Seoul (Park et al., 1990, p. 60), 54% of the respondents reported that they were affiliated with Protestant (41.6%) or Catholic (12.3%) churches in Korea. A Chicago survey also indicates that 52.6% were Christians in Korea (Hurh & Kim, 1990). Their heavy Protestant background clearly separates Korean immigrants from other Asian immigrant groups.

As discussed elsewhere (Min, 1992a), three major factors seem to have contributed to the overrepresentation of Christians among Korean immigrants. First, the Christian religion is very strong among urban, middle-class people in South Korea; and, as previously noted, Korean immigrants have been drawn largely from the urban, middle-class segment of the Korean population. Second, many Christians fled from North Korea to South Korea before and during the Korean War, and North Korean refugees, who have no strong kin and regional ties in South Korea, have immigrated to the United States in greater proportion than the general population in Korea (I. Kim, 1981). Moreover, many North Korean refugees have immigrated to the United States during recent years, especially for the benefit of visiting their relatives in North Korea. Third, Korean Christians, who are more Westernized than other Koreans, are more likely to choose immigration to the United States than are Korean Buddhists, Confucians, and those not affiliated with a religion. In this connection, it is interesting to note that Korean Buddhist immigrant women in the United States showed a significantly higher level of stress than Korean Christian immigrant women (Shin, 1992). This has also contributed to the heavy Christian background of Korean immigrants.

NEW TRENDS

Prospective immigrants report their intended place of residence in the United States in their pre-departure visa interview. Immigration data based on this report provide information on the distribution of Korean immigrants in the United States. Almost 60% of Korean immigrants have settled in seven major states — two West Coast states, four East Coast states, and Illinois. Of course, California has received more Korean immigrants than any other state; approximately 20-30% of annual Korean immigrants choose California as the state of residence. It is important to note that the proportion of Korean immigrants who have chosen one or another city of California as an entry point increased from approximately 20% in 1970 to almost 30% in 1979 and was stable throughout the 1980s. This suggests that Los Angeles and its neighboring areas as a major Korean enclave began to attract a large number of Korean immigrants at the end of the 1970s. In addition to the Los Angeles–Long Beach metropolitan area, Orange County, San Jose, San Francisco, and San Diego have also received a large number of Korean immigrants. Interestingly, the proportion of Korean immigrants settled in the state of Hawaii has steadily declined over the years. Honolulu, the center of the earlier Korean immigrants, is no longer an important Korean enclave.

In the beginning of the 1970s some 12% of annual Korean immigrants came to the state of New York. The proportion of Korean immigrants who chose New York decreased to 8% in the mid-1970s probably because of a bad economy in New York City associated with the city's fiscal crisis. It increased to more than 10% in the 1980s, and to 13% in 1989. The vast majority of Korean immigrants who have chosen New York and New Jersey have come to the New York–New Jersey metropolitan area. The New York metropolitan area, the home of approximately 100,000 Koreans, is the second largest Korean center next to Los Angeles. Roughly one-fourth of the New York City Koreans are concentrated in Flushing, and another "overseas Seoul" is in formation in the Flushing downtown area. New York has also been the major destination of Chinese and Indian immigrants. In 1985, for example, the New York metropolitan city was the destination of 27% of Chinese immigrants from mainland China and 10% of Asian Indian immigrants (Portes & Rumbaut 1990, p. 38). New York received more Chinese and Indian immigrants than any other U.S. city in the 1980s.

Illinois, Maryland, and Pennsylvania have also received a large number of Korean immigrants. Each of these three states has a major metropolitan city: Chicago, Baltimore, and Philadelphia respectively. Thus, this reflects the tendency of the new Korean immigrants to concentrate in large metropolitan areas. Other cities with a large Korean population are Washington, Atlanta, Dallas, Seattle, and Denver.

Approximately 44% of Korean Americans reside in the West Coast states. Away from the West Coast, Korean Americans are more widely dispersed in the United States than are other Asian groups. The 1990 census indicates that 80% of Japanese Americans and 70% of Filipino Americans are settled in the West (Min, 1992b). Approximately one-third of all Korean Americans live in the state of California. The proportion of Korean Americans settled in California achieved a slight increase between 1980 and 1990, and a larger proportion of Korean immigrants were settled in California in 1990 than INS data might suggest. This means that new Korean immigrants originally settled in other parts of the country have remigrated to California.

Twenty-three percent of Korean Americans reside in the states the census defines as the Northeast. Significantly, the proportion of Korean Americans settled in the northeastern region increased from 19% in 1980 to 23% in 1990. Two northeastern states in particular achieved much higher growth rates than other states in the 1980s; the Korean population in New York and New Jersey, respectively, achieved a 180% and 200% growth rate in comparison to 125% for the total Korean population in the United States. By contrast, the midwest region achieved a much lower growth rate than the national average. A picture emerging from these figures is the tendency of Koreans to concentrate in two areas, Southern California connecting Los Angeles and Orange Counties and the New York–New Jersey metropolitan area. More and more new Korean immigrants are expected to choose one of these two areas for settlement in the future.

EXPERIENCE OF KOREAN IMMIGRANT WOMEN IN A NEW LAND

Due to the recentness of their immigration, Koreans in the United States are largely foreign-born, young, and Korean-speaking. Adult Koreans are predominantly Korean born. Korean immigrants seem to agree that they also came to the United States to better their lives. Regardless of their backgrounds, few were prepared for life in the United States. In reality, Korean immigrants experienced tremendous differences between two cultures which often resulted in frustration and miscommunication. One may wonder how the Korean immigrant families adjusted themselves to the American way of life. More specifically, one might be curious about the differential patterns of cultural and social experiences among the recent Korean immigrant women.

Korean immigrant women are expected to carry out many activities with a minimum of differentiation of roles and interests. Therefore, absolute male dominant sex roles in the traditional Korean family cannot be maintained in the United States. The traditional relationships between Korean women and men are in marked contrast to American family life in terms of ideal husband and wife interaction. Additionally, there is conflict between Koreans and Americans in family role expectations. These gaps between two cultures may become a cause of hardship for Korean immigrant women and lead to problems in Korean immigrant couples.

Conflict between the husband and wife arises where the previous gender socialization needs to be changed in the context of American culture. When Korean husbands and wives start to disagree about the nature of their respective roles and about new ways of raising children, the husband may try to resolve the resulting conflict by violence against his wife.

Before immigration, there is a clear distinction between the roles of wives and husbands. The roles of driver, cook, babysitter, and shopper are rarely performed by the husbands in Korea. The majority of Koreans use public transportation; cooking is done by the wife or housemaid, and baby-sitting is done only by females. For instance, the kitchen, which in Korea is off-limits to men under normal circumstances, intrudes conspicuously in the United States home structure into the living room, which must be shared by all members of the family. These types of arrangements are apparently more distressing to the men, not only because they have had less experience than women in intense domestic environments, but also because these changes come at a time when they feel extremely vulnerable from the cultural transition.

These conflicts seem to arise because of living in a new culture. The conflicts both sexes recognize are closely related to each other. For example, in the United States domestic affairs cannot be handled by wives alone and they need help from husbands. On the other hand, husbands alone cannot solve external problems because wives are involved in socioeconomic matters. Therefore, most of the decision-making has to be done jointly. In the Korean traditional point of view, the woman's role should be limited to giving helpful advice; she should never take over the role of decision-maker. The high economic participation rate among Korean immigrant women weakens the male-dominant role of the traditional family. As wives become partners in economic activity, they no longer obediently accept the superior position of males. In this respect, the husband feels no absolute dominance over his wife, but often he expects and forces his wife to behave as if she were in Korea. This usually enrages the husband, who will then resort to violence. Even though the Korean immigrant wife may accept the traditional definition of her role, the influence of American culture could easily make her aware of the fact that an American husband is expected to share sex roles. Thus, when she feels particularly overburdened with the absolute demands of the Korean wife's role, she may ask her husband to change. This request may upset each partner. Similarly, as the wife becomes aware of American patterns of child-rearing, she could become dissatisfied with the authoritarianism of her husband. If she expresses her disagreement, this also could lead to marital discord.

At the same time, Korean husbands tend to resist transition and stick to the old authoritarian controls over their wives and children. Under these circumstances, it is difficult to maintain a stable woman-man relationship.

The high economic participation rate among Korean women, like other immigrant wives in the American history of immigration (Chafe, 1976), weakens the male-dominant role of the traditional husband. Korean immigrant wives are employed to support their family because the earnings of their husbands are usually not sufficient to meet all of the family needs (Hurh & Kim, 1984). Disadvantages in the American labor market are another reason for the high labor force participation rate of Korean married women, and a high proportion of Korean husbands turn to self-employment in small businesses such as laundromats, Korean restaurants and stores, and the like (Min, 1988; Kim & Hurh, 1983; Wong & Hirschman, 1983). Management of such small businesses is difficult enough to require the labor of unpaid family members to cut down the cost. Most of the employed wives are working particularly long hours.

It has been observed that immigrant women are expected to perform most of the household tasks, regardless of their employment status or the presence of children. In this respect, Korean immigrant husbands and wives reveal that the immigrant wives are no less traditional than the husbands. When both immigrant husbands and wives continue to believe that the wife should predominantly perform household tasks regardless of the situation, the combination of the extended full-time employment and responsibility for most of the household tasks would mean that the working wives suffer from the heavy burden of their double roles. Eventually, the wives would feel an acute sense of injustice or inequity (Hurh & Kim, 1984).

The Korean immigrant wives begin to question, and they no longer obediently and fully accept the superior position of their husbands. Husbands who are already faced with frustration caused by language difficulties, prejudice, and discrimination in the employment market find it difficult to tolerate their weakening position in the family (H. C. Kim, 1977). Husbands feel helpless when seeing their authority over their wife and children erode. Anger, thus accumulated, explodes between husbands and wives.

However, in Korean immigrant families, little possibility of role sharing or interchange between the wives and their husbands exists. Korean immigrant couples continue to exhibit sharp sex role segregation.

Korean immigrant women and men who had their marriages arranged in Korea and lived with their parents developed a pattern of adjustment that did not require intense interaction between them. For their marriage to be successful in the traditional sense, there was no need for them to get to know each other. For the first time, husband and wife may be by themselves without any other extended family members and thus may have to face each other every day. Consequently, problems they did not experience in Korea may surface and have to be confronted. This can cause intense stress in the relationships between Korean women and men.

SUMMARY

The Immigration and Naturalization Act of 1965 abolished discrimination based on national origin and Asian exclusion, which has encouraged immigration from non-European countries, particularly from Asian countries. South Korea has been one of the major source countries of the new immigrants since the liberalization of the immigration law. Koreans ranging from 30,000 to 35,000 have been annually admitted to the United States as formal immigrants since the mid-1970s. As a result, the Korean population in the United States has achieved a ten-fold increase over the last two decades, reaching nearly the one million mark in 1992.

Many new Korean immigrants have chosen the path to U.S. immigration, attracted by a higher standard of living. Whereas a better economic opportunity in the United States is a pull factor for new Korean immigration, political problems, social insecurity, and fear of another war in South Korea are push factors. South Korea has made great improvements in economic, political, and social conditions during recent years. Moreover, the possibility of major military conflicts in Korea is very slim as the North and South Korean governments have taken some positive measures to reduce tensions and establish communication during recent years. These improvements in Korea have mitigated the influx of Koreans to the United States over the last few years. In addition, the South Korean government has taken some measures to discourage the transfer of orphans to the United States. Given these changes, it is expected that the immigration flow of Koreans will continue to decrease in the future. However, a large number of high school graduates cannot go to college every year, as colleges and universities in South Korea can only accommodate one-fourth of the candidates. Thus, a better opportunity for children's education is likely to be the major pull factor for Korean immigrants to the United States in the future.

Like other new Asian immigrant groups, the new Korean immigrants are characterized by an urban, middle-class, white-collar background, and a large proportion of the Korean immigrants admitted in the early 1970s were professionals. Although revisions of the 1965 Immigration and Naturalization Act in 1976 almost put an end to Korean professional immigration, even recent family preference immigrants have much higher socioeconomic status than the Korean general population. Another important characteristic of the new Korean immigrants is their heavy Christian background. Although Christians constitute no more than 20% of the Korean population, the majority of the new Korean immigrants have come from the Christian population in Korea. Moreover, many non-Christians in Korea have started attending the Korean church in the United States. Consequently, Korean churches play an important role in Koreans' community activities in the United States.

In terms of demographic characteristics, the new Korean immigrants are characterized by a sex imbalance in favor of women, which makes an interesting contrast with the numerical dominance of men among the earlier Korean immigrants. The frequent marriages of Korean women to U.S. servicemen, the immigration of many Korean nurses in the early 1970s, and the tendency of U.S. citizens to adopt more Korean girls than boys have contributed to the sex imbalance. As with any other ethnic group, Korean immigrant women have longer life expectancies than their male counterparts. Thus, Korean women outnumber men and expect to outlive them also.

In the early 1970s the vast majority of Korean adult immigrants were young, economically active people, and few elderly Koreans immigrated to the United States. However, this trend has recently changed as more and more Korean immigrants have become naturalized citizens and thus have invited their elderly parents to join them in the United States.

Traditionally, Asian Americans have concentrated in the West Coast states, particularly in California. The new Korean immigrants are no exception to this general pattern, as 42% concentrate in the West and 32% in California. (However, the new Korean immigrants are more widely scattered away from the West than are other Asian groups.) The Los Angeles–Long Beach area in particular has become the largest Korean concentration, and a Korean territorial community known as "Koreatown" has been established close to Los Angeles downtown. The New York–New Jersey area has also attracted a large proportion of the post-1965 Korean immigrants, and another "overseas Seoul" is in formation in Flushing, New York.

Having looked at a wide range of facts, no one can reasonably argue that Korean immigrant women's and men's lives and experiences are identical. Each play different roles and experience different kinds of realities. This article offers an overview of demographic characteristics and new trends of Korean immigrant women and men in American society today. We looked at comparisons between Korean immigrant women and men to examine the ways in which their experiences are similar and different, focusing on demographics and today's trends. Sex, of course, is not the only factor affecting the demographic features of the lives of Korean immigrants, but it does play one of the most significant roles. Taking into account the sex imbalance and longer life expectancies of women, sex will continue to be a major variable in determining the future trends of Korean immigrant communities.

REFERENCES

Arnold, Fred, Urmi Minocha, & James T. Fawcett. (1987). "The Changing Face of Asian Immigration to the United States." In James Fawcett & Benjamin Curino, eds., *Pacific Bridge: The New Immigration from Asia and the Pacific Islands.* Staten Island, NY: Center for Migration Studies.

Bonacich, Edna. (1988). "The Social Costs of Immigration Entrepreneurship." *Amerasia Journal*, 9(2): 127-135.

Chafe, William. (1976). "Looking Backward in Order to Look Forward: Women, Work, and Social Values in America." In Juanita Kreps, ed., *Women and the American Economy: A Look to the 1980's.* Englewood Cliffs, NJ: Prentice-Hall.

Choy, Bong-Yung. (1979). *Koreans in America.* Chicago: Nelson-Hall.

Curino, Benjamin, James Fawcett, Robert W. Gardner & Fred Arnold. (1990). *The Fillipino Immigrants to the United States: Increasing Diversity and Change.* Honolulu, HI: East-West Center.

Fawcett, James, & Benjamin Carino. (1987). "International Migration and Pacific Basin Development." In James Fawcett & Benjamin Curino, eds., *Pacific Bridges: The New Immigration from Asia and the Pacific Islands.* Staten Island, NY: Center for Migration Studies.

Hurh, Won Moo, & Kwang Chung Kim. (1984). *Korean Immigrants in America: A Structural Analysis of Ethnic Confinement and Adhesive Adaptation.* Cranberry, NJ: Association of University Presses.

_____. (1988). "Uprooting and Adjustment: A Sociological Study of Korean Immigrants' Mental Health." In *Final Report to the National Institute of Mental Health* (Grant No. 1R1 MH40312-01). Bethesda, MD: U.S. Department of Health and Human Services, National Institute of Mental Health.

_____. (1990). "Religious Participation of Korean Immigrants in the United States." *Journal of the Scientific Study of Religion,* 29, 19-34.

Hurh, Won Moo, Kwang Chung Kim, & Hei Chu Kim. (1979). *Assimilation Patterns of Immigrants in the U.S.: A Case Study of Korean Immigrants in the Chicago Area.* Washington, DC: University Press of America.

Kim, Bok-Lim. (1978). *The Asian Americans, Changing Patterns, Changing Needs.* Montclair, NJ: Association of Korean Christian Scholars in North America.

Kim, Hyung-Chan. (1977). "Korean Community Organizations in America: Their Characteristics and Problems." In Hyung-Chan Kim, ed., *The Korean Diaspora.* Santa Barbara, CA: ABC-Clio Press.

Kim, Illsoo. (1981). *New Urban Immigrants: The Korean Community in New York.* Princeton, NJ: Princeton University Press.

_____. (1987). "Korea and East Asia: Pre-immigration Factors and U.S. Immigration Policy." In James Fawcett & Benjamin Curino, eds., *Pacific Bridge: The New Immigration from Asia and the Pacific Islands.* Staten Island, NY: Center for Migration Studies, pp. 327-345.

Kim, K. C., & W. M. Hurh. (1983). "Korean Americans and the 'Success' Image: A Critique." *Amerasia Journal.* 10.

Korean National Bureau of Statistics. (1983). *1980 Population and Housing Census, Percent Sample, Economic Activities.* Seoul: Economic Planning Board, 2(15): 3-1.

_____. (1984). *Korea Statistical Yearbook, 1984.* Seoul: Economic Planning Board, Vol. 31.

_____. (1987). *1985 Population and Housing Census.* Seoul: Economic Planning Board.

_____. (1988). *Korea Statistical Yearbook, 1988.* Seoul: Economic Planning Board.

Light, Ivan, & Edna Bonacich. (1988). *Immigrant Entrepreneurs: Koreans in Los Angeles, 1965-1982.* Berkeley: University of California Press, Vol. 35.

Min, Pyong Gap. (1983). "Ethnic Business Enterprise: Korean Small Business in Atlanta." Unpublished Ph.D. dissertation, Department of Sociology, Georgia State University.

_____. (1986-1987). "A Comparison of Filipino and Korean Immigrants in Small Business." *Amerasia Journal,* 13(1): 53-71.

_____. (1988). "Korean Immigrant Entrepreneurship: A Comprehensive Explanation." In S. H. Lee and T. H. Kwak, eds., *Koreans in North America.* Seoul: Kyungnam University Press.

_____. (1989a). "Some Positive Functions of Ethnic Business for an Immigrant Community: Koreans in Los Angeles." Final report submitted to National Science Foundation.

_____. (1989b). "The Social Costs of Immigrant Entrepreneurship. A Response to Edna Bonacich." *Amerasia Journal,* 15(2): 187-194.

_____. (1989c). "Review of Immigrant Entrepreneurs: Koreans in Los Angeles." *International Migration Review,* 23: 728-729.

_____. (1992a). "The Structure and Social Functions of Korean Immigrant Churches in the United States." *International Migration Review,* 6.

_____. (1992b). "Overview of Asian Americans." In Pyong Gap Min, ed., *Asian Americans: An Overview of Ethnic Groups*. Newbury Park, CA: Sage Publications.

Park, Insook Han, James T. Fawcett, Fred Arnold, & Robert W. Gardner. (1990). *Korean Immigrants and U.S. Immigration Policy: A Pre-departure Perspective.* Honolulu, HI: East-West Center.

Portes, Alejandro, & Ruben Rumbaut. (1990). *Immigrant America: A Portrait.* Berkeley and Los Angeles: University of California Press.

Shin, Kyung Rim. (1992). "Correlates of Descriptive Symptomatology in Korean-American Women in New York City." Unpublished Ph.D. dissertation, Department of Nursing, Teachers College, Columbia University.

Thomas, William I., & Florian Znaniecki. (1927). *The Polish Peasants in Europe and America.* New York: Knopf.

U.S. Bureau of the Census. (1983). *1980 Census of Population and Housing.* Washington, DC: U.S. Government Printing Office.

U.S. Immigration and Naturalization Service. (1960-1989). *Annual Reports.* Washington, DC: U.S. Government Printing Office.

Wong, M. G., & C. Hirschman. (1983). "Labor Force Participation and Socioeconomic Attainment of Asian American Women." *Sociological Perspectives.* 26.

Youchum, Gilbert, & Vinod Agarwal. (1988). "Permanent Labor Certifications for Asian Professionals. 1975-1982." *International Migration Review*, 22: 265-281.

6

Attitudes Toward Ethnic Identity, Marriage, and Familial Life among Women of Korean Descent in the United States, Japan, and Korea

Ailee Moon

INTRODUCTION

Most studies of Korean immigrant families in the United States indicate that traditional Korean values, strongly rooted in the Confucian philosophy, have continued to be the single most influential force shaping family structure, gender roles, and marital relations (Kim and Hurh, 1987, 1988; Min, 1992; Yu, 1987). The Confucian philosophy, among many things, dictates a male-centered patriarchal family system, filial piety, and extended family structure, emphasizing the importance of the inheritance of the family line and kinship relationships (Dawson, 1942; Kang, 1971; Lee, 1989). It also defines women as the property of men, belonging to her father before marriage and her husband after marriage, inferior and subordinate to men, and incompetent to perform major roles outside the family, confining women's roles to within the family as caregivers for their husbands, children, and parents-in-law, responsible for all household chores. Accordingly, an ideal Korean womanhood rests in being a submissive wife, sacrificial mother, and obedient daughter-in-law. Needless to say, the Confucian culture condemns women who seek out their own identity and freedom as human beings, perceive or treat men as equals, and pursue both meaningful roles in society and rights for decision-making authority in and outside the family.

Living in a Christian, industrial, and individualistic American culture, many Korean American women experience two worlds of reality, one of Korean traditionalism, which includes Confucian gender roles, and the other of American modernism, including greater freedom for women, decision-making power, and greater opportunities in family and society. In this regard, several studies of Korean immigrant wives seem to suggest that these women's lives are dominated by the former reality more than the latter, except for their participation in the labor force (Hurh and Kim, 1984; Kim and Hurh, 1987, 1988; Min, 1992; Yu, 1987). For example, Kim and Hurh (1987, 1988) reported that Korean immigrant wives were faced with the burden of double roles, the traditional Korean women's roles in the family and working women's roles outside the home. Other studies of Korean immigrant wives' work in and out of the home also found a significant lack of support from their spouses in household tasks and attributed this to Korean traditional values, especially rigid gender roles that dominate familial and marital relations (Bonacich, et al., 1987; Hurh and Kim, 1984; Kim and Hurh, 1987, 1988; Min, 1992; Yu, 1987).

Considering this background, the purpose of this chapter is to examine whether and to what extent Korean American women's thoughts and behaviors have changed from Korean traditional values and practices regarding ideal womanhood, marriage, familial life, and their actual contributions to family finance and sharing of domestic tasks. Discussion in this chapter is based on the results of empirical studies (B. Kim, 1995; J. Kim, 1995; Moon, 1995), rather than theoretical or personal observations. While the focus is on Korean American women, the research findings will also be compared with the results of two similar studies (B. Kim, 1995; J. Kim, 1995) conducted on their counterparts in Japan (Korean Japanese, hereafter) and Korea (Korean, hereafter).

Before discussing and comparing the results of the three studies, it is useful to note the similarities and differences in the characteristics of the respondents in these studies. The sample in each of these studies consists of 256 Korean American, 207 Korean Japanese, and 310 Korean women. The Korean American respondents were, at the time of survey, legal immigrants or citizens of the United States, 18 years or older, who were residing in Los Angeles County, California. Using similar age and legal status criteria, the Korean Japanese sample was drawn from 12 cities in Japan, including Tokyo (87), Saidama (27), Kanagawa (21), and Osaka (13), while Seoul was the sampling site for the Korean respondents.

The most remarkable differences between Korean American and Korean Japanese respondents are found in their place of birth versus their country of citizenship. While 94% of Korean Americans and only 10% of Korean Japanese were born in Korea, about half (51%) of the Korean Americans and nearly 96% of the Korean Japanese held Korean citizenship. Of the Korean American respondents born outside the United States, about half (51%) immigrated to America in the 1980s, and 29% in the 1970s. The extremely high rate of Korean citizenship among Japanese-born Koreans in Japan is largely attributed to the combination of the Japanese government's restrictive naturalization policy governing citizenship qualification criteria, a strong sense of Korean nationality, and the history of forced migration of Koreans to Japan during World War II.

Age distribution of the three groups shows that, overall, Korean Japanese respondents were considerably older than the other groups. More specifically, those of age 40 or younger constituted 68% of Korean American, 42% of Korean Japanese, and 61% of Korean respondents. Fifty-seven percent of Korean Americans, 63% of Korean Japanese, and 45% of Koreans respondents were currently married. While approximately three-quarters of Korean American and Korean respondents (75% and 71%, respectively) had more than high school education, only 36% of Korean Japanese had similar educational backgrounds. Finally, a major difference was found between Korean Americans and the other groups in work status: About two-thirds or 65% of Korean Americans, compared to 43% of Korean Japanese and 35% of Koreans, were working outside the home, suggesting a significant deviation from traditional Korean women's roles confining women to family life.

ETHNIC IDENTITY AND DISCRIMINATION

Despite a very high percentage of Korean-born respondents in the United States and Japanese-born respondents in Japan, similar percentages of the two groups, 66% and 62%, respectively, identified themselves as Korean, rather than Korean American or Korean Japanese, indicating strong ethnic attachment to their country of origin. Similarly, only 7% of Korean Americans and 4% of Korean Japanese considered the country of their residence, the United States and Japan, respectively, as their homeland. It is interesting that while an overwhelming majority of Korean Americans (80%) identified South Korea as their homeland, more than half (52%) of the Korean Japanese considered both South and North Korea as their homeland. This reflects the Korean Japanese community's exposure to and their ties with both South and North Korea, whereas Korean Americans have had very little or no exposure to North Korea or its people, combined with prevailing anti-communist sentiment in the Korean American community.

The studies further indicated that while 54% of Korean American respondents experienced racial or ethnic discrimination, a considerably higher 72% felt that the American legal system was, overall, fair toward them. In contrast, 92% of the Korean Japanese respondents considered the Japanese system as unfair toward them, although less than half, 46%, personally experienced ethnic discrimination in Japan.

ATTITUDES TOWARD MARRIAGE AND FAMILIAL LIFE

Table 6.1 presents the three groups' attitudes toward marriage and familial life, including attitudes toward the virtue of virginity, ideal womanhood, the importance of inheriting a family line, and traditional living arrangements. For all three groups of women, the findings suggest, overall, a significant change, at least in their value systems, if not in their actual behavior or ways of life, away from the Confucian, traditional Korean values and norms that define women's roles and lives.

Specifically, only very small percentages of all three groups, 2% of Korean Americans, 10% of Korean Japanese, and 4% of Koreans, accepted the Confucian sexism of high tolerance for men and no tolerance for women regarding sex before marriage. While most respondents believed that the rule concerning virginity before marriage should be applied equally for both women and men, the groups showed an interesting difference in their views about the virtue of remaining virgins until marriage. That is, the majority, 57%, of Korean Japanese held the belief that both men and women need not remain virgins until marriage, whereas an overwhelming majority of Korean American and Korean respondents (79% and 67%, respectively) believed both men and women should remain virgins.

Similarly, an overwhelming majority, 70% of Korean Americans, 82% of Korean Japanese, and 79% of Koreans, rejected the Confucian requirement of marriage imposed on women, believing that marriage is a woman's individual choice rather than a requirement. However, the percentage of Korean American respondents who perceived marriage as a "must," 25%, was considerably higher than the 7% of Korean Japanese and 15% of Koreans with that same belief. Fur-

Table 6.1
Attitudes Toward Marriage and Family Life

VARIABLES	U.S. (N = 256) %	JAPAN (N = 207) %	KOREA (N = 310) %
Virginity until marriage			
Both men and women should remain virgins until marriage	78.6	22.3	66.8
Only women, not necessarily men should remain virgins	1.6	10.1	3.9
Both men and women need not remain virgins (It should not be an issue for marriage)	12.9	57.0	16.5
Other	6.8	10.6	12.8
Marriage			
A must for women	25.1	6.8	14.8
Not a must, but an individual choice	69.7	82.0	79.0
Women are better off being unmarried	0.4	1.0	3.0
Other	4.8	10.2	3.3
Perception of an ideal life as a woman			
Being a good wife and mother	16.1	3.0	3.6
Being a successful career woman	4.0	19.7	12.5
Both	67.1	65.0	75.1
Other	12.9	12.3	8.9
Importance of husband, children, and self to a woman's life			
Both husband and children are critical	62.5	76.6	38.4
Only the husband is critical	3.6	0.0	8.8
Only the children are critical	3.6	3.6	9.1
Women's self is more critical than husband or children	26.7	6.6	35.7
Other	3.6	13.2	8.1
Importance of inheriting family line			
No longer important to continue a family line	47.0	58.2	50.2
Only a son, even by adoption, should inherit the family line	4.0	2.7	0.0
A daughter should inherit the family line if there is no son	43.8	26.9	47.2
Other	5.2	12.1	2.7

(continued)

Table 6.1 (continued)

VARIABLES	U.S. (N = 256) %	JAPAN (N = 207) %	KOREA (N = 310) %
Married woman living with parents or parents-in-law			
It is equally desirable to live with woman's own parents or parents-in-law	40.5	36.5	38.9
It is equally undesirable to live with either own or husband's parents	12.7	9.0	26.4
Living with husband's parents is reasonable, but living with own parents is not	3.6	30.8	16.2
Living with own parents is reasonable, but living with husband's parents is not	2.0	4.6	1.3
Other	41.2	19.1	17.2

Note: Percentages may not add to 100 due to rounding.

Source: B. Kim (1995), J. Kim (1995), Moon (1995).

ther statistical analysis of within-group difference of Korean American respondents in terms of their demographic and socio-economic characteristics indicated that those holding the traditional values regarding marriage were married respondents, significantly older, and less educated, who immigrated to the United States at significantly older ages than those with nontraditional values. Differences in family income and years of residence in America were not statistically significant for traditional and nontraditional value holders.

In response to a question about what constitutes an ideal life for a woman, only 16% of Korean Americans and even lower percentages, 3% and 4%, of Korean Japanese and Koreans indicated "being a good wife and mother," which is the traditionally defined role for Korean women, while approximately two-thirds of Korean Americans and Korean Japanese and three-quarters of Koreans identified pursuit of both a successful career and role of a good wife and motherhood as ideal for women. By pursuing multiple roles in and outside the family, most respondents in all three groups tended to have high expectations of themselves, thereby imposing heavy burdens on themselves. Statistically, Korean American respondents who conformed to the Korean traditional role of women were more likely to be married, not working outside of the home, significantly older, less educated, with a lower family income.

Furthermore, a mere 4% of Korean Americans, 3% of Korean Japanese, and none of the Korean respondents agreed that only a son, even by adoption, should inherit the family line, conforming to the traditional norms and practices in the Korean family system. In contrast, significantly higher percentages of all three groups, 47%, 58%, and 50%, deemphasized the importance of continuing a family line, whereas substantial percentages of Korean Americans (44%) and Koreans (47%), and a lower percentage (27%) of Korean Japanese indicated that if there is no son, a daughter should inherit the family line.

Finally, the table shows that most Korean Americans and Koreans, and over two-thirds of the Korean Japanese did not concur with the traditional norm of living arrangement for married women. Specifically, only 4% of Korean Americans, 31% of Korean Japanese, and 16% of the Koreans agreed that for a married woman, living with her husband's parents is reasonable, but living with their own parents is not; they thereby are rejecting the traditional living arrangement norm in the patriarchal Korean family. Instead, the majority of all three groups did not believe in differential treatments of women's and their husbands' parents in terms of living together after marriage.

FAMILY FINANCIAL AND HOUSEHOLD CHORE RESPONSIBILITY SHARING

Table 6.2 presents the findings on the respondents' actual contributions to family finances and their sharing of household chores with other family members, especially spouses, among 150 Korean Americans and 135 Korean Japanese living with a spouse or partner. It shows that the respondents' families relying on men as the sole source of family income, reflective of the most important role and responsibility of men in a traditional Korean family, constituted only one-third or 34% of both groups. About 60% of Korean Americans and 35% of Korean Japanese were engaged in a nontraditional Korean women's role of contributing to the family economy by working outside of the home.

Table 6.2
Family Financial and Household Chore Responsibility Sharing

VARIABLES	U.S. (N = 150) %	JAPAN (N = 132) %	KOREA (N = 310) %
Contribution to Family Finances			
Husband only	33.6	33.7	NA
Both husband and wife	59.7	34.6	NA
Wife only	2.0	5.3	NA
Other (e.g., husband and son, wife and son, relatives)	4.6	26.4	NA
Household Chore Responsibility			
Wife only, almost always	64.6	78.1	NA
Wife and husband share	28.0	9.0	NA
Husband only, almost always	2.7	0.5	NA
Other	4.7	12.4	NA

NA: Not available.

Source: See Table 6.1.

Despite these high percentages of respondents, especially for Korean Americans, who shared the family financial burden with their husbands or partners, only 28% of the Korean Americans and an even lower 9% of the Korean Japanese reported sharing household chores with their husbands or partners almost equally, while the housework burden is almost exclusively borne by women for

65% of the Korean Americans and a higher 78% for the Korean Japanese respondents.

CONCLUSION

Before concluding, it must be pointed out that the results discussed in this chapter are limited in their generalizability beyond the sample groups and the scope and depth of coverage of respondents' attitudes and behaviors. For example, the selection of Los Angeles and Seoul as sampling sites, both urban and the most populous cities in their respective countries, combined with the employment of a nonprobability sampling method, raises concern about the samples' representativeness of the study population. Furthermore, the selected aspects of women's attitudes and behaviors are far from adequate to fully understand their beliefs and actual ways of life on a wide spectrum of individual, familial, social, economic, political, and religious life.

Due to the inherent limitations of cross-sectional studies, the study results only reflect the status of respondents' attitudes at the time of survey, and are unable to assess the nature and pattern of change over time. The exclusive focus on women also raises questions about whether and how men's attitudes and behaviors have changed compared with the women's, as well as on their influence on the women's attitudes, and vice versa. These limitations, therefore, have implications for future research on the topic, including use of a more scientific and representative sampling method, expansion of the conceptual scope of issues covered, use of both quantitative and qualitative approaches of inquiry, design of a longitudinal study, and inclusion of men for comparison

Given these limitations, the study results, nevertheless, suggest that the attitudes of the majority of women in the studies do not concur with Confucian-rooted Korean traditional values and norms governing women's gender roles in marriage and the family. Considering that the attitudes of respondents in Korea are not necessarily more traditional than that of the Korean Americans and Korean Japanese, a shift away from Korean traditionalism toward modern, western feminism seems to be an universal, irreversible trend in the three countries. From this generalization, one can further argue that the influence of American socioeconomic and cultural settings should not be overstated in understanding Korean American women's thoughts and behaviors, refuting the general assumption that it is the immigration and assimilation into American society, characterized by less sexism, more egalitarianism and individualism, and greater opportunities for women in almost all aspects of life, that explains their current attitudes.

As discussed earlier, although greater employment opportunities and earning potential for women in the United States have significantly contributed to the high rate of Korean American women's participation in the labor force and improved their families' economic status, domestic work was still performed primarily by women. This finding is indicative of the heavy burden of double roles imposed on Korean American women, supporting the findings of previous researchers (Kim and Hurh, 1987, 1988; Min, 1992; Yu, 1987). This also suggests the potential for inconsistencies between women's own thoughts and behaviors, confirming the notion that beliefs are necessary, but constitute an insufficient condition for actions.

REFERENCES

Bonacich, E., et al. (1987). "Korean Immigrant Working Women in the Early 1980s." In E. Y. Yu & E. H. Phillips, eds., *Korean Women in Transition: At Home and Abroad*. Los Angeles: California State University.

Dawson, M. M. (1942). *The Basic Teachings of Confucianism*. New York: New Home Library.

Hurh, Won Moo, & Kwang Chung Kim. (1984). *Korean Immigrants in America: A Structural Analysis of Ethnic Confinement and Adhesive Adaptation*. Cranberry, NJ: Association of University Presses.

Kang, H. (1971). *The Making of Confucian Society in Tokugawa Japan and Yi Korea: A Comparative Analysis of the Behavior Patterns in Accepting the Foreign Ideology, Neo-Confucianism*. Washington, DC: American University Press.

Kim, B. (1995). "Life of Korean Women Residing in Japan and Their Awareness toward the Unification." *Journal of Women's Studies* [In Korean], 12, December, 171-204.

Kim, J. (1995). "An Empirical Study on the Korean Women's Attitudes toward Women's Lives and Reunification Issues." *Journal of Women's Studies* [In Korean], 12, December, 105-145.

Kim, K. C., & W. M. Hurh. (1987). "Employment of Korean Immigrant Wives and the Division of Household Tasks." In E. Y. Yu & E. H. Phillips, eds., *Korean Women in Transition: At Home and Abroad*. Los Angeles: California State University.

_____. (1988). "The Burden of Double Roles: Korean Immigrant Wives in the USA." *Ethnic and Racial Studies*, 11: 151-167.

Lee, K. K. (1989). *An Analysis of the Structure of the Korean Family*. 11th ed. Seoul, South Korea: Il-Ji Publishing Co.

Min, P. C. (1992). "Korean Immigrant Wives' Overwork." *Korean Journal of Population and Development*, 91: 557-592.

Moon, A. (1995). "Korean American Women's Attitudes toward Gender, Ethnic Identity, and Unification of Korea." *Journal of Korean Women's Studies* [In Korean], 12, December, 147-170.

Yu, E. Y. (1987). "Korean American Women: Demographic Profiles and Family Roles." In E. Y. Yu & E. H. Phillips, eds., *Korean Women in Transition: At Home and Abroad*. Los Angeles: California State University.

part three

KOREAN AMERICAN WOMEN WORKING OUTSIDE OF THE FAMILY

The following chapters in Part Three examine issues related to working Korean American women, especially married women, including the nature and pattern of work and overwork, and the influence of work status and employment type on conjugal power relations and marital satisfaction.

Several studies of Korean immigrant wives' work outside the home and domestic work suggest that significant spousal support is lacking because Korean traditional values, especially rigid gender roles, prevail in their family life. In "Work Status, Conjugal Power Relations, and Marital Satisfaction among Korean Immigrant Married Women," Hye Kyung Chang and Ailee Moon present the findings of an empirical study of 200 Korean immigrant married women's conjugal power relations, marital satisfaction, and their attitudes toward gender roles and marital relations in relations vis-à-vis their work status and the labor market in which they work. They conclude that married Korean immigrant women's work status and type of employment have no significant bearing on their conjugal power relations and marital satisfaction, indicating that working wives' contributions to the family economy do not necessarily enhance their decision making power in the family.

In "The Burden of Labor on Korean American Wives in and outside the Family," Pyong Gap Min examines the extent to which Korean immigrant wives overwork and analyzes the factors that contribute to the differentials in Korean immigrant wives' shares of housework, based on interviews with 298 Korean married women in New York City. A large majority of Korean immigrant wives in New York City are found to take an economic role, and an overwhelming majority Korean working wives are involved in excessively long hours of work compared to their husbands. Moreover, Korean immigrant working wives are responsible for most of housework. As expected, the amount of time Korean immigrant wives spend for paid work and the number of their cohabiting extra adult members significantly reduce their share of housework. Years of education Korean immigrant wives received have a moderate, but statistically significant negative effect on their proportion of housework. However, neither their length of residence in the United States nor gender role attitudes have a significant effect on their share of housework.

In "Family and Work Roles of Korean Immigrant Wives and Related Experiences," Kwang Chung Kim and Shin Kim analyze the family and work roles of Korean immigrant wives in light of their high employment rate, based on interview data collected from Korean immigrant adults in the Chicago area. Ironic as it sounds, the traditional gender role orientation seems to justify their employment. When they are employed in marginal occupations with the traditional gender role orientation, the employed wives are inevitably burdened with the double roles of family and work. The employment of wives accelerates the emergence of the independent nuclear family. At the same time, when both husbands and wives work, as in most Korean immigrant families, the married couples are busy with a full set of the major adult roles. The findings suggest that the independent nuclear family and the set of adult roles also create strain in intergenerational relationships. The authors further discuss the implications of these related events.

7

Work Status, Conjugal Power Relations, and Marital Satisfaction among Korean Immigrant Married Women

Hye Kyung Chang and Ailee Moon

INTRODUCTION

Studies have shown that when American women work outside the home, gender relations within the family change, particularly affecting domestic power relations between husband and wife, as well as their marriage (Blood & Wolfe, 1960; Blumstein & Schwartz, 1985; Hertz, 1986; Mirowsky, 1985; Oppenheimer, 1977; Ostrander, 1984; Rubin, 1976; Safilios-Rothschild, 1970). This suggests that while conjugal power relations are structurally conditioned by patriarchal culture, they are also an arena for negotiation and change as women become economically active.

In the past decade, several studies have examined labor force participation of immigrant married women and their marital lives before and/or after immigration to the United States (Boyd, 1989; Kibria, 1994; Moallem, 1991; Zhou, 1992). Among most immigrant ethnic groups, few married women held jobs in their country of origin, although labor force participation varied across countries. After arriving in the United States, however, many married women join the labor force. Their work outside the home provides indispensable income for poor families and faster economic mobility for more affluent ones (Gold, 1989; Pedraza, 1991; Perez, 1986; Pressar, 1987). Along with the income benefits, their employment often changes family life, including child rearing practices, living arrangements, division of domestic labor, and conjugal power relations.

South Korea is a good example of the countries in which married women's prevailing non-participation in the labor force contrasts sharply with their immigrant counterparts in the United States. In fact, the 1990 census indicated that 56% of Korean American women 16 years or older worked outside the home (U.S. Bureau of the Census, 1994). Also, Min (1992) found that 70% of Korean married women in New York City worked outside the home, as opposed to only 20% in South Korea. Furthermore, the 1990 census showed that approximately 29% of Korean American men and 20% of women 16 years and older were self-employed or unpaid family workers, much higher than the 9% and 6% of all American men and women, and 10% and 8% of all Asian Pacific Islanders (U.S. Bureau of the Census, 1994).

While many Korean families turn to self-employment to overcome U.S. economic and cultural hurdles (e.g., language and cultural barriers; racial and ethnic discrimination in hiring and promotion; low wages in the general labor market; lack of transferability of work experience, education, and skills acquired in Korea), willingness of the spouse, children, and cohabiting family members to provide unpaid labor has been an equally important consideration. In fact, a number of studies of Korean ethnic entrepreneurship found that the women are crucial to starting and maintaining small Korean family businesses: their availability and willingness to work long hours as unpaid workers are major factors in achieving economic success (Aldrich & Waldinger, 1990; Dallalfar, 1989; Hurh & Kim, 1984; Kim & Hurh, 1987, 1988; Lee, 1988; Light & Karegeorgis, 1994; Min, 1992; Yu, 1987).

Several studies of Korean immigrant wives' work outside the home and domestic work suggest that significant spousal support is lacking because Korean traditional values, especially rigid gender roles, prevail in their family life (Bonacich, 1987; Hurh and Kim, 1984; Min, 1992; Yu, 1987). However, little empirical evidence is available to support or refute the claim that the work status of these women affects their family and marital relations. Nor was empirical research conducted on the effect of variations in occupation or employment sector in which the women engaged.

For these reasons, this chapter presents the findings of the most recent empirical study (Chang, 1995) of Korean immigrant married women's conjugal power relations, marital satisfaction, and their attitudes toward gender roles and marital relations in relations vis-à-vis their work status and the labor market in which they work.

THE LOS ANGELES STUDY

The study sample comprises 200 Korean immigrant married women who resided in Los Angeles County, California, in 1994. It was selected on the basis of gender, age, immigrant status, location of residence, length of marriage, and years of U.S. residence. Specifically, study participants were between ages 30 and 50, born in South Korea, lived there until they immigrated, and had been married at least five years. To control for the effect of divorce, remarriage, and separation, only women whose current marriage was their first and who were currently living with their husbands were eligible. In addition, participants were legal immigrants and had lived in the United States at least five but no longer than twenty-five years.

Because participants' work status and employment sector were the study's major independent variables, it employed a nonprobability quota sampling method on the basis of work status, employment sector, and age to obtain an equal number of respondents, or 40, for each of the five sample subgroups. The five subgroups were: (1) women not working (NW, hereafter); (2) self-employed as a helper with no control over the business (HELPERS); (3) self-employed with control over operation and finance of the business (CONTROL); (4) wage-earner in the Korean ethnic labor market (KEM); and (5) wage-earner in the general labor market (GLM).

Age was used as a criterion not only to control for age effect but also because it is a good proxy of several important contextual variables, such as attitude toward traditional Korean family relations, and length of marriage and U.S. residence. Thus, each subgroup has 20 respondents from age 30 through 39 and 20 respondents from age 40 through 50. Data were collected in 1994 in face-to-face interviews, using a structured questionnaire.

It should be noted that there were no significant differences among the five groups of respondents with respect to their age and health status, their husbands' age, health status, and education completed in Korea, numbers of children and family members, and years of marriage. For example, the mean age of all respondents was 39.4, ranging from 38.2 for NW to 40.6 for GLM; the average length of marriage was 14.2 years, ranging from 12.7 for NW to 15.4 for HELPER. On the other hand, significant group differences were found in the length of U.S. residence, respondents' level of Korean education, respondents' and their husbands' experience of U.S. formal education, home ownership, and association with Koreans. For example, while respondents had lived in the United States for an average of 14 years, this ranged from 12 years for KEM to 17 years for GLM. A remarkable group difference was evident in the percentage who had lived in the United States 10 years or less: 5% for GLM; 23% for HELPER; 25% for CONTROL; 38% for KEM; and 45% for NW. The percentage of respondents who owned their home ranged from 43% for KEM to 78% for GLM. Furthermore, respondents who indicated associating "always" or "more" with other Koreans varied from 48% of GLM to 95% of NW and KEM. As this shows, the two groups of employed respondents showed a consistent and intuitively reasonable pattern in their differences: Generally, GLM, compared to KEM, had lived in the United States longer, were more educated and economically better-off, in terms of home ownership, and associated more with non-Koreans than Koreans. This would be expected given the respective workplace demands and conditions.

Conjugal Power Relations, Work Status, and the Employment Sector

Conjugal power, measured by the 6-item Blood-Wolfe Marital Power Scale (Blood & Wolfe, 1960) supplemented by 9 items developed by the authors, reflects who makes the final decision about various areas of family and marital life. Table 7.1 depicts the findings on the primary decision maker(s) for each of 15 items by group, using a 5-point Likert scale, ranging from husband's opinion being far more important to wife's opinion being far more important. The table shows several decision making patterns. Except for six items (items 7, 8, 10, 12, 14, and 15), the majority of respondents in all five groups indicated both spouses' opinions were equally important. Specifically, respondents in all five groups dominated decisions regarding decorating the house, whether and what to buy for their and their husbands' parents and relatives, and which social organizations the wife should join, while husbands dominated in two items, which social organization they should join and what job they should take.

A most striking finding was that non-working respondents (NW) exercised more decision making power than the employed (KEM or GLM), as much power as the self-employed as HELPER, and only slightly less power than the self-employed with CONTROL, although differences were not statistically significant. For example, except for items 1, 6, and 14 (whether or not the wife should

Table 7.1
Responses to the 15 Decision-Making Items by Group (%)

Decisions and Degrees of Opinion	NW	Helper	Control	KEM	GLM
1. Should the wife work?					
Husband far more important	7.5	0.0	2.5	2.5	2.5
Husband more important	5.0	10.0	7.5	7.5	0.0
Both equal	55.0	52.5	42.5	52.5	50.0
Wife more important	17.5	5.0	5.0	17.5	22.5
Wife far more important	15.0	32.5	42.5	20.0	25.0
2. What house or apartment to buy or rent					
Husband far more important	7.5	5.0	0.0	5.0	2.5
Husband more important	5.0	10.0	7.5	5.0	2.5
Both equal	75.0	72.5	85.0	80.0	95.0
Wife more important	10.0	7.5	7.5	10.0	0.0
Wife far more important	2.5	5.0	0.0	0.0	0.0
3. What health/life insurance to purchase					
Husband far more important	2.5	5.0	5.0	5.0	2.5
Husband more important	25.0	15.0	5.0	7.5	2.5
Both equal	67.0	72.5	85.0	80.0	85.0
Wife more important	5.0	2.5	5.0	7.5	7.5
Wife far more important	0.0	5.0	0.0	0.0	2.5
4. Which car to buy					
Husband far more important	5.0	7.5	5.0	7.5	5.0
Husband more important	3.0	22.5	20.0	7.5	17.5
Both equal	57.5	67.5	72.5	82.5	75.0
Wife more important	7.5	0.0	2.5	2.5	0.0
Wife far more important	0.0	2.5	0.0	0.0	2.5
5. How to discipline children					
Husband far more important	0.0	0.0	0.0	2.5	2.5
Husband more important	7.5	7.5	0.0	7.5	2.5
Both equal	75.0	57.5	82.5	72.5	82.5
Wife more important	10.0	12.5	7.5	7.5	7.5
Wife far more important	7.5	22.5	10.0	10.0	5.0
6. How many children to have					
Husband far more important	2.5	0.0	0.0	0.0	2.5
Husband more important	5.0	15.0	2.5	7.5	0.0
Both equal	87.5	77.5	77.5	77.5	90.0
Wife more important	2.5	2.5	17.5	10.0	5.0
Wife far more important	2.5	5.0	2.5	5.0	2.5

(continued)

Table 7.1 (continued)

Decisions and Degrees of Opinion	NW	Helper	Control	KEM	GLM
7. How to decorate the house or apartment					
Husband far more important	0.0	2.5	0.0	0.0	0.0
Husband more important	0.0	2.5	2.5	2.5	2.5
Both equal	20.0	17.5	32.5	45.0	40.0
Wife more important	40.0	27.5	32.5	20.0	30.0
Wife far more important	40.0	50.0	32.5	32.5	27.5
8. Buying gifts for the husband's family on special occasions					
Husband far more important	2.5	2.5	0.0	2.5	0.0
Husband more important	5.0	12.5	7.5	5.0	5.0
Both equal	30.0	30.0	30.0	42.5	47.5
Wife more important	42.5	22.5	25.0	27.5	35.0
Wife far more important	20.0	32.5	37.5	22.5	12.5
9. Which religious organization to join					
Husband far more important	5.0	12.5	2.5	10.0	5.0
Husband more important	5.0	5.0	5.0	2.5	7.5
Both equal	75.0	70.0	85.0	80.0	82.5
Wife more important	7.5	5.0	5.0	5.0	2.5
Wife far more important	7.5	7.5	2.5	2.5	2.5
10. Which social organization the husband should join					
Husband far more important	22.5	22.5	22.5	20.0	25.0
Husband more important	52.0	40.0	47.5	47.5	52.5
Both equal	25.0	37.5	27.5	32.5	22.5
Wife more important	0.0	0.0	2.5	0.0	0.0
Wife far more important	0.0	0.0	0.0	0.0	0.0
11. When to dine out					
Husband far more important	0.0	0.0	0.0	2.5	0.0
Husband more important	7.5	15.0	7.5	10.0	7.5
Both equal	72.5	62.5	67.5	70.0	82.5
Wife more important	10.0	15.0	15.0	10.0	5.0
Wife far more important	10.0	7.5	10.0	7.5	5.0
12. What job the husband should take					
Husband far more important	32.5	32.5	32.5	40.0	40.0
Husband more important	55.0	45.0	45.0	42.5	40.0
Both equal	12.5	22.5	22.0	17.5	20.0
Wife more important	0.0	0.0	0.0	0.0	0.0
Wife far more important	0.0	0.0	0.0	0.0	0.0

(continued)

Table 7.1 (continued)

Decisions and Degrees of Opinion	NW	Helper	Control	KEM	GLM
13. Where to go on vacation					
Husband far more important	0.0	2.5	0.0	0.0	2.5
Husband more important	12.5	15.0	2.5	10.0	2.5
Both equal	82.5	70.0	95.0	72.5	92.5
Wife more important	2.5	2.5	2.5	15.0	2.5
Wife far more important	2.5	10.0	0.0	2.5	0.0
14. Which social organization the wife should join					
Husband far more important	2.5	0.0	0.0	0.0	2.5
Husband more important	15.0	27.5	7.5	15.0	0.0
Both equal	32.5	47.5	25.0	32.5	35.0
Wife more important	40.0	15.0	45.0	40.0	37.5
Wife far more important	10.0	10.0	22.5	12.5	25.0
15. Buying gifts for the wife's family on special occasions					
Husband far more important	0.0	0.0	0.0	0.0	0.0
Husband more important	2.5	12.5	2.5	5.0	0.0
Both equal	32.5	37.5	22.5	37.5	35.0
Wife more important	37.5	22.5	40.0	37.5	45.0
Wife far more important	27.5	27.5	35.0	20.0	20.0

work, how many children to have, and which social organizations the wife should join), NW reported greater decision making power than GLM. It is also noticeable that the percentage of NW whose opinion was more important than their husbands' regarding whether the wife should work was lowest, 32.5%, among the five groups.

Of further interest are the responses to items 10 and 14, which ask whose opinion weighed more regarding joining social organizations in the case of the wife and husband, respectively. In the case of husbands' joining, with the exception of CONTROL (2.5%), none of the respondents in the other four groups indicated having more decision making power than their husbands. In contrast, considerable percentages of husbands had more power than their wives in deciding which social organizations the wives should join: 2.5% for GLM; 7.5% for CONTROL; 15% for KEM; 17.5% for NW; and 27.5% for HELPER. This suggests that while most respondents enjoyed considerable decision-making power over family or family-related matters, some respondents' social activities outside the home were subject to their husbands' approval, whereas husbands were free to decide for themselves what social clubs to join.

MARITAL SATISFACTION, WORK STATUS, AND THE EMPLOYMENT SECTOR

Table 7.2 presents percentage distributions of responses to 25 items of Hudson's Index of Marital Satisfaction (IMS) (Hudson, 1982). The percentage of respondents who indicated "rarely or a little of the time" felt their husbands did

Table 7.2
Responses to the 25 Marital Satisfaction Index Items by Group
(N = 200) (%)

Feelings & Satisfaction	NW	Helper	Control	KEM	GLM
1. My husband is affectionate enough					
Rarely or a little of the time	17.5	15.0	12.5	27.5	20.0
Some of the time	22.5	25.0	30.0	25.0	30.0
Most or a good part of the time	60.0	60.0	57.5	47.5	50.0
2. My husband treats me badly					
Rarely or a little of the time	97.5	100.0	90.0	87.5	87.5
Some of the time	2.5	0.0	7.5	7.5	12.5
Most or a good part of the time	0.0	0.0	2.5	5.0	0.0
3. My husband really cares for me					
Rarely or a little of the time	10.0	12.5	12.5	12.5	7.5
Some of the time	15.0	27.5	15.0	30.0	7.5
Most or a good part of the time	75.0	60.0	72.5	57.5	85.0
4. I would not choose the same husband if I could marry again					
Rarely or a little of the time	72.5	70.0	67.5	57.5	55.0
Some of the time	22.5	17.5	15.0	20.0	22.5
Most or a good part of the time	5.0	12.5	17.5	22.5	22.5
5. I can trust my husband					
Rarely or a little of the time	5.0	5.0	12.5	10.0	15.0
Some of the time	12.5	17.5	20.0	20.0	5.0
Most or a good part of the time	82.5	77.5	67.5	70.0	80.0
6. Our relationship is breaking up					
Rarely or a little of the time	95.0	95.0	92.5	82.5	77.5
Some of the time	2.5	2.5	5.0	5.0	15.0
Most or a good part of the time	2.5	2.5	2.5	12.5	7.5
7. My husband does not understand me					
Rarely or a little of the time	97.5	82.5	77.5	70.0	65.0
Some of the time	0.0	12.5	15.0	17.5	17.5
Most or a good part of the time	2.5	5.0	7.5	12.5	17.5
8. Our relationship is good					
Rarely or a little of the time	5.0	5.0	12.5	17.5	20.0
Some of the time	17.5	27.5	25.0	25.0	10.0
Most or a good part of the time	77.5	67.5	62.5	57.5	70.0
9. We have a very happy relationship					
Rarely or a little of the time	12.5	15.0	15.0	22.5	25.0
Some of the time	20.0	30.0	47.5	27.5	20.0
Most or a good part of the time	67.5	55.0	37.5	50.0	55.0

(continued)

Table 7.2 (continued)

Feelings & Satisfaction	NW	Helper	Control	KEM	GLM
10. Our life together is dull					
Rarely or a little of the time	87.5	87.5	77.5	75.0	67.5
Some of the time	7.5	10.0	15.0	12.5	22.5
Most or a good part of the time	5.0	2.5	7.5	12.5	10.0
11. We have a lot of fun together					
Rarely or a little of the time	30.0	50.0	47.5	42.5	40.0
Some of the time	37.5	20.0	25.0	27.5	27.5
Most or a good part of the time	32.5	30.0	27.5	30.0	22.5
12. My husband does not confide in me					
Rarely or a little of the time	97.5	95.0	97.5	90.0	95.0
Some of the time	0.0	5.0	0.0	5.0	5.0
Most or a good part of the time	2.5	0.0	2.5	5.0	0.0
13. Our relationship is very close					
Rarely or a little of the time	16.0	17.5	25.0	30.0	17.5
Some of the time	22.5	17.5	12.5	27.5	17.5
Most or a good part of the time	62.5	65.0	62.5	42.5	65.0
14. I cannot rely on my husband					
Rarely or a little of the time	92.5	75.0	85.0	72.5	67.5
Some of the time	7.5	17.5	5.0	12.5	15.0
Most or a good part of the time	0.0	7.5	10.0	15.0	17.5
15. We do not have enough interests in common					
Rarely or a little of the time	80.0	62.5	65.0	55.0	67.5
Some of the time	15.0	25.0	17.5	22.5	20.0
Most or a good part of the time	5.0	12.5	17.5	22.5	12.5
16. We manage arguments and disagreements well					
Rarely or a little of the time	22.5	25.0	20.0	30.0	27.5
Some of the time	20.0	35.0	37.5	30.0	20.0
Most or a good part of the time	57.5	40.0	42.5	40.0	52.5
17. We manage our finances well					
Rarely or a little of the time	15.0	22.5	25.0	37.5	17.5
Some of the time	50.0	35.0	35.0	25.0	35.0
Most or a good part of the time	35.0	42.5	40.0	37.5	47.5
18. I should never have married my husband					
Rarely or a little of the time	92.5	90.0	87.5	80.0	85.0
Some of the time	2.5	5.0	7.5	5.0	12.5
Most or a good part of the time	5.0	5.0	5.0	15.0	2.5

(continued)

Table 7.2 (continued)

Feelings & Satisfaction	NW	Helper	Control	KEM	GLM
19. We get along very well					
Rarely or a little of the time	5.0	10.0	17.0	12.5	15.0
Some of the time	22.5	22.5	20.0	27.5	12.5
Most or a good part of the time	72.5	67.5	62.0	60.0	72.5
20. Our relationship is stable					
Rarely or a little of the time	7.5	7.5	20.0	12.5	15.0
Some of the time	7.5	27.5	17.5	35.0	15.0
Most or a good part of the time	80.5	65.0	62.5	52.5	70.0
21. My husband is pleased with					
me as a sex partner					
Rarely or a little of the time	17.5	15.0	22.5	22.5	10.0
Some of the time	30.0	30.0	37.5	37.5	30.0
Most or a good part of the time	52.5	55.0	40.0	40.0	60.0
22. We should do more things					
together					
Rarely or a little of the time	47.5	40.0	37.5	37.5	32.5
Some of the time	27.5	27.5	27.5	27.5	35.0
Most or a good part of the time	25.0	32.5	35.0	35.0	32.5
23. The future looks bright for					
our relationship					
Rarely or a little of the time	10.0	10.0	15.0	17.5	15.0
Some of the time	27.5	25.0	25.0	35.0	17.5
Most or a good part of the time	62.5	65.0	60.0	47.5	67.5
24. Our relationship is empty					
Rarely or a little of the time	90.0	80.0	77.5	80.0	82.5
Some of the time	7.5	15.0	15.0	12.5	5.0
Most or a good part of the time	2.5	5.0	7.5	7.5	12.5
25. There is no excitement in					
our relationship					
Rarely or a little of the time	65.0	60.0	55.0	60.0	77.5
Some of the time	10.0	27.5	27.5	27.5	12.5
Most or a good part of the time	25.0	12.5	17.5	12.5	10.0

Note: $p \leq 0.01$.

not understand them (Item 7), an indicator of good marital relations, was the highest, 97.5%, for NW, 82.5% for HELPER, 77.5% for CONTROL, 70% for KEM, and the lowest, 65%, for GLM. This implies that working outside the home, especially labor market employment, engendered a sense of misunderstanding or lack of spousal support, encouraging marital conflict. Furthermore, the data indicate that many respondents and husbands lacked good communication or conflict management skills. The percentage of respondents who reported they and their husbands managed arguments and disagreements well most or a good part of the time was quite low, especially for HELPER and KEM groups, only 40% for both, as compared to 57.5% for NW, 52.5% for GLM, and 42.5% for CONTROL.

While most respondents in all five groups seemed reasonably satisfied with their marriage, the data showed much room for improvement. For example, responses to items 8 and 9, which measure the overall quality of marital relations, suggest that some respondents suffered unhappy marital lives. Twenty percent and 17.5% of GLM and KEM, respectively, indicated they "rarely or a little of the time" had a good relationship with their husbands compared to 5% for NW and HELPER, and 12.5% for CONTROL. Conversely, 25% and 22.5% of GLM and KEM, as opposed to 12.5% of NW and 15% of HELPER and CONTROL, felt happy with their husbands rarely or a little of the time. These findings suggest that wives employed by others are more likely to have marital problems than wives working in family businesses and non-working wives.

ATTITUDE TOWARD GENDER ROLES, WORK STATUS, AND THE EMPLOYMENT SECTOR

Finally, Table 7.3 depicts respondents' attitudes toward gender roles within and outside the family, measured by 5 items concerning traditional norms and values (Lee, 1989). As might be expected, the 12.5% of NW who agreed or strongly agreed that a wife should not work outside the home (Item 3), though very low, was still significantly higher than the 0.0% for KEM and GLM, and 2.6% and 2.5% for HELPER and CONTROL. This view, which radically departs from the traditional role expected of married Korean women, seemed to reflect the reality of the multiple roles many married Korean women carry in the United States as well as their changing values regarding gender roles (Kim & Hurh, 1987, 1988; Min, 1992).

Table 7.3 shows mixed or inconsistent results regarding attitudes toward traditional gender roles. Specifically, the overwhelming majority of all five groups, ranging from a high of 85% for NW to a low of 72.5% for GLM, agreed that husbands should have more financial responsibility for supporting the family than wives (item 4), as traditional norms maintain. Similarly, the majority, except among those in GLM, agreed that when a wife and her husband disagree on important family matters, the husband should make the final decision (item 1), also a traditional view. However, the percentage varied considerably among the groups from a high of 69.2% for HELPER to a low of 47.5% for GLM.

In contrast, responses to item 5 suggest that many respondents did not believe child-rearing to be primarily the wives' responsibilities, deviating from tradition. Again, however, group differences were considerable: only 15% of GLM and 20% of KEM, compared to 46.1% of HELPER, 42.5% of NW, and 30% of CONTROL, agreed that child-rearing should primarily be a wife's job. These findings, along with those of the previous section, suggest that respondents less willing to perform traditional roles, especially among the employed, were more likely to experience marital conflict and a less satisfactory marital life.

Table 7.3
Responses to the 5 Values/Attitudes about Gender Roles and Marital Relations Items by Group

Value/Attitude Items and Categories	NW	Helper	Control	KEM	GLM
1. When a wife and husband disagree on important family matters, the husband should make the final decision					
Strongly disagree	10.0	5.1	12.5	7.9	17.5
Disagree	25.0	25.6	35.0	23.7	35.0
Agree	40.0	56.4	47.5	52.6	45.0
Strongly agree	25.0	12.8	5.0	15.8	2.5
2. No matter how unhappy marital life is, women should avoid divorce under any circumstance					
Strongly disagree	13.2	10.5	29.7	15.4	23.7
Disagree	52.6	52.6	35.1	48.7	42.1
Agree	21.1	21.1	24.3	23.1	15.8
Strongly agree	13.2	15.8	10.8	12.8	18.4
3. A wife should not work outside the home					
Strongly disagree	27.5	20.5	42.5	20.0	57.5
Disagree	60.0	76.9	55.0	80.0	42.5
Agree	12.5	2.6	2.5	0.0	0.0
Strongly agree	0.0	0.0	0.0	0.0	0.0
4. A husband should have more financial responsibilities for supporting the family than the wife					
Strongly disagree	0.0	0.0	10.0	5.0	10.0
Disagree	15.1	17.5	10.0	12.5	17.5
Agree	57.5	50.0	57.5	42.5	57.5
Strongly agree	27.5	32.5	22.5	40.0	15.0
5. Child-rearing should primarily be a wife's job					
Strongly disagree	12.5	10.3	12.5	20.0	17.5
Disagree	45.0	43.6	57.5	60.0	67.5
Agree	37.5	41.0	27.5	15.0	15.0
Strongly agree	5.0	5.1	2.5	5.0	0.0

CONCLUSION

Findings of this study suggest that married Korean immigrant women's work status and type of employment had no significant bearing on their conjugal power relations and marital satisfaction. Working respondents' contributions to the family economy did not seem to enhance their decision making power in the family. Rather, working outside the home, especially for GLM, seemed to be a source of marital conflict. In fact, NW in general tended to exercise greater conjugal power, hold more traditional attitudes toward gender roles, and be more satisfied with marital life than working respondents. Furthermore, the finding that among the five groups, GLM, who were least satisfied maritally, also held the least traditional values regarding gender roles, seemed to imply that married Korean immigrant women are expected to perform traditional Korean women's roles in order to maintain good marital relations regardless of their economic contribution to the family.

However, in the absence of data on husbands' attitudes toward traditional gender roles as well as their own assessment of marital satisfaction, no conclusion can be drawn regarding the importance of attitude toward gender roles as an explanation for variations in conjugal power relations and marital satisfaction. Considering the small sample size (40 for each group), combined with neglect of other variables in analysis, the lack of significant differences among the five groups in their conjugal power and marital satisfaction should not be over-interpreted. Results presented in this chapter are indeed only the first from many steps of analysis ahead for examining what factors contribute to married Korean immigrant women's conjugal power relations and marital satisfaction. We believe, however, that the findings cast serious doubt on the general belief that married women's participation in the labor force empowers them and enhances the quality of their marital life.

REFERENCES

Aldrich, H., & R. Waldinger. (1990). "Ethnicity and Entrepreneurship." *Annual Review of Sociology*, 16: 111-135.

Blood, R., & D. M. Wolfe. (1960). *Husbands and Wives: The Dynamics of Married Living*. New York: Free Press.

Blumstein, P., & P. Schwartz. (1985). *American Couples*. New York: Pocket Books.

Bonacich, E., et al. (1987). "Korean Immigrant Working Women in the Early 1980's." In E. Y. Yu & E. H. Phillips, eds., *Korean Women in Transition: At Home and Abroad*. Los Angeles: California State University, pp. 219-247.

Boyd, M. (1989). "Family and Personal Network in International Migration: Recent Developments and New Agendas." *International Migration Review*, 23: 638-670.

Chang, H. (1995). *The Effect of Employment Status, Occupation, and Employment Sector on Conjugal Power Relations and Marital Satisfaction Among Korean Immigrant Married Women*. Unpublished doctoral dissertation, Department of Sociology, University of California, Los Angeles.

Dallalfar, A. (1989). "Iranian Immigrant Women in Los Angeles: The Reconstruction of Work, Ethnicity, and Community." Ph.D. dissertation, University of California, Los Angeles.

Gold, S. (1989). "Differential Adjustment Among New Immigrant Family Members." *Journal of Contemporary Ethnography*, 7: 408-434.

Hertz, R. (1986). *More Equal Than Others*. Berkeley and Los Angeles: University of California Press.

Hudson, W. W. (1982). *The Clinical Measurement Package: A Field Manual*. Chicago: Dorsey Press.

Hurh, Won Moo, & Kwang Chung Kim. (1984). *Korean Immigrants in America: A Structural Analysis of Ethnic Confinement and Adhesive Adaptation*. Cranberry, NJ: Association of University Presses.

Kibria, N. (1994). "Household Structure and Family Ideologies: The Dynamics of Immigrant Economic Adaptation Among Vietnamese Refugees." *Social Problems*, 14: 81-96.

Kim, K. C., & W. M. Hurh. (1987). "Employment of Korean Immigrant Wives and the Division of Household Tasks." In E. Y. Yu & E. H. Phillips, eds., *Korean Women in Transition: At Home and Abroad*. Los Angeles: California State University.

_____. (1988). "The Burden of Double Roles: Korean Immigrant Wives in the USA." *Ethnic and Racial Studies*, 11: 151-167.

Lee, H. K. (1988). "Socioeconomic Attainment of Recent Korean and Filipino Immigrant Men and Women in Los Angeles Metropolitan Area, 1980." Ph.D. dissertation, University of California in Los Angeles.

Lee, K. K. (1989). *An Analysis of the Structure of the Korean Family*. Seoul: Il-Ji Publishing Co., 11th ed.

Light, I., & S. Karegeorgis. (1994). "The Ethnic Economy." In N. Smelser and R. Swedberg, eds., *Handbook of Economic Sociology*. Princeton, NJ: Princeton University Press.

Min, P. G. (1992). "Korean Immigrant Wives' Overwork." *Korean Journal of Population and Development*, 2: 23-36.

Mirowsky, J. (1985). "Depression and Marital Power: An Equity Model." *American Journal of Sociology*, 91: 557-592.

Moallem, M. (1991). "Ethnic Entrepreneurship and Gender Relations Among Iranians in Montreal, Quebec, and Canada." In A. Fathi, ed., *Iranian Refugees and Exiles Since Khomeini*. Costa Mesa, CA: Mazda Publishers, pp. 180-199.

Oppenheimer, V. (1977). "The Sociology of Women's Economic Role in the Family." *American Sociological Review*, 42: 387-405.

Ostrander, S. A. (1984). *Women of the Upper Class*. Philadelphia: Temple University Press.

Pedraza, S. (1991). "Women and Migration: The Social Consequences of Gender." *Annual Review of Sociology*, 17: 303-325.

Perez, L. (1986). "Immigrants' Economic Adjustment and Family Organization: The Cuban Success Re-examined." *International Migration Review*, 20: 4-20.

Pressar, P. (1987). "The Dominicans: Women in the Household and the Garment Industry." In N. Foner, ed., *New Immigrant in New York*. New York: Columbia University Press, pp. 103-129.

Rubin, L. B. (1976). *Worlds of Pain*. New York: Basic Books.

Safilios-Rothschild, C. (1970). "The Study of Family Power Structure." *Journal of Marriage and the Family*, 32: 539-552.

U.S. Bureau of the Census. (1994). Characteristics of the Asian and Pacific Islander Population in the United States. 1990 Census of Population and Housing Subject Summary Tape File (SSTF) 5.

Yu, E. Y. (1987). "Korean-American Women: Demographic Profiles and Family Roles." In E. Y. Yu & E. H. Phillips, eds., *Korean Women in Transition: At Home and Abroad*. Los Angeles: California State University, pp. 183-197.

Zhou, M. (1992). *New York's Chinatown: The Socioeconomic Potential of an Urban Enclave*. Philadelphia: Temple University Press.

8

The Burden of Labor on Korean American Wives in and outside the Family

Pyong Gap Min

A society's view of gender can undergo remarkable changes to accommodate varied circumstances and demands. Work is perhaps one of the most misunderstood and underestimated facets of women's lives. Even now, the dominant gender ideology leads people to believe that not only do women work less than men, but that they are also too inexperienced to work as much and as effectively as men. One of the major changes made in American family life in the twentieth century is a great increase in the labor force participation rate of married women. In the year 1890 only 6% of American married women worked outside of the home. However, the labor force participation rate of married women increased to 32% in 1960, 50% in 1980, and then 57% in 1988 (U.S. Bureau of the Census, 1989, p. 385). Only one out of every eight married women with a pre-school child participated in paid employment in 1950. This figure skyrocketed to more than one out every two women by 1985 (O'Connell & Bloom, 1987, p. 2).

An important research issue with regard to the increased economic role of the wife is the relationship between work and family roles. To what extent has the increase in the wife's economic role led to a decrease in women's housework and child care tasks and the increase in their husband's housework roles? Many social scientists have conducted survey studies to answer this question (Coverman & Sheley, 1986; Hardesty & Bokermeier, 1989; Huber & Spitze, 1983; Kamo, 1988; Pleck, 1977, 1985; Ross, 1987). A major conclusion consistently supported by these studies is that women still bear the main responsibility for housework and child care regardless of their employment status. Of course, there has been a steady increase in the amount of time men spend with their families in the United States over the last thirty years. However, most U.S. couples tend to maintain the sexual division of labor even in the realm of housework. Thus, men tend to focus on repair and maintenance services, whereas women take care of traditional household tasks such as cooking, dish-washing, and cleaning.

A radical increase in the labor force participation rate of married women and no significant decrease in their housework and child care responsibilities mean overwork and role conflicts on the part of working women. A number of studies have shown that working women suffer from stress, role strain, and other forms of depression due to their divided attention to paid and house work (Fox & Nichols, 1983; Hall & Hall, 1980; Harrison & Minor, 1978; Katz & Piotrkowski, 1983). Men with spouses working full-time outside the home spend more time on housework and child care than those with full-time housewives. Thus, not only working women but also their husbands experience stress and role strain as a result of job and family demands. However, working wives express a greater amount of stress and strain in discharging work and family obligations than do husbands because the former are mainly responsible for undertaking household chores and taking care of children (Googins & Burden, 1987; Radloff, 1977).

Almost all studies on work-family relations are based on white middle-class samples. Thus, as Piotrkowski and his colleagues rightly indicated, "descriptive research needs to be conducted on minority families" (Piotrkowski et al., 1988). This chapter will bridge this research gap by examining work-family relations using a sample of Korean immigrant couples in New York City.

Under the impact of the Confucian ideology, people in South Korea have maintained a strict gender division of labor. Although urbanization, industrialization, and Westernization have led to great changes in the traditional family system in South Korea during recent years, they have not much revised the traditional ideology of marital role differentiation. Even at present only a small proportion of married women in South Korea participate in the labor force, and the husband's involvement in child care and housework is almost negligible (Choe, 1985; Min, 1988). However, the immigration of Korean women to the United States has led to a radical change in their economic activities. The majority of Korean immigrant married women participate in the labor market, and most of them work exceptionally long hours (Kim & Hurh, 1988; Min, 1990). Although Korean immigrant women are active in their economic roles, they and their husbands are not likely to have changed their traditional gender role attitudes substantially. Thus, Korean immigrant married women assume most of the housework, although most of them work long hours outside the home (Kim & Hurh, 1988). The primary objective of this chapter is to demonstrate the extent to which Korean immigrant women overwork. The degree to which Korean immigrant women overwork can be better understood by comparing them with Korean women in Korea and the general U.S. population. Thus, this chapter will very often compare Korean immigrant women with the other two groups in the number of hours of paid and family work.

The secondary objective of this chapter is to analyze the factors that contribute to the differentials in Korean immigrant women's share of housework. The relative time availability theory proposes that differences in spouses' participation in family work depend upon time and skills available to either partner (Blood & Wolfe, 1960). Blood and Wolfe (1960) found that husbands of working wives contributed more to housework than those whose wives did not work, which was supported by later studies (Berk, 1985; Condran & Bode, 1982; Ericksen et al., 1979; Maret & Finlay 1984). Other studies found that the husband's paid work hours were negatively associated with his share of housework (Hartman, 1981; Nichols & Metzen, 1978; Pleck, 1985). Thus, this theory leads us to expect that the increase in the amount of time for a Korean immigrant wife's paid work leads to the decrease in the amount of time for her housework and the increase in that for her husband's housework.

Another major determinant of the division of family work is gender role orientations of both spouses, particularly those of the wife, which are largely shaped by socialization. When the wife or both partners hold more liberal gender role attitudes, the husband's share of the household tasks is greater than when they hold more traditional gender role orientations (Hardesty & Bokenmeier, 1989; Kamo, 1988; Ross, 1987). Therefore, Korean immigrant women who hold more liberal gender role attitudes are likely to bear less heavy burdens of housework than those who hold more traditional gender role attitudes.

Gender role attitudes are associated with social class and education. Partners with higher education and higher social class generally hold more liberal gender role attitudes than those with lower education. Thus, husbands with higher education and higher occupational status were found to help more with family work than others (Blood & Wolfe, 1960; Berk & Berk, 1978; Farkas, 1976). It is therefore hypothesized that Korean immigrant women's share of housework is negatively related to their and their husbands' educational levels.

Korean immigrants achieve assimilation in proportion to length of residence in the United States, although overall they achieve a low level of assimilation (Hurh & Kim, 1984; Min, 1989). As Korean immigrants achieve more assimilation, they are likely to change their more traditional gender division of family work. Therefore, Korean immigrant women's share of housework is likely to decrease as they live in the United States longer and longer.

The vast majority of Korean immigrants came to the United States invited by their family members already settled here. This suggests that a significant proportion of Korean immigrant families have one or more non-nuclear members living together (Min, 1984). The cohabiting extended family members are in most cases elderly parents, who help their adult children with baby sitting, cooking, and other kinds of housework (Min, 1984). It is also very common in Korea that an adolescent, particularly a girl, helps the mother with housework (Choe, 1985). Given this, Korean immigrant working women are likely to reduce their share of family work in proportion to the number of elderly parents and adult children living together.

METHODOLOGY

The major data source for this chapter is telephone interviews with 298 Korean married immigrant women in New York City. Approximately 22% of Koreans have the surname Kim (Korean National Bureau of Statistics, 1977), and the telephone subscription rate of Korean immigrants is very high (Shin & Yu, 1984). Kim is uniquely a Korean surname (Min, 1989), and Kims represent the general Korean population (Shin & Yu, 1984). Thus, an unbiased sample of Korean households could be obtained by simply sampling Kims from public telephone directories. Using the Kim sample technique has advantages over using ethnic directories. An ethnic directory underrepresents those Koreans well assimilated and thus provides a more biased sample than a public telephone directory. Moreover, an ethnic directory includes many Korean households who have already moved to another city or another part of the same city.

The Kim sample technique was used for sampling Korean households in New York City for this study. Five 1988 New York City borough public telephone directories listed a total of 3,313 Kim households. Six hundred and fifty of these Kim households were randomly selected. Only married Korean immigrant women were approached for the interview. One hundred and twenty-five selected households were not married families and thus not applicable for the interview. Only one married woman from each household was interviewed. In case there were two or more married couples in one household, the wife of the household head was interviewed. Two hundred and ninety-eight Korean women from the 525 households eligible for the interview were successfully interviewed by telephone. Thus, the response rate was 56.8%. Of those 227 households not interviewed, only 42 households (8%) rejected the interview, and the others were not interviewed because they were unreachable. Some prospective respondents were unreachable because they had moved to new locations since the publication of the 1988 telephone directory. Others could not be reached probably because they worked until late at night. Since a significant proportion of those unreachable households must have been unmarried households and thus ineligible for the interview, nearly 70% of those households eligible for the interview can be said to have been interviewed.

The interview schedule included 54 items relating to the respondents' and their husbands' socioeconomic backgrounds, and gender role attitudes and behavior. It took twenty minutes on the average to complete one telephone interview. The interview was conducted by two Korean bilingual students between August and November 1988. To measure the share of housework, each respondent was asked to indicate for what proportion (%) each of the following six household tasks she, her husband, and other family member(s), including housemaid(s), bear responsibility: (1) cooking, (2) dishwashing, (3) laundry, (4) house cleaning, (5) grocery shopping, and (6) garbage disposal. The following three items were provided to measure the gender role orientation:

1. In a normal family the husband works outside the home and the wife works inside.
2. The husband should make decisions on important family affairs.
3. The husband should be able to have dinner outside the home with his friends without asking his wife, if the situation dictates.

The last item was provided, since the practice of the husband eating dinner outside without asking his wife is considered to be a good indication of male supremacy in South Korea. The respondents were asked to respond to each item by choosing one of five categories: (1) strongly agree, (2) moderately agree, (3) neither agree nor disagree, (4) moderately disagree, and (5) strongly disagree. Each category was given a value from one to five in ascending order, and a scale was created by adding all three values. Thus, a lower score indicates a more traditional gender role orientation.

RESULTS

Characteristics of the Respondents

The median age of the respondents was 35. Forty-eight percent of the respondents and 74% of their husbands were found to have completed four years of college education. All the respondents were found to be Korean-born immigrants. They had been in the United States for an average of 7.4 years, which indicates that the vast majority of them immigrated to this country after the change in immigration law in 1965. They had on the average 3.79 members per household. Eighty-five percent of the respondents were found to have at least one child, and 44% of them had one or more preschool children.

Concentration in Small Business and Wife's Increased Economic Role

Seventy percent of the respondents were found to have participated in the labor force and the majority of them (56.4%) worked full-time. The labor force participation rate of Korean married women in New York City is much higher than that of married women in Korea and even higher than that of the U.S. counterpart. Only 18.8% of non-farm married women in Korea were in the labor force in 1980 (Korean National Bureau of Statistics, 1983, p. 441) and 55.8% of American married women participated in the labor force in 1987 (U.S. Bureau of the Census, 1988, p. 364). Although 42% of the respondents were engaged in paid work in Korea, many of them worked before they got married. This indicates that the immigration of Koreans to the United States has led to a radical change in Korean women's economic role.

Table 8.1
Wives' and Husbands' Labor Market Distribution and Weekly Work Hours

Labor Market	Wives	Husbands	Total
Self-employed	102 (48.8%)	172 (61.4%)	274 (56.0%)
Employed in Korean firms	76 (36.4%)	69 (24.6%)	145 (29.7%)
Employed in non-Korean firms	31 (14.8%)	39 (13.9%)	70 (14.3%)
Total	209 (100.0%)	280 (99.9%)	489 (100.0%)

Work Hours	Wives	Husbands	Total
Below 40	13 (4.8%)	46 (22.3%)	59 (12.3%)
40–49	78 (28.6%)	42 (20.4%)	120 (25.1%)
50–59	44 (16.1%)	36 (17.5%)	80 (16.7%)
60–69	72 (26.4%)	47 (22.8%)	119 (24.8%)
70 or more	66 (24.2%)	35 (17.0%)	101 (21.1%)
Total	273 (100.1%)	206 (100.0%)	497 (100.0%)
Mean hours for total	56.8	50.7	54.2
Mean hours for those working 40 hours or more	58.2	57.6	57.9

Note: Some totals do not add up to 100.0% due to rounding.

What is noteworthy about New York Korean immigrant women's economic activities is not only their high labor force participation rate, but also their high self-employment rate and economic segregation. As Table 8.1 shows, nearly 50% of the working women are engaged in a business and another 36% areemployed in Korean firms. Thus, 85% of the Korean female work force in New York City is segregated, with only 15% employed in non-Korean firms. Husbands of the respondents show even a higher self employment rate (61.4%), with only 13% employed in non-Korean firms. The vast majority of the self-employed Korean wives coordinate with their husbands for the family business.

Long Hours of Work

Korean immigrants concentrate in labor intensive small business such as the green grocery business, dry-cleaning service, and garment manufacturing. Thus they, both husbands and wives, work long hours. Table 8.2 shows that more than 50% of husbands and 40% of wives work 60 hours or more per week. Korean married women in New York City work on the average 50.7 hours per week in comparison to 56.8 hours for their husbands. The mean difference in the number of weekly work hours between husbands and wives is largely due to several wives working part time. Excluding those who work below 40 hours per week, we find there is no substantial difference between husbands and wives in the number of weekly work hours (58.2 hours versus 57.6 hours). A study conducted in 1980 (Fox & Nichols, 1983) shows that American married women worked 32.2 hours per week and 43% of those employed worked part-time. These statistics suggest that Korean Immigrant men work excessively long hours and that their wives' overwork is even more excessive compared to U.S. wives in general.

No Significant Changes in the Wife's Domestic Role

We have noted above that the vast majority of Korean immigrant wives undertake the economic role and work excessively long hours outside the home relative to U.S. wives in general. Has the increase in the Korean wives' economic role led to a decrease in their domestic role? Table 8.2 provides data that help to answer this question. Korean immigrant housewives bear almost all the responsibility for traditional domestic tasks, and their husbands' help is almost negligible. Housewives do 95% of cooking and more than 90% of dishwashing, laundry, and house cleaning, respectively. This finding comes as no surprise, considering the fact that there are few husbands in South Korea who bear responsibility for a significant proportion of family work.

Korean working wives' share of responsibility in the four major traditional domestic tasks is substantially lower than that of Korean housewives. However, Korean working wives still shoulder most household work except garbage disposal. Moreover, the decrease in the proportion of household work for Korean working wives does not result from a significant increase in their husbands' domestic role. Korean immigrant husbands do a very small proportion of domestic tasks, even when their wives undertake the economic role full-time. Korean working wives can reduce their share of housework mainly because other family members help them at home. As can be noted in Table 8.2, the proportion of household work that other family members bear has significantly increased from single-earner to dual-earner families. Other family members are largely the respondents' mothers, mothers-in-law, and children. When Korean immigrant women work outside of the home, many of their daughters are found to do a significant proportion of housework.

Table 8.2
Share of Domestic Tasks by Wife's Work Status (%)

Domestic Tasks	Families With Wife Not Working			Families With Wife Working		
	Wife	Husband	Others	Wife	Husband	Others
Cooking	94.7	2.8	2.5	78.9	8.4	12.7
Dishwashing	92.8	3.3	3.9	72.7	9.6	17.7
Laundry	93.7	3.7	2.6	63.1	13.3	23.6
House cleaning	91.4	7.2	1.4	58.9	19.5	21.6
Grocery shopping	71.9	25.6	2.5	65.2	28.6	6.2
Garbage disposal	68.1	27.2	4.7	41.8	37.8	20.4

Factors Related to Wives' Share of Housework

To test a set of hypotheses derived from theoretical discussions, the following background variables were regressed on the wife's share of housework (%): (1) the wife's weekly hours for paid work; (2) the number of extra adult members in addition to husband and wife; (3) the wife's years of education; (4) the wife's length of residence in the United States; (5) the wife's gender role orientation; and (6) the wife's age. The results are presented in Table 8.3.

Table 8.3
Regression of Background Variables on Wife's Share of Housework (N = 287)

Independent Variable	b	Beta	Independent Variable	b	Beta
Wife's work hours	-0.438	0.491***	Length of Residence	-0.028	-0.006
Number of extra adult members	-3.394	-0.170**	Age	-0.005	0.002
Years of education	-0.962	-0.132*	Intercept	108.640	
Gender role	-0.381	-0.045	R^2	0.284	

*$p \leq .05$; **$p \leq .005$; ***$p \leq .0001$.

As expected, the number of the wife's weekly hours for paid work negatively affects her share of housework and the relationship is statistically significant. This means that Korean immigrant women can reduce their share of housework in proportion to the number of work hours. The beta value indicates that the wife's weekly work hours have the most significant effect on her share of housework. The number of extra cohabiting adult members also significantly reduces the Korean immigrant wife's share of housework. As previously indicated, extra adult family members are elderly parents, parents-in-law, and/or adult children. Elderly mothers or mothers-in-law in particular bear much responsibility for housework and childcare when Korean immigrant wives work long hours outside the home (Min, 1984).

The respondents' years of education reduce their share of housework, and the relationship is statistically significant. But neither the respondents' length of residence in the United States nor their gender role attitudes has a statistically significant effect on their portion of housework. It was hypothesized that Korean immigrant women's length of residence in the United States would reduce their housework responsibility mainly by facilitating their assimilation into American society. That is, Korean immigrant women are likely to achieve assimilation in proportion to their length of residence and thus they may adopt a less rigid gender role division accepted by most American couples as they live in this country longer and longer. However, research has shown that Korean adult immigrants, male or female, have achieved a very low level of assimilation, particularly because they are economically segregated (Hurh & Kim, 1984; Min, 1989, 1991). As our data on the New York Korean community show, the vast majority of Korean adult workers are in the ethnic subeconomy. Considering the fact that Korean immigrant adults have little contact with Americans, either at the work place or through personal networks, Korean wives holding the main responsibility for domestic work regardless of their length of residence comes as no surprise.

Korean Immigrant Wives' Overwork

While most contemporary Korean immigrant wives still learn that their primary roles have to do with the care of the home and family, most of them also spend many years contributing to the economy in the form of paid employment. The majority of middle-class working women in Seoul and the large cities in Korea depend upon housemaids for cooking and other household work. Even a significant proportion of full-time housewives in Korea hire housemaids so that they can focus on childrearing. According to one study conducted in Seoul (Choe, 1985, p. 143), 51% of working wives always or mainly depend upon housemaids and another 10% partly depend upon them for cooking. In the same study, 31% of housewife respondents reported housemaids to be mainly or partly responsible for cooking. By contrast, few Korean immigrant wives depend upon maid service, although most of them spend long hours at paid work. Only 4.3% of the homes represented by the respondents were found to have a housemaid working part-time or full-time. This suggests that Korean immigrant wives spend many more hours for house and paid work than wives in Korea.

To measure more effectively the extent to which Korean immigrant wives overwork, compared to their husbands, we asked the respondents how many hours per week they and their husbands spend on their job and household work separately. Their responses are analyzed by the wife's work status and presented in Table 8.4. Full-time housewives spend 46.3 hours per week on housework in comparison to 5.2 hours for their husbands. For dual-earner couples, the wife's time on housework is reduced to 24.8 hours per week whereas the husband's time on housework has increased from 5.2 hours to 6.7 hours. For both single-earner and dual-earner families, Korean immigrant husbands spend less than their American counterparts. The 1985 study (Robinson, 1988), for example, shows that American wives spend on the average 22.4 hours per week on housework in comparison to 11.1 hours for their husbands.

Husbands of Korean immigrant wives who do not work spend 62.1 hours per week on their job and household tasks and work approximately 15 hours more than their wives. Working wives spend 75.5 hours weekly on their job and housework, which is 12 hours more than what their husbands spend. Since the vast majority of Korean immigrant wives assume the economic role, most Korean wives seem to work longer hours than their working husbands. Korean immigrant wives' overwork inside and outside of the home becomes clearer when they are compared with U.S. wives. One survey shows that American employed wives spend an average of 45.8 hours for both paid work (25.3 hours) and housework (20.5 hours), whereas their husbands spent 46.9 hours on work in both domains (Nichols & Metzen, 1978). Korean immigrant wives spend more hours than U.S. wives for paid and house work by approximately one and a half times.

Table 8.4
Husbands' and Wives' Weekly Work Hours by Wife's Work Status

Role	Family With Wife Not Working		Families With Wife Working	
	Husband	Wife	Husband	Wife
Paid Work	56.9	0	56.8	50.7
Domestic Work	5.2	46.3	6.7	24.8
Total	62.1	46.3	63.5	75.7

DISCUSSION

Although most Korean immigrant wives work outside the home, and although women and men work for the same reasons, the success with which women reach objectives and the rewards they are able to obtain are significantly different. Employed Korean immigrant wives face special stresses and dilemmas not shared by working Korean immigrant men. This may also cause frustration in their search for meaningful and well-paying jobs that can provide opportunities for advancement. Their pursuits of achievement in their work are not applauded and are continuously as well as ambiguously disapproved of by Korean immigrant society. Changes in our attitudes are always slower than social changes. The majority of American married women undertake the economic role, and a large proportion of them do so not because of their career interest but out of economic need. Since most American adults, both male and female, have not significantly changed the traditional gender role orientation, working wives are still mainly responsible for housework, which, as cited in the beginning of this chapter, causes stress and role strain.

This conflict between gender role attitudes and women's economic behavior is more serious in immigrant families than in American native families, since immigrant women usually change their economic role within a very short period of time. Our data show that 70% of Korean married women in New York City undertake the economic role in comparison to approximately 20% of married women in South Korea. What is noteworthy is not merely the fact that the vast majority of Korean immigrant married women participate in the labor market, but also the fact that most of them work exceptionally long hours, much longer hours than their American counterparts. Although most Korean immigrant women have made a radical increase in their economic role in their adjustment to a new society, their husbands maintain the traditional gender division of labor at home. Thus, Korean immigrant working wives undertake a greater share of housework than American working wives. Our data show that Korean working women spend longer hours than their working husbands for paid and domestic work. Overwork seems to be very stressful to Korean immigrant wives, particularly because they experience stress relating to their language barrier and other adjustment problems (Kim & Berry, 1985, 1986; Shin, 1992). Wives' overwork and stress may not be unique to the Korean immigrant community. Many immigrant wives from other non-European countries seem to suffer from overwork and stress (Foner, 1979; Perez, 1986; Pressar, 1987).

Regression analysis shows that the number of Korean immigrant wives' working hours, number of extra adult family members, and years of education have significant effects on reduction of their share of housework, but that their length of residence in the United States and gender role attitudes do not have significant effects. The vast majority of Korean adult immigrants work in the ethnic subeconomy. As a result, Korean immigrants seem to be slower than other immigrant groups in discarding the rigid gender role division transplanted from their native country and adopting a more flexible gender role division associated with U.S. middle-class couples. Thus, how long Korean immigrants have lived in the United States may not make much difference in changing the traditional norm that housework is mainly the wife's obligation. Korean immigrant women who accept a more modern gender role orientation would expect their husbands to help more at home. However, their husbands, not exposed to the environment conducive to revision of the traditional gender role orientation, are not ready to favorably respond to their expectations. Thus, Korean immigrant wives' gender role orientation does not significantly affect their share of housework.

The majority of Korean immigrant wives continue to work in their own homes and serve their families without earning wages or social recognition, their behavior maintained by the harmony and pleasures derived from inside the family, wishes for affection and acknowledgment from husband and children, and avoidance of frustrations and burdens of labor outside of the family. But most Korean immigrant wives do work both in and outside of their homes and expect to do so, contradicting the myth that women will be cared for by men and that homemade gourmet foods and "womanly" characteristics and appearances are the routes to a happy life.

Now, the time has arrived for Korean immigrant society to actively and explicitly promote the ideal that women should work inside and outside the family on an equal basis with men. Korean American culture will deny women the opportunity to acquire attitudes and objectives that can maximize women's potentials fully and equally as active members of Korean immigrant society, increasing the probability that Korean American immigrant women will face overwhelming obstacles in work inside and outside of the family. As long as we continue along the current norms, Korean immigrant women will continuously confront the dilemma of choosing between family and work. Korean immigrant wives, like men, should be encouraged to pursue both. Societal and family support is critically important to the alleviation of the burden of labor on Korean American women.

REFERENCES

Berk, R. A., & S. F. Berk. (1978). "A Simultaneous Equation Model for the Division of Household Labor." *Sociological Methods and Research*, 6: 431-468.

Berk, Sarah. (1985).*The Gender Factory: The Apportionment of Work in American Household.* New York: Plenum Press.

Blair, S. L., & D. T. Lichter. (1991). "Measuring the Division of Household Labor." *Journal of Family Issues*, 12: 91-113.

Blood, R. O., & D. M. Wolfe. (1960). *Husbands and Wives: The Dynamics of Married Living.* New York: Free Press.

Choe, Jae Suk. (1985). *A Study of Modern Families* [in Korean]. Seoul: Iljisa, second edition.

Condran, John, & Jerry Bode. (1982). "Washwomen, Working Wives, and Family Division of Labor: Middletown, 1980." *Journal of Marriage and the Family*, 44, 421-426.

Coverman, Shelley, & Joseph Sheley. (1986). "Change in Men's Housework and Childcare." *Journal of Marriage and the Family*, 48: 414-422.

Ericksen, Julia, William Yancy, & Eugene Ericksen. (1979). "The Division of Family Roles." *Journal of Marriage and the Family*, 41: 301-313.

Farkas, George. (1976). "Education, Wage Rates, and the Division of Labor between Husband and Wife." *Journal of Marriage and the Family*, 38: 473-483.

Foner, Nancy. (1979). "Sex Roles and Sensibilities: Jamaican Women in New York and London." *Social Science Quarterly*, 60: 35-50.

Fox, Karen, & Sharon Nichols. (1983). "The Time Crunch: Wife's Employment and Family Work." *Journal of Family Issues*, 4: 61-82.

Googins, Bradley & Dianne Burden. (1987). "Vulnerability of Working Parents: Balancing Work and Home Roles." *Social Work*, 32: 295-300.

Hall, D. T., & F. S. Hall. (1980). "Stress and the Two-Career Couple." In C.I. Cooper & R. Payne, eds., *Current Concerns in Occupational Stress*. New York: Wiley.

Hardesty, Constance, & Janet Bokermeier. (1989). "Finding Time and Making Do: Distribution of Household Labor in Non-metropolitan Marriages." *Journal of Marriage and the Family*, 51: 253-267.

Harrison, A. D., & J. H. Minor. (1978). "Inter-role Conflicts, Coping Strategies, and Satisfaction among Black Working Wives." *Journal of Marriage and the Family*, 40: 799-805.

Hartman, Heidi. (1981). "The Family as the Locus of Gender, Class, and Political Struggle: The Example of Housework." *Signs*, 6: 366-394.

Huber, Joan, & Glenna Spitze. (1983). *Sex Stratification: Children, Housework, and Jobs*. New York: Academic Press.

Hurh, Won Moo, & Kwang Chung Kim. (1984). "Adhesive Adaptation of Korean Immigrants in the U.S.: An Alternative Strategy of Minority Adaptation." *International Migration Review*, 18: 188-215.

Kamo, Yoshinori. (1988). "Determinants of Household Division of Labor." *Journal of Family Issues,* 9: 177-200.

Katz, M. H., & C. S. Piotrkowski. (1983). "Correlates of Family Role Strain among Employed Black Women." *Family Relations,* 32: 331-339.

Kim, K. C., & W. M. Hurh. (1988). "The Burden of Double Roles: Korean Immigrant Wives in the USA." *Ethnic and Racial Studies,* 11: 151-167.

Kim, U-Chul, & J. W. Berry. (1985). "Acculturation Attitudes of Korean immigrants in Toronto." In I. R. Lagunes and Y. E. Poortinga, eds., *From a Different Perspectives: Studies of Behavior Across Cultures.* Lisse, Germany: Swets and Zeitlinger.

——. (1986). "Predictors of Acculturative Stress: Korean Immigrants in Toronto, Canada." In L. H. Ekstrand, ed., *Ethnic Minorities and Immigrants in a Cross-Cultural Perspective.* Lisse, Germany: Swets and Zeitlinger.

Korean National Bureau of Statistics. (1983). *Population Characteristics.* Seoul: Economic Planning Board, Korean Government.

——. (1977). *Population Composition by Surnames: A Report on the Data from the 1970 Korean Census of Population.* Seoul: Economic Planning Board, Korean Government.

Maret, Elizabeth, & Barbara Finlay. (1984). "The Distribution of Household Labor among Women in Dual-Earner Families." *Journal of Marriage and the Family,* 46, 357-364.

Min, Pyong Gap. (1984). "An Exploratory Study of Kin Ties among Korean Immigrant Families in Atlanta." *Journal of Comparative Family Studies,* 15: 59-75.

——. (1988). "The Korean American Family." In Charles Mindel, Robert Habenstein, and Roosevelt Wright, Jr., eds., *Ethnic Families in America: Patterns and Variations.* New York: Elsevier, pp. 199-229.

——. (1989). "Some Positive Functions of Ethnic Business in an Immigrant Community: Koreans in Los Angeles." Final Report Submitted to the National Science Foundation.

——. (1990). "Problems of Korean Immigrant Entrepreneurs." *International Migration Review,* 24: 436-455.

——. (1991). "Cultural and Economic Boundaries of Korean Ethnicity: A Comparative Analysis." *Ethnic and Racial Studies,* 14, 225-241.

Nichols, Sharon, & Edward Metzen. (1978). "Housework Time of Husband and Wife." *Home Economics Research Journal,* 7: 85-97.

O'Connell, Martin, & David Bloom. (1987). *Juggling Jobs and Babies: America's Child Care Challenge.* Washington, DC: Population Reference Bureau.

Perez, Lisandro. (1986). "Immigrants' Economic Adjustment and Family Organization: The Cuban Success Reexamined." *International Migration Review,* 20: 4-20.

Piotrkowski, Chaya, Robert Rapoport, & Phona Rapoport. (1988). "Families and Work." In Marvin Sussman and Suzanne Steinmetz, eds., *Handbook of Marriage and the Family.* New York: Plenum Press, pp. 251-283.

Pleck, Joseph. (1977). "The Work-Family Role System." *Social Problems,* 24: 417-427.

——. (1985). *Working Wives/Working Husbands.* Beverly Hills, CA: Sage.

Pressar, P. (1987). "The Dominican Women in the Household and Garment Industry." In Nancy Foner, ed., *New Immigrants in New York.* New York: Columbia University Press, pp. 103-129.

Radloff, L. (1977). "Sex Differences in Depression. The Effects of Occupation and Marital Status." *Sex Roles: A Journal of Research,* 1: 249-266.

Robinson, John. (1988). "Who's Doing the Housework?" *American Demographics,* 10 (December): 24-28.

Ross, Catherine. (1987). "The Division of Labor at Home." *Social Forces*, 65: 816-833.

Shin, Eui Hang, & Eui Young Yu. (1984). "Use of Surname in Ethnic Research: The Case of Kim in the Korean American Population." *Demography*, 21: 347-359.

Shin, Kyung Rim. (1992). *Correlates of Descriptive Symptomatology in Korean-American Women in New York City*. Unpublished Ph.D. dissertation, Department of Nursing, Teachers College, Columbia University.

U.S. Bureau of the Census. (1988, 1989). *Statistical Abstracts of the United States: 1989*. Washington, DC: U.S. Government Printing Office, 109th edition.

9

Family and Work Roles of Korean Immigrant Wives and Related Experiences

Kwang Chung Kim and Shin Kim

INTRODUCTION

Like other recent Asian immigrants, a high proportion of recent Korean immigrants completed college education and/or held white-collar positions prior to their departure from Korea (Barringer et al., 1991). Such pre-immigration social backgrounds indicate that a high proportion of Korean immigrants have middle class backgrounds. A great majority of them came to the United States with their own family in the context of kinship-based chain migration. In the United States, they thus adjust themselves as members of their family rather than isolated individuals. A good illustration of Korean immigrants' family orientation is employment of wives in most of Korean immigrant families (Kim & Hurh, 1988). The wives are employed out of economic necessity in the pursuit of a high level of aspiration or life goal consistent with their middle class backgrounds: home ownership, family life in a nice and comfortable neighborhood, and good education for their children.

Employment of Korean immigrant wives is, however, a dramatic departure from the traditional role of wives in Korea, since wives in the traditional family system are expected to stay home as full-time home-makers. Their employment is thus expected to have considerable impact on family and kinship life of the employed wives and their family members. As part of the study of family and work roles of Korean immigrant wives, we will empirically examine the nature of their employment and its impact on certain aspects of their family and kinship life.

DATA COLLECTION

Data were collected in 1986 through interviewing 622 Korean adult immigrants (age 20 or older) who resided in the Chicago area. Respondents were randomly selected from those immigrants listed in the Korean Community Directory of Chicago, 1984–1985, and eight telephone directories from the city of Chicago and contiguous suburban communities. A standardized interview schedule was used as part of a larger study of Korean immigrants' adaptation and mental health (Hurh & Kim, 1988).

The sample included 334 males (53.7%) and 288 females (46.3%). The mean age of the total sample was 41.6, with the majority (78.7%) in the age category of 30–50. The average length of residence in the United States was 8.1 years. About 13% (N = 82) of the respondents had been in the United States for two years or less, while a similar proportion of them (N = 78, 12.6%) have lived in the United States for 15 years or more. The majority of the respondents (520, 83.9%) were married. Family and work roles of these married respondents, particularly married female respondents, are the major focus of this chapter.

EMPLOYMENT ORIENTATION AND OCCUPATIONAL EXPERIENCE

An interesting fact concerning Korean immigrant wives' employment is that prior to departure from Korea, a high proportion of Korean wives already anticipated or were willing to work outside the home once in the United States. Park and her colleagues conducted predeparture interviews with those in Korea who had obtained immigration visas. In the interview, a high proportion of female respondents (80%) expressed that they would be economically active in the United States (Park et al., 1990, Table 61).

Their predeparture employment orientation seems to reflect two important points about their immigrant life in the United States. First, as already noted, they wanted to achieve in the United States a lifestyle consistent with their pre-immigration middle-class backgrounds. Even prior to their immigration, however, the wives did not expect that their husbands would earn enough to maintain such a lifestyle. Such an employment expectation of their husbands in the United States forced the wives to be economically active in the United States. Second, most of the current Korean immigrants came to the United States in the 1970s and 1980s, when it was not a common practice for the wives of the urban middle class in Korea to work outside the home. Exceptions were school teachers, other professional workers, and those engaged in informal economic activities such as credit-rotation activity (ke) or real estate transactions (Lee, 1990). In such a social context, the employment orientation of a high proportion of the immigrant wives did not reflect their own desire for careerism or independence. Ironically, what is suggested is an expression of their traditional gender role orientation: willingness to sacrifice themselves for a family need.

As expected, a high proportion of immigrant wives were indeed employed in the United States. According to the 1986 data, two-thirds of the female respondents (198, 68.8%) were employed. Of the employed female respondents, proportionally more married female respondents (163, 74.8%) were employed than unmarried female respondents (32, 51.4%). When elderly wives (over 55 years old) are excluded from the sample, data analysis demonstrates that virtually all of the young and middle-aged wives were working outside home.

Timing of their employment is also very interesting. Ideally, they should have been gradually more employed as they stayed longer in the United States and were more assimilated. Contrary to such an expectation, Table 9.1 demonstrates that a majority of Korean immigrant wives were employed from the first year of their immigrant life in the United States. In subsequent years, the proportion of employed wives slightly increased. As a whole, the proportion of the employed wives remained high regardless of length of residence in the United

States. This pattern of Korean wives' employment demonstrates three interesting facts. First, most Korean wives were forced to work outside the home from the beginning of their American life. Second, once they were employed, most of them remained employed. This observation indicates that employment of Korean wives was not a temporary arrangement, but a long-term or life-long experience. Third, since virtually all of the husbands in Korean immigrant families were employed with few exceptions (e.g., students, elderly immigrants), the employment pattern of wives indicates that in a great majority of Korean immigrant families both husband and wife were employed.

According to the 1986 data, employed Korean wives were distributed into the following four types of occupations: (1) professional/technical occupations, (2) sales or administrative support occupations, (3) self-employed small business, and (4) service/manual occupations. Professional/technical workers included those in various occupations such as school teachers, artists, technicians, physicians, accountants, and lawyers. But a high proportion of professional/technical workers were nurses. Those in sales or administrative support occupations included various types of clerical workers and salespersons working for small businesses or some big corporations like insurance companies. Most of those in small business participated in daily business operation with their spouses. The workers in service/manual occupations were housemaids, cleaning ladies, and low-skilled workers employed by garment, electronic, and other manufacturing plants. If a full-time job is defined as working 35 hours a week or more, most of employed wives (151, 92.6%) worked full-time. The working hours were particularly long for those in self-employed small business. It was common among small-business owners to work for seven days a week and more than 50 hours a week.

Table 9.1
Length of Residence and Proportion of Employed Korean Wives

	Length of Residence (years)						
	1–2	3–4	5–6	7–8	9–10	11–12	13+
N	19	20	17	19	24	32	31
%	57.6	80.0	68.0	67.9	80.0	86.5	77.6

Recently the proportion of the employed white and African American wives has been steadily increased in the United States. But even in 1995, only slightly more than half of American wives (58%) were employed and a high proportion of these employed wives worked part-time. As compared with the employed white and African American wives, Korean immigrant wives were proportionally more employed and worked longer hours. With some exceptions of those in profession/technical occupations, however, the employed Korean wives were generally employed in the marginal lines of occupations characterized by low wage, low skill and little mobility opportunity. Since a high proportion of the employed wives came to the United States with college degrees, their occupations suggest that many of them were underemployed in American labor market.

How does employment of Korean immigrant wives affect their family life and kinship life? We will empirically examine the question in terms of the following three specific topics: (1) emergence of the independent nuclear family, (2) employed wives' performance of housework, and (3) intergenerational relationships.

EMERGENCE OF THE INDEPENDENT NUCLEAR FAMILY

Goode (1963) contends that as a society becomes industrialized, the independent nuclear family (the conjugal family) emerges as the dominant type of family. The industrial economy generally hires workers based on their individual ability and performance. When workers are so hired, they have their own source of income independent of their (extended) family. The head of the extended family then gradually loses the ability to control family members. This situation weakens the traditional family system and stimulates the emergence of the independent nuclear family. As Korean society is rapidly industrialized, the independent nuclear family is also expected to emerge in Korea as the dominant type of family, replacing the traditional extended family. Emergence of the independent system would have been, however, much more accelerated for Korean immigrants by the massive employment of Korean immigrant wives. It is, therefore, expected that most Korean immigrants currently maintain an independent nuclear family. In this chapter, the issue of the independent nuclear family is examined in terms of (1) residential pattern of Korean families, (2) family financial management, (3) child care, and (4) performance of housework.

Three-quarters of the respondents in the 1986 sample (458, 74.5%) lived only with members of their own nuclear family (married couples or couple with children). About 10 percent of the respondents (52%, 8.5%) reported that their parent(s) lived with members of their nuclear family. Since most of the parent(s) temporarily lived with their married children in response to parent(s)' need or the respondents' family need, we would consider this form of residence as an extended form of the nuclear family. It was then observed that a great majority of the respondents (83%) maintained residentially independent nuclear family systems. Most of the remaining respondents lived alone or with siblings or others.

The respondents in occupations other than small business were asked to state their annual individual earnings and family income in 1985. The two types of income were then compared with the national median family income in 1985 which was slightly below $30,000. A big difference between the two types of income was observed. Only one-fifth (60, 20.2%) of them individually earned $30,000 or more in 1985, while the majority of respondents (180, 60.0%) reported that their annual family income in 1985 was $30,000 or less. If we define the national median family income as the income good enough for family support, the majority of those in non–small-business occupations showed that their families were financially self-supporting. Since income of small business families is generally higher than non–small-business families, it can be stated that most of the respondents in the sample maintained financially self-supporting nuclear families.

Along with family finance, child care and performance of housework are the two important family tasks. Table 9.2 shows the division of child care activities in the respondents' families. Physical care of children (changing children's clothes, providing children's meals) and training of children for artistic skills were in general the sole responsibility of wives. In the majority of the respondents' families, the wife alone thus performed those three tasks of child care, whether she was employed or not. The proportion of the wives who alone performed the two tasks of physical care (changing children's clothes and providing meals) was, however, significantly smaller among the employed wives than among the non-employed wives. This demonstrates that some of the employed wives were able to shift some of the child care burden to their husbands, to the children themselves, or to relatives. In three other tasks of child care (teaching children proper attitudes, helping with homework, and giving rides to children), a smaller propotion of the employed wives performed these jointly with their husbands than non-employed wives. These findings again show that although the wives bore a heavy burden, the wives and their husbands together performed most of the child care activities in their families.

Table 9.2
Distribution of Respondents by Employment of Wife and Types of Child Care

			1	2	3	Total	Chi-Square
Changing	Wife Not	N	66	5	11	82	
children's	Employed	%	80.5	6.1	13.4	100	10.2**
clothes	Wife	N	153	30	67	250	df = 2
	Employed	%	61.2	12.0	26.8	100	
Providing	Wife Not	N	76	4	6	36	
children's	Employed	%	88.4	4.6	7.0	100	10.8**
meals	Wife	N	195	25	55	275	df = 2
	Employed	%	70.9	9.1	20.0	100	
Teaching	Wife Not	N	26	60	0	86	
proper	Employed	%	30.2	69.8	0	100	5.7
attitude	Wife	N	54	223	4	281	df = 2
	Employed	%	19.2	79.4	1.4	100	
Helping	Wife Not	N	36	29	3	68	
with	Employed	%	52.9	42.7	4.4	100	11.8
homework	Wife	N	79	112	42	233	df = 2
	Employed	%	33.9	48.1	18.0	100	
Help	Wife Not	N	50	17	2	69	
develop	Employed	%	72.5	24.6	2.9	100	5.3
artistic	Wife	N	134	68	23	225	df = 2
skills	Employed	%	59.6	30.2	10.2	100	
Giving	Wife Not	N	34	45	2	81	
rides to	Employed	%	41.9	55.6	2.5	100	15.9***
children	Wife	N	55	171	28	254	df = 2
	Employed	%	21.7	67.3	11.0	100	

**p < .0; ***p < .001.

(1) Wife alone; (2) Husband alone or both husband and wife jointly; (3) Children or other relative.

THE DOUBLE ROLES OF IMMIGRANT WIVES

Wives' employment means that they share the breadwinner's role with their husbands. When the wives do so, would their husbands also share housework with their wives? This issue is discussed in terms of the respondents' normative orientation toward housework and their actual performance of housework (Kim & Hurh, 1988).

As an indirect way to test their gender role orientation, the respondents were asked to respond to the following statement, "Woman's place is in the home." If their answer is "yes," this suggests that they continuously adhere to the traditional gender role orientation in the United States. But if they answer "no," this indicates their acceptance of a new gender role orientation. By this measure, most of the employed wives were traditional in their gender role orientation in spite of their intensive employment. Of the respondents in the families in which both husband and wife were employed (the dual earner families), two-thirds (218, 66.7%) answered "yes." No sex difference was observed in their response to the above statement. Furthermore, the proportion of the employed wives who answered "yes" to the above statement remained high regardless of length of residence in the United States. This finding suggests that most of the employed wives and husbands remained traditional in their gender role orientation no matter how long they lived in the United States.

As a way to measure the respondents' performance of housework, respondents were asked about the division of housework in their families. "Among your family members (e.g., wife, husband, and other members), how do you divide housework?" and "In your opinion, how should the housework be divided in principle?" The first question measured the actual division of housework (role performance), while the second question tests their role expectations. Five specific tasks of housework were given: grocery shopping, cleaning the house, laundry, dishwashing, and cooking. The respondents were then asked to rank their family members in terms of their performance of each of the housework tasks on a six-point scale. The performance scale is calculated by adding up the points based on the family members' performance of the five types of housework. The score system will be illustrated by the wife's performance score. For each of the tasks, the wife is assigned to the following points on the basis of the nature of her relative performance in the family: 5—the wife performs alone or is so expected; 4—the wife performs more than any other family members or is so expected; 3—the wife and other family members perform equally or are so expected; 2—a family member performs more than the wife or is so expected; 1—two other family members perform more than the wife or are so expected; 0—the wife does not perform at all or is so expected. In the same manner, the performance score of the husband or other family members is calculated.

For a systematic analysis, the scores of family role expectation and performance are calculated by adding up the points in a family member's relative performance of the four types of housework, excluding grocery shopping. Only the remaining four types of housework show high factor loadings on the same dimension in the factor analysis. The role scores thus range from 0 to 20. A separate role score was calculated for the wife, the husband and other family members as shown in Table 9.3. The role scores of these family members are calculated separately for the families in which both husband and wife were em-

Table 9.3
Family Role Expectation and Performance for Wives, Husbands, and Other
Family Members

			Wife's Family Role		Husband's Family Role		Other's Family Role	
			E	P	E	P	E	P
Dual-Earner Family	Husband	M	15.0	15.0	5.6	5.6	2.5	3.7
		SD	2.5	3.4	3.5	3.5	4.1	4.9
		n	179	180	180	180	179	180
	Wife	M	15.3	14.8	4.5	4.5	3.3	4.9
		SD	3.2	3.9	3.7	3.7	4.6	5.6
		n	145	143	143	143	145	143
Single-Earner Family	Husband	M	16.3	16.7	4.2	4.2	1.7	2.3
		SD	2.1	2.8	3.6	3.6	3.5	4.2
		n	66	66	66	66	66	66
	Wife	M	16.8	17.9	3.5	3.5	1.2	0.9
		SD	2.3	2.1	3.7	3.7	2.6	2.6
		n	44	45	45	45	44	45

E = Expectation; P = Performance.

ployed (the dual-earner family) and for the families in which husband alone was employed (the single-earner family).

Both male and female respondents indicated that it was the wives who performed housework tasks heavily in their families regardless of the wives' employment (score of 15 or more). The employed wives performed, however, slightly less (score of 15) then the non-employed wives (score of 16 or 17). The wives in both types of families were expected to perform in this way by both wives and husbands (score of 15 or 16). Both husbands and wives reported that the husbands performed housework tasks substantially less than the wives. Relatively, however, the husbands in the dual-earner families performed slightly more (score of 5) than the husbands in the single-earner families (score of 3 or 4) and the husbands were expected to do so (score of 3, 4, or 5). Table 9.3 also shows that others (children or relatives) performed housework tasks even less (score of 2 or 3) than the husbands. This analysis indicates that it was the wives who bore the major burden of performing housework tasks regardless of their employment. The husbands shared the housework tasks to a limited extent, but more than others. Thus, it was basically the wives and husbands in Korean immigrant families who performed most of house-work tasks. In sum, analysis of the three family tasks—family finance, child care, and performance of house-work—demonstrates that the respondents generally maintained functionally self-managing (independent) nuclear families.

INTERGENERATIONAL RELATIONSHIPS

Emergence of the independent nuclear family is expected to have a great deal of impact on the relationship between married children and elderly parents. The independent nuclear family means not just residential and functional independence of married couples but also a drastic shifting of the primary family/kinship tie. With emergence of the independent nuclear family, married children's relationship with their spouses (marital ties) is considered more important than any family/kinship ties. In contrast, in the traditional (Confucian) extended family, the relationship between married children (sons) and their parents is considered more important than the children's own marital relations. The independent nuclear family also means that family life is gradually shifted to a couple-centered life. Such a shift indicates that marital power gradually moves toward an egalitarian relationship between husband and wife (Kim et al., 1991). With the changing reality of the family and kinship relationship, satisfying the needs of the married couple and their children is considered the more important responsibility for married children than caring for elderly parents.

Such a shifting priority does not, however, suggest that married children abandon the cultural norm of filial piety. They are continuously committed to the significant aspects of the traditional Confucian filial norms (Hurh & Kim, 1988), but married children are now expected to satisfy their family needs before they take care of their parents' needs. Married children's care for parents' needs is, therefore, considered as a secondary concern. In this priority-shifting reality, elderly parents would often feel neglected, humiliated, slighted, or arbitrarily treated by their married children, when elderly parents adhere to the Confucian norm of filial piety. Parents' sense of neglect and mistreatment would be further intensified by the fact that there is no guarantee in the United States that the eldest son would be the most capable and willing son to take care of the parents. This situation creates a considerable degree of uncertainty for arranging the filial responsibility among married children. Such an uncertain arrangement of filial obligation among the married children and evasion of the responsibility by some married children further aggravate parents' sense of frustration and humiliation (Kim et al., 1991).

Employment of wives in Korean immigrant families is associated with another problem of intergenerational relationships. As most of young and middle-aged married couples are employed, they are burdened with the three major adult roles: marital, parental, and work. In contrast, their parents gradually lose the adult roles, starting with the loss of the work role, then the parental role, and eventually the marital role (Kim et al., 1993). Such a reality of role experiences suggests generation-segregated life conditions of Korean married children and their elderly parents. The segregated life conditions in turn suggest the development of different ways of thinking and life styles between married children and elderly parents.

With different ways of thinking and life conditions, elderly parents probably would not fully understand their children's struggling experience of managing the role activities. It would be also true that married children would be too busy and too young to understand (1) their elderly parents' stressful experience with new roles and (2) their difficulty and hardship in managing their current life with a highly limited adaptability to life in the United States. When children are generally overburdened with their adult roles and also do not fully comprehend the life experience of elderly parents, children can easily overlook the difficult life of their parents and remain unconcerned. This tendency of insensitivity to the life experience of the parents could be easily sustained by the fact that they do not need parents' help as much as their parents need their help for various activities such as financial help, transportation, grocery shopping, and health care. When these two factors (children's insensitivity and parents' need for children's help) are combined, elderly parents may suffer in numerous ways as the victims of children's negligence.

DISCUSSION AND CONCLUSION

Immigrants' life experience in the United States is a joint product of two sets of variables: (1) the sociocultural factors that immigrants brought to the United States from their native country (pre-immigration factors), and (2) the structural conditions that immigrants encounter in the United States (post-immigration factors). Along with middle-class backgrounds, Korean immigrants brought to the United States from their native country the traditional (Confucian) extended family and related traditional gender role orientation. This traditional orientation seems to justify massive employment of Korean immigrant wives in the United States, when their employment was an economic necessity for family support. But their massive employment accelerated the emergence of the independent nuclear family. As Goode (1963) contends, the basic structural source of such a change in the family system has been an industrialized economy. What employment of wives in Korean immigrant families did was to speed up the process of change in the family and kinship system.

In spite of full-time employment, most employed Korean wives have accepted a heavy burden of family tasks as their obligation. If their employment conditions had been favorable or intrinsically rewarding, the employed wives could have gradually developed a sense of careerism or occupational commitment with a new gender role orientation. Such a change in their occupational orientation and gender role orientation could have led to the development of a new pattern of family and work roles—a substantial sharing of family tasks between husband and wife. In reality, however, the multiple factors associated with the immigrant wives' family and work roles (economic necessity of their employment, persistence of the traditional gender role orientation, emergence of the independent nuclear family, and the wives' unfavorable employment conditions) made Korean immigrant wives continuously employed and perennially burdened with the double roles.

Analysis of the independent nuclear family and strain in the intergenerational relationship call our attention to the structural source of intergenerational strain. Without understanding such a structural source, frustrated parents would rather blame (1) their children (sons) for their changing attitude or negligent behavior after children's marriage and/or (2) their children's spouses for the spouses' selfish or unconcerned attitude toward the parents' needs or welfare. This misplaced response of elderly parents would aggravate the relationship between married children and elderly parents by attributing the source of intergenerational strain to the personality factors of married children and their spouses. Solutions for the intergenerational strain should, therefore, come from the recognition of the changing social reality of the family and kinship system. In this respect, an interesting issue is elderly parents' preference for a separate residence independent of their married children (Kim et al., 1991; Koh & Bell, 1987). As long as married children maintain the independent nuclear family, it would also be desirable for elderly parents to maintain their own residence. With separate living arrangements, the parents and married children then need to develop a new pattern of intergenerational relationship—an Asian version of intimacy with distance.

In conclusion, massive employment of Korean immigrant wives has contributed to a series of changes in the family and kinship life of Korean immigrants in the United States. At the same time, certain aspects of their family and kinship life remain unchanged (e.g., persistence of the traditional gender role orientation). Even these non-changing aspects currently complicate Korean immigrants' family and kinship life.

REFERENCES

Barringer, Herbert, Robert W. Gardner, & Michael J. Levin. (1991). *Asian and Pacific Islanders in the United States*. New York: Russell Sage Foundation.

Goode, William J. (1963). *World Revolution and Family Patterns*. Glencoe, IL: Free Press.

Hurh, Won Moo, & Kwang Chung Kim. (1988). "Uprooting and Adjustment: A Sociological Study of Korean Immigrants' Mental Health." In *Final Report to the National Institute of Mental Health* (Grant No. 1R1 MH40312-01). Bethesda, MD: U.S. Department of Health and Human Services: National Institute of Mental Health.

Kim, K. C., & W. M. Hurh. (1988). "The Burden of Double Roles: Korean Immigrant Wives in the USA." *Ethnic and Racial Studies*, 11: 151-167.

Kim, Kwang Chung, Shin Kim, & Won Moo Hurh. (1991). "Filial Piety and Intergenerational Relationship in Korean Immigrant Families." *International Journal of Aging and Human Development*, 33: 233-245.

Kim, Kwang Chung, Won Moo Hurh, & Shin Kim. (1993). "Generation Differences in Korean Immigrants' Life Conditions in the United States." *Sociological Perspectives*, 36: 257-270.

Koh, James Y., & William G. Bell. (1987). "Korean Elderly in the United States: Intergenerational Relation and Living Arrangement." *Gerontologist*, 27: 66-71.

Lee, Hyo Chae. (1990). *Kajok Kwa Sahoe* (Family and Society, in Korean). Seoul: Kyung-Moon Publishing Company.

Park, Insook Han, James T. Fawcett, Fred Arnold, & Robert W. Gardner. (1990). *Korean Immigrants and U.S. Immigration Policy: A Predeparture Perspective*. Honolulu: East-West Center.

part four

KOREAN AMERICAN IDENTITY

The following three chapters in Part Four address both theoretical and practical issues concerning the meanings of and tensions in Korean identity in a multicultural society. They include an analysis of the components of identity development, conflicts between barriers of conservative Korean nationalism and the modern feminist framework, attitudes toward interracial and interethnic marriages, and language as a powerful part of an individual's identity.

In "Searching for and Defining a Korean American Identity in a Multicultural Society," Luke and Grace Kim analyze the components of identity development and apply them to ethnic minorities, particularly Korean Americans. They found that people grow into one or a combination of four modes of identity adjustment: assimilation, traditionalist, marginality, and bicultural integration. Conflicts between Asian/Korean American children and their parents arise from differences in cultural values. This situation may be ameliorated by both parties obtaining a bicultural perspective, which is also necessary for living in today's multicultural world and maintaining an enriching life.

Interracial marriages are becoming more and more common in the United States as different cultures and ethnicities merge together. In "Intraethnic, Interracial, and Interethnic Marriages among Korean American Women," Gin Yong Pang discusses attitudes toward interracial and interethnic love from an Asian and Korean American perspective. This chapter, which is based on interviews of young adults aged 18 to 26, explains why the ideal concept of love ("love is blind") does not follow reality. She explains Korean parents' hierarchical preferences of choice for a spouse, quotes from Caucasian men, and the negative attitudes toward relationships between Asian American women and Caucasian men to provide insight on this sensitive topic.

In "Ethnic Identities Reflected in Value Orientation of Two Generations of Korean American Women," Ailee Moon and Young I. Song investigate the value orientation similarites and differences between immigrant mothers and their adolescent daughters. Value orientation is analyzed in the context of ethnic identity. The study, which is based on the responses of 115 Korean immigrant mothers and their 89 daughters, sheds light on the points of agreement and disagreement in relation to traditional Confucian beliefs and moral standards.

10

Searching for and Defining a Korean American Identity in a Multicultural Society

Luke I. Kim and Grace S. Kim

INTRODUCTION

The United States of America is historically a nation of immigrants and a multicultural society. Because early European settlers and immigrants constituted a majority of the population, the cultural and ideological orientation in the United States has been Eurocentric. The nation has advocated the melting pot theory as a model of assimilation. A melting pot, like homogenized stew, is possible among European Caucasian immigrants even through their mixed marriages because of similar physical appearance and skin color.

However, the melting pot model does not work for people of color unless wholesale interracial marriages occur in the United States so as to mix up all the blood and cause a drastic change toward racial homogeneity, as once suggested by Arnold Toynbee, a British historian. As long as there are differences in skin color and outward physical appearance, people tend to be categorized, classified, and put in a pecking order according to skin color and physical characteristics (Kitano, 1974).

An alternative model of a multiethnic and multicultural society is that of a salad bowl (or jap-chae, a Korean dish) wherein each ingredient in the tossed salad retains its own color, texture, taste, and identity. The sum total of all the ingredients becomes a mosaic of national identities without the individual parts losing their identity. Salad dressing of oil and vinegar would induce a smooth and tasty blending and unity of the salad.

We need to strive toward a pluralistic society where we can accept and appreciate differences and similarities among diverse ethnic groups. We should promote mutual understanding and cooperation, rather than competition and pitting one against others among ethnic groups. When united, we will make a culturally enriched, colorful, and strong nation.

DEFINITION OF IDENTITY

Baumeister (1988) defined the criteria for identity as continuity as a person across time and differentiation from others.

What is ethnic identity? We use two interconnected or hyphenated words to describe our dual identity, such as Korean American, Chinese American, or African American. Douglas Kim (1993) prefers a more descriptive term "American of Korean descent."

My identity is the total sum of my being and the entirety of what I am. It is the totality of my physical, mental, emotional, social, legal, cultural, and conscious and unconscious thought processes and feelings. As we develop, we will expand and synthesize all we are, although not necessarily smoothly or without problems.

Some aspects of me are given and beyond my control. However, other characteristics are acquired or can be cultivated with effort. Identity does not form naturally by itself, but identity formation is an active process in to which we can make considerable input and define who we are. We will be able to influence the shaping of our identities.

MULTI-FACETED DIMENSIONS OF IDENTITY

Many dimensions and components of ourselves contribute to the totality of our identities. To comprehend the concept of identity more clearly, we may break down the identity into its various dimensions and components, and consider the characteristics of each dimension and ingredient and how they contribute toward the totality of identity formation.

Physical Identity

Our physical identity is made up of such factors as birth; birth order; gender; color of skin, hair, and eyes; physical appearance; and genetic factors, such as hereditary dispositions and diseases.

Our external physical appearance, especially facial features and the color of skin and hair, are readily visible, and therefore can be easily distinguished and categorized. The physical differences are the most common source of separation, bias, and discrimination.

In order to change our identity, we may attempt to modify our weight, and, to a lesser degree, our height, or even dye our hair or change our faces by plastic surgery. However, genetic factors are given and we are born with them. We have no choice in choosing our biological parents, ethnicity, and family lineage. How do we feel about our ethnicity, gender, and physical appearance? Do we accept, deny, or try to cope with it, or make up for it?

Legal Identity

Another dimension of our identities is defined by the law and our legal status in the country. Examples are date of birth; country or place of birth (American born, foreign born); legal name (original Korean name, Anglicized name, woman's name after marriage, name of adopted child, and adopted popular name, that is, pen name, movie star's name); U.S. citizenship; naturalization; dual citizenship; permanent resident status; entry as an illegal alien; foreign exchange student status; age of entry to the United States; ethnicity of spouse, biological parents, step-parents, adopted parents; social security number; inheritance rights, and so forth.

Some of the legal status characteristics are given, and others are something we can choose, change, and plan.

Professional/Occupational and Achievement-Related Identity

Usually Asians come from a historically hierarchical society and tend to be status-conscious and achievement-oriented. Often people view their self-esteem and self-identity in terms of their academic and professional achievements, degrees, and titles. Also in this capitalist society, business and financial success—millionaire or celebrity status—enhance self-esteem and self-perception as well as perceptions by others. These kinds of accomplishments contribute to a more positive self-identity.

Psychological Identity

Psychological, emotional, and life experiences are crucial in shaping and influencing identity formation. Important contributing factors are the nature and quality of relationships with parents, siblings, and extended family during the developmental age; and positive and negative identification with parents, especially with regard to their ethnicity. These psychological experiences play an important role in the development of ethnic identity. The influences of other life experiences include friends, school peers, teachers, neighbors, co-workers, girlfriends or boyfriends, husband or wife, including their ethnicities.

Also other influencing psychological experiences are experiences of prejudice and discrimination, feelings of alienation and marginality, feelings of insecurity and non-acceptance, and feelings of victimization.

Other pertinent psychological dimensions that contribute to one's identity are self-concept, self-esteem, self-affirmation, perception by others, self-denial, self-hatred, ambivalence, conscious and unconscious defensive psychological postures, especially with regard to ethnic issues, and the degree of psychological resolutions and insight into one's identity.

We are well aware that psychological factors are strongly influenced by the sociocultural environment in which we live. A child's life experiences will be very different if he/she grows up in a small town in North Dakota or in the middle of Koreatown in Los Angeles. It would make a difference if the child attends an all-white school in Minnesota or a big-city school in San Francisco where Korean and other Asian ethnic students are predominant.

In the psychological dimensions of identity, there are aspects we can choose and control, and there are areas we may or may not be able to influence as a child, such as family dynamics and parental child-rearing practices.

Cultural Identity

The transmission of cultural traditions, values, customs, rituals, and family stories through parents and extended families are very important for children in developing interest in their family history and ethnic heritage. It helps shape their cultural identity. They can further increase their understanding and knowledge of Korean culture and history by attending a local Korean weekend language school, learning the Korean language and reading books on Korean culture and literature. Many young people find it a very moving experience to visit Korea, meet relatives in Korea, and find "roots" there. There are Korean American summer camps, Korean American college leadership conferences, and other Korean American community and church programs that can help enhance the development of Korean American identity. Each year the Korean government and universities in Korea offer Korean summer culture schools for overseas students. Many high school students find Korean summer school experiences worthwhile and helpful in their search for cultural identity.

Ideological/Political/Religious Identity

Another dimension of identity is defined by where we stand ideologically and what we do in terms of social, political, and spiritual/religious actions and behaviors. The following list will tell us something about the person and his/her ideological orientation, belief system, and political/religious affiliations: Christian (Catholic, Protestant, born-again, fundamentalist, liberal, etc.), Jehovah's Witness, Mormon, Buddhist, agnostic, atheist, communist, socialist, anticommunist, Ku Klux Klan, skinhead, Aryan Brother, Crips, Bloods, Black Panther, Gray Panther, feminist, environmentalist, peace movement activist, civil rights activist, nonviolence protester, Republican, Democrat, Libertarian, conservative, anarchist, and so on.

TOTALITY OF SELF-IDENTITY

In sum, the totality of self-identity is multifaceted and dynamic. Many factors and dimensions interact together and contribute synergistically or sometimes discordantly to the development of identity. There are aspects we have no choice over because they are given. But there are many components and dimensions of identity which we can intentionally choose and influence. Positive identification with one's own ethnic identity, and the integration and synthesis of various experiences and dimensions will contribute toward a more solid sense of who we are, and the enhancement of our psychological well-being, including strong ethnic identity.

THE GRID MODEL OF KOREAN/ASIAN AMERICAN IDENTITY ADJUSTMENT

We propose a grid for four modes of Korean/Asian American identity adjustment as illustrated in Table 10.1. The four modes in the quad are assimilation, traditionalist, marginality, and bicultural integration. The four modes form a conceptual paradigm, but, in reality, people tend to adopt varying gradations and mixtures among the four types of adjustment. This is a modified version of similar paradigms previously proposed by Kitano & Daniels (1988).

As we will see later, self-identity adjustment is not fixed, and changes will occur in the different developmental phases of life, as described in the life cycle proposed by Erik Erikson (1968).

Table 10.1
Four Modes of Korean American Identity

Accept	Reject
Bicultural Integration Maintain active contact with both cultures Biculturally comfortable and competent Can easily move in and out of both cultures Bicultural perspective	**Assimilation** Mainstreaming Associate mainly with Caucasians and avoid Korean people "Banana" identity Culturally assimilated but physical appearance still a barrier
Traditionalist Emphasize "Koreanness" Reject American values and avoid American people Voluntary segregation from mainstream society	**Marginality** "Deculturation" Withdrawal from both socieities and cultures Loss of cultural identity Isolated and alienated, individualistic experience

Source: Modified; Kitano & Daniels (1988).

Assimilation

The mode of assimilation is represented by a person who is eager to assimilate into the white American mainstream. The person tends to associate with white peers only and to avoid Korean people. The person rejects Korean/Asian culture and values, including Korean food and language. He/she admires and adopts mainstream American culture and values. He/she despises Korean people and may feel ashamed of being a Korean. He/she may hide from being a Korean. This mode of adjustment is especially common during the period of kindergarten, elementary, and junior high school when children are sensitive to being different from peers. They want to be similar to, and be accepted by, their majority Caucasian peers. Some late teenagers and even adults may continue this mode of assimilation as they probably have had very negative experiences in response to being Korean Americans. Although they are trying hard to assimilate into mainstream white society, their different Asian physical appearance remains an obstacle and a barrier to complete assimilation into white society.

Traditionalist

The traditionalist strongly identifies with Korean people and their culture, while rejecting and resisting American values. He/she is proud of being a Korean and feels that everything Korean is good or "number one." The person usually associates with Korean people, eats Korean food, and maintains family relations and a Korean lifestyle. They emphasize Koreanness and Korean culture to their children. The traditionalist usually attends a Korean ethnic church for social, emotional, and spiritual support. By avoiding mainstream society, the person may be living a self-imposed "ethnic ghetto" life.

Marginality

In the mode of marginality, the person is withdrawn from both cultures. The person feels marginalized and alienated from both mainstream society and the Korean community. He/she feels a loss of cultural identity, acceptance, and belonging in both communities. They are "decultured" and live an individualistic and isolated existence. Young people during the phase of identity crisis and some interracially married Korean women may prefer this kind of existence.

Bicultural Integration

In the bicultural integration mode of adjustment, the person feels comfortable, competent, and adequate biculturally. He/she may speak the Korean language, or even if the person does not speak Korean, he/she feels proud of and is comfortable and knowledgeable with regard to Korean and American cultures. The person can move in and out of both communities easily with flexibility and appropriate cultural behavior. They view their bicultural orientation as an asset, not a liability. They feel that their lives are enriched by bicultural/multicultural perspectives (Grace Kim, 1993). We realize that this mode of bicultural integration is desirable and ideal in the conceptual scheme. However, it is not easy for American-born second-generation Korean Americans to be biculturally integrated. The 1.5 generation (those who immigrated to the United States when they were young, i.e., at an elementary or junior high school age) will have a better chance to maintain their bicultural and bilingual orientation.

Won Moo Hurh (1993) described this mode as a "cosmopolitan personality," which has had positive resolution of biculturalism, and displays flexibility, motivation, and leadership potential with a strong sense of Korean American identity. With the ascendance of the Pacific Rim countries' global economic power, such a bicultural/bilingual, cosmopolitan, "international and global" person will have an advantage in employment, business opportunities, and the political arena.

ETHNIC MINORITY IDENTITY DEVELOPMENT

Another theory of the stages of minority identity development was proposed by Derald Sue and David Sue (1990). Their ethnic identity development stages are as follows.

The Conformity Stage

The person prefers the dominant, white culture and wants to conform to his/her white peers. This person has negative beliefs about his/her own culture and has feelings of self-hatred with regard to his/her own minority ethnicity. Often young children or teenagers may feel this way when they want to be like their white peers.

The Dissonance Stage

The person experiences cultural confusion, conflict, or even an identity crisis. Denial begins to break down, which leads to questioning. The person is in conflict as a result of disparate pieces of information or experiences that challenge his/her current concept.

This stage frequently occurs among late teen and college age students who are rebellious against their parental and ethnic values, and yet are beginning to think about their ethnic identity issues in relation to dating and courting a person of the opposite sex and of a different race.

The Resistance and Immersion Stage

The person begins to reject, or react against, the dominant white society and its values as having no validity for him or her. The three common types of affective feelings the person experiences during this stage are guilt, shame, and anger. Now the person begins to show endorsement of his/her own ethnic minority and its values.

The Introspection Stage

Loyalty and responsibility to one's own ethnic group and family on the one hand, and a desire for personal independence and autonomy on the other hand, come into conflict. The person begins to recognize that there are many elements in the white American society that are functional and desirable, yet there is confusion as to how one should incorporate these elements into the ethnic minority culture and values. An introspective mode sets in for more questioning and searching.

The Integrative and Awareness Stage

One feels a sense of fulfillment with regard to one's own cultural identity. Cultural values of other minorities and dominant Caucasian groups are objectively examined and accepted or rejected on the basis of prior experiences in an earlier stage of identity development. The person in this stage attains a more synergistic and integrated bicultural orientation that is realistic and workable for them. Some call this phase the "stage of internalization" (Hall et al., 1972).

As Derald Sue & David Sue suggested (1990), we should be aware of some cautions and possible limitations in proposing any kind of ethnic identity models. Cultural identity development is a dynamic process, not a static one. Models should serve as conceptual frameworks to help us understand the process and development, but there are mixtures of the various stages and many other factors are involved.

LIFE CYCLE AND IDENTITY DEVELOPMENT

Based on experiences of his own and other second-generation Korean Americans, Douglas Kim (1993) reiterated that the nature and degree of awareness and struggle with one's own ethnic identity do change and modify in different phases of life.

Elementary and junior high school youths, for example, tend to deny and reject their ethnic identity and want to be like the dominant white peers. The children are sensitive to being different and to being ridiculed often for being different. Approval and acceptance by peers are important to them.

When they are in their late teens and college age, the issue of in-group and out-group becomes a sensitive one. Identity issues surface more acutely when they begin to date. Many of them begin to think about their identity seriously for the first time. There may be ambivalence and confusion, leading to introspection and inner struggle. Steady courtship with a member of the opposite sex of a different race and plans for an eventual marriage may precipitate a more serious crisis or some kind of resolution of ethnic issues.

By the time the second-generation Korean Americans reach adulthood, many of them appear to have accepted their ethnicity and bicultural orientation with more positive resolution. It is also noted that by the time their children have grown to be young adults, the immigrant parents tend to change and modify from their firm cultural stand. Parents become more "mellow," conciliatory, and willing to accept their offspring's more Americanized way of life. The earlier cultural conflict between the parents and growing children appears to resolve toward more mutual accommodation (Park & Sohn, 1993).

However, the above statement does not mean that the first generation of immigrants will change in their basic cultural and ethnic orientation. Even if they have lived in the United States for a long period of time, their basic core of "Koreanness" will continue, while their Western acculturation proceeds (Luke Kim, 1992). The progressive Americanization of Korean immigrants and their strong attachments are not mutually exclusive. Americanization is "added on" to their Koreanness, and does not discard or weaken the original identification. Hurh and Kim (1988) described this phenomenon as an "adhesive adaptation pattern."

OUTMARRIAGE

Outmarriage data (marriage out of one's own ethnic group) may provide another interesting angle and insight into ethnic identity issues. According to Kitano's study in Los Angeles (Kitano & Rogers, 1988), the highest rates of outmarriage of Asian Americans occurred in 1977. The outmarriage rates were Japanese (68%), Chinese (49.7%), and Koreans (31.1%). Females consistently outmarried at a higher rate than males. Since 1977 there has been a decrease in outmarriages by all groups, probably due to the fact that the population of new immigrants from Asia grew drastically. By 1984, the rates of outmarriage were Japanese (51.2%), Chinese (30%), and Koreans (8.7%). Japanese Americans have had much fewer numbers of recent immigrants and also have been in the United States longer than other Asians. This appears to be reflected in their higher rates of outmarriage than the rates of other Asian Americans. The data seem to suggest that as their generation increases (i.e., second, third, and fourth generations), they tend to outmarry more and show less attachment to their own ethnic identity.

Table 10.2
Asian/Korean Values versus American Values

Asian/Korean Traditional Values	American Mainstream Values
Family Relations	
Family-oriented	Individual-oriented
Interdependence	Independence and autonomy
Respect for parents and elders	Horizontal, democratic structure
Family loyalty and filial piety	Depends on the family and individual
Duty, obedience, acceptance	Freedom of choice, independence
Family discipline via shame/punishments	School/other agency discipline
Life Philosophy	
Family/kinship bonds, collectivism	Individualism
Success through self-discipline and will	Pragmatism, fulfilling one's potential
Sense of stoicism and fatalism	Sense of optimism and opportunism
Reciprocity and obligation	Avoidance of obligation ("going Dutch")
Status consciousness and face-saving	Self-realization; do your own thing
Living in harmony with nature	Control and conquer nature
Communication Style	
Subtle, non-verbal body language	Emphasis on verbal language
Control of feelings	Free expression of feelings
Flowery, indirect expression	Direct, explicit expression
No eye-to-eye contact	Eye contact important
Honorific language	Equality in language
Self-effacing	Self-promoting
No hugging or kissing in public	Hugging and kissing in public

DIFFERENCES IN CULTURAL VALUES BETWEEN ASIAN TRADITION AND MAINSTREAM EUROAMERICANS

We find that the most common conflict between Asian/Korean immigrant parents and their second-generation youths is due to the cultural value differences in the concept of self and family. Asian cultural values derive from the 3000-year tradition of Confucius's teachings. Confucian teachings stress work ethics (will rather than natural talent); life long self-cultivation (emphasis on higher learning and scholarship and respect for teachers); respect for elders and ancestors (importance of family lineage); priority of the interest of the family, group, and collective welfare over the interest of the individual member; and respect for and conformity to the hierarchical structure and order of the society and family.

In contrast, American democratic ideology emphasizes freedom, individuality, autonomy, independence, and equality. This different concept of the self and the family is reflected in family relations, interpersonal relationships, gender roles, communication styles, and other associated behaviors that emerge.

This difference between the primacy of the individual over the family in American culture, on the one hand, and the primacy of family over the individual in Asian culture on the other hand, are the source of recurring conflicts and disagreements between Asian immigrant parents and their American-born youths. The conflicts are manifested in constant tensions between parents and youths, with pulling and pushing, and maneuvering from both sides. Some youths may conform to parents' wishes, but many may resist or rebel.

It is a big challenge for both parents and teenagers to come to some kind of mutual understanding and "win-win" solution. What would be a win-win situation? Would Korean/Asian American values be a hybrid of two cultures or a bicultural perspective? A bicultural perspective requires flexibility, give-and-take, and the ability to move in and out of both cultures without too much conflict. Table 10.2 illustrates the differences between the two "traditional" or "model" cultures. There is a risk of describing the differences in a stereotypical manner. This is for contrast only. Also, it should be noted that there have been significant cultural changes toward Westernization among Asian countries. The global "democratic" ideology is becoming a set of common values that people aspire to across different nations and races. Thus the differences between Western and Eastern values are narrowing.

SUMMARY

In searching, defining and, developing the Korean/Asian identity, we have described the multi-faceted factors and dimensions that contribute to the totality of one's self-identity. In spite of the many givens we are born with, we have considerable choice and input that we can exercise in the shaping and directing of our ethnic identity formation processes. We have described the different modes and phases of identity development we go through as we search, define, and find our identities. Developing and maintaining a biculturally integrated "dual identity" is not an easy task, but it is a desirable and attainable goal. As a bicultural, cosmopolitan, and "globally oriented" person, one will find a more self-affirming and culturally enriching way of life.

REFERENCES

Baumeister, R. F. (1988). *Identity: Cultural Change and the Struggle for Self.* New York: Oxford University Press.

Erikson, E. (1968). *Identity: Youth and Crisis.* New York: W. W. Norton.

Hall, W. S., W. E. Cross, & R. Freedle. (1972). "Stages in the Development of Black Awareness: An Exploratory Investigation." In R. L. Jones, ed., *Black Psychology.* New York: Harper and Row.,

Hurh, Won Moo. (1993). "The 1.5 Generation: A Paragon of Korean American Pluralism." In *Korean Culture*, Vol. 14 (Special issue). Los Angeles: Korean Culture Center.

_____. (1992). Ethnic Distance and Public Opinion: Majority Americans' Perception of Koreans in the United States." Presented at the North Park College Korean Symposium, Chicago, October.

Hurh, Won Moo, & Kwang Chung Kim. (1988). "Uprooting and Adjustment: A Sociological Study of Korean Immigrants' Mental Health." In *Final Report to the National Institute of Mental Health* (Grant No. 1R1 MH40312-01). Bethesda, MD: U.S. Department of Health and Human Services, National Institute of Mental Health.

Kim, Douglas. (1993). "Korean Americans Are Able to Take Best of Both Worlds." Panel presentation at the Korean American Student Conference (KASCON) VII, San Francisco, March.

Kim, Grace. (1993). "Korean American Identity." Panel presentation at the Korean American Student Conference (KASCON) VII, San Francisco, March.

Kim, Luke I. C. (1992). "Psychiatric Care of Korean Americans." In A. Gaw, ed., *Culture, Ethnicity and Mental Illness*. Washington, DC: American Psychiatric Press.

Kitano, H. L. (1974). *Race Relations*. Englewood Cliffs, NJ: Prentice-Hall.

Kitano, H. L., & Roger Daniels. (1988). *Asian Americans: Emerging Minorities*. Englewood Cliffs, NJ: Prentice-Hall.

Park, K., & M. Sohn. (1993). "Perspective of Second Generation Child and Parent." Panel presentation at the Transition Generation Workshop, Mountain View, CA, January.

Sue, Derald, & David Sue. (1990). *Counseling the Culturally Different: Theory and Practice*. New York: Wiley.

11

Intraethnic, Interracial, and Interethnic Marriages among Korean American Women[1]

Gin Yong Pang

When I see an Asian girl with a white guy, I have an uneasy feeling, especially when the girl, appearance wise, fits the stereotype of [being] really quiet, submissive, and so on. I wonder, "Why is he dating her? What for?" I can't help looking at them. I guess it's her choice. If he looks fine, then, it shouldn't matter; but if he's on to her because of all the stereotypes, and because he could use her, then, something is wrong with it.

—"Miae Kim"[2]

INTRODUCTION

In the United States, where notions of love and ideas of freedom and individual choice dominate our social, political, and personal thought, it is difficult for anyone to imagine that romantic relationships and marriage between a man and a woman can be based on anything but individual free choice and love. So, when the *San Francisco Examiner/Chronicle's Image Magazine* published a front-page article by Joan Walsh titled "Asian Women, Caucasian Men: The New Demographics of Love" (1990), many people, in particular Asian American women and White[3] men in interracial relationships, expressed outrage at the author's assertions that there was more to interracial relationships—especially that of Asian women/White men—than "love."

As an exploratory study, this paper does not delve deeply into the subject of the social construction of love, either in general or in interracial/interethnic relationships. Some commentary, however, is necessary before we continue. I suggest that what we call "love" is not free from influences of race, gender, and class inequality in our society. Based on in-depth oral interviews with over sixty-five Asian Americans, Whites, Blacks, and biracial individuals (most of whom are students at the University of California at Berkeley, or U.C. Berkeley), I have found that socioeconomic status, "valuation" of different race/ethnic and gender groups, and "sexual/racial imagery" based on race and gender, all contribute to the "social construction" of love and meaning of interracial and interethnic relationships.

Researchers Berger and Luckman (1967) define social construction[4] as the process by which individuals come to describe, explain, or otherwise account for the world in which they live. Larry Shinagawa[5] and I also include the impact that cultural beliefs, mores, values, social institutions and structures, and agents of "authority" have on the meaning, understanding, and context in which individuals come to know and experience something. In particular, we refer to valuation, sexual/racial imagery, and socioeconomic status in the construction and shaping of personal or marital choices.

Valuation refers to the worth and esteem that society places upon individuals based upon their attributes, especially race/ethnicity and gender. It could be measured in terms of physical attractiveness, skin color, phenotype, perceptions of work attitudes, economic and educational success, or social acceptability.

Sexual/racial imagery include portrayals of sexuality of racial groups by their gender. For example, Asian or Asian American women are seen as submissive, seductive, exotic, available, and willing to please and cater to every whim of White men. Movies and plays like *Madame Butterfly*, *The World of Suzie Wong*, *Miss Saigon*, *Rambo First Blood Part II*, *Song of Singapore*, *Shogun*, and *Year of the Dragon* are only a few that portray Asian and Asian American women by these sexual/racial images. On the other hand, Asian or Asian American men are seen as sexless or as sexist pigs, unromantic, socially inept, clumsy, physically unendowed, and unable to compete sexually with White men in any way.

For this chapter, I discuss how perceptions of race, gender, and class inequality are internalized and reflected in the attitudes and interpretations that Asian Americans have about interracial and interethnic relationships. The discussion of my findings for this chapter is based on my study of one Asian American group in particular: Korean Americans.

DATA AND METHODOLOGY

There are very few studies of Korean Americans' attitudes on intermarriage or interracial/interethnic relationships. Most studies focus on the historical context or cultural conflicts of interracial marriages between Korean women and U.S. servicemen (e.g., Brewer, 1982; B. Kim, 1982; S. Kim, 1979; Rho, 1989). Very few focus on inequality, power dynamics, or resources based on race, class, and gender in these marriages or in intermarriages among Korean Americans in this country. Thus, I set out to collect data on attitudes and beliefs that Korean Americans have about intermarriage and interracial/interethnic relationships that take place in the United States.

Between January of 1989 and May 1991, I interviewed twenty single (never-been-married) Korean Americans who lived in the San Francisco Bay Area. They were chosen mainly through announcements in sociology, women's studies, Asian American studies, and ethnic studies classes. Eighteen of the twenty interviewees, at the time of the interview, were students at U.C. Berkeley and ranged in age between 18 to 26. There were eleven men and nine women in the sample; sixteen were born in Korea, four came to the United States before the age of 5. I consider these four to be in the "second generation" category with the four other U.S.-born Korean Americans. The other eleven represent what many Korean American scholars call the "1.5-generation"—those who came to the United States between the ages of about 5 and 15. So nineteen interviewees were either second- or 1.5-generation Korean Americans. One Korean American man came to this country at the age of 19.[6]

Each interview lasted from 90 to 120 minutes. The interviews were semi-structured, following a general guideline pertaining to topics of intermarriages and interracial/interethnic relationships.

One note on the sampling frame: Given the sampling frame, these Korean Americans are generally more educated, have more affluent family backgrounds, and are more liberal than the typical Korean American population. In addition, the study assesses their attitudes during one phase of their life cycle, that of young, single individuals. Attitudes and perspectives may change with age and experience. The effect of this combination of higher levels of education and class, liberality, youth, and singlehood are difficult to assess. On the one hand, this may result in presenting a more "liberal" view toward intermarriage—as is usually evident among young, affluent, middle-class individuals. On the other hand, it could also signal a more "ethnically cohesive" view than the general Korean American population because these students may exhibit heightened awareness of their ethnic heritage and culture as a result of the collegeexperience and may thereby place greater value on marriages within the Korean American or Asian American community. The degree of sampling bias is difficult to assess.

FINDINGS

My analysis of Korean Americans' attitudes toward intermarriage and interracial/interethnic relationships focuses on the following three areas: (1) the attitudes of parents and interviewees toward intermarriage; (2) the existence of "a preferential hierarchy of choice" for a spouse; and (3) the attitudes toward the relationships between Asian American women and White men. Responses to these questions and issues reveal the attitudes and beliefs that Korean Americans have toward interracial and interethnic relationships, and the ways in which they construct the meanings of various relationships that cross over race, gender, and class.

Children's and Their Parents' Attitudes Toward Intermarriage

Since today's Korean American community is largely made up of immigrants, it is not surprising that 75% (fifteen out of twenty) of the interviewees felt their parents would strongly to somewhat disapprove of intermarriage, that is, marrying outside of the Korean ethnic group. The other 25% felt their parents would somewhat approve but only under certain conditions and circumstances. The spouses' educational achievement, family background, cultural sensitivity, language skills (necessary to communicate with the parents), physical attractiveness, and race and ethnicity were all mentioned as factors that concerned their parents. Several Korean American men and women mentioned that interethnic Asian marriages raised less ire with their parents than interracial marriages. According to their parents, similarities in culture and race could help reduce differences and conflicts that might arise in marital and family relationships.

As for the interviewees, virtually no one said they disapproved, in general, of intermarriage. The majority responded, "It's up to the individual," "It's their choice," "It doesn't matter to me," "I don't care," and "If they love one another, it shouldn't matter what race people are." When asked, however, whether they would personally intermarry (both interracial and interethnic), about 80% (sixteen out of twenty) expressed many doubts and concerns, while the other 20% expressed almost no reservations about intermarrying.[7]

The majority of Korean Americans (similarly to their parents) perceived interethnic Asian marriages more favorably than interracial ones. These interethnic unions were seen as more likely to succeed, that is, not end in divorce and to be more compatible in terms of experience, culture, and race, and to be more acceptable to the family and the Korean American community.

Given the history and the continuing interracial marriages between Korean women and White and Black U.S. servicemen in South Korea—there are currently over 40,000 U.S. troops in South Korea (*Korea Report*, 1989)—there is a stigma attached to interracial relationships. Today, the Korean American community still perceives interracial relationships—particularly those of Korean/Asian women with White/Black men—as originating from dire economic or social circumstances, and as fraught with problems due to racial and cultural differences and prejudice.

Preferential Hierarchy of Choice for Marital Spouse

My father, who is an immigrant to the United States, once told my two sisters and me—all 1.5-generation—that he wanted us to marry Korean men, but if we could not find Korean men whom we could love, to marry Asian men; and if we could not find Asian men whom we could love, to marry White men, then Mexican, then Black. I questioned whether other Korean Americans grew up hearing a similar appeal, and if so, did the preferential hierarchy look the same?

Parents of Korean American Children

I asked interviewees whether their parents had a preference for whom their children should marry—having in mind, race, and ethnicity. The interviewees' parents' preferential hierarchy was nearly an exact reflection of my father's. Not surprisingly, the majority of the parents preferred, first, Korean/Korean American, then Asian American, White, and then other racial groups, like Mexicans, and finally Blacks. This pattern was consistent. Blacks were at the bottom of the preferential hierarchy.[8]

Many Korean Americans mentioned that within the broader Asian American category there was a hierarchy. Not all Asian American groups occupied equal positions of social status. After Korean Americans, Japanese Americans or Chinese Americans were preferred over Filipino Americans or Vietnamese Americans.[9] Usually, when choices reached the level of Filipino Americans and Vietnamese Americans, many Korean American men and women pointed out their parents might prefer Whites before either of these Asian American groups.

Filipino Americans were, in general, considered different from other East Asian American groups both culturally and racially. Their skin color was considered "too dark" and thus less beautiful. In addition, interviewees felt that their parents perceived the racial mixture among Filipino Americans negatively. Culturally, they were seen as very different because of the influence of Spanish colonialism.

As for Vietnamese Americans, several of the interviewees felt their parents may not approve of Vietnamese/Vietnamese American spouses because of the low social and economic status of Vietnamese/Vietnamese American people in the United States. Also, many parents were swayed negatively by images of starving and distressed Vietnamese displaced by the wars in Southeast Asia. One 21-year-old, 1.5-generation Korean American woman explains:

I think there is this world view. Certain groups are higher. Let's say, according to the Western view [of evaluating the status of Asian countries], the Japanese are the highest because they are economically superior than other Asian countries. They are much more modernized, technically advanced, not a backward nation like the Southeast Asian countries. In a way, Koreans have somewhat a similar view of seeing Southeast Asian countries as backward. But because Korea is coming out of that, if we intermarry with these people [the Southeast Asians], we would be going back and lowering our status.

For her parents, and for this young Korean American woman, issues of social and economic status that various ethnic groups occupied, and images of stability, power, and order (or lack thereof) became a conscious part of her parents' and her attitude toward certain racial/ethnic groups, and of her valuation of one group over another as potential marital partners.

Korean American Children

The preferential for marital spouses among Korean American children resembles the general pattern of hierarchy of choice for their parents. The majority (about 75%) fit the parental pattern of preferring Korean Americans first, other Asian Americans second, then Whites, followed by other non-Black racial groups, and finally Blacks. Another 15% first preferred Asian Americans in general (including Korean Americans), and the remaining 10% first preferred Whites or were open to all groups equally.

As for the preferential hierarchy within the Asian American category, the majority of the interviewees, in a way similar to their parents, expressed a slight preference for Japanese Americans or Chinese Americans over Filipino Americans; attitudes toward marrying Filipino Americans or Vietnamese Americans were more open and less severe than that of their parents.

Furthermore, four out of twenty interviewees described their parents as strongly disapproving of marriages between Korean Americans and Japanese/Japanese Americans due to the history of Japanese colonialism in Korea. None of the interviewees who were open to marrying interethnically expressed hostility toward Japanese Americans or objections to marrying Japanese Americans.

The difference in the attitudes between the Korean American interviewees and their parents reflects the generational difference of the Korean American experience. The majority of the second- and 1.5-generation Korean Americans who were born or raised in the United States do not readily identify with their parents' hostility toward Japanese Americans. First, they did not personally experience

Japanese colonialism, unlike their parents. Second, the parents gave the interviewees mixed messages about Japanese/Japanese Americans. While many parents told their children about the tragic humiliation that Koreans suffered under the Japanese during the first part of the twentieth century, they also expressed admiration for the economic success and international recognition of Japan. Third, interviewees did not so much consider the Japanese Americans as "Japanese" (as their parents did), but as "Japanese Americans" or "Asian Americans." The majority of the interviewees who are U.C. Berkeley students (a campus well known for heightened ethnic and racial consciousness) identified themselves as "Korean Americans" or "Asian Americans." They saw a lot of commonalties with Japanese Americans and other Asian American groups because of race.

Low Preference of Blacks Among Korean Americans

In the book *Mixed Blood*, Paul Spickard (1989) notes the low status of Blacks in the marital hierarchy of Japanese Americans and Jewish Americans. In a similar way, Korean Americans also relegate Blacks to the bottom or near the bottom of the preferential marital hierarchy. Virtually all the interviewees felt their parents would strongly disapprove of marriage with a Black man or woman. Usually, Blacks did not even "come into the picture," or as one Korean American woman stated, "They don't even count."[10]

In the minds of Korean American parents, interracial marriage is largely defined as a relationship involving Korean/Asian Americans with the White population or with other Asian Americans. Many interviewees felt that while marrying a White person might not please their parents, there would be certain degree of acceptance toward their decision because of the high socioeconomic and cultural status of White people. Marrying a Black person, however, would mean constant scrutiny and ostracism because of the low social, economic, and racial status of Blacks as a group.

For many Korean American parents, because Blacks represent a group of people who are so different in race and culture, it is incomprehensible to imagine their children in such relationships. One interviewee remarked that if she marries a White man, she could have a child whose skin color resembled her own or that her parents, while if she marries a Black man, the child would look "Black." She feared that the child's skin color would be a constant remainder to her parents of the degree to which she disagreed with her parents and with the norms of Korean American culture and community life. In addition, according to the interviewees, Korean American parents have internalized many racial stereotypes of Blacks as "intellectually and culturally inferior," "lazy," "sexually loose," "violent," and "criminal-like." Thus, responding both to their parents' and the Korean American community's prejudice toward Blacks as well as to their own internalized images shaped by both the Korean American community and White society, many Korean Americans found it very difficult to imagine being in a relationship or marriage with a Black man or woman.

The stigma against Black men created conflict for one Korean American woman. Eun Hee, a 23-year-old, second-generation Korean American, recalls her parents' reaction when they found out that she was in a relationship with a Black man:

When they found out I was dating John [not his real name], my mom thought that maybe what I was going through was that I was feeling sorry for Blacks, and that I was dating John because of that. My father then said to me, "You don't have to be the hero." It was really scary. I couldn't believe they were saying these things. Where do they get these things?[11]

The lack of her parents' support and approval, together with her own growing feelings of doubt and uncertainty and an awareness of the difficulties of an interracial relationship with a Black man, contributed to the dissolution of the relationship between Eun Hee and John after two years.

ATTITUDES TOWARD THE DOMINANT PATTERN OF INTERMARRIAGE AND INTERRACIAL RELATIONSHIPS: ASIAN AMERICAN WOMAN AND WHITE MAN

Although the dominant pattern of marriage among Asian Americans in the United States is still *intra*marriages, *inter*marriages are increasing (Lee & Yamanaka, 1990; Shinagawa & Pang, 1988).[12] Among the patterns of intermarriage, the dominant race/gender pattern in the intermarriages is that of Asian American women marrying White men, according to Shinagawa and Pang's (1988) study of intermarriage patterns among Asian Americans in Los Angeles County, and many other studies.[13] In my study, I asked interviewees to respond to this dominant pattern of intermarriage.

The majority of the Korean American women and especially Korean American men expressed strong reservations about, and disapproval of, this pattern of intermarriage and relationships. One Korean American man confessed that "something bothered" him, "I'm not sure why, but it doesn't look good to me. Yeah, I see quite a few couples like that where the woman is Asian and the guy is Caucasian. When I see something like that . . . it's a feeling that is close to betrayal. It seems like that Asian person is betraying her own race. Feeling that's close to that."[14]

Another Korean American man was also annoyed by seeing so many Asian American women with White men, yet rarely the reverse. He says, "Perhaps I wouldn't mind it so much if I saw just as many Asian men with White women, or Asian women with other minority men. I rarely do."[15]

Others questioned the motivations of the Asian American women and the White men involved in these relationship. As Miae Kim remarked:

When I see an Asian girl with a white guy, I have an uneasy feeling, especially when the girl, appearance wise, fits the stereotype of [being] really quiet, submissive, and so on. I wonder, "Why is he dating her? What for?" I can't help looking at them. I guess it's her choice. If he looks fine, then, it shouldn't matter; but if he's on to her because of all the stereotypes, and because he could use her, then, something is wrong with it.[16]

Another Korean American woman also explained that White men want to marry Asian women because of the image of submissiveness, passiveness, or just to have her look up to him rather than having equal terms.[17] Supporting this perspective, Joan Walsh in her article, "Asian Women/Caucasian Men"

(1990), quotes Tom Knight, a White man who is in a relationship with a Japanese American woman. He says:

I see something of a feminist backlash in it. I don't really understand it, but I know I feel less threatened by Asian women. I grew up in a culture where men acted a certain way and women acted a certain way, and I'm more comfortable with Asian culture, where interpersonal relations are more ritualized, and women are graceful, polite, and considerate.

Doubts and mistrust toward White males in these relationships arose from numerous encounters by Korean American and Asian American women with certain types of White men. In my study, many Korean American women encountered White men who, for whatever reasons, pursued and dated exclusively or predominantly Asian/Asian American women. These men were so common and identifiable that the women had special names for them; they were called "Rice Kings" or "Asianphiles," or men with an "Asian fetish" or "Asian fixation." Their motives and interests were highly suspect; the women perceived these men as demonstrating what Frank Chin and Jeffrey Paul Chan (1972) once regarded as classic examples of "racist love."[18]

Questions and doubts were also raised about the motivations on the part of Korean American and Asian American women being with White men. Questions of self-hate, the need to be "accepted by 'American' society," and the internalization of Asian inferiority, on one hand, and White superiority, on the other, were all raised as possible motivating factors in the development of certain interracial relationships.

In Joan Walsh's (1990) article, Mike Arnold, a 42-year-old White man, recognized Asian American women's sense of internalized inferiority and capitalized on it:

I get some breaks from Asian women. Their standards are lower. It's a Darwinistic world, dating-wise, and I have an inferiority complex with white women. Most of them have a big chip on their shoulders, and I don't care how liberated they say they are, they're not interested in someone who doesn't make much money. I eventually realized that being white, I could make it with an Asian woman who's more physically attractive than I am, just because she's got a cultural inferiority complex.

Ultimately, from my interpretation of the perceptions of the Korean American respondents, the issue of unequal power appears to be central to the understanding of Korean Americans' attitudes toward this dominant interracial pattern of Asian American women with White men. For Korean Americans in general, and men in particular, this interracial pattern symbolizes the unequal power and the unequivocal access that White men have to communities of women—White, Asian American, or any other—in a racist and sexist society.

In a patriarchal society—both White American and Asian American society—one could say that Asian American and White men are engaged in a struggle for power and control at many levels. A glimpse of this struggle can be seen in the most unexpected, yet common places. In a men's restroom, on the University of California campus, graffiti depicts the battle for power contained in interracial relationships (Hong, 1990). Responding to a Nazi racist slur, an

Asian/Asian American male wrote: "Fuck Nazi[s], Asians are superior." A White male countered: "Is that why your women are flocking to white men in overwhelming numbers? If that is what being superior is then 'Hail to Asian Superiority.' It keeps Asian women in my bed." No other comments followed.

CONCLUSION

In this exploratory study, I have found the interplay of two factors in determining attitudes of Korean Americans toward certain types of interracial and interethnic relationships. First, socioeconomic status differences and inequalities between the races, ethnicities, and genders within American society bring to bear an inordinate influence in the relationship choices of Korean Americans. Second, the perception—whether real or stereotypical—of those who have power, access, and control is a major factor. Although we as individuals have the ability to determine for ourselves what our choice of mates and relationships will be, social and cultural factors play a significant role in conditioning and constructing our marital and relationship choice.

NOTES

1. From Gin Yong Pang, "Attitudes toward Interracial and Interethnic Relationships and Intermarriages among Korean Americans: The Intersections of Race, Gender, and Class Inequality." Reprinted from Franklin Ng, et al., eds. (1994). *New Visions in Asian American Studies, Diversity, Community, Power.* Pullman: Washington State University Press, pp. 111–123.

In this chapter, I define "intermarriage" as marriage that involves spouses who come from different racial and ethnic backgrounds. It includes both interethnic and interracial marriages. "Interethnic marriages or relationships" involve individuals who are of the same racial background but who are members of different ethnic groups, for example, Chinese American and Japanese American. "Interracial marriages or relationships" involve individuals who are of different racial backgrounds, for example, Asian American and White. "Korean American" refers to persons of Korean descent, and "Asian American" refers to persons of Asian descent, U.S. born or foreign born, who reside in and consider the United States as their permanent residence.

2. "Miae Kim" is a 24-year-old, 1.5-generation Korean American attending U.C. Berkeley. All the names of the interviewees are fictitious.

3. It is my choice to capitalize the "w" in White and "b" in Black. White refers to people of European descent and Black refers to people of African descent. I have left the small "w" in white or "b" in Black when others have used it in their writing.

4. For more information on the phenomenological explanation of "social construction" see Peter L. Berger and Thomas Luckman, *The Social Construction of Reality: A Treatise in the Sociology of Knowledge* (1967); and Kenneth J. Gergen and Keith E. Davis, eds., *The Social Construction of the Person* (1985).

5. Larry Shinagawa is Assistant Professor and Coordinator of the Asian American Studies Program at Sonoma State University in California. I have worked closely with him on many occasions on the topic of intermarriage and interracial/interethnic relationships. I wish to thank him for his insights into the theoretical and sociological understanding of intermarriage.

6. Additional information about the Korean Americans in the sample: eighteen of them reside in California; two are from East Coast states. The majority have lived in or grown up in predominantly White suburbs. As for their families' socio-

economic status, nine come from small business backgrounds; seven from families where the parents are professionals, for example, doctors or engineers; and four others come from "working class" family backgrounds, for example, factory or garment workers, or assemblers.

7.   In the fall of 1989, Larry Shinagawa and I conducted a survey research study of 183 Asian Americans in an introductory Asian American history class at the University of California at Berkeley. Of this number, thirty-one individuals in the sample were Korean Americans: fifteen men and sixteen women. When asked about their attitudes toward interracial marriage, 13% strongly approved; 19% somewhat approved; 13% somewhat disapproved; 16% strongly disapproved; and 39% said they did not care. As for interethnic marriage, 16% strongly approved; 26% somewhat approved; 13% somewhat disapproved; 9% strongly disapproved; and 45% did not care.

8.   According to Paul R. Spickard in his book *Mixed Blood* (1989), Japanese Americans, Jewish Americans, and Black Americans also exhibited preferential hierarchy in regard to potential mates.

9.   According to a study by Larry Shinagawa and Gin Yong Pang (1990) of California, there is a pattern of Korean Americans, Chinese Americans, and Japanese Americans to intermarry with one another when they marry interethnically.

1 0.   Interview with a 24-year-old, 1.5-generation Korean American women.

1 1.   Interview with a Korean American women.

1 2.   In 1980, at a national level, 74.6% of all marriages of Asian Americans were *intra*marriages while 25.4% were *inter*marriages (Lee & Yamanaka, 1990). For the state of California, 64.6% of all marriages among Asian Americans were intramarriages while 35.4% were intermarriages (Shinagawa & Pang, 1988).

1 3.   According to Shinagawa and Pang, in the state of California in 1980, 25% of all married Asian American women and 14.4% of all married Asian American men were intermarried. Of the intermarried Asian Americans, 73% of the women were married to White men, while 54% of the men were married to White women (Shinagawa & Pang, 1988). In his 1975, 1977, 1979, and 1984 studies of marriage licenses, Kitano (1988) found that for all the years and for every one of the Asian American ethnic groups observed—Chinese American, Japanese American, Korean American, and Vietnamese American—women intermarried at a higher rate than men.

1 4.   Interview with a 22-year-old, 1.5-generation Korean American man.

1 5.   Interview with a 20-year-old, second-generation Korean American man.

1 6.   Interview with a 24-year-old, 1.5-generation Korean American woman.

1 7.   Interview with a 21-year-old, 1.5-generation Korean American woman.

1 8.   "Racist love" refers to an image created by White America of racial minority groups that is non-threatening and acceptable to Whites. These images reflect and maintain White supremacy and perpetuates the White racist social order. Such an image is often internalized by the racial minorities themselves. In the context of interracial relationships, some White men are attracted to the sexual/racial imagery of Asian/Asian American women, which is non-threatening and acceptable to their White racist and sexist perspective (Chin & Chan, 1972).

REFERENCES

Berger, Peter L., & Thomas Luckman. (1967). *The Social Construction of Reality: A Treatise in the Sociology of Knowledge.* New York: Doubleday.

Brewer, Lilia Brooks. (1982). *Interracial Marriages: American Men Who Marry Korean Women.* Ph.D. dissertation, Syracuse University.

Chin, Frank, & Jeffrey Paul Chan. (1972). "Racist Love." In Richard Kostelantz, ed., *Seeing Through Shuck.* New York: Ballantine Books, pp. 65-79.

Gergen, Kenneth J., & Keith E. Davis, eds. (1985). *The Social Construction of a Person.* New York: Springer Verlag.

Hong, Victor. (1990). A student paper at the University of California at Berkeley, December.

Kim, Bok Lim. (1982). *Women in Shadows.* La Jolla, CA: National Committee Concerned with Asian Wives of U.S. Servicemen.

Kim, Sil Dong. (1979). *Interracially Married Korean Women Immigrants: A Study in Marginality.* Ph.D. dissertation, University of Washington.

Kitano, Harry, & Roger Daniels. (1988). *Asian Americans: Emerging Minorities.* Englewood Cliffs, NJ: Prentice Hall, p. 177.

Korea Report. (1989). Washington, DC: Korean Information and Resource Center, 3(1), July, p. 15.

Lee, Sharon, & Keiko Yamanaka. (1990). "Patterns of Asian American Intermarriage and Marital Assimilation." *Journal of Comparative Family Studies,* 21(2), Summer, p. 291.

Rho, Jung Ja. (1989). *Multiple Factors Contributing to Marital Satisfaction in Korean-American Marriages and Correlations with Three Dimensions of Family Life Satisfaction—Marital, Parental, and Self-Satisfaction.* Ph.D. dissertation, Kansas State University.

Shinagawa, Larry, & Gin Yong Pang. (1990). "Marriage Patterns of Asian Americans in California, 1980." In Sucheng Chan, ed., *Income and Status Differences Between White and Minority Americans: A Persistent Inequality.* Lewiston, Maine: Edwin Mellon Press, pp. 225-282.

____. (1988). "Intraethnic, Interethnic, and Interracial Marriages Among Asian Americans in California, 1980." *Berkeley Journal of Sociology,* Spring, p. 100.

Spickard, Paul R. (1989). *Mixed Blood: Intermarriage and Ethnic Identity in Twentieth-Century America.* Madison: University of Wisconsin Press.

Walsh, Joan. (1990). "Asian Women, Caucasian Men: The New Demographics of Love." *Image Magazine, San Francisco Examiner/Chronicle,* December 2.

12

Ethnic Identities Reflected in Value Orientation of Two Generations of Korean American Women

Ailee Moon and Young I. Song

INTRODUCTION

A person's belief and value system prescribes normative behaviors and ways of thinking and also provides a framework to deal with internal and external issues. Personal beliefs and values are not static but change over time. In the process of resettlement in another country, immigrants are often faced with adjustment difficulties due to unfamiliarity with different social norms and systems, cultural and language barriers, and racial discrimination. The cultural aspect of adjustment to the host country may involve changing certain beliefs and attitudes, and these changes may be manifested in behaviors such as language use, lifestyles, and gender roles.

Ethnic identity is a person's sense of self as a member of an ethnic group; its correlation is the corresponding value system of that group. As Rotheram-Borus (1993) puts it, ethnic identity can indicate the kind of role model one is likely to follow and the types of values one will endorse. The process of developing and maintaining values is strongly influenced by ethnic and cultural factors, especially in immigrant communities. For the Korean American woman, one of the strongest cultural influences is Confucianism, the ultimate guide to social roles and relations in Asian society. Although not as literally adhered to as in the past, the Confucian doctrine is abound in the Korean family, especially in the aspects of filial piety and obedience, the importance of the family as the main unit of socialization, hierarchical relations, and patriarchal domination.

In the adjustment process of immigration, the levels of exposure and adaptation to the norms of the new culture tend to vary considerably among family members, causing ambivalence and tension within immigrant families. Tensions in Korean immigrant families seem to be most apparent between the parents who came to America as adults and their children who were either born in the United States or came at a very young age. The parents usually adhere strongly to the traditional norms of Confucian patriarchy and interdependency, such as respect for elders and clearly divided gender roles, which often conflict with their children's value orientation that has been strongly influenced by American culture, such as individualism, independence, and movement toward gender equality.

VALUE ORIENTATION OF TWO GENERATIONS

For the Korean American woman, the difference of one generation can represent a marked difference in value orientation. The different backgrounds of parents and their children give room for substantial conflict in values and resultant behavior. The older generation, raised in Korea to follow certain Confucian norms, were influenced by society as a whole. The younger generation, pulled by the two different value systems—typically Confucianism at home and western individualism outside—must choose one or the other, or attempt to meld the two together, depending on which force is greater.

In this regard, most literature on Korean immigrant families stress that the conflict of a cultural gap between the younger Americanized generation and the older generation has become a major threat to the stability of Korean immigrant family life (Hurh & Kim, 1984; Kim & Lee, 1990). Faced with the differences between the two cultures, children begin to question and challenge the traditional beliefs and values of their parents, including the absolute authority of the father, rigidly defined gender roles, and the lack of their parent's respect for the American way of life. In her model of biculturalism, De Anda (1984) indicated that it is a "dual socialization process" in which immigrants adopt and maintain their ethnic culture during their exposure and adjustment to the dominant culture.

Considering that the intergenerational differences in ethnic cultural adjustment patterns and value orientations between Korean immigrant parents and their children may lead to breakdowns of intimate family relations, an empirical assessment of the extent to which value orientations between the two groups provides useful information for better understanding the cultural and generation gaps in Korean immigrant families.

TRADITIONAL VALUE ORIENTATION IN KOREAN AMERICAN FAMILIES

The basis of Confucianism is philosophically different from the tenets of Western ideals, which emphasizes individualism. Confucianism mandates that the behavior of the individual is the reflection on the entire family (Moon & Hoang, 1997). An individual's behavior is not a reflection on her personality but the values of the family. Family or group orientation is not only an Asian value—it is prevalent in other cultures—but individualism seems solely Western. Phinney and Rohner (1987) found that dependence is encouraged in Chinese and Korean families while the American child is encouraged to be autonomous in decision-making at an early age. European children in New Zealand were found to be independent and exclusive while the Polynesian children were group-oriented. A major feature of Hawaiian families was interdependence and cooperation, and Native American and Mexican American children showed more cooperation than Caucasian American children.

Another Confucian value that limits independence is the strict mandate that one should be obedient to his or her parents. This is part of the hierarchical nature of the Confucian family. Children are taught at a very young age to respect those that are elders—uncles, aunts, older siblings—and especially their parents. Respect entails obedience and filial piety through certain behaviors like bowing, little eye contact, and the self-sacrifice of saving the best for others. Children must listen to authority figures; questioning the authority's judgment and talking back are not allowed. The effects of unquestioning obedience—limited communication and little participation in decision-making—hinder the development of individualism in a person. Differences between immigrant parents and their children in the rate and manner of adjusting to a new culture can deteriorate parent-child relationships (Table 12.1).

Table 12.1
Intergenerational Differences in Ethnic/Cultural Adjustment Patterns

Children	Parents
See more freedom of choice and become independent more quickly in America than their parents did in Korea	Find that their children become more uncontrollable. (The frustration is doubled especially for those whose immigration motive was their "children's education.")
Recognize that their parents' attitudes toward them are quite authoritarian compared to parents of their local friends	Maintain traditional hierarchical roles in the family in which obedience to the parents is paramount
Adjust to the new culture much faster than their parents, rapidly arriving at the level of social interaction of the American value system	Are still in the period of adjustment or at the level of long-term cultural assimilation

Source: Song (1996).

The child who has been brought up in a Confucian manner has a heavy weight to bear. The family uses pride and shame of the entire group to regulate an individual's behavior (Moon & Hoang, 1997). This method of psychological reward and punishment is prevalent in Asian families. Children are expected to strive for academic excellence in order to please their parents. They must maintain "face" for the whole family, not just for themselves.

As children grow older, the expectations for young men and young women become even more distinct in a Confucian family. Recognition of the male-dominated nature of Korean culture and the consequences of sexism for the lives of Korean American women and men are not new. Many minority women have learned that the main developmental objective of their lives is to establish personal and ethnic identity in order to discover their interests and direction. While Korean culture has clear expectations for men, women typically receive ambivalent messages in the process of forming their identities. Women are encouraged to listen to their interests and to develop skills for an occupation, but, on the other hand, cultural expectations proclaim, with varying degrees of subtlety, that a Korean woman must remain flexible and adaptable because her direction in life will depend largely upon the man with whom she will become identified. Women with aspirations for exploration and adventure may find conflict and confusion; as mentioned earlier, many minority women find a narrower description of how women are defined than they received during childhood and adolescence.

Korean culture explicitly encourages the man to learn to know himself and to acquire direction to pursue his values and life goals. After he experiences the struggles of identity formation, he is expected to interact with women and eventually marry to establish a family. Much has changed in the Korean American community's prescription of a woman's place and the social recognition of her abilities, but Korean culture still explicitly encourages women to follow the fundamental task of finding identity through a man. Certainly, many Korean American women resist and do not accept such a method in which to find their identities. These women strive for careers and self-definitions of identity. The Korean American culture, however, dictates that the identity of a woman is incomplete without a man and family and continues to presume that this pursuit is the younger-generation Korean girl's most important agenda in the process of developing identity.

Almost everywhere, including in the Korean American community, women have functioned primarily in the domestic sphere, assisting men in their operation in the public sphere, thereby giving men richer resources, power, and rewards. It is important at this point to examine the ways Korean American women define their ethnic identities, especially those reflected in the value orientation; and where and how Korean women's identities are sharply distinguished by generation differences.

The varying levels of exposure to mainstream American life can account for the generational differences of values. School, media, church, and the workplace are the main sources of exposure to American life and non-Confucian values. The younger generation, who either attends school or works in a company, is immersed in a very different culture from that of the older generation. Obedience to elders cannot exist in a system, such as the corporate workplace, in which the elders are one's competition. The older generation tends to enshroud itself in the Korean ways—Korean newspapers, church, and workplace—due to serious barriers in the new country, especially language handicaps. The younger generation passed its adolescence, a crucial time of identity development, in the United States, while the older generation spent that time in Korea.

This does not mean that the younger generation of Korean Americans is throwing out its ethnicity entirely. The course of achieving identity is the exposure to many different forces throughout life, but it is these college years when they make the greatest steps toward unfolding their identity (Watermann, 1982). In a recent survey by Kim, Song, and Moon (1997) of Korean American college students at the University of California, Los Angeles, and University of Illinois at Urbana-Champaign, the majority of the students identify themselves as Korean of Korean Americans, despite the different social settings the students grew up in (the Los Angeles area has more Asian and other minority populations). However, their "intensity of belongingness" to the Korean culture may be on a different level from the older generation; half of the students also affiliated themselves as Asian American, and one-third as just Americans.

THEORETICAL FRAMEWORK

Two theories are introduced here in order to explain women's identities in a given culture. For example, why is a Korean woman more likely to adopt certain value orientations? Because of culture? But the main question remains: How do we develop ethnic identities in a multicultural society such as the United States? Two different types of theories can be used to help explain how an individual comes to be the kind of person she is and, especially, how she comes to adopt particular values on the basis of her ethnic identity. The cognitive development theory claims that gender involves the interaction between biology and environment, but sees the development of gender as a process of trying to maintain identity and a sense of competence in understanding the self and the world around oneself. The other theory, social learning, emphasizes individual learning as a process of interaction with the environment, especially learning from cultural experiences since values are learned and acquired.

Developmentalists' explain how people learn to think in order to illustrate how a person develops gender and ethnic identification, and, for example, learn to be a Korean woman. As Lawrence Kohlberg (1966) indicated, basic values are not patterned directly by either biological instincts or arbitrary cultural norms, but by the individual's cognitive organization of his/her social world along gender role dimensions. Developing gender and identity is a process of making sense of the world, and it is the cognitive organization of self-identification that accounts for the existence of universals in gender role values (Kohlberg, 1966).

Learning about self is one thing; learning to follow cultural norms is another. How do Korean American women learn to follow cultural norms? Learning consists of both a cognitive dimension and an affective dimension. People do not just learn about their identities; they also learn to value themselves and people like themselves. As one learns about gender and culture, one begins to place a certain value on gender and culture as well as on the meanings that surround one.

The other approach to understanding how self and ethnic identification occurs is based on the process of social learning. Learning theory accounts for ethnic identity as a learned social behavior, which may be acquired through conditioning or observational learning and is maintained by reinforcement of various types (Bandura, 1973; Buss, 1971). People learn to become women and men in the manner their culture defines them because others reward them or provide reinforcement for behaving in value-appropriate ways, or punish them for behaving otherwise. The consequences of socialization in a given culture is the development of an individual's identity and values, which fit into the culture since that person has been shaped and modified to behave so. The social learning interpretation to socialization leads researchers to investigate how parents, families, and other institutions, such as schools, churches, and the mass media, encourage and discourage different types of values among Korean American women.

The process of identification does not stop at the end of childhood. Further educational, occupational, and domestic experiences continue the task of identity formation. The meeting of cultural expectations is even more stringent for the adult Korean woman than the Korean girl. As one steps out of childhood, rewards and punishments may become even more consequential. Younger-generation Korean women who pursue nontraditional activities often find that the only way they can succeed without tremendous opposition or disapproval is to make sure that they also play more culturally expected and defined roles.

THE STUDY

One hundred fifteen Korean immigrant mothers and their 89 adolescent daughters (ages 13-18), residing in Los Angeles County, California, responded to 15 value orientation statements as shown in Table 12.2. Seven statements are concerned with the importance of maintaining Korean ethnic/cultural heritage and identity, including Korean language, history, customs, and attitudes toward interracial dating and marriage, and 8 deal with gender differences and roles in living arrangement, education, the mother's role, premarital sex, and types of jobs.

The responses clearly indicate that both Korean immigrant mothers and their adolescent daughters highly value the importance of learning Korean language, history, and customs (items 2, 3, and 4), although teenage daughters tend to emphasize the importance of being able to speak Korean less than their mothers do (82% versus 95%). The majority of the mothers and daughters disagree that Koreans living in the United States should adopt the American way of life, even if it means giving up the Korean way of life (item 1). It is interesting to find that a considerably higher percentage of daughters (81%), compared to their mothers (62%), expressed the view that it is not necessary to give up the Korean way of life in order to adopt the American way of life. This finding seems to suggest a strong sense of biculturalism and its propriety and feasibility in a multicultural American society among the second generation of Korean immigrant families. The finding is also supported by 90% of the daughters and 89% of the parents who disagree with the necessity of giving up one's Korean heritage in order to be successful in the United States (item 5).

The two groups, however, show significant differences in their beliefs regarding interracial/interethnic dating and marriage, considering the assumption that those with a strong sense of attachment to Korean cultural identity and heritage are less likely to endorse interracial/interethnic dating and marriage. Approximately 44% and 56% of mothers indicated that Korean Americans should only date Koreans or Korean Americans (item 6) and that Koreans should marry only Koreans or Korean Americans (item 7), respectively. The disparity between these percentages (12%) suggest that 12% of the mothers would accept interracial/interethnic dating but would not endorse their children's marriage to non-Koreans. In contrast, only 11% and 16% of their daughters, significantly lower than those of their mothers, believed in dating and marrying only Koreans or Korean Americans, respectively. Overall, the findings identify the different value orientation concerning interracial/interethnic dating and marriage, not lack of respect for the Korean history, customs, and language, as a source of conflict between immigrant mothers and their teenage daughters.

In regard to their value orientations toward gender differences and role, mothers in general tend to believe more in Korean traditional gender differences and roles than their daughters. For example, while nearly two-thirds (63%) of

Table 12.2
Responses to 15 Value Orientation Statements by Korean Immigrant Mothers and Their Adolescent Daughters

Value Statement	Percentage	
	Mother	Daughter
Korean Ethnic/Cultural Identity & Heritage		
1. Koreans living in the United States should adopt the American way of life, even if it means giving up the Korean way of life.		
Agree	27.9	12.2
Disagree	61.8	81.1
Don't know/neutral	10.3	5.6
2. It is important for Korean American parents in the United States to teach their children Korean history.		
Agree	98.2	96.7
Disagree	0.9	2.2
Don't know/neutral	0.9	0.0
3. Koreans should be able to speak Korean no matter where they were born or raised.		
Agree	94.8	82.2
Disagree	4.3	13.3
Don't know/neutral	0.9	3.4
4. It is important for second-generation Korean Americans to learn about Korean history and customs.		
Agree	97.4	95.6
Disagree	2.6	3.3
Don't know/neutral	0.0	0.0
5. It is necessary to give up one's Korean heritage in order to be successful in the United States.		
Agree	5.2	4.4
Disagree	88.8	90.0
Don't know/neutral	4.3	4.4
6. A Korean American should date only another Korean.		
Agree	43.5	11.1
Disagree	53.0	84.4
Don't know/neutral	3.5	3.4
7. Koreans should only marry other Koreans.		
Agree	55.6	15.6
Disagree	40.9	76.7
Don't know/neutral	3.5	6.7

(continued)

Table 12.2 (continued)

Value Statement	Percentage	
	Mother	**Daughter**
8. Daughters should live with their parents until they get married		
Agree	62.6	25.5
Disagree	36.6	72.2
Don't know/neutral	0.9	1.1
9. Sons should live with their parents until they get married.		
Agree	46.9	22.2
Disagree	50.4	72.2
Don't know/neutral	2.6	4.4
10. To be a good mother, taking care of family is more important than pursuing a career.		
Agree	93.0	68.9
Disagree	4.3	26.6
Don't know/neutral	2.6	3.3
11. Education is more important for men than for women.		
Agree	13.1	4.4
Disagree	86.0	93.3
Don't know/neutral	0.9	1.1
12. It is important for a woman to remain a virgin until marriage.		
Agree	81.8	77.7
Disagree	17.4	15.6
Don't know/neutral	0.9	5.6
13. It is important for a man to remain a virgin until marriage.		
Agree	60.0	67.7
Disagree	35.6	22.3
Don't know/neutral	4.3	8.9
14. The husband should have more authority than the wife within family life.		
Agree	44.4	28.9
Disagree	54.8	68.9
Don't know/neutral	0.9	1.1
15. There are different types of jobs appropriate for men and for women.		
Agree	48.7	37.7
Disagree	51.3	61.2
Don't know/neutral	0.0	0.0

Note: Percentages may not add to 100 due to rounding.

mothers indicated that daughters should live with their parents until they marry, and less than half (47%) of them indicated the same belief for sons (Items 8 and 9). In other words, about 16% of mothers approved their sons' but not daughters' living outside the home before marriage. In contrast, a significantly smaller percentage of daughters believed that unmarried children must live with parents until marriage (26% for daughters and 22% for sons), with 10% of them indicating different attitudes toward such living arrangement for daughters and sons. Clearly, the wide disparity in the two groups' beliefs in living arrangement for unmarried children can be considered another source of intergenerational conflict in Korean immigrant families.

Similarly, while 82% of mothers believed in the importance of virginity for unmarried woman, a substantially lower percentage, or 60% of them, held the same belief for unmarried men (items 12 and 13). The teen daughters held similarly conservative or traditional views on the same statements, but only 10% of them indicated that the importance of virginity should apply differently for women (78%) and men (68%).

Furthermore, the overwhelming majority of both mothers (93%) and their teen daughters (69%) supported the Korean traditional role of married women, taking care of her family being more important than pursuing her career outside the home (item 10). Similarly, while less than half of both mothers and daughters agreed that the husband should have more authority than the wife within family life (44% and 29%), the finding also suggest that a considerably higher percentage of mothers held the traditional gender role and subordinate status of women in the family than their teen daughters. It is interesting to note that while only 13% of mothers and 4% of daughters agreed that education is more important for men than for women (item 11), nearly half of the mothers (49%) and 38% of the daughters expressed the view that there are different types of jobs appropriate for men and women (item 15). This finding, in part, may reflect the respondents' perception of the reality of uneven distributions of different occupations and types of jobs men and women hold in American society today.

CONCLUSION

This chapter has focused on questions of comparison, commonality, and difference across two different generations of Korean American women. Some of the questions about gender and culture were addressed by looking at specific aspects of difference and diversity among two generations of Korean American women. Overall, the findings suggest that both Korean immigrant mothers and their teenage daughters tend to hold conservative and/or traditional values reflected in their responses, while their mothers tend to be more conservative and/or traditional than their daughters. They also suggest that living arrangements and interracial/interethnic dating and marriage are three areas of major differences in value orientation between mothers and daughters, which may lead to conflicting parent-child relationships, especially when the child grows older.

Contradictions between well-earned behavior of traditional values are often found. The differences we found among the younger generation include more tolerance to interracial dating and marriage. What motivates the younger generation to be more open-minded? Each young Korean American woman probably has her own reasons. But it appears to be related to how they learn and develop gender and ethnic identification in the process of becoming Korean American women.

A recent trend of young Korean women in regarding to living at home before marriage is seen as disadvantageous, especially in the aspect of their freedom, and they may anticipate conflict in value orientation with their mothers. Instead of cultural approval, young Korean American women find that marrying Korean men and being obedient children living at home until adulthood will not provide any fulfillment toward defining their positive identities. Thus, their value orientation is not patterned directly by Korean cultural norms, but by their own cognitive organization.

Findings from the study suggest that the two generations of Korean women often do not learn or choose to be different but are forced to be different. Korean American women are forced out of certain roles and activities because their experiences as minority women have been varied through sexual and racial discrimination as well as through the influence of biculturalism.

REFERENCES

Bandura, A. (1973). *Aggression: A Social Learning Analysis.* Englewood Cliffs, NJ: Prentice-Hall.

Buss, A. H. (1971). "Aggression Pays." In J. L. Singer, ed., *The Control of Aggression and Violence.* New York: Academic Press.

De Anda, D. (1984). "Bicultural Socialization: Factors Affecting the Minority Experience." *Social Work*, March-April, 104-107.

Hurh, W. M., & K. C. Kim. (1984). *Korean Immigrants in America: A Structural Analysis of Ethnic Confinement and Adhesive Adaptation.* Cranberry, NJ: Association of University Presses.

Kim, H. C., & E. H. Lee, eds. (1990). *Koreans in America: Dreams and Realities.* Seoul: Institute of Korean Studies.

Kim, K. C., Y. I. Song, & A. Moon. (1997). "Ethnic Identity of Korean American College Students." Presented at Keimyung University International Conference of Korean Studies.

Kholberg, Lawrence. (1966). "A Cognitive-Development Analysis of Children's Sex Role Concepts and Attitudes." In E. Macaby, ed., *The Development of Sex Differences.* Stanford, CA: Stanford University Press.

Moon, A., & Hoang, T. (1997). "Korean American Families: Value Orientation and Adolescents' Attitudes toward Parents." In Y. Song & A. Moon, eds., *Korean Women Living in Two Cultures.* Los Angeles: Academia Koreana.

Phinney, J., & R. Rohner. (1987). *Children's Ethnic Socialization Pluralism and Development.* Beverly Hills, CA: Sage.

Rotheram-Borus, Mary Jane. (1993). "Biculturalism among Adolescents." In M. Bernal & G. Knight, eds., *Ethnic Identity.* Albany: State University of New York Press.

Song, Y. I. (1996). *Battered Women in Korean Immigrant Families: The Silent Scream.* New York: Garland.

Watermann, Alan S. (1982). "Identity Development from Adolescence to Adulthood: An Extension of Theory and a Review of Research." *Development Psychology*, 18(3): 341-358.

part five

MARRIAGE AND FAMILY

Part Five consists of four chapters devoted to analyses of marital and family issues facing Korean American families in a changing socioeconomic, multicultural environment. Beginning with a discussion of separation and divorce, it investigates marital conficts, divorce, domestic violence against women, parenting styles, and the problems faced by the elderly in Korean American families.

Traditional incentives that once facilitated men and women to stay married have been eroded in many Korean immigrant families. Siyon Rhee investigates this in "Separation and Divorce among Korean Immigrant Families" to broaden the knowledge of the Korean American divorce situation. She challenges the general assumption that Asian American families are stable and problem-free, and highlights that Korean immigrant families are faced with a serious, complex problem.

In "The Domestic Violence against Women in Korean Immigrant Families: Cultural, Psychological, and Socioeconomic Perspectives," Young I. Song and Ailee Moon examine whether and how wife battering in Korean immigrant families is related to Korean traditional beliefs and adjustment difficulties upon immigration to the United States, based on interviews with 150 Korean immigrant women. They investigate major factors contributing to the occurrence of wife battering in Korean immigrant families, focusing on attitudes toward traditional values, sex role rigidity, and socioeconomic stressors; and they discuss implications for the intervention and prevention of wife battering in Korean American families.

In "Korean American Mothers' Parenting Styles and Adolescent Behavior," Eunai Kim Shrake explores the patterns of Korean American parenting in relation to adolescent psychological and behavioral problems via a survey of 23 adolescents and interviews of 5 mothers. The data analysis revealed "high parental pressure with poor supervision" and "authoritarian control with low communication" as the most problematic patterns in Korean American parenting. The study's findings warrant model building studies for the effects of Korean American parenting style on adolescent behavior.

There has been a steady growth in the overall population of persons 65 years of age and older in American society, and Koreans in the United States are no exception. Although problems faced by the elderly are all serious, they are more so for the Korean American elderly because of cultural and language barriers they experience. Young I. Song's study in "Life Satisfaction of the Korean American Elderly" examines the impact of social-psychological factors, including marital status, social activity, health, religion, and reminiscence, on the life satisfaction of 104 Korean persons aged 55 and older in the San Francisco Bay Area.

13

Separation and Divorce among Korean Immigrant Families

Siyon Rhee

OVERVIEW

Terminating an unhappy marriage through obtaining a divorce is an extremely traumatic life experience for the divorcing couple and their family (Lopez et al., 1988; Song, 1991; Tien, 1985). The dramatic rise in divorce during the past two decades in the United States has attracted great interest in the study of marital instability, marital dissolution, causative factors leading to divorce, and the problems of post-divorce adjustment. Despite the increased attention and a large number of studies, there are few divorce studies specifically focused on ethnic Korean immigrants. Little information is available regarding the major factors causing separation and divorce, and on the main psychological effects of marriage dissolution on immigrant Korean individuals and their families.

The Statistical Abstract of the United States (Bureau of the Census, 1993) and the National Center for Health Statistics (1989) report that divorce rates in the United States have doubled from 2.5 per thousand population in 1965 to a phenomenal high of 5.0 per thousand in 1985, while the marriage rate was 10.1 per thousand population in 1985. The divorce rate thus has increased to a level where one out of every two marriages today ends in divorce.

Although the general public in the United States has experienced a rapid increase in divorce, some racial-ethnic groups, for instance, Chinese American families, have exhibited relatively low divorce rates and other indicators of marital solidarity (Iu, 1982). The low rates of marital dissolution among some Asian American groups have accelerated an unrealistic assumption that Asian American families in general are relatively stable and cohesive.

Surprisingly, however, the divorce rate for the Korean American group is one of the highest among various racial-ethnic groups in the United States. Tien (1985) showed that the divorce rate for Koreans in America was 4.8 per thousand population. On the other hand, according to the Korean Women's Development Institute (1986), the divorce rate in Korea was 0.6 per thousand population in 1984.

BACKGROUND

In traditional Korean society, the most important motivation for marriage was to continue the patrilineal family line and to obtain a daughter-in-law to serve the parents. The main purpose of marriage was to benefit the family, specifically that of the husband. At the same time, marriage dissolution was primarily related to ancestors, parents, or members of the family, while the personal relationship between husband and wife was of secondary importance (Iu, 1982). Until the beginning of the twentieth century, divorce had been predominantly initiated by the husband's family, giving the right of divorce only to men. The husband had several socially sanctioned reasons for expelling his wife in traditional Korea. Those, the so-called Seven Deadly Sins, included (1) failure to perform filial duties to parents-in-law, (2) failure to produce a son, (3) infidelity, (4) jealousy, (5) chronic disease, (6) garrulity, and (7) a habit of theft (Bae, 1973). Among those, a rebellious attitude of a woman toward parents-in-law or childlessness was generally considered to be the most serious offense.

Traditional family relationships and a long history of discrimination against female members of the family in Korea remained relatively unchanged until the period of World War II. For the past few decades, there has been a rapid change in the socio-economic structure in Korea. The status of Korean women has improved in many aspects, including the rights of formal education and career opportunities. However, the underlying family relationship in contemporary Korean society is still characterized by a tradition of male dominance in which the husband leads and the wife follows.

Korean women have considered divorce as something totally unacceptable, disgraceful, and shameful to the entire family. There are several factors accounting for the low rate of divorce in Korea. Those are (1) traditionally, men have had a socially accepted channel to compensate for their marital dissatisfaction by resorting to extramarital affairs or concubinage rather than terminating their marriages; (2) many women stay at home after marriage, and they never acquire or keep their acquired job skills that would enable them to be economically self-sufficient; (3) courts consistently give the father custody rights over the children. The consequence of divorce is too painful for the mother to bear; thus, she may choose to remain married in the presence of marital dissatisfaction; (4) due to various social restrictions and cultural prejudices, divorced women have much less opportunity to meet suitable partners after divorce than do men; and (5) the stigma attached to divorce is still very strong. Consequently, divorce is considered as the least preferable option in resolving marital conflicts (Shin, 1984).

Although the divorce rate in Korea is still low when compared to other industrialized countries, it has been steadily rising over the last decades (Lee, 1988). A growing economic independence of women, the growth of individualism and self-actualization, and the decline of traditional values of collectivity seem to have some effect on the general trend of rising divorce rates in Korea.

The Korean population in the United States is one of the fastest-growing ethnic minorities. The 1990 Census data and a recent population projection study show that there are approximately one million Koreans in the United States, which represents an increase of over 130% since 1980 (Yu, 1993).

A number of factors make the Koreans unique among the various Asian American groups. First, even though a small portion of the population reflects as much as five generations, the present Korean communities primarily consist of new immigrants who have lived in this country less than 15 years on the average (Korean Profile Study Committee, 1985). Second, Koreans tend to immigrate to this country as family units rather than as individuals, so that husband, wife, and children tend to enter the United States together (Min, 1984). Third, Koreans are one of the highly educated immigrant groups in the United States. Nearly 50% of Korean immigrants had received some college education in Korea before coming to the United States. College graduation rates for Korean Americans are twice as high as the U.S. average, according to U.S. Census statistics (Yu, 1993). Finally, labor force participation among Korean women is exceptionally high. A 1994 poll of 143 Korean American married women in Los Angeles conducted by the Korean American Women's Association reveals that 62.2% of the respondents are currently employed (Korea Times, July 21, 1994).

Presently, one of the problems facing the Korean community is that Korean Americans who are of marriageable age have limited opportunities to find prospective marital partners within the community. Many Korean immigrant young men prefer to marry more traditional Korean females, and they often go back to Korea to find their brides. They can find eligible candidates relatively easily within a short period of time through arrangements by their relatives or friends living in Korea. On the other hand, when Korean American females who were primarily socialized in the United States get married to men who were raised and educated in Korea, they are more likely to have serious marital problems.

MAJOR THEORETICAL ORIENTATIONS

Many researchers have attempted to explain the factors associated with divorce and the process through which couples ultimately decide to terminate their marriages. Among various theories of marital dissolution, social exchange theory and the modernization perspective seem to be useful in explaining the Korean American divorce situation.

Social exchange theory consists of two basic concepts—costs and rewards. According to Thibaut and Kelly (1959) and Homans (1961), people are likely to maximize rewards and minimize costs in an effort to achieve the most profitable outcome in their transactions. Social exchange theory suggests that the decision to terminate an intimate relationship with another is often motivated by the assumption that the alternative to an unhappy marriage is either more rewarding or less costly than to remain with the relationship. More specifically, if one perceives that terminating a marriage is going to offer higher degrees of satisfaction than the cost involved in moving out of the married relationship, one might seek divorce. On the other hand, if one anticipates higher costs in terminating the relationship, that is, facing financial difficulties, criticism of family and friends, and shame and dishonor brought to the individuals involved, one might remain married despite the existence of marital dissatisfaction.

Levinger (1979) and Spanier and Lewis (1981) further elaborated the concept of cost and reward in their micro-level social psychological analysis of marital dissolution. Levinger investigated the concept of barriers (e.g., social or religious pressure against divorce, or the presence of children), which is similar to the concept of cost in social exchange theory. He also examined the concept of attraction in marriage, which constitutes material rewards, symbolic rewards (e.g., status), and the affectional rewards (e.g., companionship, or sexual satisfaction). When there are few barriers around the marriage, and few attractions within it, the marriage may end in divorce.

Another significant theoretical orientation that has received much attention in recent years is the economic theory of marriage formulated by Becker (1973, 1974, & 1976). Becker proposes that couples tend to remain married when the utility of staying married exceeds the utility expected from divorce. If there is an increase in the expected value of positively evaluated factors (e.g., the earning level of the husband), divorce is discouraged. However, the probability of divorce increases if there is an increase in the negatively evaluated factors (e.g., the wife's earnings increase). Although Becker's theory is primarily based on economic principles, it is clear that his theory emerged from the social exchange perspective.

The modernization approach is considered as a major macro-level theoretical framework in the study of divorce. The process of modernization generally results in a breakdown of traditional values and family relationships with a strong emphasis on individual self-actualization and an ideology of egalitarianism. Goode (1956, 1963) noticed that rapid social changes, such as urbanization, industrialization, and high levels of education, are significantly related to the high rates of divorce in recent years. Basic family structures are changing everywhere as an outcome of recent social changes and modernization. Goode (1963) pointed out three major factors that contribute to increased divorce rates. Those include changes in the family value system especially among women, reduced emphasis on marital stability by kin and friends, and diverse alternatives to unhappy marriages. For example, better education and expanded job opportunities have accelerated considerable economic independence for women. Those women are likely to demonstrate greater desire for more egalitarian family relationships, emotional independence, and self-actualization.

SOCIAL AND PSYCHOLOGICAL FACTORS CAUSING DIVORCE

A variety of studies have been conducted to determine the types of problems and factors causing divorce. Goode (1956, 1963) identified the following social and psychological factors as related to the prediction of divorce: (1) marriage at a young age (usually before age 20), (2) no engagement, (3) insufficient acquaintanceship before marriage, (4) difference in religious beliefs, (5) parental divorce, (6) clear difference in the background between marital partners, (7) different expectations of a husband and wife regarding their role obligations, and (8) disapproval of the marriage by parents, relatives, or friends. Especially those who marry at a young age are likely to experience economic hardship due to the unstable employment status and low wages. This stressful situation can account for the exceptionally high rate of divorce among young couples in the United States.

Berrelson and Steiner (1964) suggested the following factors as major reasons for divorce among Americans: (1) mutual unsuitableness or incompatibility, (2) extramarital affairs, (3) sterility, (4) sexual incompetence, (5) lack of financial support, and (6) cruelty and quarrelsomeness. More recently, Albrecht and his colleagues (1983) surveyed 500 American divorced respondents and identified the major reasons leading to the termination of a marriage. The first ten reasons identified by the respondents for marital failure by rank order include: (1) infidelity, (2) loss of love, (3) emotional problems, (4) financial problems, (5) physical abuse, (6) alcohol use, (7) sexual problems, (8) problems with in-laws, (9) neglect of children, and (10) communication problems.

The above findings indicate infidelity as one of the most important reasons in precipitating divorce for many American couples, and physical abuse or problems with in-laws as relatively less important. However, problems and causes leading to divorce may vary from one culture to another.

THE CURRENT DIVORCE SITUATION IN KOREA

As indicated previously, divorce in Korea has been rising at a steady rate over the past few decades. Divorce is caused by a number of factors such as differences in personality, extramarital affairs, physical violence, excessive drinking, and problems with in-laws. Among these, husbands' extramarital affairs are the most common reason for Korean women's divorce in Korea (Shin, 1984). The second leading cause for divorce in Korea involves intergenerational conflicts with mothers-in-law. Under the influence of Confucian morality, there has been a strong expectation that the daughter-in-law should be submissive to her parents-in-law and wait on their daily needs. Although the Korean society has experienced rapid social structural changes, many Koreans still have an extended family. When the mother-in-law in the extended family structure has a high degree of domineering attitudes, conflicts seem to be inevitable.

Lee (1988) analyzed the 1985 court records of divorce by mutual agreement filed in the Seoul Family Court and found that the length of marriage prior to divorce ranged from less than 1 year to 33 years, with a mean of 8.1 years. In other words, the average divorce took place within approximately 8 years of marriage in 1985 in Seoul, Korea. The average age at the time of divorce was 37.6 years for the husband and 33.5 years for the wife. Another significant finding presented by Lee focuses on divorce initiation patterns among Korean couples. Surprisingly, 50% of the total number of divorces were suggested by both husband and wife at the same time. The percentage of husband-initiated divorces (25%) was exactly the same as that of wife-initiated divorces (25%).

Another significant finding with respect to the average age at the time of divorce can be found in the 1990 Annual Report issued by the Korean Supreme Court. According to the report, young-age divorce has steadily increased for the past few years. As high as 38.7% of the total number of divorcing men and women who obtained judicial divorces in 1989 were under age 30. These figures suggest that divorce, in general, takes place among relatively young couples in Korea. Divorce before age 30 reflects a growing awareness of self among well-educated females who tend to value their own accomplishments and aspirations instead of passively accepting the traditional expectation of sacrificing their lives for the family.

DIVORCE IN IMMIGRANT KOREAN FAMILIES

The author conducted an exploratory study with 35 divorced immigrant Korean women in Los Angeles County. The purpose of the study is to broaden our understanding of various factors leading to divorce among Korean American women, and to present baseline data on divorce initiation patterns and relevant socio-economic characteristics. The sample was obtained from community social service agencies serving Korean families in the Los Angeles area. Data were collected in 1 hour face-to-face structured interviews in 1993 and 1994.

The age range of the subjects at the time of divorce varies: those 29 and under, N = 9 (25.7%); 30–39, N = 18 (51.4%); 40–49, N = 6 (17.1%); 50–59; N = 1 (2.8%); and 60 and over, N = 1 (2.8%). The average age for the subjects at divorce was 35.8 years. The above figures show that the majority of Korean immigrant women's divorces take place among people over the age of 30. The proportion of mid-life divorce is also relatively high among immigrant Korean women. All subjects are Korean-speaking, first-generation immigrants who have resided in the United States for 8.7 years at divorce. The subjects' duration of marriage prior to divorce ranged from 1 year to 39 years, with a mean of 9.5 years. The level of educational attainment among the subjects was 14.1 years on the average. More than 60% (N = 22) of the subjects have completed at least some years of college education. At the time of interview, over 90% of the subjects were employed.

With respect to divorce initiation patterns, 62.9% (N = 22) of the total number of divorces were suggested by the wife, while 28.5% (N = 10) were initiated by the husband. On the other hand, only 8.6% (N = 3) were suggested by husband and wife at the same time. These study results indicate that the majority of divorce actions are initiated by women in the United States.

The most significant reason for divorce among the subjects was physical violence by husband (31.4%, N = 11), followed by husband's extramarital affairs (22.9%, N = 8), and husband's gambling (11.4%, N = 4). Husband's excessive drinking (8.6%, N = 3), lack of financial support from husband (8.6%, N = 3), differences in personality (8.6%, N = 3), husband's drug problems (5.6%, N = 2), and marriage fraud in relation to immigration issues (2.9%, N = 1) were identified as additional reasons for divorce. Interestingly, five subjects responded that problems with in-laws partially contributed to their divorce decisions. However, none of them considered that problem as their primary reason for divorce. These findings reveal that the problem of domestic violence is more serious than spouse unfaithfulness in causing divorce for Korean American women.

DISCUSSION

Traditional incentives that once facilitated men and women to stay married have been eroded in many Korean immigrant families. High rates of divorce among Korean immigrants can be accounted for by a number of factors that characterize the present Korean community in the United States. First, as discussed earlier, a high proportion of Korean wives who had no previous work experience and carried the traditional role of homemakers in their home country have entered the labor market immediately after their arrival. Consequently, Korean immigrant families are experiencing a rapid change in traditional role definitions in which the husband earns a living and leads the family while the wife serves her husband, children, and in-laws. Many immigrant Korean women realize that they do not have to depend on their husbands financially, and they experience a sense of independence and confidence in their ability to survive difficult times.

Second, according to the judicial system in Korea, a divorce can be effected only through mutual agreement between the husband and wife or lawsuit of one party against the other on the grounds of a legal cause for divorce (Lee, 1988). This means that in order for a divorce to be in effect, it is essential to show a mutual consent to divorce by the two parties or the legitimate causes for divorce such as an act of infidelity or spousal maltreatment. On the other hand, divorce is relatively less complicated to obtain in the United States due to the enactment of no-fault statutes in most states including the state of California (Halem, 1982). There is no need to get an agreement or permission from the spouse to finalize a divorce. Furthermore, the divorcing parties do not have to prove that their spouses caused the problems in their marriages. It takes approximately 6 months for a marital dissolution to become final in California.

Third, institutionalized discrimination against women over the issues of child custody and division of property is considered a barrier to divorce for many women in Korea. For instance, legal provisions of alimony as a form of payments to an ex-wife do not exist in Korea even when the wife has no marketable skills. Legal and physical child custody is arbitrarily awarded to the father, reflecting the tradition of the patriarchal family structure. Women are in a far disadvantageous position in the division of property as compared to men in the divorce process. In contrast, in the United States, the principle of community property and favorable treatments for women in granting child-rearing rights appear to be an attractions for many women in wife-initiated divorce. In addition, divorce is generally much less stigmatized in the United States than in Korea.

Fourth, the rate of domestic violence in Korean immigrant families is reported to be the highest among various Asian groups in Los Angeles. According to records of the Los Angeles County Attorney's office, the agency handling domestic violence cases prosecuted in Los Angeles County in each year, Korean males composed the highest percentage of Asian defendants accused of spousal abuse (Chun, 1990). Song (1992) also found in her survey of 150 Korean American women residing in Chicago that 60% of them experienced wife abuse by their husbands. According to the 1994 Semi-Annual Statistical Report of the Korean American Family Service Center in Los Angeles, problems related to domestic violence comprised the highest percentage of all office visit cases from January to July, 1994. The report also indicates that most of those who experienced physical violence considered a divorce seriously and attempted to obtain legal information about divorce. All of these findings and reports are highly consistent with those of the author. It is very likely that significant numbers of chronically abused Korean women can seek divorce as an alternative to their traumatic marital relationships.

Several studies show that variations in divorce adjustments exist among different racial-ethnic groups due to different values and cultural orientations toward divorce. Tien (1985) investigated divorce adjustments among Anglo, Chinese, and Korean Americans and concluded that there were marked differences in adjustment among the three groups studied. According to her findings, Anglo and Chinese Americans tended to consider divorce as something positive and adjusted to divorce relatively well. Many Korean subjects, however, indicated that their post-divorce relationships with their ex-spouses were worse than before the divorce, and they experienced negative feelings after divorce including anger, shame, regret and confusion. Song (1991) also found that divorce brings emotional as well as economic hardships to those women. They face complex personal, psychological, and social problems after divorce.

The author's study attempts to broaden the knowledge of the Korean American divorce situation. It challenges the general assumption that Asian American families are stable and problem-free. The present chapter highlights that Korean immigrant families are faced with a series of complex problems. However, we need to be cautious about generalizations from the findings because the sample for this study was not drawn randomly. It will be important to examine in the future the overall psychological and social effects of divorce on Korean American women and their children, and of long-term residence in America on their post-divorce adjustments.

REFERENCES

Albrecht, S. L., H. Bahr, & K. Goodman. (1983). *Divorce and Remarriage: Problems, Adaptations, and Adjustments*. Series Contribution in Women's Studies, no. 42.

Bae, K. S. (1973). *Women and the Law in Korea*. Seoul: Korean League of Women Voters.

Becker, G. (1976). *The Economic Approach to Human Behavior*. Chicago: University of Chicago Press.

_____. (1974). "A Theory of Marriage: Part II." *Journal of Political Economy*, 82 (March/April): 511-526.

_____. (1973). "A Theory of Marriage: Part I. *Journal of Political Economy*, 81 (March/April):813-846.

Berrelson, B., & G. Steiner. (1964). *Human Behavior*. New York: Harcourt Press.

Bureau of the Census. (1993). *Statistical Abstract of the United States*. 113th Edition. U.S. Department of Commerce, Economics and Statistics Administration.

Chun, E. (1990). "The Korean Battered Spouse: Where to Go for Help." *Korean Journal*, 1(3): 22-23.

Goode, W. J. (1963). *The World Revolution and Family Patterns*. New York: Free Press.

_____. (1956). *Women in Divorce*. New York: Free Press.

Halem, L. C. (1982). *Separated and Divorced Women*. Westport, CT: Greenwood Press.

Homans, G. (1961). *Social Behavior: Its Elementary Forms*. New York: Harcourt, Brace and World.

Iu, C. R. (1982). *Ethnic and Economic Correlates of Marital Satisfaction and Attitude towards Divorce of Chinese American Women*. Doctoral dissertation, School of Social Welfare, University of California, Los Angeles.

Korea Times. (1994). "A Report on Active Korean Immigrant Wives." July 21.

Korean Profile Study Committee. (1985). *Koreatown Profile Report*. United Way, Central and Western Los Angeles Region.

Korean Women's Development Institute. (1986). *Social Statistics and Indicators on Women*. Seoul: Korean Women's Development Institute.

Lee, Y. H. (1988). *The Study of Current Divorce Situation in Korea*. Doctoral dissertation, Department of Social Sciences, University of Denver.

Levinger, G. (1979). "A Social Psychological Perspective on Marital Dissolution. In G. Levinger & O. C. Moles, eds., *Divorce and Separation*. New York: Basic Books, pp. 37-60.

Lopez, F. G., V. L. Campbell, & C. E. Watkins. (1988). "The Relation of Parental Divorce to College Student Development. *Journal of Divorce*, 12(1): 83-98.

Min, P. G. (1984). "An Exploratory Study of Kin Ties among Korean Immigrant Families in Atlanta." *Journal of Comparative Family Studies*, 15(1): 59-75.

National Center for Health Statistics. (1989). *Vital and Health Statistics: Supplements to the Monthly Vital Statistics Report*. U.S. Department of Health and Human Services, Public Health Service, Center for Disease Control, Series 24(1), May.

Shin, H. S. (1984). *Korean Americans' Attitudes toward Divorce, Perceived Causes of Divorce and Adjustment to Divorce*. A thesis submitted for the degree of Master of Nursing, University of California, Los Angeles.

Song, Y. I. (1992). "Battered Korean Women in Urban United States." In S. M. Furuto, R. Biswas, D. K. Chung, K. Murase, & F. Ross-Sheriff, eds., *Social Work Practice with Asian Americans*. Newbury Park, CA: Sage Publications, pp. 213-226.

_____. (1991). "Single Asian American Women as a Result of Divorce: Depressive Affect and Changes in Social Support. *Journal of Divorce and Remarriage*, 14 (3-4): 219-230.

Spanier, G., & R. Lewis. (1981). "Marital Quality and Marital Stability: A Reply." *Journal of Marriage and the Family*, 43: 782-783.

Thibaut, J. W. & H. H. Kelly. (1959). *The Social Psychology of Groups*. New York: John Wiley.

Tien, J. L. (1985). *Divorce Adjustment Across Three Cultures: Implications for Family Therapy*. Paper presented at the Biennial Conference of the World Federation for Mental Health, July 15-21, Brighton, England.

Yu, E. Y. (1993). "The Korean American Community." In D. N. Clark, ed., *Korea Briefing 1993: Festival of Korea*. Boulder, CO: Westview Press, pp. 139-162.

14

The Domestic Violence against Women in Korean Immigrant Families: Cultural, Psychological, and Socioeconomic Perspectives

Young I. Song and Ailee Moon

INTRODUCTION

The problem of domestic violence to women in Korean immigrant families in the United States is an extension of a long history of Korean society that has tolerated such violence, compounded by additional problems and frustrations brought on by difficulties of adjustment to a new culture. Thus, in order to fully understand the domestic violence problem in Korean immigrant families, it is necessary to consider it in the context of its historical precedent and the present socioeconomic circumstances under which the violence occurs.

Although wife battering of Korean women is not a new phenomenon, it is only recently that society has begun to question the long-standing tradition that tolerates this violent behavior. Traditionally, violence against women has been justified in the context of Korean culture, which is strongly rooted in the philosophy of a male-dominated Confucianism (Phillips & Yu, 1982). Under Confucianism, it is the male who carries on the family name, provides for the aging parents, and inherits the family wealth, whereas the female is raised to leave her family upon marriage and be loyal to her husband's family. As a consequence, Koreans have long regarded male children to be far more valuable than female children from early childhood. At the same time, conformity to rigidly defined sex roles has been and continues to be the fundamental characteristic that governs the relationships of men and women in the Korean society (Yu, 1987; Yu & Phillips, 1983). While boys are taught to be tough, aggressive, and independent, girls are raised to be feminine, submissive, and dependent. In addition, Korean society has taught men not only to be served by women and to have authority over them but also to discipline their wives even through the use of violence. At the same time, it has taught women to accept their subordinate position in society, to obey their husbands, and to blame themselves for familial problems. Considering this socio-cultural background, it is not surprising that many Koreans today view violence against wives as an acceptable expression of patriarchal domination. Korean immigrants transport these traditional cultural beliefs with them to the United States, and many continue to hold on to these patriarchal attitudes toward women.

Although these Korean families immigrated to America for a better life, only a few came with clear ideas of how to adjust their lives to a foreign country, particularly with regard to the cultural differences. Therefore, any attempt to analyze the causes and remedies of the problem of wife battering among Korean immigrant couples requires a clear understanding of the nature of the conflicts during the process of their adjustment in a new economic, social, and cultural environment.

The primary objective of this chapter is to examine whether and how wife battering in Korean immigrant families is related to Korean traditional beliefs and adjustment difficulties upon immigration to the United States. For this purpose, 150 Korean immigrant women were interviewed to provide insight into the problem. The chapter begins with a brief description of the data collection method and the statistics on the frequency and severity of wife battering among the sampled women. This is followed by the examination of some major factors contributing to the occurrence of wife battering in Korean immigrant families, focusing on the attitude toward traditional values, sex role rigidity, and socioeconomic stressors, such as language and employment problems. Finally, it discusses the implications of the intervention and prevention of wife battering in Korean American families.

DATA COLLECTION METHOD AND SAMPLE

The data for this inquiry were collected through face-to-face interviews with 150 Korean immigrant women residing in Chicago in 1987. The subjects were recruited at various sites, using both random and availability sampling methods. Initially, over 200 individuals were randomly sampled from the telephone directories of several Korean American associations and from the lists of subscribers of Korean newspapers. After telephone contact, 95 individuals were identified as eligible to participate in the study by meeting two stated criteria. They (1) were currently married or had been previously married to Korean men and (2) had resided in the United States not more than ten years. Of the 95 eligible women, 72 participated in the study. For these women, in most cases, home visit interviews were conducted after telephone contact. In order to reduce potential selection biases inherent in relying on the above sampling sources available in the Korean American community, which tended to exclude those who had low profile or little contact with the community, 78 additional study participants were recruited and interviewed at several designated locations such as Korean restaurants, churches, grocery stores, and nursery schools.

The Korean immigrant women in our sample were on average 36 years old and the average length of residence in the United States was five years. Eighty-two percent of the respondents were currently married and the rest were either divorced or separated. Twenty-eight percent had completed four years of college, while approximately 50% were high school graduates.

PREVALENCE OF WIFE ABUSE AMONG THE SAMPLE WOMEN

The study shows that a significant proportion of Korean immigrant women suffered from domestic violence. Of the 150 respondents, 60% (N = 90) reported having been battered by their spouses, while the other 40% (N = 60) were found to be nonbattered women. As presented in Table 14.1, there was a wide range of wife battering in terms of frequency and severity of violence. For example, 57% (N = 51) of the battered women had been hit by their spouses with a closed fist, 24% (N = 22) had been choked, and 21% (N = 19) had been hit with an object. In two extreme cases the batterers had attempted to kill their wives. The table also reveals the considerably high prevalence of sexual abuse against these women. Thirty-seven percent of the battered, or 22% (N = 22) of all women in the study, had been forced by their spouses to have sex.

Looking at the frequency of violence, 24% (N = 22) of the battered women had suffered from violence at least once a week and an additional 37% (N = 34) had been subject to domestic violence at least once a month. As a consequence of the violence, 70% (N = 63) of the battered women indicated that they had bruises, and 19% (N = 17) had broken bones or teeth. Moreover, 9% (N = 8) of the victims experienced miscarriages and 7% (N = 6) were hospitalized as a result of domestic battering.

FACTORS CONTRIBUTING TO THE OCCURRENCE OF WIFE BATTERING IN KOREAN IMMIGRANT FAMILIES

Cultural Acceptance Factors: Traditionalism

Wife battering may occur in certain societies and groups because it is understood as a culturally accepted aspect of husband-wife interactions (Erchak, 1984; Ferraro, 1983; Lozios, 1978). It is useful to examine the ways in which the traditional Korean value system tolerates and legitimizes domestic violence against women.

Even today, a traditional Korean saying that "the real taste of dried fish and tame women can only be derived from beating them once every three days" is frequently quoted as a rationale or a justification for battering women. In this context, wife battering is justified as a means of improving the "quality" of womanhood. Unfortunately, this reflects the attitude of many contemporary Koreans that it is acceptable for a man to beat his wife when she does something that makes him angry. In this regard, a Korean scholar (Lee, 1977) pointed out that Korean women had to develop an ability to absorb insults and injuries without protest and to assume responsibility for others' faults.

As implied in Lee's observations, traditional Korean women had little choice but to blame themselves for whatever mistreatment they received, believing that they must have done something wrong to deserve such mistreatment. Logical reasoning and protest against men were considered damaging to the Korean traditional ideal of womanhood and resulted in further harm to themselves. In fact, battered women may exemplify society's old image of an ideal woman as submissive, nonassertive, self-blaming, and accepting of whatever the married life brings (Martin, 1988). In short, wife battering in Korean immigrant families, in part, is a product of the long history of the Korean tradition that demands endurance and self-blame from a wife while tolerating abusive behavior of a husband. Focusing on the findings of the present study, it is evident that Korean American women with more traditional attitudes regarding appropriate husband-wife relationships suffered from domestic violence more than those who held less

Table 14.1
Description, Severity, and Frequency of Domestic Violence Against Korean Immigrant Women

Degree		Description	% Battered Cases (N = 90)
Abusive Acts			
Moderate	1	My husband/partner destroyed my property	43.3
	1	My husband/partner threw an object at me	51.1
	1	My husband/partner threatened to hit me with an object	34.4
	1	My husband/partner threatened to hit me with his fist	56.7
Less Severe	2	My husband/partner hit me with a closed fist	56.7
	2	My husband/partner slapped me	42.2
	2	My husband/partner hit me with an object	21.1
Moderately	3	My husband/partner threatened me with a knife	15.6
Severe	3	My husband/partner threatened to kill me	22.2
	3	My husband/partner threatened to kill himself	14.4
	3	My husband/partner threatened me with a gun	4.4
Severe	4	My husband/partner forced me to have sex with him	36.7
	4	My husband/partner squeezed or pinched me	25.6
	4	My husband/partner choked me	24.4
	4	My husband/partner burned me	4.4
	4	My husband/partner broke my bone	7.8
	4	My husband/partner stabbed me	3.3
Very Severe	5	My husband/partner attempted to kill me	2.2
Resultant Injuries			
Moderate			
	1	Bruises	70.0
	1	Black eye	37.8
	1	Minor cuts or burns	30.0
	2	Cuts, burns, or bruises requiring medical attention	14.4
	2	Concussion	16.7
	2	Damage to teeth	10.0
	3	Broken bones	8.9
	3	Joint injury	3.3
	3	Spinal injury	1.1
	4	Injury to internal organs	2.2
	4	Miscarriage	8.9
	4	Emotional/mental distress requiring medical care	28.9
	5	Physical injury requiring hospitalization	6.7
Frequency of Abuse			
		At least once per day	3.3
		At least once per week	24.1
		At least once per month	37.3
		At least once per year	38.3

traditional beliefs. As shown in Table 14.2, more than one half of battered women (52%), as opposed to less than one third of nonbattered women (32%), scored "high" on their traditionalism, measured by the Traditional Family Ideology Scale (LeVinson and Huffman, 1955). As indicated by the chi-square value (6.17) and its significance level (p < .05), the differences between the two groups in terms of their traditional values were statistically significant.

A detailed appraisal of the participants' responses to the statements regarding their attitudes toward traditionalism further indicates that most of the battered women tried to fulfill the Korean traditional image of a good wife. They tended to conform to the virtues of obedience, endurance, tolerance, limited decision-making authority, and the limited role and participation of women in society in general. They viewed themselves primarily as wives and mothers rather than as individuals. Most of them also believed that they should be submissive and forgiving of their spouse's abuse. Furthermore, these traditional wives tended to view the relative success of their marriage as a reflection of their worth, both as a person and as a woman. They further expressed the view that 'leaving an abusive husband' is not a solution but a cause of more serious hardships and problems. For most of these women, divorce meant personal failure, economic insecurity, and social stigma.

Table 14.2
Attitude Toward Traditionalism by Battered and Nonbattered Korean Immigrant Women

Attitude Toward Korean Traditionalism	Battered		Nonbattered		Total	
	N	%	N	%	N	%
High (more traditional)	47	52.2	19	31.7	66	44.0
Low (less traditional)	43	47.8	41	68.3	84	56.0
Total	90	100.0	60	100.0	150	100.0

$X^2 = 6.17$; p < .05.

While wife battering has been tolerated and justified in the context of Korean culture, Korean immigrants, have to deal with two different sets of values which affect their marital life: the Korean traditional values on the one hand, and the American value system on the other. The differences between the two cultures often create confusion, identity crises, and marital conflicts.

To illustrate, it is useful to consider how a typical Korean immigrant wife becomes less willing to conform to the traditional Korean ideas of what a "desirable" husband-wife relationship is. Normally, within a few years after immigrating to the United States, she may feel that ordinary American wives, in comparison to herself, enjoy more freedom in pursuing their own interests and careers, have more authority in making important family decisions, and share household chores and social activities with their husbands. She may then come to the realization that the Korean traditional perception of a "good wife" may not necessarily be the prerequisite for a happy married life, especially in America.

This further leads to the recognition that she deserves better treatment and cooperation from her husband. While she challenges the virtue of maintaining the traditional sex role and adopts the American way of married life, marital conflicts are likely to arise when the husband is not willing to modify his traditional sex role. Therefore, it is highly plausible that the failure to reconcile these two different cultural norms and patterns of marital relationships constitutes another contributing factor for marital conflict, and hence, wife battering in Korean immigrant families.

Rigid Sex Role Socialization Factors

One of the most salient characteristics of wife batterers is their strict adherence to a rigidly defined male role. This compulsive masculinity is reflected in an attempt to maintain total dominance over their wives (Martin, 1988; Coleman & Strauss, 1986; Rosenbaum & O'Leary, 1981). Indeed, the underlying socialization patterns of male and female sex roles have been widely recognized as an important consideration in analyzing the cause of domestic violence against women. While batterers are more rigidly socialized into the male dominant sex role than nonbatterers, many battered women hold similar stereotyped attitudes regarding appropriate masculine and feminine behavior. Evidence further indicates the tendency among battered women to regard men as superior, and to regard all women, including themselves, as inferior (Martin, 1988).

As expected, Korean immigrant couples bring with them the Korean traditional pattern of a clear division of sex roles between the husband and wife. Most married women in Korea are confined to domestic roles, performing almost all of the household tasks, including cooking, babysitting, cleaning, shopping, and washing. These tasks are rarely performed by the husband, whose primary responsibility is to support the family financially as well as make important family decisions. For example, the traditional belief that men are supposed to stay away from the kitchen and laundry areas is still strongly supported by the majority of Korean men and women. In general, Korean married couples usually have little involvement in activities together at home and elsewhere. Nor do they expect to share or exchange traditionally defined sex role performances.

The rigid sex role socialization between married couples is also well reflected in the uses of the Korean language. For example, a wife speaks of her husband as uri-jip-juin, meaning "the master of our house." She may also refer to him as "the outside gentleman," pokkat-yangban in Korean. In sharp contrast, the wife is referred to as the husband's jip-saram or an-saram, meaning his "house person" and "inside person," respectively. This reflects the stratification and segregation of sex roles and interpersonal relations in Korean thought.

For many Korean immigrant families, efforts to adjust to new social and work environments require certain changes with respect to traditional lifestyles and ways of thinking. The active economic participation of Korean immigrant wives outside the home implies that the traditional role of the husband as the sole breadwinner has diminished and as a result, the "absolute male dominant sex roles in the traditional Korean family cannot be maintained intact in the United States" (Yu, 1987).

In fact, the results from our study show that a significant proportion of Korean immigrant wives, regardless of their employment status, continue to live by rigidly defined traditional sex roles. Table 14.3 summarizes the patterns of the respondents' sex role performances, measured by how each couple divides and shares household chores. As shown in the table, about 41% of all wives indicated that the Korean traditional pattern of a clear division of sex roles persisted in their family. It was also observed that while the majority of the wives performed most of the household tasks, many husbands were involved in certain tasks such as paying the bills and making decisions to buy things for the family.

More importantly, the prevalence of domestic violence was found to be higher among the couples who adhered to a rigidly defined Korean traditional sex role performance than those who did not. As indicated in the table, 58% of the wife battering cases occurred in the families with high congruency to rigidly defined sex roles, whereas only 17% of nonviolent families conformed to the rigid Korean patterns of sex role performance. The difference is significant indeed.

Table 14.3
Congruency of the Rigid Sex-Role by Battered and Nonbattered Korean Immigrant Couples

Attitude Toward Korean Traditionalism	Battered		Nonbattered		Total	
	N	%	N	%	N	%
High congruency to rigid sex-roles	52	57.8	10	16.7	62	41.3
Sharing sex-roles	25	27.8	34	56.7	59	39.3
Low congruency to rigid sex-roles	13	14.4	16	26.7	29	19.3
Total	90	100.0	60	100.0	150	100.0

$X^2 = 25.14$; $p < .05$.

The high correlation between wife battering incidence and rigid sex role is in part explained by the combination of the wives' discontent with and resentment of their husbands' strong demand for an ideal traditional Korean wifehood and the men's unwillingness to concede the absolute male dominant sex role. It is worth noting that a study of American couples also concluded that equality and sharing in marriage tend to be related to a lower incidence of wife abuse (Coleman & Strauss, 1986).

Stress-Evoking Socioeconomic Factors

There is considerable evidence to indicate that situational stresses cause domestic violence. Unemployment, job dissatisfaction, and financial difficulties, for example, are frequently associated with episodes of wife battering (Barling & Rosenbaum, 1986; Gelles, 1987). Furthermore, according to Teichman and Teichman (1989), societal upheaval (e.g., economic stress, immigration, wars) aggravates the violence potential and triggers quicker and more frequent incidents. The sources of stress and frustration among Korean immigrant couples, especially the newly arrived, seem to be the combination of many factors, including unsatisfactory employment status, language problems, and lack of socializability (Hurh & Kim, 1984; Kim & Lee, 1980). It is thus important to consider some of the major stress-evoking factors for a better understanding of the causes of wife battering in Korean immigrant families.

Upon their arrival in the United States, the majority of Korean immigrants face the harsh reality of unfavorable labor market conditions. It is well documented that many college-educated Korean immigrants hold blue-collar jobs and many professionals are either unemployed, underemployed, or turn to nonprofessional jobs mainly due to language barriers, licensing requirements, discrimination in hiring, and the lack of job information (Hurh & Kim, 1984).

Returning to the findings of the interviews, they indicate that stressful economic circumstances may have considerable bearing on marital relations and wife battering in Korean immigrant families. Table 14.4 shows a high correlation between the incidence of wife battering and the inconsistency in the pre- and post-immigration employment status of husbands. Based on the respondents' subjective judgment of employment status, 58% of wife batterers as opposed to 17% of nonviolent husbands were holding lower employment status compared to their pre-immigration employment status, and the percentage difference was statistically significant.

Table 14.4
Status Inconsistency in the Employment Status of Korean Men by Battering and Nonbattering Groups

	Men from Battering Group		Men from Non-battering Group		Total	
	N	%	N	%	N	%
Holding lower employment status compared to pre-immigration status	52	57.8	10	16.7	62	41.3
Holding same or higher employment status compared to pre-immigration status	38	42.2	50	83.3	88	58.7
Total	90	100.0	60	100.0	150	100.0

$X^2 = 25.2$; $p < .05$.

Unlike in Korea, where job discrimination against married women, in terms of hiring and wage level, is a widely accepted practice in the labor market, Korean immigrant wives find it relatively easier to obtain a low- or moderate-wage job in the United States. This enables many immigrant wives to seek employment in order to supplement their family income. For some wives whose husbands' incomes are insufficient for survival or decent family life, the decision to get a job is not a choice, but a necessity. It is also notable that a high proportion of Korean American families eventually turn to self-employed small business, such as grocery markets, liquor stores, gift shops, laundries, coffee shops, and restaurants. Such small businesses often require the labor of unpaid family members, particularly wives, to cut down the business expenses. In short, most

Korean immigrant wives, whose role in Korea had been confined to homemakers, contribute significantly to the economic well-being of their family through gainful employment and/or through helping the family businesses. In fact, a study by Hurh and Kim (1984) found that the majority of Korean immigrant wives work outside the home and most of them work long hours, with two-thirds of the working wives working an average of ten hours.

As wives become partners in economic activities, many of them no longer obediently accept the superior position of men and find it difficult to fulfill the roles of a traditional Korean wife. Indeed, the combination of extended full-time employment and primary responsibility for most of the household tasks means that working wives suffer from the heavy burdens of double roles. Eventually, the wives would feel an acute sense of unfairness. This, in fact, leads some wives to demand changes in the authoritarian attitudes of their husbands and the rigid traditional sex roles' expectation and performance.

Marital conflict arises when the husband and wife do not agree about whether and what changes should be made in their respective roles in the context of new social and work environments. For example, a wife who feels overburdened with the absolute demand of the traditional Korean wife's roles may expect her husband to share the responsibility for some of the household chores with minimal differentiation of sex roles. The husband, on the other hand, may continue to insist that the wife perform all of the household tasks, regardless of her employment status and to expect his wife to behave as if they lived in Korea. This scenario of marital conflict is apparently more stressful to the men, not only because the position of absolute male dominance is threatened but also because these changes usually come at a time when they feel insecure and frustrated in the process of cultural transition. Under these circumstances, the Korean American men, in an attempt to prove their masculinity, may follow the old pattern of harassing and punishing a "disobedient wife" through physical violence.

Previous studies have produced evidence that for many Korean immigrants, language problems and social isolation are major obstacles in the adjustment process of forming new lives in the United States and have significant bearing on the cause of wife battering (Yim, 1978; Yu, 1987). Needless to say, the language difficulty presents significant limitations for their participation in the mainstream of American social and cultural circles. Moreover, it has been suggested that social isolation of battered women constitutes part of both the cause and consequence of violence. According to Martin (1988), the batterer tends to systematically isolate the woman from others, while at the same time she withdraws to protect herself from further violence.

Results from our inquiry also support the conclusion that to some extent language problems and social isolation are directly or indirectly associated with episodes of wife battering. About one fifth of the battered women, whereas no one from the nonbattered group, reported not being able to speak English at all.

Focusing on socializability of the respondents, measured by the frequency of going out, contact with relatives or friends, physical mobility (e.g., driving a car, taking the bus), and participation in social clubs or organizations, the lack of social life was found to be significantly more evident among the battered women than among the nonbattered. For example, only 19% of battered women, compared with over 50% of nonbattered women, participated in a Korean association or other social clubs or professional organizations. The findings also show that battered women had significantly less contact with their friends and relatives than nonbattered women.

In general, many respondents seem to relate the cause of their spouse's violence to the accumulated stress and frustration resulting from cultural shock. As Yu (1987) explains, the process of immigration and cultural adjustment signified disruption of the family lifestyle of the immigrants and involves disintegration of the intra-familial relationships, loss of social identity, and major shifts in the value system and behavior patterns. In fact, the majority of the respondents indicated having experienced a cultural trauma due to disorientation, displacement, disappointment, alienation, loneliness, feelings of total inadequacy, cognitive dissonance, and/or loss of self-control during the cultural transition process. This suggests that immigration, whether motivated by the hope for a better life or flight from political or economic hardship, often results in intermingled emotions of grief, anger, loneliness, and guilt. Indeed, the process of cultural adjustment could be compared to the crisis in cultural loss.

Finally, it is useful to mention some of the variables or characteristics that are frequently related to domestic violence among non-Korean Americans but not found in the study of Korean immigrants. For example, studies on non-Korean Americans have found that unemployment, income, and education levels have considerable bearing on the occurrence of domestic violence against women (Gelles, 1987; Roy, 1977). This does not seem to hold true for Korean immigrants. Specifically, violent Korean men in our study do not differ significantly from nonviolent ones in terms of income, education levels, and employment status.

In addition, wife battering among non-Korean Americans is often associated with drinking problems and problems related to love lives (Fagan et al., 1983; Leonard et al., 1985; Rosenbaum & O'Leary, 1981; Roy 1982). However, results from our study suggest that such problems were not significant factors for Korean immigrants. Another difference between non-Korean and Korean battered women is that while about half of the former group tends to fight back physically in response to violence, it was extremely rare for the Korean women in our study to have taken such action.

IMPLICATIONS AND CONCLUSIONS

In general, victims of wife batterers stay in abusive relationships for a variety of reasons: fear of increased violence, financial insecurity, lack of support and resources, fear of loneliness, and/or desire to keep the family together. In this regard, Korean battered women are no exception. As mentioned earlier, the majority of the battered women in this study believed that leaving their violent spouses would cause more hardship, and that divorce was a sign of personal failure, which would lead to economic insecurity and social stigma. For them, it was a shame to reveal such an unpleasant private family matter, thus inhibiting them from seeking support from relatives, friends, or social workers. Moreover, most respondents had little or no knowledge about various services and resources available to help them nor how to obtain such services. It must also be pointed out that nearly half of the battered women in the study reported having reservoirs of hope, believing that the problem would be resolved without intervention. As a result, only a very small proportion of Korean families with marital problems had ever sought outside help.

These observations have several important implications especially for the prevention of domestic violence against women. First, having recognized the overall reluctance to utilize outside help, there is a great need for concentrated efforts to help them realize the usefulness and importance of getting outside intervention in the crisis of domestic violence before the problem worsens. Without outside intervention, it must be stressed, the cycle of violence is likely to increase in frequency and intensity because it has an addictive quality similar to drugs and alcohol. Furthermore, the intergenerational transmissional quality of marital violence must also be pointed out, in that over 60% of all batterers in America came from homes in which they were abused or their mothers were abused (Arias, 1984). This suggests that when nothing is done, children may grow up thinking that violence against women is acceptable behavior, and become batterers or victims of violence. Therefore, it is of great importance to enable abused mothers to realize that their children pay a high price indeed unless they take some action to prevent further violence, emphasizing that outside intervention does decrease the repetition of violence.

Second, there must be increased effort from both Korean American and non-Korean American social service organizations to reach out to and help the victims of domestic violence. The effort to reach out to the victims is essential because abused Korean immigrant women tend to be isolated, self-blaming, and uninformed about the existence of various services and resources available to assist them. Additionally, in order to provide effective assistance to Korean immigrant battered women, there must be a Korean American community–based comprehensive social service agency which provides not only professional counseling and referral services but also shelters staffed by Korean-speaking professionals. This is expected to overcome the language and cultural barriers of many Korean immigrant women, thereby making these services more accessible and helpful to them. The services provided by the Korean American community-based agency must include: (1) clinical counseling and shelters; (2) comprehensive and detailed information about the organizations that offer additional support, resources, and advocacy to enable battered women to help themselves, such as legal assistance, counseling, and medical care; (3) referrals to the organizations that can help the victims with other specific problems; (4) assistance in getting help from other service organizations, such as the provision of transportation, filling out forms, and translation; (5) case management; (6) counseling and rehabilitational programs for the batterers; (7) educational programs for the Korean American community for the prevention of domestic violence.

Third, it is important to have the whole Korean American community, both men and women, realize the legal interpretations and consequences of domestic violence, stressing the fact that in America wife battering is not acceptable behavior but a crime. Unfortunately, many Korean immigrants are not aware that in most states domestic violence is a felony and that the police do take legal action against it. Nor are they aware that calling the police and the arrest of batterers have been documented to be the most effective intervention, at least short-term, in deterring further violence. A clear understanding of the legal implications of domestic violence, as well as undertaking effective intervention will bring about considerable reduction in the occurrence of wife battering in Korean immigrant families.

Fourth, in order to stop violence against women, it must be emphasized that battering men also need help. Otherwise, the violence is likely to recur. These men are often insecure individuals in a foreign environment who know only one way to express their feelings of anger, frustration, disappointment and vulnerability—through violence. To convince battering Korean American men that they need professional help, however, is a challenging task because many of them do not consider violent behavior at home to be a problem, especially a problem that requires professional diagnosis and treatment. Nevertheless, for the preventive efforts to be successful, it is crucial to have these men learn and practice better ways to deal with stress, anger, and frustration, other than with their fists.

Finally, there must be increased efforts to improve the communication and stress-coping skills of Korean immigrant couples and to encourage them to express their feelings and ideas about many relevant issues, such as the perception of a happy marital life, how to better adjust their family life and ways of thinking in a new cultural and living environment, and how to deal with marital and nonmarital problems. In this regard, the provision of specialized marriage counseling sessions for Korean immigrant couples on a regular basis will be especially helpful in preventing domestic violence in the early stage of marital conflict.

In conclusion, it must be emphasized that any serious effort to attack the problem of domestic violence in Korean immigrant families requires strong support and commitment from within the Korean American community, including community leaders, media, service agencies, and concerned individuals, who possess the means and resources to prevent and help the victims of domestic violence. Without their effort, intervention from outside the Korean American community with its severely limited resources can only make minimal impact on the problem. The organized effort of the Korean American community to mobilize badly needed resources to provide various educational and social service programs for the intervention and prevention of domestic violence against women can make a significant contribution to improving the quality of family and marital life of many Korean immigrant families. In so doing, the community must send out a clear message, especially for those who view wife battering as normal or accepted behavior, that it has adopted a new norm assuring the safety of everyone, regardless of gender.

REFERENCES

Arias, I. (1984). *A Social Learning Theory Explication of the Intergenerational Transmission of Physical Aggression in Intimate Heterosexual Relationships.* Unpublished doctoral dissertation, State University of New York, Stonybrook.

Barling, D. H., & A. Rosenbaum. (1986). "Work Stressors and Wife Abuse." *Journal of Applied Psychology,* 71: 346-348.

Coleman, D. H., & M. A. Strauss. (1986). "Marital Power, Conflict, and Violence." *Violence and Victims,* 1: 139-153.

Erchak, G. (1984). "Cultural Anthropology and Spouse Abuse." *Current Anthropology*, 25: 331-332.

Fagan, J. A., et al. (1983). "Violent Men or Violent Husbands: Background Factors and Situational Correlates." In D. Finkelhor et al., eds., *The Dark Side of Families*. Beverly Hills, CA: Sage.

Ferraro, K. J. (1983). "Rationalizing Violence: How Battered Women Stay." *Victimology: An International Journal*, 8: 203-214.

Gelles, R. J. (1987). *The Violent Home*. Newbury Park, CA: Sage.

Hurh, Won Moo, & Kwang Chung Kim. (1984). *Korean Immigrants in America: A Structural Analysis of Ethnic Confinement and Adhesive Adaptation*. Cranberry, NJ: Association of University Presses.

Kim, B. S., & S. H. Lee, eds. (1980). *The Korean Immigrant in North America*. Montclair, NJ: The Association of Korean Christian Scholars in North America.

Lee, I. H. (1977). "Women's Liberation in Korea." *Korea Journal*, 17: 4-11.

Leonard, K. E., et al. (1985). "Patterns of Alcohol Use and Physically Aggressive Behavior." *Journal of Studies on Alcohol*, 46: 279-282.

LeVinson, D., & P. Huffman. (1955). "Traditional Family Ideology and Its Relation to Personality." *Journal of Personality*, 23: 251-273.

Lozios, P. (1978). "Violence and the Family: Some Mediterranean Examples." In J. P. Martin, ed., *Violence and the Family*. Chichester: Wiley.

Martin, M. (1988). "Battered Women." In N. Hutchings, ed., *The Violent Family: Victimization of Women, Children, and Elders*. New York: Human Sciences Press.

Phillips, E. H., & E. Y. Yu, eds. (1982). *Religions in Korea: Beliefs and Cultural Values*. Los Angeles: Center for Korean-American and Korean Studies.

Rosebaum, A., & K. D. O'Leary. (1981). "Marital Violence: Characteristics of Abusive Couples." *Journal of Consulting and Clinical Psychology*, 49: 63-71.

Roy, M. (1977). "A Current Study of 150 Cases." In M. Roy, ed., *Battered Women — A Psychological Study of Domestic Violence*. New York: Van Nostrand Reinhold.

_____. (1982). "Four Thousand Partners in Violence: A Trend Analysis." In M. Roy, ed., *The Abusive Partner: An Analysis of Domestic Battering*. New York: Van Nostrand Reinhold.

Teichman, M., & V. Teichman. (1989). "Violence in the Family: An Analysis in Terms of Intepersonal Resource-Exchange. *Journal of Family Violence*, 4: 129-142.

Yim, S. B. (1978). "Korean Battered Wives: A Sociological and Psychological Analysis of Conjugal Violence in Korean Immigrant Families." In H. Sunoo & D. Kim, eds., *Korean Women in a Struggle for Humanization*. Memphis, TN: The Korean Christian Scholars Publications.

Yu, E. Y. (1987). "Korean-American Women: Demographic Profiles and Family Roles." In E. Yu & E. H. Phillips, eds., *Korean Women in Transition: At Home and Abroad*. Los Angeles: Center for Korean-American and Korean Studies.

Yu, E. Y., & E. H. Phillips, eds. (1983). *Traditional Thoughts and Practices in Korea*. Los Angeles: Center for Korean-American and Korean Studies.

15

Korean American Mothers' Parenting Styles and Adolescent Behavior

Eunai Kim Shrake

INTRODUCTION

The image of Asian American students as the "model minority," "whiz kids," and as "problem-free" in popular media as well as academic literature (Sue & Sue, 1983; Smith, 1985; Sue, 1980) resulted from their relatively high level of academic achievement.

This academic success of Asian American students has drawn considerable attention from scholars who are interested in explaining the different patterns of academic achievement and the factors contributing to the academic performance of minority students. Some scholars have identified macro sociocultural factors, such as traditional cultural values and socioeconomic status of Asian Americans in the host society (Gibson & Bhachu, 1988; Ogbu, 1987), while others identified micro factors such as interpersonal interactions between parents and child (Stevenson & Lee, 1990; Schneider & Lee, 1990) as the primary factor for Asian American students' academic success.

Yet, this high achievement profile of Asian American students and subsequent research findings that stress the positive influence of parental/cultural values on the academic achievement of Asian American students may have overshadowed possible psychosocial as well as behavior problems of this group of students. What often goes unreported is that many Asian American youth belong to high-risk categories for high school dropouts, substance abuse, and juvenile delinquency. Many are already involved in those problem behaviors.

In spite of recent reports on the increasing rate of high school dropouts, substance abuse, teen pregnancy, and gang activity among Korean American adolescents (Kim, 1992; Yu, 1986; Astom, Prendergast & Lee, 1989), and in spite of some speculations on cultural/parental pressure to succeed as being a stress factor that may lead young Asian Americans in general, and Korean Americans in particular, to the development of mental as well as behavioral problems (Sue, 1980; Sue & Zane, 1985; Yu, 1986; Pang, 1991), little attention has been focused upon the possible relationship between parental behavior and the development of problem behaviors of Korean American adolescents.

The lack of concern and the lack of empirical research on this matter is particularly problematic for Korean Americans considering their relatively short immigration history, which has begun to reveal a widening cultural gap between first-generation parents and second-generation adolescents. Presumably, familial cultural conflict may be expressed as tension between parents and children, which may arise from conflicts in ideologies of upbringing and in patterns of parental control. Thus, it is plausible to expect that intergenerational cultural conflict may negatively influence adolescents' perception of parents' behavior, which may exacerbate the parent-adolescent relationship and thus contribute to the adolescent problem.

Although studies addressing this issue of intergenerational cultural conflict in relation to parenting practices among Korean Americans are sparse, the weight of anecdotal evidence clearly suggests that Korean American adolescents experience heightened cultural conflict arising from the struggle between the pressure of their rather rigid and demanding parents and their own desire for independence. Given this particular situation in which Korean American adolescents find themselves, it would not be surprising to see increasing problems among Korean American youth in the future should there be no deliberate attention and effort to examine Korean American parenting practice.

Children's psychosocial and/or problem behavior, as their academic success or failure, should be viewed as the result of a multilevel process of interactions among parents, school, and peers. However, given the gross importance of the parent-child relation during the adolescent period and the lack of information on Korean Americans concerning this issue, the link between adolescents' psychosocial development and parental behavior needs more attention if we want to unravel the specific mechanism through which Korean American parenting practices influence Korean American adolescents' behavior.

I will focus on the general parental factors influencing the adolescent psychosocial development, with special emphasis on problem behavior, in the next section. Later I shall be concerned with identifying the problems specific to Korean American parenting as perceived by both Korean American adolescents and parents themselves. Although this chapter focuses on Korean American parenting, the issues raised may be relevant to other Asian Americans to the extent that they share a similar cultural as well as immigrant context.

PARENTING AND ADOLESCENT DEVELOPMENT

It has been argued that a primary issue for parents and adolescents during the adolescent period is the negotiation of independence and connectedness (Youniss & Ketterlinus, 1987, cited in Montemayor & Flannery, 1991). According to the psychoanalytic view, conflict and detachment rather than harmony and connectedness characterize parent-adolescent relations during this stage of development (Blos, 1979; Erikson, 1959; A. Freud, 1969; all cited in Baumrind, 1991). Consequently, psychoanalytic theorists often have portrayed adolescence as a period of "storm and stress," implying that some problem behavior in adolescence may be a normative manifestation of the detachment process.

More recently, however, empirical studies from both clinical and psychosocial approaches argue against the psychoanalytic view that the detachment process is inevitable or desirable during adolescence. Instead of evidence indicative of a preponderance of adolescent detachment, many empirical studies have found that adolescents who feel relatively closer to their parents scored higher on measures of psychosocial development such as self-esteem and social competence, and scored lower on measures of problem behavior such as drug use, depression, and deviant behavior than their peers who feel more detached from their parents (e.g., Barnes, 1984; Maccoby & Martin, 1983; cited in Steinberg, 1991: 725). Drawing upon this empirical support, they have concluded that the most crucial task for adolescents is not detachment but balance between independence and connectedness. Further, unlike the unduly pessimistic view of the adolescent problem of psychoanalytic theories, theories based on these empirical studies have argued that adolescent problem behavior is a pattern or trait that is preceded by the social, environmental, and interactional factors that facilitate these behaviors, and thus it can be prevented or averted (Reid & Patterson, 1989; Jessor & Jessor, 1977).

Based on the latter view, a great deal of research has focused on the respective socializing influences of parents and peers as antecedents and correlates of adolescent problem behavior (e.g., Huba & Bentler, 1980; Kandel & Andrews, 1987; cited in Windle, 1991: 840). Notwithstanding peer influence, which is frequently described as leading to adolescent deviant behavior, theories of deviance such as social control theory (Hirschi, 1969), social learning theory (Akers, 1973; Bandura, 1971), or social interaction model (Patterson & Dishion, 1985) have emphasized in one way or another that poor parenting is the most prominent variable contributing to adolescent problem behavior. Loeber and Dishion (1983), for example, identified the parenting variable as the most consistent and powerful predictor of antisocial behavior of adolescents. Further, Patterson and Dishion (1985) found evidence indicating that poor parenting practice had a more salient and independent influence on delinquent behavior in adolescence when both peer and parenting influences were considered simultaneously.

In support of the idea that parental influence has the primary effect on adolescent behavior, researchers have examined various dimensions of parental behavior in an attempt to find effective parenting styles that may foster positive adolescent development while preventing problem behavior. Some researchers have focused on the warmth, nurturing, or support dimension of parenting (e.g., Rohner, 1986), while others have emphasized responsiveness and control dimensions (e.g., Baumrind, 1991; Maccoby & Martin, 1983). Still others who are inclined toward clinical studies on juvenile behavior (e.g., Patterson, 1986; Patterson & Stouthamer-Loeber, 1984; Loeber & Dishion, 1983) have identified parental discipline and monitoring as the prime components of effective parenting against antisocial or delinquent behavior in adolescence.

With respect to the warmth or support dimension, Barnes and Windle(1987) found that high parental support is inversely associated with problem behavior in adolescence. In addition, Simons, Robertson, and Downs (1989) reported that children with rejecting parents, compared to children with nurturing parents, are more apt to report deviant behavior.

Baumrind has used both responsiveness and control aspects of parenting in her typology of parenting styles: Authoritative, Authoritarian, Permissive, and Neglecting (Baumrind, 1991). Among others, she defined authoritative parenting as both responsive and demanding, while authoritarian parenting is controlling but not responsive. Later, in her study on adolescence, Baumrind (1991) found that adolescents with authoritarian parents were less competent, less prosocial, lower in school performance, and had more internalizing problem behaviors (withdrawn, anxious, depressed) than those with authoritative parents. Steinberg et al. (1989) also indicated that authoritative parenting has a positive effect on the psychosocial maturity of children, while Yee and Flanagan (1985) discussed the negative relationship between authoritarian parenting and adolescents' levels of self-esteem.

Taken together, Belsky et al. (1991), in their literature review, found that cooperation and compliance develop among children whose parents showed shared control, sensitivity, and responsiveness (authoritative), while noncompliance and aggression appear to be fostered by coercive and demanding patterns of parenting (authoritarian). In addition, Rollins and Thomas (1979) reported that children's self-esteem and prosocial behavior are negatively associated with coercive control attempts of parents, implying that coercive control, restrictiveness, and authoritarian parenting can be presumed to be responsible for children's antisocial behavior.

In their clinical research on parenting and antisocial behavior of adolescents, Loeber and Dishion (1983) found that the most consistent and powerful predictors of later juvernile delinquency were parenting practices which specifically related to inconsistent discipline and poor parental supervision. Though poor parental disciplinary practices such as too little control and cruel, harsh, and violent punishment may increase the risk for adolescent problem behavior, Patterson and Dishion (1985) suggested that parental monitoring is thought to be more crucial since the failure to monitor contributes to the lack of control over the child's associations with delinquent peers, which in turn leads to the failure to discipline antisocial or delinquent behavior.

While such arguments certainly seem plausible, it should be noted that much of the research has been conducted on samples of Anglo American adolescents, thus excluding ethnic minorities in general and Asian Americans in particular.

Though it shares certain essential features with Anglo American parenting, minority parenting should be operationalized somewhat differently depending upon the cultural or ethnic context reflecting the unique cultural and survival strategies that determine the way parents actually behave toward their children and the way children interpret their parents' behavior. As an example, Trommsdorff (1985) has argued that parental practices such as strict control and discipline do not necessarily always function negatively nor do they necessarily induce disturbances in adolescent development in every cultural context.

For example, Asian American parents, specifically Korean American parents, perceive that their ethnic survival lies in their children's education. Accordingly, many Korean American parents seem to exercise strict control over children in order to assure their children's academic success. This may account in part for many Korean American adolescents' perceptions of their parents as highly controlling and authoritarian. Interestingly however, some research findings show that, unlike many Anglo American adolescents who tend to associate strict parental control with parental hostility, Korean American adolescents still perceive their parents as warm, caring, and nonrejecting (Rohner, Hahn, &

Rohner, 1980; Rohner & Rohner, 1983; Rohner, Hahn, & Koehn, 1992).

This unique feature of Korean American parenting and the adolescents' perception of their parents' behavior would be an exemplary case that Anglo American–parenting measures fail to explain since they do not take into account the cultural or ethnic milieu in which these subjective views are embedded. Unfortunately, in spite of the recognition of the differences in ethnic minority parenting (Baumrind, 1991), research concerned with more culturally sensitive indices for ethnic minority parenting, particularly for Korean Americans, has been virtually absent.

PERCEIVED PROBLEMS IN KOREAN AMERICAN PARENTING

Given the abundant evidence that parenting behavior has a primary effect on adolescent deviance ranging from delinquency to psychopathology, and also given the increasing reports of problem behavior among Korean American adolescents, there is a need for research investigating the factors specific to Korean American parenting that contribute to problem behavior and the extent to which these factors influence deviant behavior of Korean adolescents.

Though general parental anxiety about parenting practices has been frequently reported as a common problem for most Korean American parents (Kim, Sawdy, & Meihoefer, 1982; Nah, 1993), except for some speculations that Korean parenting practices often presented as high academic pressure, authoritarian control, and lack of proper supervision may have adverse effects on adolescent behavior, there have been few studies conducted on the problem of Korean American parenting in relation to psychological and behavior problems of Korean American adolescents.

In an attempt to find empirical support for the perceived problems in Korean American parenting, I conducted a survey of 23 Korean American high school students (seventh through eleventh grade) and interviews with 5 mothers from a Korean church in Orange County, California. The student sample comprised 14 male and 9 female students. All the mothers who participated in the interview had a child attending a high school in this area. As a group, the participants did not differ much from each other in terms of socioeconomic status and educational levels. Most of the sampled students reported that they were from middle- or upper-middle-class backgrounds, and all the mothers were college graduates. The reason why I interviewed mothers only was that, even though there is some evidence that in the United States the Korean father's role in childrearing is increasing (Yu & Kim,1983), when asked who their primary caretakers were, Korean American adolescents typically identified their mothers (Rohner, Hahn, & Koehn, 1992). In addition, as McCord (1991) noted, compared with fathers, mothers are more influential in affecting adolescent behavior.

Data on the students' perceptions of parental behavior were collected through a survey questionnaire comprised of 43 items. Out of the 43 items, 28 questions were authoritarian vs. authoritative indices, 5 were indices for discipline, 7 were for parental monitoring, and the remaining 3 questions were for parental pressure to succeed. For the construction of the survey questionnaire, Schaefer's (1965) Children's Reports of Parental Behavior Inventory (CRPBI) and the parenting questionnaire of Lempers et al. (1989) were selectively combined. In addition, 3 items indicative of parental pressure that may pertain to Korean American parenting context were designed and used as supplemental indices.

To collect the mothers' data, an open-ended questionnaire was used for the interview. The questionnaire consisted of 9 items related to the (1) main emphasis of their parenting; (2) self-evaluation of their level of parental pressure; (3) parental monitoring practice; (4) level of communication with their children; and (5) general perceptions of the problems in Korean American parenting.

On the basis of those speculations as well as my own survey and interview data, I will examine in this section the perceived problems in Korean American parenting in three areas: parental expectations versus parental pressure, authoritarian parenting versus low communication, and poor supervision/monitoring. The focus of the analysis will be on finding the patterns of problems in Korean American parenting practice perceived by both adolescents and the mothers themselves, and their implications for the adolescents' psychosocial behavior. In analyzing the data, emphasis will be given to gender differences.

PARENTAL EXPECTATIONS VERSUS PARENTAL PRESSURE

It is often said that probably the most important factor distinguishing the new Korean immigrants from other Asian groups may lie in their intention to provide greater educational as well as occupational opportunities for their children (Kim, Sawdy, & Meihoefer, 1982). Anecdotal evidence shows that there are several immigrants' myths concerning children's education commonly held by many Korean American parents. Among others, many Korean parents say that they came to the United States to provide better education for their children (Kim et al., 1987). Whether this statement is simply a myth or not, most researchers who have studied Korean American parents agree that parents hold extremely high and sometimes unreasonable educational expectations for their children (Kim, 1980, 1983; Rohner et al., 1980).

A large body of literature addresses the positive relationships between parental expectations and children's educational achievement among Asian Americans (Mordkowitz & Ginsberg, 1987; Stevenson & Lee, 1990; Lee, 1987). However, the problem of these studies lies in their focus solely on academic achievement, ignoring other areas of child development. In other words, these studies did not pay sufficient attention to how children perceive those expectations and translate them into their psychosocial behavior.

Recently, however, a few researchers have discussed the manifested problems of low self-esteem, high-achievement anxiety, and low social skills in relation to parental pressure found among some high achieving Asian American students. For example, Schneider and Lee (1990) addressed the psychological cost of parental pressure among Asian American students. In their comparative study of parental environments between Asian American and Anglo American students, Lee and Schneider found that from an academic perspective, Asian American parents' high expectations showed positive outcomes, though unfortunately achieved at certain costs. Examining students' interview results, they suspected that Asian American children lack social skills because they are forced to spend much time studying rather than participating in social activities.

However, it is Pang who recognized the mechanism through which parental pressure influences children's psychological development. In her study of test anxiety as it relates to students' perceptions of parental pressure, parental support, and pleasing parents, Pang (1991) found that although there were no ethnic differences in the students' perceptions of parental pressure, Asian American students reported stronger desires to please their parents and exhibited significantly higher test anxiety than their Anglo American counterparts. She concluded that pleasing parents may be an indirect way that students internalize parental pressure, and that this internalization of parental pressure may influence children's achievement anxiety and lowered self-esteem. Further, this conclusion led her to speculate that Asian American students' high academic performance may mask psychological problems such as low self-concept, depression, frustration, and desperation.

This external locus of control in terms of pleasing parents for Asian American adolescents was well supported by Liu and others' interviews with Asian American high achievers. In interview after interview, Liu et al. (1990) found that these teenagers explained their drive to excel in terms of the shame that can befall their parents should they fail, and the glory they bring to their families when they succeed. Thus, they concluded that this external locus of control may intensify the perceived parental pressure, which in turn is likely to cause psychological problems among Asian American adolescents.

The external locus of control by the adolescents and the low level of satisfaction by parents are also evidenced in the following wishes in the New Year's Eve prayer written by a 13-year-old Korean American girl:

Dear Jesus,
This year I would very much like to get all A's. It would please my mom. Plus, please show my mom that a B does not make a very big difference if everything else is A plus.

It comes as no surprise that this girl seems to suffer from lack of confidence and emotional insecurity.

Unfortunately, there has been no clear distinction in many studies between strong parental expectation and negative parental pressure. Henceforth, it is my assumption that the distinction may lie in the way parental expectation is perceived by children along with other parental dimensions. For example, strong expectations combined with low levels of parental satisfaction as well as overemphasis on achievement without proper supervision or help may function as negative pressure on children, thus leading them to unnecessarily high anxiety and, in the worst case, to deviant behaviors such as cheating, lying, and involvement in gang activities.

Both seem to be the case in Korean American parenting. Indeed, Yu and Kim (1983) noted that Korean American parents report that they focus more on motivating their children than on providing actual supervision and help. Aldwin and Greenberger (1987) also reported that in counseling situations, even in the area of academic problems, Korean American parents reportedly do not provide more support for their children than do Anglo American parents. In addition, despite the high educational expectations for their children, many Korean American parents are not effusive in their reinforcement for academic excellence. For example, many Korean American adolescents I interviewed noted that their parents get upset or ground them when they get poor grades, while when they bring good grades, they tell the youth to do even better and that their other grades should be as good.

According to my survey, a majority of students (78%) revealed that their parents push them to excel at school while 61% responded that they do not receive any parental supervision or help in doing school work. Also, more than 65% of the respondents reported that their parents are not interested in what they are learning at school other than the grades. There was a slight gender difference in the perception of parental pressure and receiving parental help. More girls (88%) than boys (71%) reported their parents are pushy, and also slightly more girls (67%) than boys (57%) complained about lack of parental help. No significant gender difference was found in adolescents' perceptions of the lack of parental interest other than school grades.

Overall, these findings clearly support Yu and Kim's argument that Korean American parents are pressuring children without providing proper help. I also suspect that this lack of proper supervision and concern for a balanced adolescent development may give those adolescents an intensified feeling of parental pressure, thus causing increased psychological turmoil since they are left alone in achieving academic excellence as well as other areas of adolescent development. Concerning gender difference, it is not clear why girls feel more parental pressure. I can only speculate that the differential socialization goals for girls, which demand additional virtues such as submissiveness, femininity, and chastity, may limit the areas of girls' social activities, and thus, intensify the girls' perceptions of parental pressure.

It is not clear whether this negative perception of parental pressure actually influences adolescents' behavior negatively. Nevertheless, my survey data showed that approximately one third of all students identified parental pressure as the major reason for involvement in gang activities among Korean American adolescents, while the remaining two thirds perceived peer pressure to be the major reason. Since this trend was similar across genders, it seems clear that Korean American adolescents perceive parental pressure as problematic. This, at least partially, implicates parental pressure as a cause of adolescent deviance.

The low level of satisfaction with their children's school performance was also evidenced by the interviews with the mothers. When asked how they think about their child's B grade, 4 out of 5 mothers replied that it is "not a good" grade. By no coincidence, they rated their parental pressure as higher than other ethnic mothers except one mother who showed a contradiction between her conscious effort not to push her son and her overt frustration with her son's low academic performance in the following quotation:

Unlike other Korean mothers, I tried not to push my son to just get good grades because I thought his being popular among his peers was more important. He is now in eleventh grade and I found out that his grade is not good enough to enter a college. It is too late to reverse everything. Now, I feel ashamed and depressed since I think I ruined my son's future by not pushing him hard enough. I can't blame anyone but myself.

Interestingly, however, many mothers admitted high parental pressure as a problem factor in Korean American parenting. When I asked their opinions on the general problem of Korean American parenting, considering recent media reports on the delinquent behavior among Korean American adolescents (e.g., the "Tay" murder incident), though they recognized the problems in broader areas other than parenting (e.g., bicultural context of immigrant community, schools' failure in moral education, and developmental stage of adolescents), they also identified high parental pressure as the major problem. Stressing its impact on psychological and behaviorial problems of children, one mother addressed the problem of parental pressure in a summary fashion:

We, Korean American parents, tend to pound it into our children's heads that it is their duty to do well in school overly emphasizing our sacrifice for them. In doing so, we tend to forget the tremendous psychological burden children may have. To please their parents, many children may study hard, but probably many also may give up and get involved in deviant behavior.

As complimentary evidence for the negative effect of parental pressure, one mother expressed her experience with one high-achieving student:

Once I took my son and his friend to a miniature golf. My son's friend is known to be a top student at his school. During the game, he looked overly anxious to win. When he noticed that he was losing the game, he acted almost crazy. My son told me he was like that because his mother pushed him to be the first all the time. When I visited his home, I happened to hear him saying to his dog held in leash, "My life is no better than yours." Later, I heard that he became rebellious to his mom.

Findings thus far suggest a general consensus of students and mothers on the perception of the problems of parental pressure in Korean American parenting. That is to say, both mothers and students seem to recognize high parental pressure as one of the major problems in Korean American parenting that may increase the likelihood of adolescent problems.

AUTHORITARIAN CONTROL VERSUS LOW COMMUNICATION

Authoritarian control and subsequent poor communication were also frequently criticized problems in Korean American parenting. As discussed in the previous section, it is often argued that authoritarian control by parents is negatively correlated with children's school performance as well as prosocial behavior. In contrast, in their cross-ethnic study, Dornbusch et al. (1987) found that this general argument railing against authoritarian parenting did not adequately fit Asian American parenting, since many Asian American students performed well in school though they reported more authoritarian parenting than their Anglo American counterparts. Unfortunately, being primarily concerned with academic performance, this study tells us little about the psychological and behavioral aspects of adolescent development.

Though there has been no empirical research directly relating parenting style to adolescent psychosocial behavior for Asian Americans, a number of studies have shown that Asian American parents, especially mothers, tend to be more restrictive by exerting more parental control over their children than do Anglo American mothers (Lin & Fu, 1990). For instance, Chiu (1987) found that Chinese American mothers tended to be more protective, more restrictive, and more authoritarian than Anglo American mothers in their parenting style, while Pettengill and Rohner (1985) addressed the highly authoritarian parental control perceived by Korean American adolescents.

The perception of authoritarian parenting by Korean American adolescents was well supported by my survey results. Responding to the Children's Reports of Parental Behavior Inventory, many students scored higher on authoritarian indices than on authoritative indices. For example, approximately 69% of all respondents replied that their parents "often" or "very often" get upset when the respondents talk back and tell them not to argue with their parents, and feel hurt when they don't follow parents' advice. In addition, almost 70% of the respondents indicated that their parents insist on their obedience and 56% of them complained that their parents "often" or "very often" try to impose parents' values on them.

Overall, the data suggest that Korean American parents seem to be perceived as highly authoritarian by their children. Not unexpectedly, a significant gender difference has emerged in these authoritarian indices. Except for the variable "parents get upset when they talk back," girls scored higher than boys in other variables. Fully 78% of girls compared to 64% of boys related their parents' high demands for obedience, and 67% of girls reported of their parents' hurt feelings while 57% of boys did so. However, the most significant gender difference was revealed in the variable indicating parents' imposing values: 78% for girls compared to 43% for boys. One possible explanation of this gender difference is the impact of cultural beliefs on parenting. That is to say, Korean traditional values reflected in a rigid gender typing may still affect Korean American parenting, resulting in more authoritarian control over girls. If this holds true, Korean American adolescent girls may be more vulnerable to psychological problems such as low self-esteem, high anxiety, and depression since Rosenthal (1987) suggested that immigrant adolescent girls from a cultural background with sharply differentiated gender roles are more likely to be at risk than girls from a culture with less gender role differentiation. However, due to the small sample size, it is rather hasty to conclude that girls perceive their parents as more authoritarian and are thus more vulnerable to internalized problem behaviors.

Mothers also seem to recognize the authoritarian way of their parental behavior. In the following quotation, one mother admitted her outright authoritarian parenting as a problem:

Often I think I shouldn't impose what I think is right on my child. Also I know I shouldn't say just "No, No, No" without listening to him. But it is really hard not to do that. We tend to believe we are right just because we are parents. We were raised in that way. I feel my whole system is made that way. Breaking the cycle is hard, isn't it?

As Chiu (1987) noted, the authoritarian control by Korean American parents may be intended to protect rather than to inhibit the child. Unfortunately, children may interpret their parents' strict control as parental hostility and rejection.

As a matter of fact, Pettengill and Rohner (1985) found that Korean American adolescents perceived strict parental control in association with great parental hostility and rejection. Following Rohner's theory of parental acceptance-rejection, which postulates that rejected children are more likely to develop an impaired sense of self-esteem and self-adequacy than accepted children (Rohner, Hahn, & Rohner, 1980), their strong perception of authoritarian control may raise a problem for Korean American adolescents. Furthermore, strict authoritarian control can be detrimental to adolescents' psychosocial maturity since it may hamper adolescent development in terms of independence and self-control.

It should be also pointed out that, perceiving their parents as authoritarian, many Korean American adolescents seem to suffer from the lack of communication or negative communication between themselves and their parents. According to my survey, 61% of the adolescents reported that their parents rarely listen to their ideas or opinions, and 65% complained that their parents do not let them share their worries with parents. Also, fully 70% indicated that they are not included in family decision-making. Although the dissatisfaction with parent-adolescent communication was slightly lower for girls than for boys, the survey results quite clearly point to a general lack of communication between Korean American parents and their adolescent children.

This lack of communication is more frequently mentioned by mothers and is revealed as a serious problem in the following comment:

Often I find myself being the only person talking when it comes to mother-child conversation. Only response they give is "Yeah, Yeah," or "Okay, Okay, I got that, mom." I know it is because whenever I talk to them it ends up with scolding or nagging. Since they don't talk back, they seem to be listening, but I know they are ignoring me.

This low level of communication can be, for the most part, attributed to authoritarian parenting. For example, within the traditional Korean family, communication is often unidirectional, flowing from parents to children without allowing the children's interruption (Lee & Cynn, 1991). Strom et al. (1987) also indicated that many Korean American parents, especially fathers, hold the traditional belief that there should be a distance between adults and children in order to maintain children's respect for parents, and they tend to be unwilling to listen to their children's expressions of worries and anxiety. Obviously, this authoritarian attitude of parents deteriorates the parent-adolescent relationship, and in the worst case, to the point of alienation and parental rejection, thus undermining the level of communication between parents and adolescents.

Reflecting this authoritarian culture, one mother describes the psychological mechanism through which negative communication affects adolescent deviance:

Korean American parents expect children to just listen and say, "Yes." Probably, this authoritarian way of communication makes our children incompetent to be assertive. I often notice my son having a hard time to say "No" to his peers though he knows he should say "No." I guess this lack of courage to say "No" may be partly responsible for the gang involvement of Korean American adolescents.

Coupled with these cultural attitudes, a language gap also creates emotional as well as intellectual distance between parents and adolescents (Yu & Kim, 1983) lessening the quality of communication. As studies on the Korean American family disclose, Korean American adolescents often speak fluent English but speak Korean poorly or not at all, and this makes establishing meaningful communication with Korean-speaking parents difficult (Lee & Cynn, 1991; Rohner & Rohner, 1983; Rohner, Hahn, & Rohner, 1980). Over time, this language gap associated with parent-adolescent culture conflict may deteriorate the quality of communication.

Given the importance of communication in helping adolescents strike a balance between separateness from and connectedness to their parents for their healthy psychosocial development, and also to facilitate the development of higher levels of moral reasoning in adolescents (Barnes & Olson, 1985), this negative finding of parent-adolescent communication compounded with highly authoritarian parenting seems to foretell a serious problem in Korean American adolescent development.

PARENTAL SUPERVISION AND MONITORING

The lack of parental supervision or poor monitoring of Korean American parents has been also blamed for adolescents' delinquent behavior. For instance, a Korean American probation officer at the Los Angeles County Probation Department, in an interview, pointed out that despite the strong concerns for their children, many Korean American parents seem to be unable to monitor their children's emotional conflicts, antisocial behavior, school activities, or peer relations occurring outside the home. The discrepancy between parental concern and actual monitoring practices appears to be a serious problem in Korean American parenting and is evidenced in my student survey. My survey results revealed that although many students (65%) showed that their parents are concerned with where they are and whom they are with, only 35% of them indicated that their parents actually find that they misbehave outside the home and only 48% reported that their parents provide proper supervision. A significant gender difference was revealed in the actual monitoring variable in terms of parents' perceiving misbehavior. Only 11% of girls compared to 50% of boys reported parents' finding that they misbehave. Since there were no such differences in other two monitoring variables, I can only speculate that this gender difference may be explained in terms of girls' sophistication in dealing with parents rather than parents' differential monitoring practices according to gender.

This lack of supervision or poor monitoring is probably a result of the lengthy absences of both parents from home due to the long hours of work required for Korean American parents to support the family (Kim & Hurh, 1985). Addressing the issue of parental absence, mothers also admitted the problem in monitoring practice in the interview:

We say we came to the U.S. for our children's education. In reality however, we are too busy building up our businesses to provide proper supervision for our children. As for my husband and I, we are working 7 days a week and almost 10 hours a day. Since I don't have enough time to monitor my kids, I try to observe their mood swings or behavior changes whenever possible. However, due to the lack of time we spend together, it is not an easy job.

According to Crouter et al. (1990), parental monitoring, at one level, implies conscious supervision of the child. At another level, however, parental monitoring is a relationship property. In order to provide effective monitoring, parents should make an effort to establish communication channels with children through which children willingly share their experiences and activities with the parents. This may have serious implications for Korean American parenting. Given the low level of communication, children are not likely to talk about what they are doing and whom they are involved with outside the home, and parents will probably not be able to find out. This leads, in turn, to the parents' failure to supervise children's out-of-home activities. Stressing the linkage between poor supervision and poor communication, one mother expressed her concerns for juvenile behavior:

Since I don't have enough time and energy to check up on my son, I often ask him to talk about his day. His typical answer is "It was O.K." or "Nothing much." He rarely talks about what's going on in his life outside the home. What if he gets involved with bad friends? Since there is no communication, there is no way I can find the problem. Sometimes, that makes me really worried.

However, the problem of poor supervision seems especially serious as it is related to parental pressure for academic excellence. When students were asked how their parents react if they say they studied at the library when they came home very late, almost a half of the respondents answered "often" or "very often" they got excused. In this sense, not simply poor monitoring but the pattern of parental pressure with poor supervision seems to be the problem in Korean American parenting.

CONCLUSION

Primarily, the findings of the present research provide support for the general speculations that Korean American parenting practice may be characterized as "high academic pressure," "authoritarian control," "low communication," and "poor supervision." More significantly however, the patterns of problems in Korean American parenting seem to emerge through data analysis. Due to the small sample size, it is rather hasty to draw any conclusions. However, since the data analysis suggests that the above characteristics of parenting are interrelated thus complicating the problem, it leads us to speculate that the problem patterns of Korean American parenting can be summarized as "parental pressure with poor supervision" and "authoritarian control with low communication."

Both problem patterns in Korean American parenting should be understood in the light of the sociocultural background of recent Korean immigrants. On the one hand, Korean American parents originated in a culture that places high value on education, with a highly competitive educational system. As such, it seems quite natural for parents to put strong academic pressure on children. On the other hand, with a Confucian philosophy that stresses deference to elders and teachers, they have brought expectations for both school and community to share the responsibility of supervision of children. Thus, many Korean American parents may not assume total responsibility for the supervision of their children as one mother exhibited her disappointment as follows:

In Korea, to supervise children is not just the parents' job. Since children stay long hours at school, teachers do much of the supervision. Also many adult members of the society take partial responsibility. Whenever they see child's misbehavior, even though they are total strangers to that child, they scold or discipline that child. In America, nobody seems to hold that kind of authority nor does care for others.

In spite of this cultural dilemma, many Korean American parents still tend to honor the Korean cultural ideology that stipulates the unquestionable right and responsibility of parents to exert authority over their children, while discouraging children from questioning authority and expressing feelings or new ideas. Undoubtedly, this cultural tendency is attributable to the problem patterns of "high parental pressure with poor supervision" and "authoritarian control with low communication" in Korean American parenting. Given this cultural understanding, both problem patterns of parenting may be generalized to recent immigrant parents from East Asia who share a similar sociocultural background.

Concerning the possible relationship between these patterns of parenting and adolescents' problem behavior, the data supporting this relationship must be considered somewhat tentative, since the student survey data do not include variables of problem behavior. However, as the interview data suggested, it is speculated that these parenting patterns may be problematic in that they may have an indirect effect on adolescents' behavior problems by driving them to a psychological edge.

Unfortunately, this study focused on identifying specific problems in Korean American parenting and did not measure all the variables that are relevant in finding an association between parental behavior and adolescents' psychosocial behavior. To find this association, more structured data collections for dependent variables such as adolescents' self-esteem, social competence, and problem behavior should be conducted.

However, this study resulted in reasonable suspicions that there may be a relationship between the Korean American parenting pattern and adolescents' problem behavior and also that this parenting pattern may be found in other Asian American parenting. In this sense, this study warrants model building studies for the effect of Asian American parenting on adolescents' psychosocial behavior.

REFERENCES

Akers, R. L. (1973). *Deviant Behavior: A Social Learning Approach.* Belmont, CA: Wadsworth.

Aldwin, Carolyn, & Ellen Greenberger. (1987). "Cultural Differences in the Predictors of Depression." *American Journal of Community Psychology,* 15: 789-813.

Astom, G.A., M. L. Prendergast, & Harvey Lee. (1989). "Substance Abuse Among Asian American Youth." *Prevention Research Update,* 5.

Bandura, A. (1971). *Social Learning Theory.* Morristown, NJ: General Learning Press.

Barnes, Howard L., & David H. Olson. (1985). "Parent-Adolescent Communication and the Circumplex Model." *Child Development,* 56: 438-447.

Barnes, G. M., & M. Windle. (1987). "Family Factors in Adolescent Alcohol and Drug Abuse." *Pediatrician,* 14: 13-18.

Baumrind, Diana. (1991). "Parenting Styles and Adolescent Development." In R. M. Lerner, A. C. Petersen, & J. Brooks-Gunn, eds., *Encyclopedia of Adolescence,* Vol. 2.

Belsky, Jay, L. Steinberg, & Patricia Draper. (1991). "Childhood Experience, Interpersonal Development, and Reproductive Strategy: An Evolutionary Theory of Socialization." *Child Development,* 62: 647-670.

Chiu, Lian-Hwang. (1987). "Childrearing Attitudes of Chinese, Chinese American, and Anglo American Mothers." *International Journal of Psychology,* 22(4): 409-419.

Crouter, Ann C., S. MacDermid, S. McHale, & M. Perry-Jenkins. (1990). "Parental Monitoring and Perceptions of Children's School Performance and Conduct in Dual- and Single-Earner Families." *Developmental Psychology,* 26(4): 649-657.

Dornbusch, S. M., P. L. Ritter, P. H. Leiderman, D. F. Roberts, & M. J. Fraleigh. (1987). "The Relation of Parenting Style to Adolescent School Performance." *Child Development,* 58: 1244-1257.

Gibson, Margaret A., & Parminder K. Bhachu. (1988). "Ethnicity and School Performance: A Comparative Study of South Asian Pupils in Britain and America." *Ethnic and Racial Studies,* 11(3): 239-262.

Hirischi, T. (1969). *Causes of Delinquency.* Berkeley: University of California Press.

Jessor, R., & S. L. Jessor. (1977). *Problem Behavior and Psychosocial Development: A Longitudinal Study of Youth.* New York: Academic Press.

Kim, Bok-Lim C. (1980). *The Korean American Child at School and at Home: An Analysis of Interaction and Intervention through Groups.* Washington, DC: U.S. Department of Health, Education, and Welfare.

_____. (1983). "The Future of Korean American Children and Youth." In Don T. Nakanishi & Marsha H. Nakanishi, eds., *The Education of Asian and Pacific Americans: Historical Perspectives and Prescriptions for the Future.* Phoenix, AZ: Oryx Press.

Kim, Bok-Lim C., Michael R. Sawdy, & Barbara C. Meihoefer. (1982). "Facilitation Roles with Non-Native Korean American Children." *Social Work in Education,* 4(2): 17-33.

Kim, Sophia Kyung. (1992). "Parental Pressure Blamed for Cheating at Palos Verdes." *Korea Times* (English edition), March 16, pp. 1, 7.

Kim, L. C., & W. M. Hurh. (1985). "The Wives of Korean Small Businessmen in the U.S.: Business Involvement and Family Roles." In I. S. Lee, ed., *Korean American Women: Toward Self-Realization.* Mansfield, OH: Association of the Korean Christian Scholars in North America.

Kim, Yui-Kyung, Elaine H. Kim, Charles J. Kim, & In-Sook Hong. (1987). *Aidle Taemune: Mikuk Iminkwa Janyukyoyuk (For Children's Education: Korean Immigrants and Child-rearing).* Seoul, Korea: Yong Hak.

Lee, Julie & Virginia Cynn. (1991). "Issues in Counseling 1.5 Generation Korean Americans." In Courtland Lee & B. Richardson, eds., *Multicultural Issues in Counseling: New Approaches to Diversity.* Alexandria, VA: American Association for Counseling and Development.

Lee, Yong Sook. (1987). *Academic Success of East Asian Americans: An Ethnographic Comparative Study of East Asian American and Anglo American Academic Achievement.* Seoul: American Studies Institute, Seoul National University Press.

Lempers, J. D., D. Clark-Lempers, & R. L. Simons. (1989). "Economic Hardship, Parenting, and Distress in Adolescence." *Child Development*, 60: 25-39.

Lin, Chin-Yau & Victoria Fu. (1990). "A Comparison of Childrearing Practices among Chinese, Immigrant Chinese, and Caucasian-American Parents." *Child Development*, 61(1): 429-433.

Liu, W.T., Elena S. Yu, Ching-Fu Chang, & Marilyn Fernandez. (1990). "The Mental Health of Asian American Teenagers: A Research Challenge." In A. Stiffman & Larry E. Davis, eds., *Ethnic Issues in Adolescent Mental Health*. Newbury Park, CA: Sage Publications.

Loeber, Rolf & Thomas J. Dishion. (1983). "Early Predictors of Male Delinquency: A Review." *Psychological Bulletin*, 94: 68-99.

Maccoby, E. E., & J. A. Martin. (1983). "Socialization in the Context of the Family: Parent-Child Interaction." In E. M. Hetherington, ed., *Handbook of Child Psychology*, Vol. 4. New York: Wiley.

McCord, Joan. (1991). "Family Relationships, Juvenile Delinquency, and Adult Criminality." *Criminology*, 29(3): 397-417.

"Meeting the Challenge of High-Risk Asian Youth in the 90s." (1990). Conference Summary, Asian Youth Substance Abuse Project.

Montemayor, Raymond, & Daniel J. Flannery. (1991) "Parent-Adolescent Relations in Middle and Late Adolescence." In R. M. Lerner, A. C. Petersen, & J. Brooks-Gunn, eds., *Encyclopedia of Adolescence*, Vol. 2.

Mordkowitz, E. R., & H. P. Ginsburg. (1987). "The Academic Socialization of Successful Asian-American College Students." *Quarterly Newsletter of the Laboratory of Comparative Human Cognition*, 9: 85-91.

Nah, Kyung-Hee. (1993). "Perceived Problems and Service Delivery for Korean Immigrants." *Social Work*, 38(3): 289-296.

Ogbu, J. (1987). "Variability in Minority School Performance: A Problem in Search of an Explanation." *Anthropology and Education Quarterly*, 18(4): 312-334.

Pang, Valerie Ooka. (1991). "The Relationship of Test Anxiety and Math Achievement to Parental Values in Asian-American and European-American Middle School Students." *Journal of Research and Development in Education*, 24(4): 1-10.

Patterson, G. R. (1986). "Performance Models for Antisocial Boys." *American Psychologist*, 41: 432-444.

Patterson, G. R., & T. J. Dishion. (1985). "Contribution of Families and Peers to Delinquency." *Criminology*, 23: 63-79.

Patterson, G. R., & M. Stouthamer-Loeber. (1984). "The Correlation of Family Management Practices and Delinquency." *Child Development*, 55: 1320-1327.

Pettengill, Sandra M., & R. P. Rohner. (1985). "Korean American Adolescents' Perceptions of Parental Control, Parental Acceptance-Rejection and Parent-Adolescent Conflict." In Isabel R. Lagunes & Ype H. Poortinga, eds., *From a Different Perspective: Studies of Behavior Across Cultures*. Lisse, Germany: Swets & Zeitlinger.

Reid, John B., & G. R. Patterson. (1989). "The Development of Antisocial Behavior Patterns in Childhood and Adolescence." *European Journal of Personality*, 3: 107-119.

Rohner, E. C., & Rohner, R. P. (1983). "Socio-economic Status and Children's Perceptions of Maternal Acceptance-Rejection in Korean American Immigrant Families." In J. B. Deregowski, S. Dziurawiec, & R. C. Annis, eds., *Expiscations in Cross-Cultural Psychology*. Lisse, Germany: Swets and Zeitlinger.

Rohner, R. P. (1986). *The Warmth Dimension: Foundations of Parental Acceptance-Rejection Theory*. Beverly Hills, CA: Sage.

Rohner, R. P., Byungchai C. Hahn, & Uwe Koehn. (1992). "Occupational Mobility, Length of Residence, and Perceived Maternal Warmth among Korean Immigrant Families." *Journal of Cross-Cultural Psychology*, 366-376.

Rohner, R. P, Byungchai C. Hahn, & E. C. Rohner. (1980). "Social Class Differences in Perceived Parental Acceptance-Rejection and Self-Evaluation among Korean American Children." *Behavior Science Research*, 15(1): 55-66.

Rollins, Boyd C., & Darwin L. Thomas. (1979). "Parental Support, Power, and Control Techniques in the Socialization of Children." In W. R. Burr, Reuben Hill, F. I. Nye, & Ira L. Reiss, eds., *Contemporary Theories about the Family*, Vol. 1. New York: Free Press.

Rosenthal, D. A. (1987). "Ethnic Identity Development in Adolescents." In J. S. Phinney & M. J. Rotheram, eds., *Children's Ethnic Socialization*. Newbury Park, CA: Sage.

Schaefer, Earl S. (1965), "Children's Reports of Parental Behavior: An Inventory." *Child Development*, 36(1): 413-424.

Schneider, Barbara., & Yongsook Lee. (1990). "A Model for Academic Success: The School and Home Environment of East Asian Students." *Anthropology and Education Quarterly*, 21: 358-377.

Simons, R. L., J. F. Robertson, & W. R. Downs. (1989). "The Nature of the Association Between Parental Rejection and Delinquent Behavior." *Journal of Youth and Adolescence*, 18(3): 297-310.

Smith, E. M. J. (1985). "Ethnic Minorities: Life Stress, Social Support, and Mental Health Issues." *The Counseling Psychologist*, 13(4): 537-579.

Steinberg, L. (1991). "Parent-Adolescent Relations." In R. M. Lerner, A. C. Petersen, & J. Brooks-Gunn, eds., *Encyclopedia of Adolescence*, Vol. II.

Steinberg, L., Elmen, D. Julie & Nina S. Mounts. (1989). "Authoritative Parenting, Psychosocial Maturity, and Academic Success among Adolescents." *Child Development*, 60: 1424-1436.

Stevenson, Harold W., & Lee, Shin-ying. (1990). *Contexts of Achievement: A Study of American, Chinese, and Japanese Children, Monographs of the Society for Research in Child Development*, 55(1-2).

Strom, Robert, S. H. Park, & S. Daniels. (1987). "Child Rearing Dilemmas of Korean Immigrants to the United States." *Scientia-Paedagogica-Experimentalis*, 24(1): 91-102.

Sue, D. (1980). "Asian Americans." In N. D. Vacc & J.P. Wittmer, eds., *Let Me Be Me: Special Populations and the Helping Professional*, Muncie, IN: Accelerated Development.

Sue, D. W., & S. Sue. (1983). "Counseling Chinese Americans." In D. R. Atkinson, G. Morten, & D. W. Sue, eds., *Counseling American Minorities: A Cross-Cultural Perspective*. Dubuque, IA: Brown.

Sue, S., & N. Zane. (1985). "Academic Achievement and Socioemotional Adjustment among Chinese University Students." *Journal of Counseling Psychology*, 32(4): 570-579.

Trommsdorff, Gisela. (1985). "Some Comparative Aspects of Socialization in Japan and Germany." In I. R. Lagunes & Ype E. Poortinga, eds., *From a Different Perspective*. Lisse, Germany: Swets & Zeitlinger.

Windle, Michael. (1991). "Problem Behavior in Adolescence." In R. M. Lerner, A. C. Petersen, & J. Brooks-Gunn, eds., *Encyclopedia of Adolescence*, Vol. 2.

Yee, D. K. & C. Flanagan. (1985). "Family Environments and Self-Consciousness in Early Adolescence." *Journal of Early Adolescence*, 5(1): 59-68.

Yu, Eui-Young. (1986). "Juvenile Delinquency in the Korean Community of Los Angeles." *The Korea Times*, Los Angeles.

Yu, Kuen, & Luke Kim. (1983). "The Growth and Development of Korean American Children." In Gloria Powell, ed., *The Psychosocial Development of Minority Group Children*. New York: Brunner/Mazel.

16

Life Satisfaction of the Korean American Elderly[1]

Young I. Song

INTRODUCTION

The dramatic change in the American demographic structure has stimulated a growing awareness of the need for better understanding of the conditions and circumstances of older minority persons from different ethnic heritages. However, it is generally known that older minorities, especially the Asian American elderly, receive much less attention from both researchers and service providers. Asian American elderly problems and needs have oftentimes been ignored by gerontologists, social planners, and service providers.

Some early studies examined attempted to deal specifically with the problems of the Korean American elderly. But factors associated with life satisfaction among the Korean American aged have not been investigated. The case of the Korean American elderly, being one of the newer immigrant groups from Asia, is a prime example of this minimal attempt at identifying their individual characteristics and problems. Traditionally, care of the aged has not been a social problem in Korea because it has always been the responsibility of children to take care of their elders. Changing patterns of lifestyles among the Korean American elderly also affect their level of life satisfaction.

There is perhaps no other construct in gerontology that has been as widely investigated as life satisfaction among the aged (Palmore, 1968; Toseland & Rasch, 1980; Herzog and Rodgers, 1981; Lowry, 1984). Extensive investigations have been conducted regarding the biological, psychological and social correlates of an individual's well-being, of which life satisfaction is one of the major components (Mussen 1982; Veroff et al., 1981; Edwards & Klemmack, 1973). Evidence has shown that individual well-being is related to a variety of factors (Medley, 1976).

This chapter examines the relationship of the social-psychological factors of social activity, socioeconomic status, marital status, gender, health, religion, and reminiscence to the life satisfaction of the Korean American elderly. These variables were chosen because they are among the most salient predictors of life satisfaction (George & Bearon, 1980; Herzog & Rodgers, 1981). For the purpose of this study the selected variables are defined as follows:

1. Life satisfaction—the assessment of the overall conditions of one's life derived from a comparison of one's aspirations with one's actual achievements (Campbell et al., 1976).
2. Social activity—the level of activity with family and non-family.
3. Socioeconomic status—a gradated scale of income ranging from less than $5,000 to $30,000.
4. Health—defined by the individual through self-reports.
5. Marital status—defined in terms of whether an individual is single, married, divorced, or widowed.
6. Religiosity—defined in terms of how important the practice of religion and religious activities are to the individual.
7. Reminiscence—defined in terms of how important the process of reminiscing contributes to social functioning.

CONCEPTUAL FRAMEWORK

This chapter will be guided by activity theory (Havidhurst, 1968a, 1968b). This theory will provide an opportunity for the exploration of views of individual behavior in the later stages of the life cycle. Investigators of life satisfaction and well-being in older people have attempted to identify specific measures of life satisfaction by trying to systematically explain the social phenomena associated with the aging process through the theories of disengagement (Cumming & Henry, 1961) and activity. These are perhaps the two most widely used theories as prescriptions for aging.

The major tenet of disengagement theory states that aging is an inevitable process in which the individual and society make a gradual and mutual withdrawal from each other. This theory suggests that society must go on and that, for it to do so, older people must abandon their societal roles in order to prevent death from disrupting the normal functioning of society. As such, the elderly withdraw, younger individuals assume the roles abandoned by the elderly, and society continues (Manual, 1982).

Conversely, the activity view posits that the norms of middle age remain consistent throughout the later years of life, and that successful aging is dependent on the extent to which the roles and relationships of middle age can be sustained (Havighurst, 1968a, 1968b; Lemon, Bengston & Peterson, 1976). Thus, the major proposition of activity theory is that morale and life satisfaction are a function of continued active participation. Hence, the more meaningfully involved the elderly are, the more satisfied they are.

MEASURES OF LIFE SATISFACTION

There are a number of studies indicating that among older adults, current good health, secure socioeconomic standing, and high levels of social activity are associated with strong feelings of satisfaction (Toseland & Rasch, 1980; Herzog & Rodgers, 1981). Research into the social-psychological aspects of aging has been concerned with discovering factors associated with successful aging.

Okun et al. (1984) found that social activity is positively and significantly related to high levels of life satisfaction. In addition, researchers found that informal activities and activities with friends were not related to life satisfaction as consistently as formal activities and activities with neighbors. Lee and Lassey

(1980) concluded that regardless of the amount of interaction with relatives or neighbors, high levels of life satisfaction tended to increase when social activity involved club and church participation (Kivett, 1982; Ainlay & Smith, 1984).

Various studies supply a great deal of evidence that non-familial activity or social participation is a much stronger predictor of life satisfaction than is familial participation. Edwards & Klemmack (1973), and Lemon, Bengston & Peterson (1976) in their studies found no correlation between familial participation and life satisfaction. But Edwards & Klemmack (1973) did find nonfamilial participation to be their second best predictor of life satisfaction.

Another study has shown that religion plays an increasingly important role in the lives of the elderly and that indices of mental well-being such as happiness, feelings of usefulness, and personal adjustment increase with religious activity and interests (Koenig et al., 1988). Other researchers have found a positive relationship between religion and life satisfaction (Taylor, 1986; Thorsen & Cook, 1980).

It is believed that the thoughts and self-concepts of elderly persons, which tend to be dominated by events in the distant past such as their developmental years and early adulthood, contribute significantly to well-being in late adulthood (Merriam, 1980; Molinari & Reichlin, 1985). Researchers have found that reminiscing is positively correlated with successful aging as it assists in the maintenance of self-esteem, reaffirming a sense of identity, working through and mastering personal losses, and contributing positively to society (Merriam, 1980; Molinari & Reichlin, 1985).

Health is considered by many researchers to be the strongest predictor of life satisfaction (Lowry, 1984; Jackson et al., 1982a, 1982b; Kivett, 1982; Toseland & Rasch, 1980). The likelihood that one is very satisfied with life rises as personal health increases. Hence, it is clear that health status is the most important concern of older people as they evaluate their satisfaction with life. Coward and Kerchoff (1978) found that good physical health, the ability to function independently, participate in enjoyable social activities, and conserve income—all factors contributing to an overall sense of well-being—are central to life satisfaction. Those individuals with poor health have consistently shown lesser life satisfaction (Edwards & Klemmack, 1973; Palmore & Snyder, 1974).

THE KOREAN ELDERLY IN THE UNITED STATES

An important element in the adjustment of older Koreans who have migrated to the United States, namely their successful aging, has received relatively limited attention in the planning of community-based services for minority aging. Perhaps planners and service providers have tended to overlook the service needs of immigrant Korean elderly because of their comparatively small numbers when contrasted to other aging Americans, or by reason of the commonly held assumption that Asian Americans seem to take care of their own or rarely become social problems (Kalish & Yuen, 1971).

The 1990 U.S. Census (*Korea Times*, 1991) reported a total of 798,849 Koreans residing in the United States, of whom 36,747 persons, or 4.6%, were 60 years of age and older. Considering a continuous inflow of immigrants from Korea and a natural increase among Korean Americans, it is estimated that by the end of the century the Korean population in the United States will be over a million persons, of whom an estimated 46,000 (4.6%) will be 60 years and older.

In the United States, a country in which the national percentage of elderly persons aged 60 and older hovers around 15.7%, the 4.6% of Koreans who are elderly may not seem impressive. However, there seems to be a number of problems that could influence the life satisfaction of the Korean American elderly. The overall increase in the elderly population poses serious problems for the American youth-oriented society. Problems related to jobs, money, security, social relationships, and leisure time will likely become worse as the elderly population increases. Watson (1983) believes that the demand for public and private dollars will overburden our current welfare system and efforts to sustain the increasing proportion of functionally dependent people will fall short. Colen and Soto (1979) believe that social and human service agencies will be unable to meet the needs of the elderly and sustain the elderly in a manner that permits them to live out their lives in dignity.

Population growth is also manifested in the Korean elderly. Although problems for the elderly are very serious, they can be more serious for the Korean elderly because of their limited access to resources. A major concern of all people is satisfaction with life. Old age should be a time in life when one can reap the harvest of his/her efforts. What follows is a description of this study's methodology for taking a closer look at this important human condition.

METHODOLOGY

Respondents

The target population for this investigation were Korean persons aged 55 and older. The study was conducted in the San Francisco Bay Area. Of the 641 older Koreans from a list of three different locations of senior housing, and an up-to-date directory of Korean senior citizen associations of the San Francisco, Oakland, and San Jose areas, 150 were selected for the study. The sample was then stratified into the young-old, ages 55 to 74, and the old-old, those 75 and over. This stratification considers age as a significant variable of life satisfaction.

Instrumentation and Procedure

Data were collected by face-to-face interviews in the subjects' residential settings. The Life Satisfaction A and B Indexes were administered and demographic information was obtained from a separate questionnaire not included in the Life Satisfaction Indexes. The Life Satisfaction Index A (LSIA) provided a measure of life satisfaction (Neugarten et al., 1961). The Life Satisfaction Index B (LSIB) consists of 12 open-ended and checklist items that are scored on a three-point scale. The items in both these instruments are shown to reflect different components of life satisfaction. The respondents were given a general explanation by this researcher and/or by two research assistants who are Korean-speaking graduate students.

The sampling strategy chosen to select the subjects for the study was a systematic stratified random sampling. A random numbers table was used to select one out of every four names from the original 641 for study. Once selected, a two-by-two factorial design (table) was constructed. This stratification considers gender and age as significant variables of life satisfaction. The sample was divided into four categories: young-old and old-old men; and young-old and old-old women. A total of 150 elderly were approached to be interviewed: 18 could not be reached due to incorrect addresses while 16 could not be reached due to incorrect telephone numbers. In 14 cases, the interview was never completed. A final total sample of 104 was included in the data analysis reported in this chapter.

RESULTS AND DISCUSSION

The sample consisted of 58 women, 35 young-old and 23 old-old, and 46 males, 31 young-old and 15 old-old. The mean ages of the young-old women and men are fairly close, while the mean ages of the women in the old-old category is 3 years higher than the men. Marital status differs sharply between elderly men and women. Among the men, 82% (N = 38) were married, while only 31% (N = 18) of the women were married. The reasons for this result are that women tend not to remarry because of cultural constraints, and that they live longer than men. Another reason that the elderly women may remain unmarried may be the relatively short supply of available men from whom to choose a marital partner.

The median number of years of education completed by the respondents in the sample was middle school graduate. There were more subjects (N = 14) in the young-old category who received some college education than in the old-old category (N = 6). Furthermore seven of the respondents chose "no answer" for their highest grade of school completed and they did not specify what this meant when they were asked for clarification. These findings may indicate that some of the respondents may not have accurately reported their actual conditions or were too embarrassed to report that they had no formal educational background at all.

The median income of this sample was $500–$999 per month for both men and women. Within the young-old category, 54% (N = 36) had earnings in this income bracket. Within the old-old category 58% (N = 22) earned $500–$999 per month. Among the young-old category, 36% (N = 24) earned less than $500 per month. Many aged Americans consistently fall below the income of other age groups in the adult population. According to these findings the Korean elderly are no exception. Many Korean elderly have an income below $6,000 a year, which places them below the poverty level. However, these findings contradict the existing data that indicates that, as one gets older, one's income decreases.

Mean scores for life satisfaction A and life satisfaction B are displayed in Table 16.1. This table also summarizes the mean life satisfaction scores for the young-old and old-old categories by gender. Overall, men had higher life satisfaction A and B scores than women. Among the women, the young-old had higher life satisfaction than the old-old.

In order to examine the strengths of the correlations between the variables, a Pearson correlation coefficient matrix was computed. Table 16.2 shows the values reported in that matrix. Religion was strongly correlated to life satisfaction A ($r = .73$; $p < .05$). Further findings revealed that those individuals with higher religiosity mean scores had higher levels of life satisfaction than those with lower religiosity scores. This study also revealed that there are no significant gender differences in religiosity scores among females and males, regardless of age stratification.

Table 16.1
Life Satisfaction Mean Scores (Scale A and B) by Category and Gender

	Mean Scores (Scale A)				Mean Scores (Scale B)			
	N	Male	N	Female	N	Male	N	Female
Young-old (55–74)	31	27.98	35	24.59	31	14.82	35	13.69
Old-old (75 and over)	15	24.47	28	21.60	15	12.84	28	12.52

For the variable social activity, there was the positive relationship between life satisfaction and social activity. As shown in Table 16.2, the data revealed a marginally significant correlation to life satisfaction A ($r = .29$; $p < .05$), life satisfaction B ($r = .37$; $p < .05$). A one-way analysis of variance indicated that there was no significant difference among life satisfaction (A) scores according to social activity (F-value = 1.7347; $p > .05$) and life satisfaction (B) scores according to social activity (F-value = 1.4047; $p > .05$).

An unexpected finding in the study was the unusually strong relationship between life satisfaction and economic status. As shown in Table 16.2, the data revealed a strong correlation to life satisfaction A ($r = .83$; $p < .001$), life satisfaction B ($r = .62$; $p < .05$). Further, the one-way analysis revealed that there was significant difference among life satisfaction scores and socioeconomic status (F-value = 6.7147; $p < .05$). Research findings by Jackson et al. (1982b) support these results. These findings are consistent with those of Edwards & Klemmack (1973) who have consistently found socioeconomic status to be one of the strongest predictors of life satisfaction, even when all other factors are controlled.

Table 16.2 shows that socioeconomic status and religion were significantly correlated to life satisfaction. Socioeconomic status was most strongly correlated to life satisfaction A. This is followed by religion ($r = .73$; $p < .05$). Education showed a weak, but significant correlation to life satisfaction A ($r = .31$; $p < .05$). In life satisfaction B, the religion variable showed a strong correlation ($r = .85$; $p < .001$). Education showed a weak but significant correlation ($r = .20$; $p < .05$).

A t-test was computed to measure the differences in life satisfaction A, life satisfaction B, economic status and religion based upon the respondents' gender. No significant difference was found between men and women on the religion variable on the life satisfaction measures A and B. No significant difference was found between the men and women on the religion variable ($t = -1.73$; $p \geq .05$). The .05 significance level was determined in the t-test.

In order to assess the relationship between life satisfaction and social activity, socioeconomic status, marital status, age, health, religion, and reminiscence, a multiple regression analysis was utilized. The variables religion and socioeco-

Table 16.2
Pearson Correlation Coefficient Matrix

	Life Satis-faction A	Life Satis-faction B	Relig-ion	Socio-econo-mic status	Educa-tion	Social acti-vity	Remi-nis-cence	Health
Life satis-faction A	1.00							
Life satis-faction B	.78	1.00						
Religion	.73	.85	1.00					
Socio-econo-mic status	.83	.62	.17	1.00				
Education	.31	.20	-.15	.19	1.00			
Social activity	.29	.37	.28	.58	.24	1.00		
Reminis-cence	.33	.31	-.01	.26	.10	.34	1.00	
Health	.42	.34	.23	.51	.13	.50	.27	1.00

nomic status accounted for 68% of the variance in life satisfaction; significance at the .05 level was determined by the F-test (F = 6.8259). These variables were followed by reminiscence (R^2 = 39). In life satisfaction B, social activity and religion accounted for 53% of the variance.

A t-test was used to measure the impact of health on life satisfaction. The data showed that those individuals who reported they had health problems had lower levels of life satisfaction than those who did not have health problems (t = -5.71; p < .01). These findings are consistent with those of other researchers who have found health to have a significant impact on life satisfaction. (Lowry 1984; Toseland & Rasch 1980; Jackson et al. (1982a, 1982b).

Another finding revealed by these data is that reminiscence is a significant variable in explaining life satisfaction. Reminiscence appears to contribute to life satisfaction of the elderly in that it is sometimes used as a means to reduce stress and as a source for solving current life problems. Of the 104 subjects in the sample, 101 stated that they reminisced. Only three subjects stated that they did not reminisce. Further findings indicate that of the 101 subjects who reminisced, 94, or 91% of the sample, used reminiscence to solve current problems. More women (N = 66; 63.5%) than men (N = 48; 46.2%) used reminiscence to solve current problems.

CONCLUSIONS AND IMPLICATIONS

This section will focus upon the major conclusions of this analysis. Each hypothesis will be addressed and the implications of this study will also be discussed.

Hypothesis 1: There is no significant relationship between life satisfaction levels and social activity.

This hypothesis was rejected, which indicates that there is a significant relationship between life satisfaction and social activity. The Pearson correlation matrix indicated that social activity was positively correlated to life satisfaction A ($r = .29$; $p < .05$) and life satisfaction B ($r = .37$; $p < .05$). These findings are consistent with those of Okun et al. (1984), who found the strongest relationship between social activity and life satisfaction. This suggests that, for the Korean elderly, remaining socially active with family and friends provides stimulation and purpose to life that contributes to their psychological well-being. These findings also indicate that the elderly prefer continued engagement with members of society rather than being isolated and restricted from participating within the community. In addition, this study revealed that the young-old (55–74) had greater levels of social activity than old-old (75 and over), regardless of gender. However, it is interesting to note that in both categories, young-old and old-old men had higher levels of social activity ($r = .37$; $p < .001$) than did the women ($r = .19$; $p < .001$). One explanation for this difference in levels of social activity by gender is possibly that men may acquire larger social circles and friendship ties than do women.

The major factor that contributes to the low level of social activity among women is that they are expected to take care of grandchildren or other domestic chores. The majority of women (72%) indicated that they do not have much individual freedom other than once or twice a week when their adult children can take care of their own children. Many of these women (74%, N = 43) are reluctantly babysitting their grandchildren due to the lack of availability of other existing daycare resources.

The decline in social activity among the old-old (75 and over) is attributable to many factors, the major one being health status. Statistically, it has been found that good health declines with age (Stephens & Christianson, 1986). As a consequence, some elderly people develop health problems that limit their physical capabilities, and in some instances, the increase in health problems reduces their mental stamina and willpower to remain actively involved. This phenomenon appears to be more common for elderly women than for men.

These findings suggest that social activity can contribute to life satisfaction, in that it may reduce loneliness and isolation. One explanation for this finding suggests that among the Korean American elderly, satisfaction with life is not only determined by degree of involvement in social activity but by many other factors. Perhaps this is due to the fact that the Korean American population, in general, tends to have much less opportunity for socialization and social service programs for the Korean elderly than for their white counterparts (Stephens & Christianson, 1986).

Hypotheses II: There is no significant relationship between life satisfaction levels and socioeconomic status.

This hypothesis was rejected, which indicates that there is a significant relationship between socioeconomic status and life satisfaction A scores. This relationship was positively and very strongly correlated ($r = .83$; $p < .001$). It was found that the elderly with higher levels of socioeconomic status had higher levels of life satisfaction than those with low socioeconomic status. Further, the results of the one-way analysis of variance revealed that there was a significant difference among life satisfaction scores for socioeconomic status (F-value $= 6.7147$; $p < .05$). These findings suggest that economic level is a strong and salient predictor in explaining life satisfaction.

Hypothesis III: There is no significant relationship between life satisfaction levels and marital status.

This hypothesis was rejected. The findings of this study revealed that there is a significant relationship between marital status and life satisfaction A scores. There appears to be a significant difference among scores of life satisfaction B for marital status (F-value $= 3.8557$; $p < .05$). These results suggest that the companionship which marriage provides is important to life satisfaction, in that it may reduce loneliness.

Hypothesis IV: There is no significant relationship between life satisfaction levels and gender.

A significant relationship was found between life satisfaction A scores and gender. A possibility exists that the relationship between gender and life satisfaction is the result of an intervening variable. It was found in this study that greater social activity is positively correlated to life satisfaction. In addition, it was noted that men tend to have greater levels of social activity ($r = .54$; $p < .05$) than women ($r = .31$; $p < .05$). Consequently, it would appear that it is the increased levels of social activity that explain the significant difference between men and women in life satisfaction. These findings contradict other researchers who found no direct link between gender and life satisfaction (Liang 1982). Differences found in this study continue to reveal diversity among the elderly population.

Hypothesis V: There is no significant relationship between life satisfaction levels and health.

This hypothesis was rejected. This analysis indicates that health was a significant predictor of life satisfaction. The results showed that those elderly who indicated they had health problems had lower levels of life satisfaction than those who did not have health problems ($t = -5.31$; $p < .01$). The stepwise regression analyses that accounted for 43% of the variance also revealed that health is a significant factor in predicting life satisfaction.

Hypothesis VI: There is no significant relationship between life satisfaction and religion.

This hypothesis was rejected. The results of this study indicated that there was a very strong and positive relationship between life satisfaction A and religion (r = .73; p < .05). These results are consistent with other researchers who suggest that religiosity is important to the psychological well-being of minority elderly (Thorsen & Cook, 1980; Jackson et al., 1977).

Hypothesis VII: There is no significant relationship between life satisfaction levels and reminiscence.

This hypothesis was rejected. The results of this study indicated that reminiscence is a significant factor in explaining life satisfaction. Reminiscence appears to contribute to the psychological well-being of the elderly. This result is one of the interesting findings revealed by these data. The findings indicate that a preoccupation with nostalgia or reflections of the past is important to the Korean American elderly. In particular, almost every one of these study participants lived through the most tremendously dramatic periods in the history of Korea and additional drastic changes after immigrating to the United States. These Korean elderly people have survived through Japanese colonization, the Korean War, and painful memories as a people in a divided country.

Atchley (1977) proposes that an increased incidence of reminiscing occurs with advanced aging. This is certainly true for the Korean elderly who have a great repertoire of past experiences, especially events back in Korea. These findings could be a significant contribution in that they provide greater information about the utility of reminiscing to the well-being of this particular population. One can suggest that increased incidence of reminiscing may contribute, in some instances, to a decrease in depressive thoughts caused by language and cultural barriers and may enhance expressions of serenity.

In conclusion, the findings of this study support the basic tenets of activity theory, in that the more meaningfully involved the elderly are, the higher life satisfaction can be achieved. Then, it is very important that programs using the Korean language be created for the Korean elderly to foster continued engagement in a variety of meaningful, culturally sensitive activities in order to maximize emotional well-being or life satisfaction. In such activities, the Korean elderly can have an opportunity for socialization with other Korean groups. There are tremendous needs for programs to assist the Korean elderly person in adjusting to major changes associated with the aging process, such as loss of friends.

Additionally, Korean elderly have great difficulties in adjusting to the new cultural environment in the United States, such as their lack of familiarity with the social system, existing services, and the dominant language as well as their loss of status due to immigration and aging. There is also a further need for programs to tap the reservoir of skills, talent, and knowledge that Korean elderly persons have so that they can continue to utilize their capacities and potentials for achieving self-actualization and contributing to the Korean American communities and society at large.

The findings suggest that active involvement in the church and other religious activities is extremely valuable, as such religious involvement can create social acceptance and approval, and minority elderly may feel a great need to belong. Korean churches have become the focal points of communal interaction, providing a variety of social and psychological functions. Especially for the elderly Koreans, church is the principal place of social activity. In other words, the Korean American elderly place unusually strong emphasis on active participation in the church because involvement is not just for religious activities but also for social and cultural activities. This study provides additional evidence to dispute the theoretical contention that disengagement must take place in order for one to successfully age. No empirical evidence found in this study to support the tenets of disengagement theory (Lowenthal & Boler, 1965).

Since these results indicate that religion significantly contributes to the life satisfaction of the Korean American elderly, churches need to serve as a crucial resource in enabling the Korean American elderly to cope with the oppressive forces of discrimination caused by racism and ageism. Churches can also serve as a supportive network for the development of leadership for this subpopulation, in providing opportunity for validation of self-esteem, and in offering psychological and spiritual encouragement and hope for a more dignified life.

Some may view the need to explore social support in relation to life satisfaction among Korean American elderly as unwarranted because of the existence of informal social support. In the Korean family, strong family traditions and the influence of Confucianism may be seen as a buffer to prevent the potential for disrespect. In actuality, overworked adult children in the Korean immigrant community do not have time to provide the much needed emotional, social, and financial support for their elderly parents. Excessive work patterns of Korean immigrants may cause another serious problem for the elderly. Many adult children do not have time to fill any of these supporting roles. Without that support, the elderly can easily fail, because they are too fragile to cope with the difficulties caused by their aging and cultural differences.

In addition, this study suggests that more outreach is needed to assist the Korean American elderly in utilizing many existing facilities and services where they have been ignored or excluded historically. Efforts should also be made to furnish more services and programs in or near the areas where large concentrations of Korean Americans reside and near to public transportation. Very often Korean elderly people cannot get their full benefits because those programs are often inaccessible, impersonal, and inadequate. This is particularly true with the Korean American elderly who may experience difficulty in achieving access to existing services. Jackson (1980) and Liu and Yu (1985) note that minority elderly are singled out for differential and inferior treatment.

A further major implication of this study is the need to improve programs related to income security. The study indicates that economic status is the strongest predictor of the level of life satisfaction. These findings suggest several possible explanations. One may be the sociocultural circumstances of the elderly in the sample. It could be the case that these Korean American elderly have not been smoothly integrated into the new life in America, with the extremely limited amount of resources they have to maintain self-worth. Korean American elderly turn to economic security mainly because of their disadvantages in society. Most of them cannot find levels of social status similar to the majority elderly in any other areas. Korean American elderly believe that their language and cultural barriers have less serious negative effects on them if they have acquired economic security. As for other subgroups among the Korean American community, other ways to achieve perceived high social status appear to be virtually non-existent. For survival in the new land, they are apt to place economic survival above other issues such as social standing among the majority population in the larger community.

This chapter has also clearly identified some important factors of life satisfaction among the Korean American elderly that have implications for helping professionals and researchers. First, the growing number of Korean elderly people requires that individuals who serve the elderly take a greater interest in understanding and serving this special minority among minority groups. A person who serves the Korean American elderly must go further than just understanding the basic needs of the client in order to be effective. The professional must be knowledgeable and familiar with certain significant cultural patterns, beliefs, norms, and lifestyles that are inherent within the Korean community.

NOTE

1. From Young In Song, "Life Satisfaction of the Korean American Elderly." *Korea Journal of Population and Development*, 21 (2). Reprinted with permission.

REFERENCES

Ainlay, Stephen C., & Randall D. Smith. (1984). "Aging and Religious Participation." *Journal of Gerontology*, 39: 357-363.

Atchley, Robert C. (1977). *The Social Forces in Later Life: An Introduction to Social Gerontology*. Belmont, CA: Wadsworth.

Campbell, A., P. Converse, & W. Rogers. (1976). *The Quality of an American Life*. New York: Russell Sage Foundation.

Colen, J. N., & D. L. Soto. (1979). *Service Delivery to Aged Minorities: Techniques of Successful Programs*. Sacramento: California State University.

Coward, M. D., & N. Kerchoff. (1978). "Relationships of Demographic Variables and Mental Health Indices to Satisfaction and Functioning." Technical Memo (NIH Grant #20707), Survey Research Center.

Cumming, E., & W. Henry. (1961). *Growing Old*. New York: Basic Books.

Edwards, J. N., & D. L. Klemmack. (1973). "Correlates of Life Satisfaction: A Re-Examination." *Journal of Gerontology*, 28: 497-502.

George, Linda, & Lucille B. Bearon. (1980). *Quality of Life in Older People: Meaning and Measurement*. New York: Human Sciences Press.

Havighurst, R. J. (1968a). "A Social-Psychological Perspective on Aging." *Gerontologist*, 8: 67-71.

_____. (1968b). "Personality and Patterns of Aging." *Gerontologist*, 8: 20-23.

Herzog, Anna, & Wilard Rodgers. (1981). "The Structure of Subjective Well-Being in Different Age Groups." *Journal of Gerontology*, 36(4): 472-479.

Jackson, James S., Linda M. Chatters, & Harold Neighbors. (1982a). "The Mental Health Status of Older Black Americans: A National Study." *Black Scholar*, 13: 21-35.

Jackson, J. J. (1980). *Minorities and Aging*. Belmont, CA: Wadsworth.

Jackson, J. S., J. D. Bacon, & J. Peterson. (1977). "Life Satisfaction Among Black Urban Elderly." *Journal of Aging and Human Development*, 8: 169-177.

Jackson, Maurice, Bohdan Kolodz, & James L. Wood. (1982b). "To Be Old and Black: The Case for Double Jeopardy on Income and Health." In Ron C. Manuel, ed., *Minority Aging: Sociological and Social Psychological Issues*. Westport, CT: Greenwood Press.

Kalish, R., & S. Yuen. (1971). "Americans of East Asian Ancestry: Aging and the Aged." *Gerontologist*, 11: 37.

Kivett, Vira S. (1982). "The Importance of Race to the Life Situation of the Rural Elderly." *The Black Scholar*, 13: 13-21.

Koenig, Harold, James Kvale, & Carolyn Ferrel. (1988). "Religion and Well-Being in Later Life." *Gerontologist*, 28: 18-27.

Korea Times. (1991). San Francisco edition, June 13, p. 1.

Lee, Gary R., & Marie L. Lassey. (1980). "Rural-Urban Differences Among the Elderly: Economic, Social and Subjective Factors." *Journal of Social Issues*, 36(2): 62-71.

Lemon, Bruce, Vern Bengston, & James Peterson. (1976). "An Exploration of the Activity Theory of Aging: Activity Types and Life Satisfaction Among In-Movers for a Retirement Community." In Cary S. Kart & Barbara B. Manard, eds., *Aging in America*. New York: Alfred A. Knopf.

Liang, Jersey. (1982). "Sex Differences in Life Satisfaction Among the Elderly." *Journal of Gerontology*, 31(1): 100-108.

Liu, W. T., & E. Yu. (1985). "Asian/Pacific American Elderly: Morality Differentials, Health Status, and Use of Health Services." *Journal of Applied Gerontology*, 4(1): 35-64.

Lowenthal, M., & D. Boler. (1965). "Voluntary versus Involuntary Social Withdrawal." *Journal of Gerontology*, 20: 363-371.

Lowry, Janet Huber. (1984). "Life Satisfaction Time Components Among the Elderly." *Research on Aging*, 6(3): 417-431.

Manuel, Ron C. (1982). "The Study of the Minority Aged in Historical Perspective." In Ron C. Manuel, ed., *Minority Aging: Sociological and Social Psychological Issues*. Westport, CT: Greenwood Press.

Medley, Morris L. (1976). "Satisfaction with Life Among Persons 65 Years and Older." *Journal of Gerontology*, 31: 448-455.

Merriam, S. (1980). "The Concept and Function of Reminiscences: A Review of the Research." *Gerontologist*, 20: 604-609.

Molinari, V., & R. Reichlin. (1985). "Life Review Reminiscence in the Elderly: A Review of the Literature." *International Journal of Aging and Human Development*, 20: 81-91.

Mussen, C., et al. (1982). "Early Antecedents of Life Satisfaction." *Journal of Gerontology*, 28: 629-634.

Neugarten, B., R. Havighurst, & S. Tobin. (1961). "The Measurement of Life Satisfaction." *Journal of Gerontology*, 16: 134-143

Okun, A., W. Stock, M. J. Haring, & R. Witter. (1984). "The Social Activity/Subjective Well-Being Relation." *Research on Aging*, 6(1): 36-42.

Palmore, E. (1968). "The Effects of Aging on Activities and Attitudes." *Gerontologist*, 8: 259-263.

Palmore, E., & E. Snyder. (1974). "Correlates of Life Satisfaction Among the Aged." *Journal of Gerontology*, 29: 454-458.

Stephens, S., & J. Christianson. (1986). *Informal Care of the Elderly*. Lexington, MA: D. C. Heath.

Taylor, Robert. (1986). "Religious Participation Among Elderly Blacks." *Gerontologist*, 26: 630-636.

Thorsen, James A, & Thomas Cook. (1980). *Spiritual Well-Being of the Elderly*. Atlanta, GA: Charles C. Thomas.

Toseland, Ron, & J. Rasch. (1980). "Correlates of Life Satisfaction: An AID Analysis." *International Journal of Aging and Human Development*, 10(2): 203.

Veroff, Joseph, E. Dowane, & R. A. Kulka. (1981). *The Inner American: A Self Portrait from 1957 to 1976*. New York: Basic Books.

Watson, Wilbur H. (1983). "Selected Demographics and Social Aspects of Older Blacks: An Analysis with Policy Implications." In R. L. McNeely & John L. Colen, eds., *Aging in Minority Groups*. Beverly Hills, CA: Sage Publications.

MENTAL HEALTH ISSUES

Korean immigrant families face multiple problems in adjusting their lives to a new cultural and socioeconomic environment, and in the process they experience enormous emotional and psychological strain. The following two chapters in Part Six, therefore, focus on mental health issues relevant to Korean American families and women, including the implications for clinical treatment of mental problems.

Luke I. Kim provides a comprehensive picture of "The Mental Health of Korean American Women." His work shows that Korean American women, as adult immigrants, are generally resourceful, adaptable, and resilient people who are strong in survival skills and determined to succeed in fulfilling their American dreams, for both themselves and their children. However, they experience psychological strain and anxiety, and they feel that they are paying too high a price for a comfortable life. Below the surface are tensions and conflict with regard to changing gender roles in marriage and in relationship with the rapid Americanization of the younger generation.

"Hwa-Byung" has been identified as a culture-bound syndrome not classifiable according to the prevailing Western psychiatric diagnostic system. In "Korean Women's Hwa-Byung: Clinical Issues and Implications for Treatment," Mikyong Kim-Goh identifies common precipitating factors, help-seeking patterns, clinical courses, and treatment outcomes of Korean American women with Hwa-Byung and illustrates how they relate to contemporary mental health treatment practices.

17

The Mental Health of Korean American Women

Luke I. Kim

What can we say about the mental health of Korean immigrant women in the United States? How does their mental health compare with that of women in Korea? Is the stress of cultural adjustment and the pressures of economic survival and family changes so great that the prevalence of psychological or psychiatric problems among Korean American women may be greater than those among women in Korea? No studies have been conducted to answer these questions. However, a higher incidence of mental disorders was discovered among immigrant populations in an early study of Eastern Europeans who migrated to England and the United States after World War II (Murphy, 1965). Also, the prevalence of major depression and/or post-traumatic stress syndrome among Vietnamese and Cambodian women in the United States is close to 70% of the ethnic population (Flaskerud & Anh, 1988).

There have been few systematic surveys or epidemiological studies done on the mental health and psychological well-being of Korean American women in the United States. The only exceptions are survey studies on Korean immigrants in Los Angeles (1984), and Chicago (1987, 1988) conducted by Professors Won Moo Hurh and Kwang Chung Kim of Western Illinois University. They were not prevalence or diagnostic studies of mental health, but interview studies attempting to correlate among mental health and three social variables: (1) social/cultural adaptation (assimilation and ethnic attachment), (2) family relations, and (3) work-related experiences (income earning and job satisfaction). I will summarize the methodology and findings of the studies in some detail because there are few other research data available.

For the survey study (Hurh & Kim, 1987, 1988), a list of 11,726 Korean households was compiled as the target population based on the 1985 Korean Community Directory of Chicago. A random sample of 1,000 households was selected from the master list as prospective respondents. Letters were mailed to them requesting their cooperation. Out of this group, a total of 622 (334 men, 288 women) were selected as study subjects. Twenty-five trained interviewers made arrangements for appointments, either at home or in their work places, and conducted the interviews. The one-and-a-half-hour structured interviews with each subject included, among other things, administering four measuring scales regarding health, depression, and sense of well-being (The Center for Epidemiological Studies—Depression Scale, The Health Opinion Survey, the Memorial University of Newfoundland Scale of Happiness, and the Cantril Self-Anchoring Striving Scale).

The study produced many interesting findings, but discussion will be limited to the findings related to women. Information based on the qualitative analysis of interviewers' comments will be reviewed first.

After each interview, the interviewers were instructed to write down their observations, feelings, and opinions about the interviewing process and sociopsychological problems of the family presented. Then the interviewers' comments were categorized into three mental health profiles in terms of a general sense of mental well-being: poor, medium, and good mental health. This categorization was based on the interviewer's a subjective and impressionistic review and thus, is not suitable for statistical analysis.

Poor Mental Health (PMH) Profile (comments on 15 cases): example

Mrs. K. was in the poorest mental health condition I have ever observed. Her body was covered with scars and bruises resulting from her husband's beatings. He battered her because she didn't work, and even when she worked, he still continued to beat her, saying that she didn't earn enough. "If you want to file divorce, go ahead, but I am not going to divorce you," said her husband. Mrs. K. felt she was deceived into marrying him and everyday has been a hell ever since. She told me that she wanted to take revenge but did not know how.

Medium Mental Health (MMH) Profile (comments on 58 cases): example

Mrs. Y's husband owned and managed a laundry shop, but he was killed by a robber one night. With 3 children she had to struggle hard to survive—physical strain and mental stress during the past several years. Eventually she reopened the laundry shop and life seemed to return to somewhat normal for Mrs. Y and her children. Mrs. Y said that she would have never made it without social supports from relatives, her children, and, most of all, her faith in God.

Good Mental Health (GMH) Profile (comments on 37 cases): example

Mrs. L was a very pleasant person to talk to—she was friendly and always smiling. Her husband was employed in a skilled occupation with a good income. They were saving money to open a business for themselves someday. They have two small children and Mr. L's parents were also living with them. Since they had a one-bedroom apartment, the bedroom was given to the grandparents and the rest of the family used the living room for sleeping. Despite these living conditions, Mrs. L seemed to be very satisfied with life and optimistic about their future. Especially the family members, including her in-laws, appear to get along well. In fact, her family reminded of me an ideal family with warmth and laughter. She expressed that her life in America is better than in Korea, because in America, honest hard work is a more important factor than education-social status for earning money.

In reviewing the mental health profiles in each of the three categories, the following salient features emerged:

Poor mental health category: The immigrants' mental health is most vulnerable in the early stage (1–2 years) of their migration (the "exigency" stage). Commonly observed factors are: economic hardship, English language problems, family conflicts, social isolation, and family violence. Usually women are more vulnerable in family conflicts.

Medium Mental Health category: In contrast to the PMH group (i.e., financial, job, and language problems), psychological factors predominate in this group. Job and economic factors have improved but marital or intergenerational family conflicts may surface. Social network and support (family, kin, friends, fellow Koreans) appear to be an important factor for positive mental health. Ethnic attachment becomes increasingly important, even to the extent that many of the respondents entertain the thought of returning to Korea. As the length of stay in the United States extends, the source of mental stress varies and has a differential impact on the immigrants. The sense of existential ambivalence ("Did I make a mistake in migrating to this country?") might have affected the male immigrants more seriously than female immigrants. Male immigrants seem to be more vulnerable to the existential uprooting (the loss of social belonging, status. and power) than are female immigrants.

Good Mental Health category: This group shows a high degree of expressed or observed life satisfaction. With few exceptions, most of the respondents in this category have been in the United States for ten years or longer. A majority of them at least have no perceived financial stress, and relatively no problem with language. Also they show: (1) a lack of existential ambivalence, and an optimistic definition of their life situation, (2) good family relations and social supports, (3) active involvement in the Korean American community, and (4) social interaction with Americans.

Unfortunately, the interviewers did not make observational comments on all study subject families. Therefore, not all subjects could be categorized, making it difficult to estimate what percentage of the study subjects is represented in each mental health category. However, the above described vignettes provide some picture of the kind of mental health problems the families presented.

Information on the quantitative data with regard to general life satisfaction is interesting and informative. The findings are as follows:

A question was asked, "Taking everything into consideration, how well are you generally satisfied with your immigrant life?" The respondents (male and female) indicated that they are very satisfied (11%); somewhat satisfied (40.7%); and only 10.1% of the respondents indicated dissatisfaction. The remainder (37.3%) fell in the middle, that is "sometimes satisfied, other times dissatisfied."

In response to another question about life satisfaction using a scale of 0 to 10, with 10 representing the top, only 10.5% of the respondents indicated less than the mid-point value 5, and about 62% indicated more than the value of 6 in the scale. However, as we will discuss later, the life satisfaction appears to vary depending on the stage of immigration in this country.

Surprisingly, however, the mean score of overall demoralization measured by the Studies Depression Scale is moderately high: 12.32 (SD = 7.82) for men, and 12.88 (SD = 9.53) for females. These scores are 3–4 points higher than for white Americans and other Asian Americans (Kuo, 1984). It suggests that, while most Korean immigrants feel relatively satisfied with their lives, they do experience a moderate degree of stress and demoralization.

PSYCHOSOCIAL VARIABLES AND MENTAL HEALTH

Of the psychosocial variables examined, the work-related variables (i.e., income earning and job satisfaction) are the strongest correlates of the male respondents' mental health. To a lesser degree, family life satisfaction is also positively related to the men's mental health. However, except for the variables of association with Korean friends and regular reading of American newspapers, the sociocultural adaptation variables in general (ethnic attachment and assimilation) have little effect on the mental health of the male subjects.

For the female subjects, married status, high levels of education, and occupation have high positive correlation with their mental health. However, unlike the male subjects, family-life satisfaction and ethnic attachment variables (Korean church affiliation, kinship contact, Korean neighbors, regular reading of Korean newspapers), are found to be moderately correlated with the female's mental health. Even for the employed women, the effect of work-related variables on their mental health is more limited and different than that of their male counterparts. In fact, high individual earnings are negatively associated with the mental well-being of employed women, whereas the opposite is true for the employed men. Therefore, the mental health correlates of Korean female immigrants are far more complex than initially assumed.

Professors Hurh and Kim interpreted the interesting findings as follows:

Most of the employed wives carry a double-burden of performing the household tasks and working outside home due to the immigrants life conditions (financial needs and opportunity) and persistence of the traditional sex-role ideology (woman as a homemaker). Hence, the immigrant wives' employment outside the home means additional work, which in most cases, bring no intrinsic reward. This may explain why the employed females complain of more somatic impairment than the non-employed female. A little additional income does not seem to compensate her additional work which is usually secondary to her husband's.

The study shows that two-thirds (68.8%) of the female respondents were found to be currently employed. Of the study sample, 63% were represented by the "two-income family." Only 21.5% of them were one-income (husband alone). A total of 7.4% of the respondents indicated that the wife was the only employed person in the family. The employed husbands and wives were found to work usually more than 45 hours a week.

The data did not show a breakdown of the nature of employment. However, it is assumed that to run a small family business, such as dry-cleaning shop, store, or grocery, not only the women but the whole family, including teenage children, may work.

Given this high rate of labor participation, how do the Korean immigrants feel about their employment and family life? About 80% of the all respondents said that they feel satisfied with their family life because of a higher living standard, especially with dual-employment income. Other positive factors mentioned were: convenient living facilities, the quality of family relations, good food, and educational opportunities for children.

However, at the same time, 63% of the respondents expressed negative and dissatisfied aspects of their family life. The most frequently mentioned were time pressure, heavy work load, physical and psychological exhaustion, little time to rest, worrying about the Americanization of their children, limited opportunities for social activities, conflict in marriage, and problems with in-laws. Many feel that they are paying too high a price for the quality of life. Again, we can say that the Korean immigrants are generally satisfied but pay a high price with considerable stress and strain.

The above data were collected 10 years ago. However, the Los Angeles riots in April 1992 decimated Koreatown and devastated Korean Americans in Los Angeles. Hate crimes against Korean immigrants spread across the country. Many Korean Americans are now dismayed, more demoralized, and have lost confidence in American life, compared to 8 years ago when the study was conducted.

STAGES OF ADJUSTMENT OF MIGRATION

The empirical data indicate the following stages of post-migration adjustment and level of life satisfaction over time (Hurh & Kim 1988):

1. The exigency stage: an initial vulnerable period (first one or two years) due to culture shock, language problems, jobs, and struggle for survival.
2. The resolution and optimism stage: mental health and life satisfaction improve with more confidence and mastery gained in the new environment.
3. The stagnation stage: life satisfaction reached a plateau around the fifteenth year or thereabouts after migration. Life satisfaction remains flat or even decreases somewhat thereafter. Old-timer residents exist in a state of "existential limbo." They may feel that they have not been able to realize their American dreams.

In the stage of stagnation, some Korean Americans have attained and secured a good professional career, and yet they are unhappy or feel their lives to be meaningless. They may also experience the "glass ceiling" phenomenon and institutional racism in their work environment. Many of them want to go back to Korea for better opportunities and to make professional contributions to the Korean society. I know several immigrant couples who are considering going back to Korea. Quite often, husbands wish to return to Korea, but wives are reluctant to go back. Some of the wives say that they have more freedom, choices, and autonomy in this country than living in Korea, and that they are afraid of going back to the more male-dominant and hierarchical Korean society.

SOURCES OF STRESS

What are the sources of stress for Korean American women in this country? What kind of mental health problems do they have? What kind of professional help are they seeking, and what kind of help is being offered to them?

In order to gain a wider perspective on the mental health issues of Korean American women, I conducted a telephone interview survey with 14 Korean American psychotherapists on the East coast, West coast, and the Midwest.

They are psychiatrists, psychoanalysts, clinical psychologists, psychiatric social workers (S. Chang, M. Chang, M. C. Cho, C. S. Chung, C. Chung, B. L. Kim, W. J. Kim, S. C. Kim, K. O. Kim, H. A. Kim, C. H. Lee, S. E. Lee, Y. S. Park, and D. S. Rue, personal communications, February 1993). They have been working actively with Korean American women in their clinical practice. Some of them are in private practice, some in public mental health clinics, two work with shelter programs for Asian battered women, and one works at a child guidance center.

The survey of these 14 therapists indicates some of the common difficulties observed among Korean American women who seek help from therapists. Of course, problems of individuals are all different, and therefore we have to individualize each clinical case.

Psychiatrists are more likely to see disturbed clients who need medication as well as psychotherapy. They cite anxiety, panic attacks, depression, phobia, somatization, and obsessive-compulsive traits as common presenting symptoms. They also see cases of more serious mental disorders, such as schizophrenia, manic depressive mood disorder, and major depression with psychotic features.

The surveyed psychiatrists said that the ratio of their clients is two-thirds women and one-third men. One-third of the clients receive psychotropic medication. Types of therapy are 30% crisis intervention, 30% short-term or intermediate-term psychotherapy, and 10% long-term psychotherapy or psychoanalysis.

Frequent sources of stress are cultural and gender-role conflicts in the marriage, serious communication problems with spouse and children, and emotional isolation. Some second-generation young adult Korean Americans (age 20–30 years old) seek help for dealing with their struggle with identity issues and their conflicts with Korean parents and their values. For long-term therapy, problems areas are achievement failure, career conflict, and issues of intimacy and sexuality.

Female therapists cited the following factors as the most frequent sources of stress among Korean American women: powerlessness, helplessness, victimization, and spousal abuse, as well as lack of support and understanding by spouse. Some of the victimized women feel powerless but at the same time have difficulties dealing with their own anger and aggressive feelings. Also, those women who had a history of early childhood deprivation and had depended on husbands emotionally tend to experience more emotional disturbance and anxiety when their husbands are demoralized and feel despair in their newly adopted country.

Two social workers (M. Kim & K. O. Kim, personal communications, February 1993) working with battered wives or sexually abused women said that there are cases of incest and child molestation committed by Korean men. This is contrary to a perception that there are no or very few cases of incest or child molestation among Asians or Koreans. They say that it is such a taboo that nobody wants to talk about it.

Teenage gangs, violence, drugs, and school drop-out are increasing among Korean American teenagers, especially in Los Angeles and New York. The parents are so busy with making a living that they do not have time to supervise children, and the children are more or less on their own. They have serious latchkey problems, and parents have lost control over the children (Yu, & Kim, 1983; M. Chang, personal communication, 1993).

VULNERABILITY AND RESILIENCY

The intensity of the stressful events and the individual's coping skills determine the impact of the stressful events on the individual's functioning. The outcome is also affected by two additional factors: the person's vulnerability and resilience. One's resiliency buffers the negative impact of stress.

Protective factors of resilience are (1) personal resources, such as intelligence, education, social skills, and coping strengths, (2) social support from family and extended family, (3) role models available who exhibit positive coping behaviors, and (4) community support and religious beliefs.

Having gone through war and refugee life experiences, Koreans are strong in their survival skills and their resiliency in the face of an adverse environment. Also, Korean American immigrant women have some advantage in that they are relatively well educated as an immigrant group, have a strong work ethic, and have support from relatives who are already in the United States. Moreover, many of them attend Korean Christian churches that provides them with additional support.

THE ROLE OF THE KOREAN CHRISTIAN CHURCH

An amazing phenomenon is that Korean ethnic churches are springing up all over the country. It is estimated that there are close to 2,000 Korean ethnic churches in the United States. Seventy-seven percent of Korean immigrants attend Korean churches (Hurh & Kim, 1988). Korean church plays an important role as an extended family. Not only does the church offer opportunity for spiritual growth, but it also provides fellowship and emotional and social support. People exchange the latest information on jobs, housing, school, recreation, and the like. Many churches also offer classes on Korean language and culture for the younger generation.

All the therapists surveyed indicated that church is an important part of Korean American life. They supported affirmatively the role that the church plays in providing spiritual, emotional and social support, and networking. Some therapists indicated, however, that, for more serious or deeper mental health problems, church may impede the healing process by fostering denial mechanisms or offering simple magical solutions to mental health problems ("God will take care of me," "All I need is to pray more") and by depriving members of the opportunities to confront the problem and grow in their inner resources and problem-solving skills.

HELP-SEEKING BEHAVIOR IN MENTAL HEALTH

As is the case with other Asian American clients, Korean women usually do not seek mental health professional treatment until the problem reaches a crisis point. By the time they come to see mental health professionals, they have gone through and exhausted all other avenues, such as prayer meetings, pastors, acupuncture and herbal medicine, and internist medical doctors. They come to the mental health professional as a last resort.

By the time they come to mental health professionals, they are very disturbed and in a crisis. They want a quick fix for their problems. They hope that the therapist can solve the problem for them. They are not familiar with the concept of psychotherapy or counseling, and they drop out of counseling after one or two sessions, unless they receive some concrete benefit with immediate symptom relief. Furthermore, they often seek medications. Therapists need to educate clients about psychotherapy and counseling.

The surveyed therapists indicate that self-referred Korean American clients are few in number; and the great majority of the clients are referred by court, community agencies, school, law enforcement agencies, or by family.

LOS ANGELES RIOTS AND THE MENTAL HEALTH OF KOREAN AMERICANS

The Los Angeles riots in April 1992 played havoc with Korean Americans. About 2,200 small businesses owned by Korean Americans in Los Angeles were burned and destroyed. Korean Americans were targeted as a scapegoat by rioters who vented their frustrations and anger over their lives in inner city poverty and neglect. The media further inflamed the problem by choosing to focus on the Korean-black conflict rather than addressing the main cause: demoralization caused by inner-city poverty and decay.

Many of the Korean American victims were so shocked and devastated by the destruction that they were totally paralyzed. They had lost everything—financially and psychologically. Right after the riots, Korean American psychiatrists, psychologists, clinical social workers, and volunteers, under contract to the Federal Emergency Management Agency (FEMA), offered on-site emotional debriefing and counseling. Also, the clinical staff of the Los Angeles Asian Pacific Counseling Center responded to emergency situations and provided educational and outreach activities. Many victims were initially skeptical of the usefulness of counseling, saying that what they needed was financial assistance and rehabilitation, not psychological counseling. Nevertheless, about 100 to 150 Korean American victims were seen by the clinicians. Eighty percent of them experienced severe insomnia, hyperarousal, anxiety, and somatic symptoms. These symptoms resembled post-traumatic stress syndrome. Group sessions were offered to them to help desensitize their panic and anxiety. Many of them were helped significantly by anti-anxiety medications and sleeping pills. Some of them also suffered agitated depression following the initial shock (M. C. Cho & C. Chung, personal communication, February 1993).

Rehabilitation of the Los Angeles Koreatown, as well as individual family businesses, will take a long time. Government financial assistance and insurance payments are slow and are stalled in a bureaucratic mess. The majority of the victims have not yet recovered financially and emotionally, and have not been able to reestablish their businesses. At this time of writing, more than one year later, only 25% of them had resumed their business activities. Many were bankrupt, and others had left Los Angeles and moved to other states.

Clinicians also observed that more marital problems surfaced after the riots. The victims became more irritable and agitated, and many exploded in temper, causing more family conflicts. Husbands and wives blamed each other for their plight. Some of them are now being seen at the Asian Pacific Counseling Center for further therapy and counseling.

SOME PSYCHOLOGICAL ISSUES FOR KOREAN AMERICAN WOMEN

Changing Roles in Marriage

In traditional Asian countries, culture has been heavily influenced by Confucian teaching. According to Confucianism, women are to follow "three obediences"—to obey father at home, husband after marriage, and sons when widowed. Additionally the Confucian teaching promoted "Four Virtues": chastity, reticence, a pleasing manner, and domestic skills (McGoldrick et al., 1989). However, modernization with western influences in Korea has drastically changed women's role for the last two decades, although many remnants of traditional teachings linger on. Also, one needs to be reminded that although there is an external or formal appearance of women's propriety in their public behavior, there is an informal behind-the-scenes and actual power in the house by women.

Although the women's movement progresses slowly, the position of women in Korea has made steady improvement, especially with the attainment of higher education by a great number of young women. There are many prominent women in literature, arts, and sciences. Many of them have achieved economic success in small business and financial dealings such as the "keh" system. After migrating to the Unites States, Korean immigrant women are further influenced by Americanization which offers more freedom and employment opportunities. However, changes often create marital conflict and role identity crises. To be effective and assertive is contrary to the traditional teaching of passive conformity and modesty.

Now in America, two-thirds of Korean women are employed, as indicated previously. And yet they are responsible for domestic tasks as well. Also, mothers are considered the primary educators of children and are held responsible for their success. Korean women are, by and large, resourceful individuals, probably helped by the adaptability and intensity of the women's determination to achieve success for the family.

On the other hand, many of the first-generation Korean *men* are underemployed, have suffered a loss in status and prestige, and often are discriminated against in the new country. Many of them are discouraged and become ineffective. Frustrated, men may resort to drinking, playing golf, or to doubling their authoritarian stance in the family to foster their deflated ego. This may cause more domestic conflicts and even domestic violence.

One scenario is that wives become the emotional and economic backbone of the family. Parental (primarily motherly) sacrifice for the benefit of the children has always been a pivotal Korean value. Mothers will, at times, play a mediating role between their husbands, who are having difficulty accepting the American culture, and their children, who are rebelling against father, by tacitly choosing the children's side.

Anger and Aggression of Women

A common stereotype of woman conjures up images of softness, nurturance, and passive compliance. Instead of allowing the expression of anger, culturally approved feminine behaviors inhibit women's expression of anger, even when they are betrayed or victimized. The "virtues" of self-sacrifice and service to others may lead many women to decision making that simply is not in their own best interests. Or they may express anger indirectly through such behavior as moodiness and acting like a "manipulative bitch" (Nadelson & Zimmerman, 1992).

How can a woman express aggression in a more appropriate way? Psychoanalytic theory holds that women and men begin life with the same quantity of aggression. Women's lifelong task, then, is to divest themselves of their direct aggression in order to achieve "femininity." To achieve the "female ego ideal," women strive to sublimate anger and be someone who is not "overtly aggressive" (Nadelson et al., 1982). Aggressive feelings may be turned inward, leading to depression.

Depression

Depression is an important subject for all women across nations and races. All the literature points out that clinical depression is much more common in women than in men universally. A number of explanations for female predominance have been offered. One is the artifact hypothesis, which holds that the response set and labeling process serve to overestimate the number of females with depression. Also there may be a biological basis as a contributing factor, such as endocrine changes in pre-menstrual syndrome, post-partum depression, and menopausal depression.

Another theory (Weissman & Klerman, 1982) is that there are two proposed pathways in the psychosocial explanation of depression. The first pathway is the "social status hypothesis," which holds that psychological disadvantage, social bias, and inequities lead to legal and economic helplessness, dependency on others, and chronically low self-esteem, low aspiration, and, ultimately, clinical depression.

The other pathway is called the "learned-helplessness hypothesis." It proposes that socially conditioned, stereotypical images produce in women a nonassertive cognitive set that is further reinforced by societal expectations. The classic "femininity" values are nothing more than a variant of "learned helplessness." Young girls learn to be helpless during their socialization and thus develop a limited response repertoire when under stress. These self-images and expectations are internalized in childhood so that the young girl comes to believe that the stereotype of femininity is expected, valued, and normative.

I think that the above general hypothetical explanations of depression apply to all women, but more particularly to Asian women because of the Asian cultural reinforcement. It is important to know that clinical depression in Asian women frequently manifests itself not as sad and depressed feelings, but as somatic symptoms, which include headaches, dizziness, insomnia, stomach upset, and impaired memory and concentration. Often Asian women go to different medical doctors thinking that they have medical problems. Once depression is diagnosed and anti-depressant and supportive therapy are given, the majority of clients improve from depression.

Haan-Ridden Life for Korean Women

Anger, bitterness, resentment, and grudges are frequently experienced emotions among Koreans, but more so among Korean women. A unique Korean folk term for these feelings of suppressed anger is "Haan." Haan, the feelings of suppressed anger and grudges, is a victimization syndrome. A Haan-ridden person feels that he/she has been victimized and unjustly treated (uh-gul ha-da) (Kim, 1990, 1992). Korean psychotherapists as well as Korean theologians have been interested in the concept of Haan recently. Some Korean psychiatrists think that Haan is deeply imprinted in the collective subconscious of Koreans, who have suffered much and endured oppression and pain in their history. Koreans are said to be people of pain and suffering. Haan is not a passive process of suffering with acceptance and resignation, but an active process of suffering with a will to endure pain, to overcome and to triumph someday.

The concept of Haan is especially essential in understanding Korean women who have been oppressed individually and collectively in a male-dominant society. For example, brutal treatment by husbands or in-laws is often mentioned by Haan-ridden women (Min & Lee, 1986). Haan is an important and dynamic contributing factor to the development of clinical depression, as well as the culture-bound syndrome, Hwa-byung, which will be further discussed in Chapter 18.

Haan has become a rallying, focal point for the new Asian women's liberation theology. Theologian Hyun Kyung Chung has been a powerful voice in articulating Haan and connecting it with Korean women's pain (Chung, 1990; Shim, 1990).

Historically, Korean women have been taught the concept of Palja, fate and destiny, to overcome pain and suffering. A teaching of fate, Palja, makes women think that what happens in their lives is something beyond their control, and something that they have to accept and endure. Many Korean women's beautiful but painful poems, songs, and novels are rich in the expression of, and are reflective of, feelings of Haan.

Throughout history Korean women have untangled the complex webs of Haan through their survival wisdom and endurance. Korean shamans are known to be more sympathetic to Haan-ridden women by helping the release of Haan through Mudang (shaman dancing) and Haan-pu-ri (release of Haan) in the Korean tradition. Some say that the frequent, ritualistic anti-government demonstrations by Korean students are a form of Haan-pu-ri.

Feelings of personal Haan and feelings of victimization are very important issues to be explored in psychotherapy with Korean women. To understand Korean women, one has to understand their Haan (B. L. Kim, personal communication, February 1993).

Jeong-Filled Life

As Haan is to pain, Jeong is to love. I think that Jeong is the most important and enriching part of interpersonal and affective life that we experience as we grow up in Korea. There are no exact English words for Jeong. Jeong embraces feeling, empathy, affinity, attachment, bonding, affection, and love. There are different kinds of Jeong: motherly love, mo-jeong; friend's love, woo-jeong; romantic love, ai-jeong, and so forth. When you have established woo-jeong (Jeong as a friend), you can expect a lifelong friendship. In times of social upheaval, calamity and unrest, Jeong is the only sustaining force in human relationships (Kim, 1990,1992). Jeong is an emotional bond and inter-personal glue that connects people together. When we live in the individualistic American society in which people are lonely and isolated from each other, we begin to appreciate the importance of Jeong as a source of enduring love, affection, and joy. In working with Korean women in psychotherapy, I find it helpful and important to explore areas of Jeong relationships in their lives.

ANGER, SELF-ASSERTION, AND WOMEN'S SELF-HELP GROUPS

I have indicated above that women's feelings of suppressed anger and aggressive expressions have been a universal issue for women in general. As a way of dealing with the issue, the promotion of assertive communication skills has become popular in recent years. An emphasis has been on expressing oneself in an assertive and effective way, yet not in an aggressive or confrontational way. The woman who conforms to the traditional feminine role is basically a non-assertive woman. In Korean and in other Asian cultures, communication is often subtle, indirect, and non-verbal. Adding to this, Korean women are supposed to be gentle, soft-spoken, and yielding when they speak.

I also have seen Korean American women who are nonassertive most of the time, and then once in a while explode in an aggressive way. Nonassertiveness is a problem with many women of different ethnic backgrounds. However, nonassertiveness occurs more widely among Asian women. Traditional culture reinforces this. Non-assertiveness contributes to low self-esteem and depression. I think that Korean American women need to improve their communication skills and learn to be more assertive, not passive or aggressive. There are many good books on assertive communication for women (Butler, 1976; Cambrill, & Richey, 1980; Learner, 1989). Better yet, it will be helpful to take a course on communication skills at an adult school or through a university extension program.

Consciousness-Raising Group

As an outgrowth of the women's movement, an increasing number of consciousness-raising groups (Brodsky, 1981) have appeared among American women. The group provides a setting where women can share their personal experiences and find commonalties for understanding what hitherto was private discontent. An increasing number of women's self-help and support groups have arisen for similar purposes. Other self-help groups include wellness groups, health groups, and conflict management groups. These groups can be helpful in dealing with women's issues and improving self-esteem, although they are not alternatives to individual psychotherapy if the problem is deep and serious. Korean or Asian American women would benefit from such self-help, support group experiences.

Feminist Therapy

The role of the gender of the therapist for female clients has been much discussed. "Feminist therapy" asserts that a woman therapist will be more empathetic and supportive of women clients because, presumably, the therapist has experienced similar problems related to sex discrimination and stereotyping. Feminist therapy is often advocated as a personal and political growth process due to the social roots of women's psychological problems (Gilbert, 1980; Fodor & Rothblum, 1984).

However, Nadelson and Zimmerman (1992) stated that having a female therapist for a female client may help establish a working therapeutic alliance in the initial phase, but these bonds alone cannot resolve the client's problems. This is true of the ethnic matching in therapy. A client may seek a therapist of the same ethnic background for similar reasons of shared values and understanding. However, it can be deceptive in that, if unexplored, it can help the client avoid dealing with pathology and maladaptive behavior. It can lead to "shared blind spots."

I am struck by the realization that there is much similarity between the Korean concept of Haan and the issue of women's suppressed anger focused on by feminist therapy. Suppressed anger and psychology of victimization must be a prominent issue for women regardless of ethnic background. Certainly the issue of gender and the type of therapy needs to be further explored and studied.

SUMMARY

In this chapter, I have not covered the mental health of elderly Korean women (a topic in another chapter), and Korean American women of 1.5 and second generations.

We can say that Korean American women, as adult immigrants, are generally resourceful, adaptable, and resilient people who are strong in survival skills and determined to succeed in fulfilling their American dreams, for both themselves and their children. Surveys show that the majority of them are generally satisfied with their life in the United States. However, at the same time, they experience psychological strain and anxiety and feel that they are paying too high a price for their comfortable life. Many of them are employed and carry the dual burden of homemaker and wage earner. However, below the surface of their apparent comfortable living, there are tensions and conflict with regard to changing gender roles in their marriage and in relationship with their rapidly Americanizing younger generation.

As time passes by, there will be more psychological and emotional issues emerging among Korean American women. Especially after the LA riots, Korean immigrants' American dreams have been shattered. They are worried about their future in this country. As a politically weak minority, Korean Americans may be easily scapegoated and targeted again for hate crimes. Korean Americans need to mobilize themselves to have more political voice and power. Negative stereotyping, low self-esteem, unresolved Haan, and lack of control over their lives would further their sense of demoralization and negative mental health.

REFERENCES

Brodsky, A. (1981). "The Consciousness-Raising Group as a Model for Therapy with Women." In W. Howell & M. Bayes, eds., *Women and Mental Health*. New York: Basic Books, pp. 572-580.

Butler, P. (1976). *Self-Assertion For Women*. New York: Harper & Row.

Cabrill, E., & C. Richey. (1980). "Assertion Training for Women." In C. L. Heckerman, ed., *Evolving Female: Women in Psychosocial Context*. New York: Human Sciences Press, pp. 222-267.

Chang, M. (1993). Personal communication.

Chang, S., M. C. Cho, C. S. Chung, C. Chung, B. L. Kim, W. J. Kim, S. C. Kim, K. O. Kim, H. A. Kim, C. H. Lee, S. E. Lee, Y. S. Park, & D. S. Rue. (1993). Personal communications, February.

Cho, M. C., & C. Chung. (1993). Personal communications, February.

Chung, H. K (1990). *Struggle to Be the Sun Again: Introducing Asian Women's Theology*. Maryknoll, NY: Orbis Books.

Flaskerud, J. H., & N. T. Anh. (1988). "Mental Health Needs of Vietnamese Refugees." *Hospital and Community Psychiatry* 39(4): 434-437.

Forder, I., & E. Rothblum. (1984). "Strategies for Dealing with Sex-Role Stereotypes." In C. Brody, ed., *Women Therapists Working with Women: New Theory and Process of Feminist Therapy*. New York: Springer, pp. 86-95.

Gilbert, L. A. (1980). "Feminist Therapy." In A. Brodsky & R. Hare-Mustin, eds., *Women and Psychotherapy*. New York: Guilford Press, pp. 245-266.

Hurh, Won Moo, & Kwang Chung Kim. (1984). *Korean Immigrants in America: A Structural Analysis of Ethnic Confinement and Adhesive Adaptation*. Cranberry, NJ: Association of University Presses.

_____. (1988). "Uprooting and Adjustment: A Sociological Study of Korean Immigrants' Mental Health." In *Final Report to the National Institute of Mental Health* (Grant No. 1R1 MH40312-01). Bethesda, MD: U.S. Department of Health and Human Services, National Institute of Mental Health.

_____. (1987). "Korean Immigrants in the Chicago Area: A Sociological Study of Migration and Mental Health." *Interim Report for National Institute of Mental Health*. Bethesda, MD: U.S. Department of Health and Human Services, National Institute of Mental Health.

_____. (1990). *Korean Ethos: Concept of Jeong and Haan*. Paper presented at the Winter Meeting of the American Academy of Psychoanalysis, San Antonio, TX.

Kim, L. I. C. (1992). "Psychiatric Care of Korean Americans." In A. Gaw, ed., *Culture, Ethnicity and Mental Illness*. Washington, DC: American Psychiatric Press.

Kim, M., & K. O. Kim. (1993). Personal communications, February.

Kim, S. C. (1985). "Family Therapy for Asian Americans: A Strategic Structural Framework." *Psychotherapy*, 22(25): 342-348.

Kuo, W.H. (1984). Prevalence of Depression among Asian-Americans." *The Journal of Nervous and Mental Disease*, 172(8): 449-457.

Lerner, H. G. (1989). *The Dance of Anger*. New York: Harper & Row.

McGoldrick, M., N. Garcia-Preto, P. M. Hine, & E. Lee. (1989). "Ethnicity and Women." In M. McGoldrick, C. Anderson, & F. Walsh, eds., *Women in Families*. New York: W. W. Norton, pp. 169-199.

Min, S. K., & H. Y. Lee. (1986). "A Diagnostic Study of Hwabyung." *Journal of the Korean Medical Association*, 29: 653-1986.

Murphy, H. B. M. (1965). "Migration and Major Mental Disease." In M. B. Lantor, ed., *Mobility and Mental Health.* Springfield, IL: Charles C. Thomas.

Nadelson, C., M. Notman, J. B. Miller, & J. Zilbach. (1982). "Aggression in Women: Conceptual Issues and Clinical Implications." In M. Notman & C. Nadelson, eds., *The Woman Patient,* Vol 3. New York: Plenum Press.

Nadelson, C., & V. Zimmerman. (1992). "Culture and Psychiatric Care of Women." In A. Gaw, ed., *Culture, Ethnicity and Mental Illness.* Washington, DC: American Psychiatric Press, pp. 501-516.

Shim, S. S. (1990). *A Clinical Case Study of "Haan" Experiences Among Korean Immigrants in Southern California.* Ph.D. Dissertation, School of Theology at Claremont.

Weissman, M., & G. Klerman. (1981). "Sex Differences and Epidemiology of Depression." In E. Howell & M. Bayes, eds., *Women and Mental Health.* New York: Basic Books.

Weissman, M., & G. Klerman. (1982). "Depression in Women: Epidemiology, Explanations, and Impact on the Family." In M. Norman & C. Nadelson, eds., *The Woman Patient,* Vol 3. New York: Plenum Press.

Yu, K. H., & L. I. C. Kim. (1983). "The Growth and Development of Korean American Children." In G. Johnson-Powell, J. Yamamoto, & A. Romero, eds., *Psychosocial Development of Minority Children.* New York: Brunner/Mazel, pp. 147-158.

18

Korean Women's Hwa-Byung: Clinical Issues and Implications for Treatment

Mikyong Kim-Goh

Although Hwa-Byung has been a well-recognized and familiar condition among Korean health and mental health professionals for many years, it was virtually unknown to non-Korean researchers until Lin (1983) identified several Hwa-Byung patients among a group of Korean American psychiatric patients in the Seattle area and raised the question of whether Hwa-Byung was a "culture-bound syndrome." Hwa-Byung is a unique Korean folk illness designation, indicating a physiological as well as psychological outcome of chronic repression or suppression of negative emotions. The term *Hwa-Byung* is a Korean pronunciation of two Chinese characters: Literally "Hwa" stands for fire or anger, while "Byung" means sickness, thus Hwa-Byung came to be known as the "anger syndrome" (Lee, 1977).

In a study of 100 Hwa-Byung patients in Korea, Min (1989) found that the majority of them were middle-aged or older married women of lower socioeconomic and educational classes. Major symptoms included anxiety and depressive syndrome and somatic complaints of chest oppression, indigestion, heat or hot sensations, headaches, something pushing up in the chest, palpitations, epigastric mass, and talkativeness. Although Hwa-Byung patients were reluctant to be treated as psychiatric patients, most of them were aware that the etiology of their illness was psychological. Diagnostically depressive, anxiety and somatization disorders were most frequently observed (Min, 1989).

While Min (1989) has suggested that the symptom patterns and pathogenesis of Hwa-Byung are unique and should be regarded as a "culture-bound" syndrome not classifiable according to the prevailing Western psychiatric diagnostic system, some others have argued that there seems to be a substantial overlap of the symptom manifestation, clinical course, and treatment responses between Hwa-Byung and major depression as defined in the Western diagnostic system (Lee, 1977; Lin, 1983; Lin et al., 1991). In discussing the intricate relationship of culture to symptom presentation in clinical practice, Lin (1983) suggested that Hwa-Byung may be "a culturally patterned way for Korean patients suffering from major depression to express their distress through somatic symptoms." This idea was supported by the recent study in which Lin and colleagues (1991) found that 12% of their sample of 109 Korean Americans were reportedly suffering from Hwa-Byung. Since most Hwa-Byung patients in their study manifested symptoms that were compatible with the diagnosis of major depression according to the American Psychiatric Association's *Diagnostic and Statistical Manual of Mental Disorders* (DSM-III-R) criteria, they suggested that Hwa-Byung could be considered as a high-risk factor for major depression among Koreans and Korean Americans.

The following case examples illustrate three Korean women living in the United States whose symptom manifestations were identified as Hwa-Byung by the patients themselves and by a treatment team at Asian/Pacific Counseling & Treatment Center in Los Angeles, an outpatient mental health clinic. These cases are presented in order to identify common precipitating factors, help seeking patterns, clinical courses, and treatment outcomes of Hwa-Byung patients, and to illustrate how they relate to contemporary mental health treatment practices.

Case 1

Mrs. Kim, a 56-year-old married woman, had experienced her first episode of Hwa-Byung 11 years ago, soon after her oldest son had committed suicide. She began to complain that there was a heavy block of metal hanging on her chest, causing palpitation and indigestion, and painfully described a feeling of a "bloody mass pushing up to the throat." She said a bus on the street looked to her like a "huge fireball." Her other symptoms included heat sensation, excessive tiredness, general body weakness, and occasional fainting. Mrs. Kim sought help from a local pharmacist who gave her minor tranquilizers. After a religious prayer retreat, the epigastric mass reportedly vanished. One year later, the patient migrated to the United States with her family.

During the first four years of immigration, Mrs. Kim remained asymptomatic and managed to work at a factory. However, she soon began to complain of body weakness and lack of strength to walk. Her fainting also became more frequent. Each time, Mrs. Kim was rushed to a hospital emergency room, where she was medically cleared and subsequently referred to an Asian mental health clinic. During the first interview with a Korean American therapist, Mrs. Kim presented physical symptoms such as severe headaches, dizziness, psychomotor retardation, and walking difficulty. She called her problem Hwa-Byung and attributed the symptoms to the death of her son. However, she initially told the therapist that her son had died in an auto accident. It took a while before she was able to reveal her son's suicide and her obsessive thoughts about him. Mrs. Kim revealed that her own mother also had suffered from Hwa-Byung after losing a 2-year-old son.

Due to the prominence of vegetative signs, antidepressant and antianxiety medications were prescribed by a psychiatrist at the clinic. In therapy, Mrs. Kim was allowed to grieve the son's death, and share her feelings of shame and guilt as well as the betrayal of the dead son. In order to describe the pain that she was experiencing, the patient beautifully quoted the Korean saying: "A dead husband will be buried in the mountain; a dead son will be buried in the mother's heart." Through supportive psychotherapy combined with a medication regimen, Mrs. Kim became less depressed and was able to walk again on her own, although some somatic complaints such as body weakness, backache, and tiredness remained. She began to talk less about the dead son and was able to focus her attention on her current relationships with her husband and a surviving son.

Case 2

Mrs. Park is a 61-year-old married Korean woman who immigrated to the United States 10 years ago. She first visited the Asian mental health clinic three years ago through a referral by her family physician. Her presenting problems included dizziness, severe headaches, nausea, diarrhea, shakiness and weakness of limbs, indigestion and insomnia. Initially she denied having any problems in her life. However, after further questioning, the patient reported that her symptoms were due to Hwa-Byung that dated back to 30 years ago, when she first discovered her husband's extramarital affair. Since then, the patient frequently had become bed-ridden with multiple physical complaints and was unable to care for her children, who, as a result, were cared for by maids. Despite her husband's continuing womanizing behavior, Mrs. Park stayed in the marriage for the "sake of [her] children." During this time, the patient was seen by numerous medical doctors, including neurologists and psychiatrists, for her physical symptoms such as chronic headaches, weakness of body, and indigestion. Each time she was medically cleared and reassured of her health. However, over the years, Mrs. Park became quite dependent on medications to relieve her anxiety.

Since her family moved to the United States, the patient's condition slightly improved until she recently discovered her husband's infidelity once again. Her physical symptoms reappeared and she began to seek help from physicians, at times asking for surgery to "eliminate [her] headache." In therapy, Mrs. Park primarily focused on her somatic problems and was very reluctant to disclose the conflicting aspect of her life. However, the therapist was able to gather the following background information from the patient through several sessions. Mrs. Park was born to a well-to-do family in North Korea. Her father was a gold miner, a very rich and influential man in town. Mrs. Park's mother died when the patient was 9 years old. Apparently the patient grew up as her father's favorite child. During the Korean War, however, the patient escaped to South Korea with her brother, and her father remained in the North. While working as a maid, she met her husband. The patient revealed that she married him only because he had raped her. She thought that no other men would find her worthy of marrying once she had been raped. Therefore, from its beginning, the patient's marital relationship was very distant and conflict-ridden.

In treatment, Mrs. Park briefly joined a women's support group, but did not continue, feeling that her problem was "too different" from others'. She would dominate the group with all her physical and familial problems, seeking attention from others, and became discouraged when her needs were not being met. However, the patient continued medication treatments and individual therapy where she was able to talk about her feelings of guilt for neglecting the children. She maintains minimal insight into her problem of marital conflict and somatization.

Case 3

Mrs. Lee, a 54-year-old widow, had developed Hwa-Byung five years ago, soon after her husband's death. During her husband's funeral, she had an unexpected visit from a woman who claimed to be her husband's long-term mistress. To make matters worse, the patient found out that her late husband had diverted money for his mistress, leaving virtually none for the patient and her children. Suddenly the patient felt weak all over her body and subsequently lost consciousness. Since then, Mrs. Lee had been experiencing insomnia, ruminating thoughts, palpitation, and indigestion. Although she had always been healthy and active, Mrs. Lee became immobilized after the incident.

Mrs. Lee was referred to the Asian mental health clinic by a friend one year after the onset of her symptoms. During the first interview with a Korean American therapist, Mrs. Lee burst into tears hysterically and cried throughout the session. She presented physical symptoms such as pain and weakness in the body, severe headaches, palpitations, heat sensation, and insomnia. The patient expressed feeling anxious and fearful. She attributed her problem to the shock of discovering her late husband's extramarital affair, and she verbalized feelings of mortification and hatred toward him. However, she felt even more frustrated because her target of anger was no longer alive. Around this time, she was also medically diagnosed with diabetes and hypertension.

Mrs. Lee grew up in a poor family with five children. Being the only girl, she was allowed to complete only an elementary school education while her brothers went on to college, which the patient states became her "hahn." For financial reasons she was forced at 23 to marry her late husband, who was 18 years her senior. The marriage was turbulent, but the patient never suspected her husband's infidelity. Mrs. Lee and her family immigrated to the United States in 1985 and soon after that her husband was diagnosed with terminal cancer. The husband demanded to go to Korea for medical care. Out of sympathy, and to grant his last wish, the patient agreed to his demand, and during his last year of life, the husband made several trips back and forth from the United States to Korea, using up all their life savings. The patient now thinks that her husband's demand to get care in Korea was only an excuse to be with his mistress. After her husband's death, the patient lived with her son, who was abusive and alcoholic. The son blamed the patient for her husband's decision not to leave any money for the family. Although the patient has two daughters who are married, she did not feel welcomed by either of them. Being destitute and feeling hopeless, the patient was in a desperate condition when she sought help from the mental health clinic.

In therapy, the patient was quite talkative and tearful. With medication from a psychiatrist, the patient was able to sleep better at night. However, she would report seeing black clouds or a human figure when she closed her eyes. At times she was so frightened that she felt paralyzed and choked by the figure. After discussion with the therapist, Mrs. Lee applied for public funding and moved into a boarding care home. She became more relaxed and less depressed although some of her physical complaints remained. She regularly attended a Korean women's therapy group and developed the support system that she needed. The patient says she sometimes shouts and yells at her dead husband when angry, and it makes her feel better. Now she is looking forward to finding an apartment for herself.

DISCUSSION

Hwa-Byung seems to be a socially recognized and accepted form of a help-seeking behavior in Korea, an "illness behavior" in Kleinman's (1977) terms. It represents an effective way for Koreans to identify and communicate their problems in living as well as negative emotions, without the risk of losing face. Koreans are not used to discussing their emotions openly with others, particularly if this involves sexual feelings or anger. Instead, they tend to somatize their emotional and psychological problems. In fact, Hwa-Byung implies a social milieu that restricts expression of such negative feelings. An individual may use Hwa-Byung as a communication tool in relationships, and a basis of secondary gain, that is, to escape social responsibility, draw sympathy from family, and control the people around her/him. This tendency to somatize is even more prominent among women in Korean culture.

The women illustrated in the case examples share common character structures such as dependency, passive-aggressiveness, and avoidant personality traits that may be a reflection of the prolonged familial and societal oppression of women. Historically, Korean women have been oppressed by parents, husbands, in-laws, and social systems. They had no recourse to appeal injustice and had to swallow and suppress their anger and resentment. According to Confucianism, which has had a significant influence on the Korean value system for the past several centuries, a woman's role is clearly defined. One of these prescribed roles demands that a woman is subordinate first to her father before the marriage; second, to her husband after the marriage; and third, to her eldest son after the death of her husband. Traditionally Korean women are not allowed to have personalities or identities of their own. Oftentimes, a Korean woman is not addressed by her own name as a separate and unique individual, but rather is called by titles in relation to others, that is, somebody's daughter-in-law, wife, mother, daughter, or sister. Due to their own socialization experiences, parents tend to show favoritism toward their male children, a practice that often has a devastating effect on girls' self-concepts and perpetuates sexism. The differential attitude and treatment of genders in the family and the society at large seem to have a significant influence on how men and women express and cope with negative feelings. The exceptionally high rate of alcoholism among Korean males (Lee et al., 1990a; Lee et al., 1990b) may be a good example of a socially and culturally reinforced help-seeking behavior that is widely used to communicate and to cope with difficulties in living. For Koreans, divorce brings a sense of shame and disgrace to the whole family. Whatever the reason for divorce may be, the woman is more likely to be blamed for it. Moreover, most married women are financially dependent on their husbands, and there are very few employment opportunities available in society for middle-aged women with children. Such an economic dependency on the part of a woman places her in a powerless position, often forcing her to endure and hold on to an unsatisfactory and abusive marriage. Therefore, it is understandable that despite her husband's ongoing infidelity, Mrs. Park felt that she had no choice but to stay in her marriage, using her children as an acceptable excuse.

Although the label Hwa-Byung is uniquely Korean, its symptom pictures are by no means bound to the Korean culture. The tendency to somatize is also prominent in other Asian cultures that demand the repression or internalization of anger (Kleinman & Lin, 1981; Nguyen, 1982; Tseng, 1975; Ying, 1990). In discussing frequent somatization among the Chinese, Kleinman (1977) claimed that high stigmatization of mental illness led to somatization. Another study found that nearly 70% of the psychiatric outpatients in Taiwan presented somatic complaints to the psychiatrist at their first visit (Tseng, 1975). Like the Korean women presented in this paper, patients in Tseng's (1975) study seemed to use physical complaints as a legitimate metaphor to indirectly express personal and interpersonal problems. Many Koreans find mental illness in the family difficult to accept, and they consider it shameful for the whole family. They often keep it as a secret for fear that the patient could never find a marriage partner if the illness is known to the public. This is one of the reasons why Korean people seldom seek psychiatric help until their conditions deteriorate to the point of requiring an urgent and intensive care. As presented in the case examples, the mentally ill Koreans often ask for help from friends, family physicians, or non-mental health professionals, such as a pharmacist or religious leaders, before they seek psychiatric care.

A Korean concept that is inseparable from the etiology of Hwa-Byung is that of Hahn. Min (1989) stated that "Hwa-Byung [is] an individualized illness behavior and expression of Hahn." Hahn is a Korean traditional affective expression, an "individual and collective emotive state of Koreans, involving feelings of anger, rage, grudge, resignation, hate and revenge. [It is a] form of victimization syndrome of Korean people, with feelings of injustice and indignation suppressed and endured" (Kim, 1991). Hahn of the powerless people, that is, suppression of desire, sense of failure, despair, vengeance, and pessimism, can be inherited for generations. Although Hahn is to become an incentive and energy source to endure the hardships once sublimated (Kim, 1991) the outcome does not necessarily justify the process. Mrs. Lee who had a "Hahn" feeling for her lack of formal education made sure that all her children, including her daughters, went to college. She supported them by working various jobs and managing businesses, while trying to maintain her unsatisfying marriage. In other words, Mrs. Lee's children's educational success came at the expense of her own needs and well-being. In all three case examples, there were traumatic and identifiable precipitating events, e.g., death of a son, rape, spousal infidelity, which seemed to have triggered the onset of Hwa-Byung in each patient. The patients' reactions to these precipitating events are quite similar to those experiencing major depressive disorders or post-traumatic stress syndrome, except for the excessive somatic complaints by Hwa-Byung patients in addition to the typical depressive and anxiety symptoms.

Based on the Los Angeles County data on depression, women were nearly twice as likely to be depressed as men, and the prevalence of depression was strongly related to family income (Fredrichs et al., 1981). Similarly, recent psychiatric epidemiology studies in Korea (Lee et al., 1990a; Lee et al., 1990b) reveal that Korean women suffer from major depression almost twice as often as men and are more than twice as likely to have diagnosable anxiety disorder. In another study of Chinese psychiatric patients, those patients who presented somatic symptoms usually belonged to a lower social class, while those who presented emotional problems came from the upper class (Tseng, 1975). Therefore, the general characteristics of Hwa-Byung patients as middle-aged or older women with a lower socioeconomic status seem to support the hypothesis that Hwa-Byung may be in fact a depression expressed in a somatic manner, and that the explanation for a higher occurrence of Hwa-Byung in Korean women than in their male counterparts may be a higher vulnerability to depression in general.

Despite the growing Korean American population and their emerging psychosocial needs, very few studies on Korean American mental health are available at this time. In a research done in Seattle, Korean Americans had the highest mean score on the Center of Epidemiological Studies Depression Scale (CES-D) among Asian groups, higher than blacks or Hispanics (Kuo, 1984). Interestingly, however, the Korean American women in the study were less depressed than their male counterparts. Recently, Lin and colleagues (1991) found a similar phenomenon in that women were not overrepresented in their study of Hwa-Byung in the Korean American sample. It could be that the stress associated with migration overrides the importance of other risk factors related with Hwa-Byung. For instance, upon their immigration to the United States, those with a higher socioeconomic status in Korea often have to restart their careers just as others do. Therefore, Korean men who used to enjoy higher positions in general may be facing the downgrading of their status after immigration to the United States, while females may be experiencing greater economic opportunities.

IMPLICATIONS FOR TREATMENT

First of all, mental health professionals need to know how to deal with the family's denial of mental illness and resistance to psychiatric treatment. In general, Korean Americans are very sensitive to the loss of face. Mrs. Kim's case of initially describing her son's death as caused by an auto accident is a good example. Until enough trust has been developed in the therapist-patient relationship, Korean American women would be very reluctant to reveal family secrets that may cause shame and disgrace. It is essential to create a safe and supportive environment, and to attempt to establish a good rapport with the patient on the first contact. The patient's manner of presenting her problems to the therapist not only serves the primary function of informing the therapist of her problem, but reveals also the patient's way of relating to the therapist as influenced by her orientation to therapy, her conceptualization of the problem, and her usual pattern of help-seeking.

Tseng (1975) recommended that therapists provide psychological education for somatic patients to help them conceptualize and orient their problems within a psychological framework. Initially it is essential to fulfill the patient's needs, whether physical or emotional, making her feel comfortable in relating to the therapist. Due to the multiple physical complaints that Hwa-Byung patients present, a team approach involving psychiatrists as well as non-M.D. clinicians is useful in the treatment of Hwa-Byung patients. Like any other patients with somatic complaints, Hwa-Byung patients should be referred to a physician for a thorough physical check-up in order to rule out any organic condition before assuming that the problem is somatic. Cultural sensitivity and awareness on the part of the therapist are crucial in understanding the patient's world view as well as the meaning of the illness to her and to the family. At the beginning stage of therapy, the therapist needs to actively listen and acknowledge physical complaints as valid and real. Later the patient can be approached by gradually inquiring about her present life situation as well as past history. By this means of inquiry, a dynamic understanding of the patient's problems can be achieved, and comprehensive treatment can be formulated and carried out even though the patient may continue to complain of somatic symptoms. The therapist needs to be aware of the underlying meaning of the patient's somatic complaints, rather than remaining confined to the manifest problem as presented by the patient.

In terms of the clinical courses and treatment outcomes of Hwa-Byung patients, there seems to be a significant overlap with major depression. The supportive nature of psychotherapy has been helpful in replacing the patient's sense of hopelessness with new hope and meaning in life. As with most depressive patients, Hwa-Byung patients have experienced significant loss in their lives, and oftentimes they were not allowed to grieve for the loss. Providing a warm and non-critical environment for them to express and verbalize their sadness as well as anger is critical in helping the Hwa-Byung patients resolve the grieving process. All three patients responded positively to antidepressants and antianxiety medications.

In conclusion, Hwa-Byung seems to be a culturally constructed illness category specific to Koreans and Korean Americans that substantially overlaps with major depressive disorder in terms of symptom manifestation, clinical course, and treatment responses. The studies of gender difference in the prevalence of Hwa-Byung show mixed results among Koreans and Korean Americans. It will be of great interest to study the effect of immigration, acculturation to Western society, and generational differences on the prevalence and presentation of Hwa-Byung in Korean Americans. The relationship between the personality make-up and Hwa-Byung can be another fascinating issue for investigation. Finally, systematic future research could help further clarify the relationship between Hwa-Byung and contemporary Western psychiatric diagnoses such as major depression, somatization disorder, and post-traumatic stress disorder.

REFERENCES

Fredrichs, R. R., C. S. Aneshensel, & V. A. Clark. (1981). "Prevalence of Depression in Los Angeles County." *American Journal of Epidemiology*, 113(6): 691-699.

Kim, L. (1991). "Korean Ethos: Concept of Jeong and Haan." Paper presented at the Scientific Meeting of Pacific Rim College of Psychiatrists, Los Angeles.

Kleinman, A. M. (1977). "Depression, Somatization and the New Cross-Cultural Psychiatry." *Social Science and Medicine*, 11: 3-10.

Kleinman, A. M. & Lin, T. Y. (1981). "Introduction." In A. Kleinman & T. Y. Lin, eds., *Normal and Abnormal Behavior in Chinese Cultures*. Dordrecht, The Netherlands: Reidel, pp. 13-23.

Kuo, W. H. (1984). Prevalence of Depression among Asian-Americans." *The Journal of Nervous and Mental Disease*, 172(8): 449-457.

Lee, C. K., Y. S. Kwak, J. Yamamoto, H. Rhee, Y. S. Kim, J. H. Han, J. O. Choi, & Y. H. Lee. (1990a). "Psychiatric Epidemiology in Korea Part I: Gender and Age Differences in Seoul." *Journal of Nervous and Mental Disease*, 178(4): 242-246.

____. (1990b). "Psychiatric Epidemiology in Korea Part II: Urban and Rural Differences." *Journal of Nervous and Mental Disease*, 178(4): 247-252.

Lee, S. H. (1977). "A Study on the Hwa-Byung (Anger Syndrome)." *Journal of Korea General Hospital*, 1: 62-69.

Lin, K. (1983). "Hwa-Byung: A Korean Culture-Bound Syndrome?" *American Journal of Psychiatry*, 140: 105-107.

Lin, K., J.K.C. Lau, J. Yamamoto, H. Kim, K. Cho, & G. Nakasaki. (1991). "Hwa-Byung: A Community Study of Korean Americans." Unpublished article.

Min, S. K. (1989). "A Study of the Concept of Hwabyung." *Journal of Korean Neuropsychiatric Association*, 28(4): 604-616.

Nguyen, D. S. (1982). "Psychiatric and Psychosomatic Problem among Southeast Asian Refugees." *Psychiatric Journal of University of Ottawa*, 7: 163-167.

Tseng, W. S. (1975). "The Nature of Somatic Complaints Among Psychiatric Patients: The Chinese Case." *Comprehensive Psychiatry*, 16(3): 237-245.

Ying, Y. (1990). "Explanatory Models of Major Depression and Implications for Help-Seeking Among Immigrant Chinese-American Women." *Culture, Medicine and Psychiatry*, 14: 393-408.

part seven

ISSUES FOR THE FUTURE

In this final section, attention is focused on two critical global issues for women of Korean descent in the United States and elsewhere: the military comfort women, and reunions of Korean families separated by war. In concluding this entire book and its topic, the last chapter is devoted to a final analysis and overview of modern feminist issues facing Korean American women.

Alice Yun Chai's article "Korean Feminist and Human Rights Politics: The *Chongshindae/Jugunianfu* ("Comfort Women") Movement" examines the *Chongshindae/Jugunianfu* issue from a Korean–Asian Pacific feminist perspective. The *Chongshindae/Jugunianfu* were women (primarily Koreans) who the Japanese military euphemistically drafted as military "comfort women" during the Pacific War officially as laborers, but primarily to serve as sex slaves. The article discusses the historical links between Japan's Pacific War military sex slaves and their contemporary parallels; the reasons why this military sex slavery issue has been buried for almost half a century; the social context for politicization of the issue; and the global feminist and grassroots coalition politics—the *Chongshindae/Jugunianfu* movement in Korea and Japan that has recently spread to other East and Southeast Asian countries.

Ten million family members were separated between North and South Korea since the Korean War in 1950 and the subsequent division of land that divided them. Many Koreans migrated to the United States and Canada, and over four thousand individuals have managed to visit their separated families in North Korea. Based on the first survey and personal interviews of these families, Sook Ja Paik and Dong Soo Kim report in "Revisioning of Family Reunions: A Case of Korean American Women and Their Families Separated by War" perspectives of the families separated by circumstances, search efforts, first visit experiences, and future reunion prospects, particularly through the eyes of the women.

In "Modern Feminist Issues Facing Korean American Women: A Global Perspective," Young I. Song provides an overview of the past, present, and future of sexism in the Korean American community. From a feminist perspective, she illustrates the patterns and effects of sexism on women's attitudes and behaviors in various aspects of Korean American women's lives, including self image, self-esteem, relationships with men, and economic activities. Acknowledging that many Korean American women experience psychological conflicts between personal achievements and "feminine" responsibilities, she emphasizes the importance of the women's clear understanding of the conditions, the different ways that male dominance affects their lives, and the need to discover ways to achieve equality between Korean American women and men.

19

Korean Feminist and Human Rights Politics: The *Chongshindae/Jugunianfu* ("Comfort Women") Movement[1]

Alice Yun Chai

HISTORICAL LINKS AND CONTEMPORARY PARALLELS OF JAPANESE COLONIAL EXPANSION AND SEXUAL EXPLOITATION OF WOMEN

Karayuki-san (Foreign-Bound Women)

There is a thread of continuity in Japan's colonial and neocolonial capitalist expansion and the systematic commodification of women's bodies. Officially sanctioned red-light districts existed in Japan from as early as 1617 (Kunimitsu & Sugimura, 1980). This long tradition of legalized prostitution only became illegal in 1956, when the Law for the Prevention of Prostitution was passed (Association of Anti-Prostitution Activity, 1984; Kim, 1980).

During Japan's colonial expansion, women went abroad to serve as prostitutes for Japanese stationed overseas. They went northward to Siberia, westward to China, southward to Southeast Asia, and all the way to India and even Africa. From the beginning of the Meiji period (1868–1912), daughters of poor Japanese peasant families from two peninsulas of Kyushu were recruited as overseas prostitutes, a practice that continued to the end of the Taisho period (1912–1926) (Yamasaki, 1972). These women were known as *Karayuki-san*, "foreign-bound" (literally "China-bound"). The wartime conscription of women to serve as sex slaves for the Japanese overseas military units can be considered a continuation—or culmination—of this Japanese system of officially sanctioned prostitution.

Military Sex Slaves of the Pacific War

Some terminological questions need to be clarified before discussing the historical origins of Japanese military sex slavery, the establishment of *wianso/iansho* ("comfort centers"), the methods of procurement, and the working conditions and treatment of military sex slaves during and after the war.

Terminology

During the Pacific War, the Japanese euphemism for military sex slaves was *Jugunianfu* (military "comfort women"), and the term has continued to be used in postwar Japan. Koreans, on the other hand, have more commonly used the term *Chongshindae* (women's "volunteer corps"), rather than *Chonggunwianbu* (military "comfort women"), to refer to the same women. Women who did only factory or service work were referred to as *Kunro Chongshindae*. When first recruited, many women and their families were told that the women were going to work in factories of hospitals at manufacturing or service jobs. But once they were transported to the occupied territories and the battlefront, they realized that they had been deceitfully drafted as military sex slaves.

To make matters more complicated, some of the *Chongshindae/Jugunianfu* performed nonsexual labor during the day and sexual services as night. In addition, some women in their early teens were initially employed as factory or service workers, then forced into sexual slavery within a year or two. Consequently, in Korea, the term *Chongshindae* has been used interchangeably with *Chonggunwianbu* ("military comfort women").

In order to avoid ambiguity, the Korean Council for Women Drafted by Japan for Sexual Slavery (hereafter, the Korean Council) has decided to reserve the term *Kunro Chongshindae* ([women's] "labor volunteer corps" for those who performed only manual labor as factory workers, domestic workers, and nurses; and to use the term   in Korean is thus equivalent to *Chonggunwianbu* ("military comfort women"). We will hereafter defer to both Japanese and Korean customary usage and use the terms *Chongshindae* (in Korean) and *Jugunianfu* (in Japanese) to refer to sex slaves drafted by the Japanese Imperial Army during the Pacific War.

Historical Origins of Japanese Military Sex Slavery

The Japanese Imperial Army first recruited military prostitutes during the Russo-Japanese War (1904–1905) and the Sino-Japanese War (1894–1895). The personal testimonies of some former military sex slaves who went public in both North and South Korea indicate that 30 women, 20 of them Korean, were drafted and taken to the Guangdong area of China soon after the Japanese landed troops in Shanghai in 1932 (Korean Council, 1992a). More recently, the Fact-Finding Team for the Truth About Forced Korean Laborers found documents in the National Archives in Tokyo that provided evidence of the Japanese Imperial Army's direct operation of military brothels (employing mostly young Korean women) starting as early as 1933 (*Honolulu Star-Bulletin*, December 7, 1992). However, military sex slavery did not become an official, large-scale operation until after the Nanjing Massacre of December 1937.

After the Japanese army invaded China in 1937, attempts were made to obtain prostitutes in order to prevent soldiers from gang-raping women in the occupied territories of Manchuria. Because of the reluctance of procurers to release Japanese prostitutes in large numbers, and the rapid spread of venereal disease among Japanese prostitutes and soldiers, young Korean women were drafted as military sex workers. Korean women were known to be socially secluded and strictly indoctrinated with the Confucian ideals of virginity and feminine chastity. In fact, in the southern province of Cholla, the Japanese policy formed a Virgin Girls Club *(Ch'onyohoe/Shojokai)* to provide drafters for the military brothels in accordance with the Draft Order for Virgin Girls (Shojo, 1992).

Institutionalization of the "Comfort Centers"

After the Nanjing Massacre of December 1937, in which 115,000 Chinese civilians were killed, the first military *wianso/iansho* ("comfort center") was set up in Shanghai. For the first such establishment in Shanghai, 80 of the 104 women recruited in 1938 were Koreans, most of them daughters of Korean migrant coal miners in northern Kyushu, Japan (Korean Council, 1992a; Ki Chan Kim, 1992). These early military brothels were initially managed by the Japanese Imperial Army's Recreation Division. However, due to the negative reaction of the public, many were later handed over to private firms under the direct supervision of the military (Senda, 1992; Suzuki, 1990). Between 1938 and 1945, the Japanese Imperial Army systematically recruited Korean women to be sent to wherever Japanese troops or large numbers of male laborers were working in coal mines, military factories, and construction sites. Some documents and personal testimonies have surfaced in recent months that establish the fact that, during the Pacific War, *wianso/iansho* were present in colonized Taiwan and Korea, and in the occupied territories of Manchuria, Sakhalin, Guangdong, Myanmar (formerly Burma), the Philippines, Indonesia, Malaysia, Sumatra, Papua New Guinea, and the Pacific Islands, as well as in the Japanese islands of Kyushu, Honshu, Hokkaido, and Okinawa (Nishino, 1992; *Asahi Shimbun*, July 21, 1992, Aug. 14, 1992; *Chungang Ilbo*, March 1, 1992; Yun, 1991).

Social Backgrounds and Methods of Procurement

It is believed that from 80 to 90% of the estimated 80,000 to 200,000 *Chongshindae/Juguianfu* during the war were Korean women. As early as 1941, 20,000 Korean women were in China alone as sex slaves to 700,000 Japanese soldiers (Suzuki, 1990).

During the early years of the war, they were recruited mostly from impoverished peasant families in Kyongsang and Cholla provinces in southern Korea. However, as the war intensified and spread to Southeast Asia and the South Pacific, women were recruited indiscriminately from cities and villages in all parts of Korea, especially toward the end of the war. Since the most sought-after draftees initially were unmarried women between 17 and 20, fearful Korean parents hurriedly married their daughters off during the war, even to men of undesirable or dubious backgrounds. Consequently, after the war, there was a tremendous increase in marriage annulments and divorces among Korean wartime brides (Senda, 1992). However, toward the end of the war, females as young as 12 and as old as 30—even married women and nursing mothers—were forcibly sent to the battlefronts as *Chongshindae/Juguianfu* (Senda, 1992; *Korea News Review*, January 25, 1992).

The Japanese Army lured, threatened, and kidnapped women from farms, schools, streets, restaurants, marketplaces, wells, riversides, factories, and even from homes to supply the sexual needs of the military (Yun, 1991). Recruiters lured some women and their families with false promises of well-paying jobs in factories, military bases, and hospitals, and three meals of white rice a day (Go, 1992). Others were threatened by recruiters and sometimes persuaded even by their own families to offer themselves to save their fathers and brothers from being conscripted into the Army or to work in the coal mines and other forms of slave labor in Manchuria and Kyushu, Japan.

Wartime Working Conditions and Postwar Treatment by the Japanese Army

In general, *Chongshindae/Jugunianfu* were treated as sexual commodities and slaves rather than as human beings with basic human rights. For instance, since women had no official place in the Japanese military except as nurses, the "comfort women" were shipped to battlefronts and to mining towns, military factories, and construction sites like food rations, simply labeled "military supplies," without any record of their names or identities through which they could be traced (Korean Association of Women Theologians, 1991). Upon arrival, the women were pressured into sexual slavery in a way that resembled gang rape. Japanese soldiers referred to them as *nuku-ichi*, "29-to-1," a reference to the number of men each woman was expected to service each day. In truth, the number was more likely to be 40 or even 100 men a day. In one story, one woman is said to have had sex with as many as 300 soldiers a day, especially on those days when military units were transferred to new locations (Tamai, 1984; Senda, 1992). Probably for this reason, Japanese soldiers referred to the "comfort centers" as "sanitary public lavatories" (Go, 1992).

Many women who tried and failed to escape were killed, as were some women who became pregnant or contracted venereal disease. In any attempt to cover up the presence of *Chongshindae/Jugunianfu*, the army massacred many of them as it retreated. Others were merely abandoned without knowledge of Japan's defeat. Some were offered to the Allied Occupation Forces as military prostitutes (Go, 1992).

Under these atrocious, inhuman working conditions, it is not surprising that some researchers estimate that as many as 75 to 90% of *Chongshindae/ Jugunianfu* became casualties of war, as a result of diseases such as gynecological infections, venereal disease, and tuberculosis, or mental disorders caused by poor physical and medical care, desertion, and physical and sexual violence committed against them by the Japanese military.

Postwar Treatment by the Confucian Culture of Korean Society

Japan's defeat in 1945 did not mark the end of the ordeal for the "comfort women" who survived. Since many of them had become physically and mentally ill as a result of their enslavement, they lacked the health or resources to return home, or else they were too ashamed to return. Of those who remained in place, some resorted to prostitution in order to survive. Those who managed to return to Korea also led a bitter existence. Some of them also became prostitutes because no other alternatives were available (Yun, 1991).

Considered "fallen women" by a Confucian society that regarded lifelong chastity for women as more important than life itself, some committed suicide aboard ships carrying them to Shimonoseki, rather than face a homecoming of humiliation and social isolation (Go, 1992). Most of the survivors were impoverished and remained unmarried or barren, some no doubt wishing they had died in the war.

Japayuki-san (Japan-Bound Women)

The *Chongshindae/Jugunianfu* issue is not merely a question of past history that has been buried for almost half a century. It has an important impact on present-day Korean and other Asian and Pacific societies and some implications for the future, since it is interconnected with military expansion, colonialism, capitalist development, and patriarchal social organization (Kelker, 1992).

During the 1970s, Japanese men visited Asian countries such as Korea and Taiwan for so-called sex tours in pursuit of cheap female sexual companions. During the 1980s, Japanese men have also been able to enjoy cheap (or exotic) sexual encounters without even leaving the county because of the many young *Japayuki-san* ("Japan-bound" women) from the Philippines, Thailand, Taiwan, Korea, Hong Kong, Indonesia, and increasingly from Latin American countries such as Brazil in recent years. These women, also known as *dekasegi kanko no josei* (female migrant [sex-]tour workers), have been coming to work in Japan's entertainment industry, as waitresses, bar hostesses, performers, and often unwilling prostitutes (Yamaguchi, 1989).

According to statistical records covering the period from 1980 to 1985, the number of 15- to 34-year-old women coming to Japan from the Philippines, Taiwan, Thailand, and Latin America has surpassed the number of men in the same age range (Iyori, 1987). Nearly one half of all Filipinos entering Japan were "entertainers" in 1989 (Randolf, 1991). However, many of these "entertainers" end up working as bar hostesses and being forced—as illegal aliens—into degrading sex-related work (Ohshima & Francis, 1989). They are being recruited, with or without their prior knowledge, to work as prostitutes in Japan's flourishing sex industry, as well as in the international tourist trade in their homelands, catering to Japanese, European, and American male visitors, including American soldiers stationed in military bases in the Philippines, Korea, and Okinawa. As poor foreign women from the poorer Asian counties, the *Japayuki-san* occupy the lowest rung in the Japanese social hierarchy. The international division of labor, based on racial, sexual, and economic stratification, places Asian migrant women in an extremely vulnerable situation (Go, 1988).

Similarities and Differences Among *Karayuki-san* *Chongshindae/Jugunianfu*, and *Japayuki-san*

There are many points in common among the *Karayuki-san*, the *Chongshindae/Jugunianfu*, and the *Japayuki-san*. Because of the historical continuity and some structural similarities among the three groups, it is important to analyze how military and economic expansion exploits the colonized, the economically disadvantaged, and women and to understand the relationship between the specific characteristics of recruitment patterns and the degrees of sexual enslavement of women (Go, 1992). All three groups consist of women who are daughters of economically disadvantaged families from colonized/neocolonized Third World countries (Go, 1992).

A significant feature for all three groups of women is the intervention of the militaristic/patriarchal state and/or state-backed sex industry in their procurement. Both their recruiters and the recipients of their sexual services have been ruling-class and colonial military men. The sex industry cooperates with the state and benefits from government support (Kim, 1980; Gay, 1985). During the Pacific War, Japanese soldiers in military uniforms, using the power of their weapons, took colonized women to occupied territories and war zones for sexual exploitation. Currently, many Japanese men in business suits, using the power of their currency, sexually exploit women from other Asian countries, either by making sex tours to those countries or by luring them into Japan's own sex industry.

Despite differing contexts and circumstances, the everyday living and working conditions of these three groups of women show similarities: inadequate housing, either low wages or none at all, long working hours with few days off, lack of freedom, inadequate medical and welfare benefits, and, for many, the need to do extra manual labor in addition to their sexual labor (Go, 1992).

The important factor that distinguishes the "comfort women" from the other groups is that they were directly recruited by the Japanese Imperial Army. In fact, Imperial Ordinance no. 519 (the *Josei Teishin Kinro Rei*, "Women's Volunteer Labor Ordinance"), issued on August 22, 1944, gave official recognition to the already well-established practice (*Korea Herald*, February 8, 1992; *Chungang Ilbo*, February 8, 1992). The proclamation was issued in an attempt to shore up the flagging morale of the Imperial Army (Suzuki, 1990).

The conscription of the *Chongshindae/Juguatanfu* and the institutionalization of the *wianso/iansho* within the framework of the Japanese Imperial Army thus amounts to a state crime approved by the Emperor, administered by the Japanese colonial military government, and supported by the prevailing sexist, racist, and classist attitude that young, poor, colonized women are sexual commodities at the mercy of men and the state (Go, 1992).

There is some evidence that the *Chongshindae/Juguatanfu* were considered by the Japanese Army to be the female counterpart of *kamikaze* soldiers, who offered their lives for the Emperor. One photograph shows a group of "comfort women" wearing plain white headbands *(hachimaki)* with a picture of the Japanese flag *(hinomaru)* and the word *kamikaze* with a picture of the Japanese flag *kamikaze* printed on them (Chon, 1992).

Furthermore, it may be postulated that Japan's institutionalization of *Chongshindae/Juguatanfu* was one facet of its attempt to control the Korean population by assimilation, on the one hand, and dispersal overseas, on the other. Many thousands of young Korean men and women were drafted as soldiers, coal miners, factory workers, and as sex slaves. Some have even speculated that the *Chongshindae/Juguatanfu* policy was genocide insofar as it left thousands of young Korean women of childbearing age infertile (Chung-myon Kim, 1992).

WHY HAS THE ISSUE OF *CHONGSHINDAE/JUGUNIANFU* BEEN BURIED FOR ALMOST HALF A CENTURY?

There are several reasons why the issue of *Chongshindae/Juguatanfu* has been ignored in Korea-Japan relations for almost half a century.

Confucian Cultural Ideology

In Korean tradition, a woman's chastity has been considered more valuable than even life itself. The feminine ideal requires virginity before marriage and chaste behavior after marriage. A woman who loses her virginity becomes "damaged goods," unmarriageable and socially ostracized. This Confucian ideology leads the victims of sexual exploitation to silently endure their *haan*, the unresolved pain and anguish caused by injustice inflicted on the innocent and the powerless. The internalized oppression resulting from Confucian socialization made it almost impossible for most of the surviving *Chongshindae/Jugu012nianfu* to return to their home villages and families, or even to talk about their experiences (Yun, 1991; Kim, 1992). Thus the former "comfort women" who never returned to Korea but stayed in the foreign lands where they worked as sex slaves during the war, kept silent for almost half a century. Until they began in recent years to receive support and encouragement from feminist organizations in Korea, the former *Chongshindae/Jugu012nianfu* have been unable to realize that they are survivors rather than merely victims of sexual violence.

Denial and Irresponsibility of the Japanese Government

During the war, the Japanese Army intentionally camouflaged the presence of the *Chongshindae/Jugu012nianfu* by not keeping accurate or honest records, instead labeling them as military supplies. Immediately after Japan's defeat, the military appears to have destroyed most of the documents proving that the Imperial Army played a direct role in recruiting the "comfort women" and in administering the "comfort centers."

The Japanese government avoided raising the issue during the drafting of the 1965 treaty normalization relations between Korea and Japan. Even as recently as July 1992, the Japanese government announced that there was no available hard evidence (*tegakari*, something that could be grasped in the hands) proving that the Japanese Imperial Army had engaged in forcibly recruiting Korean women into military sex slavery during the Pacific War.

The Militaristic/Capitalist Sociopolitical Structure and the Indifference of Korean Society Toward the Issue After the War

The militaristic postwar sociopolitical structure in South Korea, caused by the division of the country after the Pacific War, actively promoted sex tourism in order to obtain foreign currency and, consequently, may have been in no position to criticize the Japanese government over military prostitution during the war (Matsui, 1975). Moreover, during the negotiations for the 1965 treaty, leaders of the Korean government were eager to gain Japan's economic and technical assistance in reconstructing after the Korean War. Such assistance was urgently needed for restoring the political stability that had been undermined by the division of the Korean peninsula after the Pacific War. Therefore, Korean government officials, many of whom had cooperated with the Japanese colonial government officials during the war, did not bring up issues related to the Japanese colonization of Korea, such as the *Chongshindae/Jugu012nianfu* (Senda, 1992).

It is also probable that the Korean people in general did not want to recall the painful experiences of Japanese colonization and did not feel any particular empathy with the "comfort women," since the majority of the latter were daughters of marginalized, poor Korean farmers.

Classism of Korean Women and Racism and Classism of Japanese Women

The class consciousness of upper- and middle-class Korean women, and the sense of racial or ethnic superiority on the part of Japanese women, prevented either group from identifying strongly with the *Chongshindae/Jugunianfu* and taking up their cause as a feminist issue until the late 1980s. In addition, the internalized oppression caused by Confucian patriarchal socialization led ordinary Japanese women to identify more closely with male relatives who fought in the Pacific War than with either Japanese prostitutes or poor, rural, colonized Korean *Chongshindae/Jugunianfu*. Some women even thought it unnecessary to bring up the subject insofar as it could be considered one of the necessary evils or "unfortunate incidents" of a brutal war. Perhaps they rationalized that anything can happen in times of war, and that there has always been a relationship between militarism, on the one hand, and prostitution and/or sexual violence against women, on the other.

GLOBAL FEMINIST AND GRASSROOTS COALITION POLITICS: THE *CHONGSHINDAE/JUGUNIANFU* MOVEMENT

Even though works on the *Chongshindae/Jugunianfu* by Japanese journalists, historians, and former recruiters had begun to appear in the early 1970s, most former soldiers of the Japanese Imperial Army waited until recently to tell their stories anonymously on "hotlines" set up between January and March 1992 in Tokyo and other cities in Japan. Some former soldiers in their late seventies and their eighties called the hotlines because they wanted to tell their stories before they died (*Jugunianfu 110 Ban*, 1992). Even though books had already been published on the topic, it was the Korean Church Women United and the Japan Women's Christian Temperance Union who first made the general public aware of this long-suppressed history and made it into a political issue, helping spread the movement to other parts of Asia, such as North Korea, Taiwan, the Philippines, Thailand, and Myanmar (Burma) (*Honolulu Star Bulletin*, August 10, 1992). Their activities, and the Japanese government responses to them, focused world attention on the *Chongshindae/Jugunianfu* as an instance of the gross violation of the human rights of women by the Japanese Imperial Army.

Recent Events: Direct Actions of Women's Coalition Politics

This darkest page in the history of Korea-Japan relations became a political issue after a coalition of Korean women's groups, Japanese women's groups, and the Uri-Yosong network of Korean women residing in Japan conducted investigative exposure trips, public forums, and television programs both in Korea and Japan that featured the personal testimonies of former Korean "comfort women" (*Jugunianfu Mondai Uri-Yosong* Network, 1991). The Korean groups collected their oral histories, retrieved public records, and collected research data to reveal the truth. The coalition group in Japan raised funds for a network of lawyers supporting the lawsuit filed against the Japanese government by nine Korean former "comfort women."

The following paragraphs will present a chronology of important events that galvanized the *Chongshindae/Jugunianfu* movement in Korea and Japan, a movement that later spread to the Philippines, Taiwan, Thailand, North Korea, and other parts of the Asia/Pacific region (Carter, 1992).

On January 7, 1988, upon hearing of the Korean government's plan to send an emissary to Emperor Hirohito's funeral, over 200 members of women's groups—Korean Church Women United, the Korean Association of Women Theologians, the Women's Studies Research Committee of Ewha Woman's University, the Advocacy and Research Committee on the *Chongshindae* Issue, the Federation of University Women Students, the YWCA of Korea, and the Federation of Korean Women's Associations—drafted a protest letter that included a statement on the issue of the *Chongshindae/Jugunianfu*. Then the members staged a demonstration march at Tapkol Park (formerly Pagoda Park), the site where a nationwide demonstration was launched for national independence against Japanese colonial rule on March 1, 1919 (Suzuki).

In February 1988, Professor Yun Chung-ok and two members of the Korean Church Women United made an investigative exposure trip to Japan, visiting Fukuoka in northern Kyushu, Sapporo and Hakodate in Hokkaido, Tokashiki Island in Okinawa, and Kashiwa-shi on the outskirts of Tokyo. In 1989, Professor Yun also made exposure trips to Thailand and Papua New Guinea (Yun, 1991).

In April 1988, the International Conference on "Women and Tourism," sponsored by the Korean Church Women United, was held on Cheju Island, Korea. Korean and Japanese women have been writing and demonstrating both in Japan and Korea against sex tourism since the 1970s (Korean Church Women United, 1983). As early as 1977, the Asian Women's Association was formed to protest the Japanese sex tours to South Korea. It holds monthly study meetings, engages in protest actions, and maintains links with other women's groups both in Japan and abroad. And in April 1986, the Japan Women's Christian Temperance Union opened a shelter called HELP to provide assistance to migrant women workers in Japan (Iyori, 1987). A workshop held in 1985 entitled "Solidarity Among Migrant Women" at the NGO (Non-Governmental Organizations) Forum in Nairobi, Kenya, organized by the World Council of Churches, had already called for strengthening international solidarity and government involvement to deal with the flow of women overseas (Iyori, 1987). At the 1988 conference on Cheju Island, Professor Yun Chong-ok of Ewha Woman's University made a presentation on the *Chongshindae/Jugunianfu* issue that enabled participants from Korea and Japan to make the historical connection between the *Chongshindae/Jugunianfu* and sex tourism (Takahashi, 1992) .

In June 1990, the Korean Church Women United responded in anger to a Japanese Diet member's announcement that the *Chongshindae/Jugunianfu* would be treated as unrelated to other issues involving Koreans recruited for forced labor by the Japanese colonial government.

On November 16, 1990, the Korean Council for Women Drafted by Japan for Sexual Slavery was officially formed under the leadership of Professor Yun Chung-ok. The Korean Council is a coalition of 36 women's organizations dedicated to exposing the truth about this aspect of the Japanese colonization of Korea and restoring the human dignity of the victims who have had to live in *han*-ridden silence and shame for almost half a century.

However, the most important event, which raised the consciousness of people everywhere, including many Japanese, was the first public testimony by a former Korean *Chongshindae/Jugunianfu*. On August 14, 1990, a female Korean atomic bomb victim brought Kim Hak-soon, a 67-year-old, childless widow and former "comfort woman" in Manchuria, to tell her story at the offices of Korean Church Women United. This woman's courageous decision created the momentum to unleash a series of activities and an outpouring of angry responses in both Korea and Japan.

In a series of public forums in December 1991 sponsored by the Japanese Women's Network Group, she told audiences in several Japanese cities her story:

My whole body and soul still shiver just thinking and talking about my experience as a *Chongshindae* woman, even when I saw that Japanese flag, the *hino-maru*, as I was boarding the Japan Airlines flight to come here. As a living witness, my blood boiled when I heard the Japanese government denying its role in the *Chongshindae* system on the television newscast and their refusal to teach history correctly to younger generations. As a former *Chongshindae*, when I refused to have sex with soldiers, they said that they would kill me because I was under orders from the Emperor, the commanding officer, and the soldier himself, a soldier of the Japanese Imperial Army.

It took just one courageous woman's action to raise public awareness and encourage other former *Chongshindae/Jugunianfu* and their relatives to come forward with their stories. In addition, some former Japanese government officials and schoolteachers, who were directly or indirectly responsible for recruitment, have come forward publicly to ask for forgiveness (Senda, 1992).

Since 1983, Yoshida Seiji, a former chief of the National Service Labor Recruitment branch office in the southern Japanese port of Shimonoseki in Yamaguchi Prefecture, has written two books on his war crimes involving Korean *Chongshindae/Jugunianfu*. He was the first Japanese to publicly confess and to apologize to Koreans on visits to Korea in 1983 and again in August 1992 as an invited guest of the Fraternity of Survivors and Relatives of Pacific War Victims of Korea. He considers the *Chongshindae/Jugunianfu* to be "the most serious war crime in the twentieth century." He admitted that between 1942 and 1945, with assistance of the Japanese police, he had "hunted"—mostly in the Cholla provinces—approximately 5000 Koreans, including 1000 Korean women aged 18 to 30, some of them nursing mothers, and then handed them over to the Japanese Imperial Army at Shimonoseki (*Honolulu Star Bulletin*, August 12, 1992; Yoshida, 1983).

On December 6, 1991, three former "comfort women," joined by six more on April 7, 1992, filed a lawsuit in Tokyo district court in conjunction with lawsuits filed by thirty-five members of the Fraternity of Survivors and Relatives of Pacific War Victims of Korea. The first public hearing of this lawsuit was held on June 1, 1992, at Tokyo district court (Korean Council, 1991).

On January 8, 1992, members of the Korean Council marched in protest in front of the Japanese Diet. The following Wednesday, January 15, 1992, members of the Korean Council were joined by 400 people, including members of the Fraternity of Pacific War Victims' families and six other organizations, in the first of a series of weekly demonstrations in front of the Japanese Embassy in Seoul, the longest-running weekly demonstrations in South Korea's history (*Chungang Ilbo*, Nov. 16, 1992). Professor Yun Chung-ok announced that the Korean Council would continue the weekly demonstrations until the Japanese government met the six demands in the lawsuit made by the nine former *Chongshindae/Jugunianfu*.

On January 17, 1992, public outrage was created by testimonies from former *Chongshindae/Jugunianfu*, and the discovery of wartime documents by Yoshimi Yoshiaki of Chuo University at the Self-Defense Department a few days before Prime Minister Miyawa's visit. He was then obliged to promise that the Japanese government would conduct an investigation and publicize its report on the issue of Korean *Chongshindae/Jugunianfu* (*Shisa Journal*, January 30, 1992).

Between January and March 1992, the Korean Council installed a hotline in Seoul to encourage women victims, relatives, and those responsible for drafting *Chongshindae/Jugunianfu* to come forward with their testimonials and records. During the three-month period beginning January 24, a total of 390 people responded, of whom 155 were either victims or their relatives, including 74 former "comfort women" who came forward and entered their names in the government's registry of surviving *Chongshindae/Jugunianfu* (Chongshindae Task Force, 1992; Hangyore Shinmun, February 6, 1992). Members of the research committee of the Korean Council have conducted life-history interviews of 39 former "comfort women."

During the same period, between January 14–16 and March 30–31, 1992, hotlines were set up in Tokyo, Osaka, Kyoto, and Fukuota by the Japanese Women's Network Group (a network of sixteen Christian and women's groups in Japan), a coalition of three groups of Korean women residents in Japan, and other Japanese grassroots organizations such as Nihon no Sengo Sekinin o Hakkiri Saeseru Kai (Association for Japan Taking Clear Postwar Responsibility). The Osaka hotline alone, *Jugunianfu* Number 110, received 230 calls on March 30–31, 1992. Sixty-one of the callers, most of whom were Japanese military personnel and associated civilian workers, confessed personal involvement in the Japanese military's *Chongshindae/Jugunianfu* system.

One of the purposes of these hotlines was to gather facts from former "comfort women," Japanese soldiers, officials, and citizens who were involved in the *Chongshindae/Jugunianfu* system in order to raise the political consciousness of the general public and compel the Japanese government to accept the demands made by the plaintiffs in the lawsuit filed by the Korean former "comfort women."

On February 4, 1992, Professor Grant Goodman of the University of Kansas released documents entitled "Comfort Women and Comfort Center Management Regulations," recorded in February 1943 in Manila. These documents clearly state that comfort center management fell under the supervision of Japanese military communication officers (*Hangyore Shinmun*, February 6, 1992).

Between February and March 1992, Professor Lee Hyo-jae of the Korean Council addressed audiences in New York City, Washington, D.C., and Los Angeles, at the invitation of Korean American Women United and the Women's Association for the Commemoration of the March First Korean Independence Movement (*Chungang Ilbo*, March 10, 1992). On April 1, 1992, the latter Women's Association launched a petition drive aimed at building a monument to the *Chongshindae/Jugunianfu*. The Los Angeles chapter of Korean American Women United subsequently sent three delegates to Pyongyang for a September 1–6, 1992, meeting entitled "Women's Role in Peace in Asia."

On May 2, 1992, a mutual support of former "comfort women" called the Mugunghwa Chamae Hoe [Hibiscus Sisters Association] was formed in Seoul, Korea.

On May 13, 1992, the Human Rights Commission of the United Nations announced in Geneva that it would conduct a fact-finding investigation on the *Chongshindae/Jugunianfu* issue. Furthermore, the Commission's Working Group on Contemporary Forms of Slavery, composed of the Coalition Against Trafficking in Women and the International Abolitionist Federation, placed the issue on the official agenda for its August 15, 1992, meeting. Three delegates from the Korean Council and one former "comfort woman" testified at the meeting (*Chungang Ilbo*, August 11, 1992; Lee, 1992).

In June 1992, Professor Yun Chung-ok and members of the *Jugunianfu* Investigation Group (Jugunianfu Mondai o Kyumeisuru Kai) made trips to former Manchuria to locate the graves of "comfort women."

On July 6, 1992, a Japanese government spokesperson offered an apology that admitted official Japanese Army involvement in the recruitment of "comfort women" and the administration of "comfort centers." However, the statement neither recognized forced recruit-ment nor offered any compensation to the individual victims. At a press conference the next day, the Korean Council denounced the insincere attitude of the Japanese government and the inadequacy of any statement that denied the coercive patterns of recruitment and sexual enslavement.

Also in July 1992, documents surfaced from Indonesian war-crime tribunals held in Sumatra. This was the first documented evidence of forced recruitment, and it revealed that a total of 300 Dutch women had been coerced into Japanese military sex slavery under the threat of death to themselves and their families (*Asahi Shimbun*, July 21, 1992).

On August 10–11, 1992, nearly 100 women participants, including 9 former South Korean *Chongshindae/Jugunianfu* and 30 delegates from Korea, Japan, Taiwan, Hong Kong, the Philippines, and Thailand, met in Seoul under the sponsorship of the Korean Council. The participants founded the Comfort Women Issue–Asian Solidarity Conference to continue networking, cooperative research, and advocacy work. Calling this issue the most atrocious crime committed against women, these participants from six Asian and Pacific countries passed a resolution with five demands to be sent to the Japanese government, other relevant governments, non-governmental women's groups, and the United

Nations Human Rights Commission (Soon Han Choe, 1992; Carter, 1992; Yang, 1992).

Between August 3 and 28, 1992, four Non-Governmental Organizations, including the World Council of Churches and the International Education Development, testified before the UN Human Rights Commission's Subcommission and decided to request that Professor Theo van Boven, a UN-appointed expert on compensation for victims of gross violations of human rights, prepare a report by August 1993. He subsequently visited Japan and Korea between December 3 and 11, 1992, to conduct investigations (Hi-kyong Kim, 1992).

On September 1–6, 1992, women of Korean Japanese ancestry from South Korea, Japan, and the United States, attended a conference in Pyongyang entitled "Women's Role in Peace in Asia." This was the third in a series of conferences initiated in February 1991 by Japanese women. North and South Korean former "comfort women" gave their personal testimonies. Some of the North Korean women testified to being drafted as early as 1929, much earlier than the South Korean women (*Hangyore Shinmun*, September 6, 1992). Such conferences have provided a valuable opportunity for Japanese and South Korean women from non-governmental organizations to meet face to face with North Korean women who share their two major concerns: national unification and the *Chongshindae/Jugunianfu* issue (*Yosong Shinmun*, October 30, 1992).

On October 13, 1992, infuriated by the Japanese government's attitude, a coalition of Korean women's groups submitted an open letter to Japanese Prime Minister Miyazawa protesting the proposed establishment of a welfare fund for former *Chongshindae/Jugunianfu* and demanding that Japanese government representatives visit surviving women victims and take responsibility for respecting the human rights of the people of the Asia-Pacific region. The Japanese government issued no response (Korean Council, 1992c).

SUMMARY AND CONCLUSION

The central task of those engaged in active research on the *Chongshindae/Jugunianfu* issues is to recover evidence and rewrite the history of these ordinary Korean women, whom Professor Yun Chung-ok calls "the central figures of the history of Korea" (Lee & Kim, 1991) a combination of documents from official archives and personal testimonies from surviving witnesses has made it increasingly difficult for the Japanese government to deny any official role in the forcible and/or deceitful recruitment of large numbers of women as sexual slaves for the Japanese military and colonial government. The true picture is slowly emerging.

For feminists, there is a broader need to place this issue in a comprehensive analysis of the sexual exploitation of women and to build a global political coalition to liberate women from sexual, economic, political, and racial oppressions. Japan's colonial and sexual exploitation of Korean and other Asian and Pacific women is not just past history. Its postwar economic strength has allowed Japan to continue exploiting foreign women as a source of cheap labor and sexual services, no longer just overseas but in Japan itself.

The *Chongshindae/Jugunianfu* issue is on the cutting edge for the contemporary women's movement in Korea, Japan, and other parts of the Pacific and Asia. For the first time in the history of Korea-Japan relations, Korean and

Japanese women have engaged in formally organized coalition activities with the common goal of recovering and correcting Japan's official accounts of its colonial history. It is hoped that such coalition politics will help bring about a reconciliation between Japanese women, Korean women residing in Japan, Korean women elsewhere, and women in other Pacific and Asian countries by leaving a legacy of shared struggle for justice, peace, and freedom to future generations.

Monetary restitution for the "comfort women" would be welcome, but not before the Japanese government officially acknowledges its crimes against humanity and issues a formal apology. When a young male Japanese reporter asked her how much she was seeking in compensation, Shim Mija, one of the former "comfort women," gave the following angry response before fainting at a March 1992 public forum in Japan.

I did not come all the way here to ask for money. Neither any kind of apology by anybody nor any amount of money will bring back 69 years of my lost life. I struggled hard to survive, waiting for this day when I could tell the truth to the whole world so that others' lives will be saved. We can save all of our and our children's lives by including the living truth of my experience in history books for future generations so that this kind of injustice against all of our humanity will not be repeated again! (*Zenkoku Fujin Shimbun*, March 25, 1992)

Nevertheless, the Japanese government is considering setting up a fund to provide economic and medical support for former *Chongshindae/Jugunianfu*, a kind of *mimaikin* (a monetary gift to a sick person). The government also recently said it planned to include a yet-undetermined amount of money in the next year's budget to create a foundation that would funnel money to the Japanese Red Cross (*Hangyore Shinmun*, July 8, 1992). In response, the Korean Council strongly protested the idea of the Japanese government paying *mimaikin* for damaging women's bodies, finding it extremely humiliating. Instead, it announced plans to raise funds from Koreans in order to conduct its own investigations and to pay for living expenses, medical bills, and housing for *Chongshindae/Jugunianfu* survivors in order to be able to refuse Japan's token handout. A nationwide fund drive began on March 1, 1993, on the anniversary of the March First (1919) Korean independence movement. Among the recent donors was a Buddhist monk who turned over all of his life savings and a Buddhist lay woman who donated a piece of her property to be used to provide housing for surviving *Chongshindae/Jugunianfu* (Korean Council, 1992b; Ik-rim Choe, 1992; *Hangyore Shinmun*, August 30, 1992).

Korean women residing in Japan, who have been actively involved in this issue, feel that they came to understand more clearly their own present social condition by placing their *Chongshindae/Jugunianfu* foremothers within the larger framework of Japan's historical colonization and contemporary neocolonization that they still experience in their everyday lives (Yun et al., 1992). Japanese feminist historian Suzuki Yuko (1990) writes, "Japanese women also have an obligation to see justice done for our Korean sisters. Our own liberation is bound together with correcting injustices done to these Korean sisters, thus affirming our own identity as women and as caring human beings."

Indeed, it is only by retrieving and validating the whole experience of the *Chongshindae/Jugunianfu* that all of our humanity can be restored. Only then can we revitalize our strength and enlarge our vision, enabling us to continue our common struggle to change the world into a better and more humane place to live for us all and for future generations.

NOTE

1. From Alice Yun Chai, "Asian-Pacific Feminist Coalition Politics." Reprinted from *Korean Studies*, Vol. 17, by permission of the publisher. © 1993 by University of Hawaii Press.

I want to express my sincere appreciation to Yun Chung-ok, Lee Hyo-jae, Park Jin Sook, Yu Choon Ja, Cho Sung Sook, and Kye Young Bok, David K. S. Suh, and Yun Chong Koo of Korea, and to Yang Ching Ja, Park Hwa Mi, Suzuki Yuko, Takahashi Kikue, Shima Yoko, Matsui Yayori, and Aiko Carter, Kuniko Funabashi, Yumi Lee, Emiko Terazawa, Chung Mo, Etsuko Chida, and Lisa Go of Japan, for giving their encouragement and support in doing the research and acquiring the resource materials for this paper.

I also want to thank Pauline Sugino, Ji Sun Chang, Freda Hellinger, Katsue Akiba Reynolds, and Joel Bradshaw for their editorial assistance and help with romanization, and the faculty, students, and staff members of the University of Hawaii Women's Studies Program for their moral and technical support.

I am also very grateful to Ellen Chapman, Shiro Saito, Kyungmi Chun, Lan Hiang T. Char, Masato Matsui, Alice Mak, Jonathan Okamura, Glenda Roberts, and Katherine Yoshimura of the University of Hawaii's Hamilton Library for their assistance in searching the literature and in romanization.

Finally, I want to express my deep appreciation to the surviving "comfort women" and others who have been actively involved in the *Chongshindae/Jugunianfu* issue in Korea, Japan, and other parts of Asia and the Pacific. They provided the inspiration for my research and advocacy work.

REFERENCES

Asahi Shimbun. (1992). " 'Cha no settai o,' jitsu wa iansho ['To serve tea,' but really a comfort center]." July 21, p. 11.
_____. (1992). "Oranda josei mo ianfu [Dutch women also comfort women]." July 21, p. 1.
_____. (1992). "Iansho, malay hanto zeniki ni [Comfort centers were all over the malay peninsula]." August 14, p. 23.
Association of Anti-Prostitution Activity. (1984). *Anti-Prostitution Activities in Japan.*
Carter, Aiko. (1992). "Comfort Women Contesting History." *Japan Christian Activity News*, pp. 4-8.
Choe, Ik-rim (1992). "Chongshindae nanum ul chip konrip" [Construction plan for house of sharing for surviving former *Chongshindae/Jugunianfu*]. *Hangyore Shinmun*, September 27, p. 14.
Choe, Soon Han. (1992). "Chongshindae munje haegyol: Aju yondae kyolsong [Resolving the comfort women issue: Asian solidarity organizing conference]." *Chosun Ilbo*, August 12.
Chon, Hymoyong. (1992). "Shinmun nonp'yong: Chongshindae podo [Newspaper editorial: Chongshindae news report]." *Hangyore Shinmun*, January 22.
Chongshindae Task Force, Asia Section Chief. (1992). *Iljeha kindae wianbu shilt'ae chosa* [Report on actual conditions of military comfort women under Japanese colonization], pp. 8-9. Seoul: Ministry of Foreign Affairs.

Chungang Ilbo. (1992). "Chongshindae kongshik chosa p'alp'yo: Ilwang ui chongshindae," February 8.
_____. (1992). "Iljongbu posang yogu tanch'ae shiwi ittara [Continuing demonstra-
tions demanding Japanese government compensation]," November 16.
_____. (1992). "The Japanese Emperor's Direct Role in the Comfort Women Order,"
February 8.
_____. (1992). "Local News of Los Angeles," March 1.
_____. (1992). "The Chongshindae Will Testify at the Human Rights Commission of
the United Nations: Korean Delegates Sent to Geneva on August 15, 1992,"
August 11.
Gay, Jill. (1985). "The 'Patriotic' Prostitute: Her County Promotes Her as an Economic Asset." *The Progressive,* pp. 34-36.
Go, Lisa. (1992). "Jugunianfu, Karayuki, Japayuki: A Continuity in Commodification." *Japanese Militarism Monitor,* 53: 9-16.
_____. (1988). "An Overview of Filipino Migration." *Women from Across the Seas:
Migrant Workers in Japan.* Tokyo: Asian Women's Association, p. 78.
Hangyore Shinmun. (1992). "Chongshindae kyokpun ui monjitsok ch'ongjung
hunukkim kwa han-sum [Audience reacts with tears and sighs as witnesses tell
stories with indignation]," September 6, p. 5.
_____. (1992). July 8, p. 15.
_____. (1992). "Chongshindae kwalli kyonjik palgyon [Discovery of documents re-
lating to the management of comfort women]," February 6.
Honolulu Star-Bulletin. (1992). "Sex-slave Procurer Rips Japan's Stand," August 12,
p. A19.
_____. (1992). "Former WWII Sex Slaves Around Asia Join Efforts," August 10, pp.
4-8.
_____. (1992). "World War II 'Comfort Women' Papers Found by Group," December
7, p. A7.
Iyori, Naoko. (1987). "The Traffic in 'Japayuki-san.'" *Japan Quarterly,* 84-88.
Jugunianfu 110 ban [Jugunianfu hotline number 110]. (1992). Tokyo: Meiseki
Shoten, pp. 154-156.
Jugunianfu Mondai Uri-Yosong Network. (1991). *Kono han o haku tame ni: Gen
jugunianfu kim haksoon-san no hanashi o kiku atsumai o oete [In order to re-
solve han: After the meeting to hear former Jugunianfu Kim Haksoon's story],*
December 9, pp. 5-10. Tokyo.
Kelker, Govind. (1992). "On the Question of 'Comfort Women.'" Paper presented at
the Comfort Women Issue-Asian Women in Solidarity Conference.
Kim, Chong-hyok, & Wha-shik Tae. (1992). "The Exposure of Chongshindae at the
Japanese Court." *Chungang Daily,* May 28, p. 8.
Kim, Hi-kyong. (1992). "U.N. Chongshindae munje pongyok kaeip [U.N. fully in-
volved in Chongshindae issue]." *Donga Ilbo,* December 12.
Kim, Il-myon. (1980). *Nihon hisei aishi [Sorrowful History of Japanese Women],*
pp. 184-192. Tokyo: Gendaishi Shuppan-kai.
Kim, Jae-on. (1992). "Chastity as a Social Ideal in Korea: Comparative and Histori-
cal Explorations." Paper presented at the First Pacific Basin International Con-
ference on Korean Studies, Honolulu, July 27-August 2.
Kim, Ki Chan. (1992). "Chongshindae Nun 'P'iya' So Shijak Toetta [Chongshindae
started as 'p'iya]." *Chunggang Ilbo,* August 15.
Kim, Kyong-yong (1992). "Chongshindae arirang: Muryo ch'ulhyon [Chongshin-
dae arirang: Benefit performance]." *Donga Ilbo,* October 15, p. 13.
Korea Herald. (1992). "Hirohito OK'd Mobilization of 'Comfort Girls.'" February 8.
Korea News Review. (1992). "Bitter Experiences Not Forgotten," January 25, p. 5-7.

Korean Association of Women Theologians. (1991). *Biblical Look at the Suffering of Chongshindae Women.* Seoul: Korean Association of Women Theologians.

Korean Church Women United. (1983). "Kisaeng kwangwang: Chonguk sagae chi-yok shilt'ae chosa [Kisaeng sex tourism: The nationwide four-district survey]." *Resource Collection.* Seoul.

Korean Council for Women Drafted by Japan for Sexual Slavery. (1991). *Chong-shindae munje charyojip* [Chongshindae issue resource collection], vol. 1. Seoul: Korean Council for Women Drafted by Japan for Sexual Slavery.

_____. (1991). "*Chongshindae*-Related Data: Statement Submitted for the Lawsuit Against the Japanese Government to Compensate Korean World War II Victims." Filed on December 6. Seoul: Korean Council for Women Drafted by Japan for Sexual Slavery.

_____. (1992a). "Chongunwianbu yonp'yo [Chronology of military comfort women]." (Manuscript). Seoul: Korean Council for Women Drafted by Japan for Sexual Slavery.

_____. (1992b). "Our Position on Japan's Plan for These Surviving Former Chong-shindae/Jugunianfu," October 17. Seoul: Korean Council for Women Drafted by Japan for Sexual Slavery.

_____. (1992c). "Open Letter to the Prime Minister Miyazawa of Japan, October 13, 1992," *Japan Christian Activity News,* November, pp. 3-4.

Kunimitsu, Shiro, & Akira Sugimura. (1980). *Baishun no rekishi: Kage no nihonshi* [History of prostitution: Dark side of japanese history]. Tokyo: Nihon Shokan.

Lee, Suk Ku. (1992). "The United Nations Sets to Investigate the Truth Surrounding the Issue of Chongshindae." *Chungang Ilbo,* May 15.

Lee, Yoo-Lim, & Hee-Jung Kim. (1991). "Interview with Professor Yun Chung-ok, Chongshindae: The Shame of a Nation." *The Ewha Voice,* p. 2.

Matsui, Yayori. (1975). *Why I Oppose Kisaeng Tours: Exposing Economic and Sexual Aggression Against South Korean Women.* Tokyo: Femintem Press.

Nishino, Rumiko. (1992). "Chugoku tohokubu no ashiato o tadoru [Following the trail in northeastern China]." *Zenkoku Fujin Shimbun,* July 10, p. 5.

Ohshima, Shuzuko, & Carolyn Francis. (1989). *Japan Through the Eyes of Women Migrant Workers.* Tokyo: Japan Women's Christian Temperance Union, p. 128.

Randolf, David S. (1991). "Filipino Workers in Japan: Vulnerability and Survival." *Kasarinian: A Philippine Quarterly of Third World Studies,* 6: 10.

Senda, Kako. (1992). *Jugunianfu to tenno* [Military comfort women and the Emperor]. Kamogawa Booklet. Kyoto: Kamogawa Shuppan.

Shisa Journal. "Criticism Against the Japanese Diplomacy of Apology," January, 30, 1992, pp. 6-7.

Shojo, Khoshutsu Reijo. (1992). "Ch'onyo konch'ul yongjang, kugyosaeng 'chongshindae chingbal'" [Drafting of elementary school girls as *Chongshindae*]. *Donga Ilbo,* January 15.

Suzuki, Yoko. (1990). "Sins Against Women." *New York City Tribune,* April 27.

Takahashi, Kikue. (1992). "Ima naze, jugunianfu mondai [Why now, the *Jugunianfu* issue?]." *Agora* 174, May 10, pp. 31-38.

Tamai, Noriko. (1984). *Hinomaru o koshi ni maite* [Wearing the hinomaru around the loins]. Tokyo: Gendaishi Shippankai, p. 86.

Yamaguchi, Akiko. (1989). "'Dekasegi kanko' ni kuru kankoku no onnatachi [Korean women who come as migrant sex-tour workers]." *Ajia to josei kaiho* [Asia and women's liberation]. October 20, Special Issue, *Ajia kara no dekasegi joseitachi* [Female migrant workers from Asia], pp. 16-17.

Yamasaki, Tomoko. (1972). *Sandakan hachiban shokan* [Sandakan number 8 brothel]. Tokyo: Chikuma Shobo, pp. 7, 258.

Yang, Sun Hi. (1992). "Chongshindae Investigation Needs an International Network: Asian Network Seminar on Victims' Personal Testimonies of Women from Involved Asian Countries." *Chungang Ilbo*, August 13.

Yoshida, Seiji. (1983). *Watakushi no senso hanzai: Chosenjin kyosei renko* [My war crimes: Forced recruitment of Koreans]. Tokyo: Sanchi Shobo.

Yosong Shinmun. (1992). *"Chongshindae wonhondul ui nok tallaenda* [Healing the han-ridden spirits of *Chongshindae*]," October 30.

Yun, Chung-ok. (1991). "Jugunianfu no ashiato o totte [Following the footsteps of the military comfort women]." *Chosenjin jugunianfu: Inpeisareta rekishi ni ima koso hikari o* [Korean military comfort women: Bringing to light the suppressed history]. Special issue of *Kankoku josei mondai shiryoshu* [Collection of resource materials on Korean women's issues], 8: 34-55. Tokyo: Zainichi Kankoku Minshu Josei Kai.

Yun, Chung-ok, et al. (1992). *Chosenjin josei ga mita ianfu mondai* [The comfort woman issue from the perspective of Korean women]. Tokyo: Sanichi Shobo, pp. 3-6.

Zenkoku Fujin Shimbun. (1992). "A Profile of Shim Mija-san." March 25, p. 1.

20

Revisioning of Family Reunions: A Case of Korean American Women and Their Families Separated by War[1]

Sook Ja Paik and Dong Soo Kim

The family is the most intimate context of human life and is the basic unit of modern society. Thus the family is a natural life space and structure for most people. Traditionally Asian societies have cherished the values of the family, especially in the form of large and extended kinship relationships. Even after being transplanted in North America, Asian communities today rely heavily on mutual support and cooperation among family members for their survival and prosperity.

When the family, as a close natural support system, breaks down for various natural and/or human-made causes, people are bound to suffer a great deal from the loss or undue disruption of major ties, network, and meaning in their lives. Especially when forced upon them by sudden natural disasters, violent conflicts, and wars, the impact of the involuntary disruption or separation of family life tends to be pervasively destructive and long-lasting.

In this century alone, the international community witnessed immense destruction, dispersion, and suffering of family lives through two world wars in 1914 and 1939. In recent decades, numerous families were separated, dispersed, and lost between the China mainland and Taiwan; North and South of Korea; the western and eastern parts of Europe; among Soviet Jews; displaced Palestinians; Indo-Chinese refugees; some Cuban and other Central Americans; and most recently the Iraqi Kurds. They have in most cases become separated from their family members for a long period or even permanently by external forces, not by choice.

The United Nations Universal Declaration of Human Rights and the International Covenants on Human Rights (II) as an embodiment of ideals of civilized human society declared that the family was society's natural basic grouping and it had rights for protection from society and government. In order to help resolve the problem of family separation in the same spirit, the Geneva Agreement (August 12, 1949) guaranteed the reunion of separated families in its Fourth Agreement, Article 26. Also, the Protocol Concerning Supplement to the Geneva Agreement and Protection of Victims of International Conflicts (Protocol 1, June 10, 1977) stipulated proper service provisions for, and rights of, separated families in its Articles 32 and 74. With the establishment of separated family provisions of the Geneva Agreement as international law, the 18th International Red Cross Conference (Toronto, 1952) adopted a resolution that each national Red Cross serve as a mediating agency to help reunite separated families as a humanitarian task. Subsequent International Red Cross (IRC) and other conferences[2] adopted resolutions with regard to separated families. Thus the international community recognized the family as an important basic human right by international agreement and that separated families have a guaranteed right to contact and reunite with their families by international law.

HISTORICAL BACKGROUND

Before the turn of the century Korea, as a small "hermit" kingdom, was invaded by several foreign powers on numerous occasions; and since 1910 she was occupied and colonialized by Imperial Japan. During Japanese rule, many Koreans voluntarily or involuntarily moved to Manchuria, the eastern part of Russia, and other countries as political or economic refugees. In 1945 at the conclusion of World War II, which defeated Japan, Korea was "liberated" by the Allied Forces. In order to receive the surrender of the Japanese Armed Forces, the Korean peninsula was divided along the 38th parallel—North by the then Soviet Forces and South by the U.S. Supreme Command. This supposedly temporary arrangement of divided occupation was since fortified by the ideological confrontation of the Cold War between the free and communist worlds. In spite of the fact that Korea had been one nation for thousands of years with the same language, culture, race and ethnic ethos, both rival North and South leaders set up socialistic and capitalistic regimes, respectively, under supporting foreign auspices. Both in North and South there was violent strife and numerous political conflicts between the ideological camps. Many people had to hide, flee, or escape from the other side. Especially many landlords, Christians, and collaborators with the Japanese from the North took refuge in the South. In 1950 when the Korean War broke out on the peninsula, it caused extensive casualities and destruction, and forced the movement of millions of civilians and soldiers in both directions.

In this tragic process of the 3-year military conflict involving a total of 19 international fighting forces, 16 of which were under the United Nations' "police action," millions of Korean people were separated from their families. According to one Korean Red Cross report, the total number of separated family members between the North and South was estimated at about ten million (Korea Red Cross, 1976, p. 178). Another report estimated the following breakdown.

South-bound refugees before the war	3,500,000
Refugees during the war	1,000,000
Personnel kidnapped or ran to North	84,000
Unaccounted for or lost during the war	303,000
Northern POWs released in South	27,000
Koreans detained in Sakhalin (Saghalien)	40,000
Korean residents shipped to North from Japan	100,000
Total about	5,054,000

Counting both sides, separated and seeking, of about five million, the total estimated separated families may have amounted to about ten million between the North and South ("Oh! You're Alive," 1983; p. 283). Here the separated families may have included direct blood relations like parents, children, brothers and sisters, grandparents/grand-children, and kinships such as uncles and aunts, cousins, and nieces and nephews who were separated and divided due to the exploitation, division, and war instigated by foreign powers (Lee, 1985; p. 232). By extension, spouses and direct in-laws may have also been affected parties.

The most peculiar and tragic nature of these ten million families was their separation from the closest ties of their lives for some 40 years. They had no communication between themselves whatsoever, not even knowing whether the other side was still alive or not. Typical cases of their separation were that male heads of the households left for the South or the North, leaving the families behind; or young single men left their families or were taken away often without even notifying their families at a critical juncture of the fighting or imminent threat of arrest or draft. As a result, many women with young children and/or wives were left behind. These women were the main victims of the separation, waiting forever for their bygone husbands, sons, or fathers. As dramatized by the recent best seller, *The Three Day Promise* (Chung, 1990), the young man from the North, who now resides in the United States as a successful surgeon, took 33 years to keep his promise to return in three days to his mother and two sisters. There are millions of such women and men in both the North and South who for almost half a century lived and died without having any prospect for reuniting with their families or returning home from their "temporary escape."

On both sides of Korea, any individual attempt to contact families on the other side, let alone visit with them, was a crime punishable by national security laws. The separated family issue has been an exclusive government domain and politically exploited in the past 40 years. In spite of continuous political propaganda from both sides and then full-dress Red Cross talks with numerous rounds of preliminary, delegates, and working level meetings since 1971, only two staged meeting between separated families ever took place—for a couple of hours with less than 50 selected visitors from exchange delegates in the North and South capitols in 1985 (Korea Red Cross, 1986, pp. 178-237). This means only one brief encounter between 100 separated family members or less than 0.001% of ten million suffering people. As small step as it was, it was a significant first official step for family reunions. Their document pledges that "The Inter-Korean Red Cross talks are intended in the spirit of humanitarianism to resolve the pains of dispersed families. The Red Cross Societies in the South and the North made an oath to transcending the difference of ideology and structure between two" at the present time (Korea Red Cross, 1991, p. 10).

On December 13, 1991, the Agreement on Reconciliation, Nonaggression, and Exchange and Cooperation Between the South and the North was signed by both governments in Seoul. This historic agreement was the fruit of five high-level contacts between prime ministers of the South and the North that began in September, which in turn was followed by eight preparatory meetings since February 8, 1988. It has the first official provisions for reunions of separated families and in part it states: "article 18: Both parties shall permit free correspondence, reunions, and visits between family members and other relatives dispersed south and north, shall promote the reconciliation of divided families on their own and shall take measures to resolve other humanitarian issues (Reconciliation Agreement, 1992, pp. 30–32).

In spite of the poor outcomes in the past 40-plus years, this political agreement seemed to promise a major breakthrough for family reunions in the near future. Very recently both sides followed up this provision by reaching a tentative agreement to allow about 100 of the oldest separated members to visit their families from both sides (*The Korea Times*, May 8, 1992).

Even though any nongovernmental or private attempt to make contact with or to visit the separated families on the other side in Korea is still strictly forbidden and virtually impossible, there are two private nonprofit organizations in North America that have made significant humanitarian contributions for the cause of separated families throughout the United States, Canada, and elsewhere. They are the Organization for the Reunification of Separated Korean Families based in Toronto since 1980, and the One Korea Movement Committee for Separated Koran Families in Los Angeles founded in 1987. The cooperating counterpart in the North is a semi-governmental agency, The Committee for Aid to Koreans Abroad in Pyongyang. Working together, they have helped Koreans find about 6000 separated family members in the North and have arranged for a little over 4000 persons to visit their families in the North and one North Korean to visit in America in the past 10 or 11 years.[3] Those fortunate and daring enough to have visited their families have experienced tremendous joy, relief, and reflection after all the years of anxiety, worry, and uncertainty. Their experiences may serve as a pivotal cast for about ten million people on the Korean peninsula and elsewhere who are long awaiting to reunite and reconcile with their lost families in the coming years. As pioneers in this venture, their identity, perception, post-visit opinions, and requests have never before been systematically assessed, largely because of the confidential nature of their visits and the legal liability of the cooperating organizations.

WOMEN'S PERSPECTIVE

A unique aspect of this tragic separation experience is that women have suffered more physical and emotional burdens than have their male counterparts. Most, if not all, men who voluntarily or involuntarily abandoned their families eventually remarried in resettlement, while women were left with young children to rear and old parents to take care of with little or no resources. Historically, women have been exploited as men's possessions and for men's sexual needs under the paternalistic family system, or controlled and constrained morally as a model for a wise mother and good wife. Women are surrounded by a male-dominant environment and described through male-dominant standards. Gilligan (1982) wondered why women scored less than men in moral standards. She found that women had a different perspective from men in that women considered contextual or situational variables when they decided moral judgment. Women tend to care for, feel responsible to, and include others in their moral decisions. Furthermore, women tend to attach more values and meaning to relationships, connectedness, and intimacy. According to Surrey (1984), girls have taken a different developmental process because of their physical, cultural and social situations. Girls find themselves and develop their self-concept through continual close relationships with their mothers, while boys find themselves different from mothers and are encouraged to separate and individuate themselves from mothers. Therefore, according to a feminine psychological perspective, women's experiences and developmental processes are different in that men's developmental process emphasizes separation, autonomy, and individuation, whereas women mature and develop their self concept through relationships with others (Miller, 1984; Surrey, 1984; Kaplan, 1984; Stiver, 1985).

According to this women's psychology, self is not a separated, individuated entity. It is rather a "self-in-relationship" (Miller, 1984) or a relational self (Surrey, 1984). Women seem to have special ability to be sensitive to others' needs and to respond to them. Women contribute to building human relations and take an important role to enhance the development of others. Women gain their power by giving themselves in relationships. It is quite different from the power men exercise through authority and control. In other words, women express themselves in relations, exercise and exhibit their ability in caring for others, and develop self and gain satisfaction through relationships. Thus women represent reconciliation rather than division, and cooperation rather than competition. Therefore, women who lost their close family ties may have suffered much more.

PURPOSE AND METHODOLOGY

The purpose of this study is to examine the collective experiences of the family reunions among those Korean American and Korean Canadian citizens or residents who have already visited their families in North Korea. Particularly, 44 women's opinions were analyzed from 223 mail survey respondents, supplemented by personal interviews.

The survey instrument is a four-page anonymous questionnaire with mostly structured, composite items and a few short open-ended items, which is accompanied by a cover letter by one of the researchers and by one of the coordinators of the cooperation organizations. The instrument contains (1) subjects' demographic data; (2) factual information about separation and the first visit; (3) feelings about the visits; (4) impressions about North Korea; (5) perceptions about unification prospect; and (6) requests and suggestions to various parties. Through the cooperation of the two organizations mentioned above, survey instruments were sent out in January 1992, to all those known families that the organization helped visit in North Korea. With certain qualifications,[4] the instruments were mailed to 600 individuals and 198 individuals affiliated with the Toronto organization and Los Angeles organization, respectively. When both husband and wife visited North Korea, only one questionnaire was sent. Perhaps female visitors may be underrepresented, assuming a male-dominant culture among Koreans. Out of the mailing from the Toronto organization, 148 questionnaires (24.6%) were returned and 75 responses (37.8%) were received from the Los Angeles organization respectively.[5] A total of 223 cases (175 U.S. citizens or residents; 35 Canadian citizens or residents; and 13 missing) represents a 27.9% response rate.[6] There seems to be no serious subgroup differentials or non-response bias that would threaten the homogeneity of representativeness of the sample.

MAJOR FINDINGS

In this study a total of 44 female cases have been used for various analyses.

Demographic Characteristics

Ages of female subjects range from 47 to 73, with the median age being 62. This means their average age when they were separated from their families was about 20, assuming that most left home in 1950 when the war started. Their years of immigrant life ranges from 4 to 39, with a median of 18 years. Their immigrant status is as in Table 20.1. The majority are naturalized U.S. citizens. It is interesting to note that 18 (40.9%) of the female subjects are non-citizens, legal aliens in either the United States or Canada.[7] This may be due to the language proficiency requirement in some cases or due to their preference for Korean citizenship in some other cases. The educational level of women is lower than that of men as indicated in Table 20.1. The median educational level of female subjects is high school while that of male subjects is college graduate.

Table 20.1
Immigrant Status and Educational Level of Respondents

Immigration Status	Female Subjects		Male Subjects	
	N	%	N	%
U.S. Citizen	20	45.5	105	64.4
U.S. Resident	16	36.4	32	19.6
Canadian Citizen	6	13.6	24	14.7
Canadian Resident	2	4.5	2	1.2
Total	44	100.0	163	100.0
Educational Level				
Elementary school graduation	4	9.3	6	3.7
Middle school graduation	9	20.9	12	7.4
High school graduation	12	27.9	23	14.1
Some college	5	11.6	27	16.5
College graduation	8	18.6	51	31.3
Graduate school	5	11.6	44	27.0
Total	43[a]	100.0	163[a]	100.0

[a]Respondents who did not indicate their educational levels were not included.

Family Separation and Search Efforts

Most female subjects (19; 43.2%) were separated in 1950. The circumstances under which they came to be separated were varied. Primary reasons given were to take a supposedly brief refuge (46.5%), to escape to the South during the war (30.2%), and to follow husband or to marry (11.6%). Obviously, no male subject indicated marriage as a reason.

Their search efforts for the lost families have been long and slow. The very first attempt was by a single subject in 1974. Most separated families, however, started to look for their lost families from 1988 to 1989 (31; 73.8%), clearly reflecting realistic problems they had to face then. For their efforts, most found their separated families during the recent years of 1989 to 1990 (28; 68.3%). Since those who could not find their lost families were not included in this study, there is no way to assess their number or proportion. From personal interviews, however, it is clear that a significant number of persons have been anxiously waiting for news about their separated families for more than two years. All kinds of speculation abound, including indiscriminatory bombing and prevalent malnutrition and disease.

When asked why they have delayed their search for such a long time even after their resettlement in the United States and Canada, various reasons were provided as in Table 20.2. The reasons they gave indicated that there was no well-publicized service information by any organization, and they had prevailing fears, some of which may have been drawn out by concerns about the safety of families and relatives either in the North or South as well as worries about possible violation of laws either in Korea or in the United States or Canada.

Family Reunion Experience and Impression

Most female subjects visited their separate families for the first time in 1991 (26; 63.4%), even though one subject managed to visit as early as in 1980. This means that they have taken more than a painful 40-year journey to find and meet their separated families again. Using the typical average (median or mode) length, this long process is depicted in Figure 20.1.

Figure 20.1
Time Lapse between Family Separation and Reunion Visit

Family Separation		Search Initiation	Family Found	First Time Visit
-----|---------------/		/------|-----------------|----------------------------|------------		
1950		1988	1989	1991

Since the majority of subjects again delayed their visit even after they found their separated families, they were asked why they took such a long time. Even though four subjects said they did not take any length of time, 24 subjects (54.5%) cited as their reasons for waiting an official invitation from the North which was required for their entry into North Korea. Twenty-one subjects (47.7%) indicated personal reasons such as expenses, vacation time, sickness; and four subjects (9.1%) the reason of community suspicion and opposition from the family.

Most subjects (33; 78.6%) who indicated the number of visitations reported only once, even though eight (19.0%) subjects visited two to three times and one subject five times. When they visited for the first time, they must have had strong desire and expectation to meet the closest family members. The closest family members they hoped to see may indicate the level of interruption of family relationships in terms of loss of intimacy. Because of the time lapse, many of them could not meet their closest family members. Family members whom they hoped to meet and whom they actually met are listed in Table 20.2 according to the assumed closeness of their relationships. The majority of them looked for their brothers and sisters. The proportion of people who met their siblings was larger than the proportion of people who met their parents. In considering the ages of the parents, this discrepancy was as expected, Interestingly, spouses ranked very low as the closest family member in both the female and male categories. In the case of the female subjects, it was most likely that they either fled with their husbands or that they were single then.   It is almost inconceivable for women to have left their husbands behind. On the other hand, if they did, they might have given up their hope to meet their husbands, assuming they had remarried. In the case of male subjects, it can be explained in several different ways.[8] The total number of family members and relatives that met ranged from 4 to about 43, with a median of 15.

Their travel from the North American continent usually takes Tokyo–Beijing–Pyongyang or Seoul–Hong Kong–Beijing–Pyongyang routes instead of a direct Seoul–Pyongyang route, which is only about 130 miles.   Once they arrive at Pyongyang by a Chinese or North Korean Civic Airline, they are cordially accommodated in one of the western-style A-class hotels, and their entire itinerary is escorted by "guides" dispatched from the Committee for Aid to Koreans Abroad. Pyongyang is the completely rebuilt ancient capital of Korea with memorable scenic beauty and grand modern facilities. Almost always the visitors stay a few days in Pyongyang and surrounding areas for sightseeing and then they are allowed to visit their old hometown. In some cases the family members sought are brought into Pyongyang to meet with the visiting family members. The typical length of stay in Pyongyang is 10 days; a sightseeing sidetrip for 3 days; and visiting their hometown for 4 days.   However, 25 subjects (56.8%) did not report they ever visited their old hometown, and 21 subjects (47.7%) said they visited other places that are presumably new hometowns for their families now. Since there had been mass relocations during and after the Korean War, many families lost ties to the old residence and contacts with relatives within North Korea.

For most subjects, visiting with their families after 40-some years' absence was an emotionally overwhelming experience beyond any description. Some subjects reported that they had so much to talk about that they could not express much, flooded by tears, memories, and mourning. One of the universal complaints was that the visit was too short and too controlled. Many wished they had more freedom and privacy. The overwhelming majority (32 subjects or 72.7%), however, felt that the trip was "highly beneficial"; 9 subjects (20.5%) felt "some benefits"; only 3 (6.8%) said it was "so-so"; and no one "regretted" the trip.   The primary reason for such positive feelings, despite many complaints, was that now they could be relieved of their lifelong nostalgic melancholia by knowing and accepting the new reality. The subjects who felt "so-so" expressed that they felt sorry that they could not help their relatives economically; and they also felt that they missed their relatives more than ever before as a result of the visit.

Future Prospects

One of the most tragic natures of the Korean family separation or division is that, in spite of the intensive and extensive victimization of their fate, their rights are not respected and they are virtually helpless in the reconciliation process. In fact they are still being blamed as a political liability or failure by one side or both sides of Korea. Until recent years, they could not even mention

Table 20.2
Reasons for Delay of the Separated Family Search, Cases of Family Members Contacted in North Korea, and Family Members Looked for and Met in North Korea

Reasons	Women N	%	Men N	%
Did not know where and how	15	35.7	64	40.5
Fear of harm to family in North	18	41.9	61	38.5
Fear of harm to family in South	10	23.3	25	15.8
Violation of South Korean laws	9	20.9	28	17.7
Fear of political exploitation	8	18.6	25	15.8
Violation of American/Canadian laws	2	4.6	14	8.9
Other reasons	3	7.0	10	6.4
Total	43		158	

	Women				Men			
Relations	Looked		Met		Looked		Met	
	N	%	N	%	N	%	N	%
Parents	10	24.4	2	4.8	44	28.6	23	15.2
Brothers & Sisters	18	43.9	25	59.5	82	53.2	95	62.9
Spouse	2	5.0	1	2.4	3	1.9	1	0.7
Children	4	9.7	4	9.5	11	7.1	13	8.6
Grand-children	0	0.0		1.0	0.6	0.0		
Aunts & Uncles	2	4.9	3	7.1	6	3.9	8	5.3
Cousins	1	2.4	1	2.4	3	1.9	3	2.0
Nephews & Nieces	4	9.7	5	11.9	2	1.3	7	4.6
In-laws	0	1.0	2.4	2.0	1.3	1.0	0.7	
Total	41	100.0	42	100.0	154	100.0	151	100.0

Note: Since some subjects did not indicate any reasons and some indicated more than one reason, the percentage was based on those who responded, not on the number of responses.

their agony and suffering as legitimate political issues in Korea. Now as a privileged few who could visit their families, they appeal to both Korean governments for their human rights to reunite with loved ones. They "strongly agreed" that the recent agreement by the high level talks should help facilitate and expedite family reunions (44 subjects, 100%). Also, 42 subjects (95.5%) "strongly agreed" that the separated family issue should be resolved as the first priority from a humanitarian point, and that both South and North governments should ban any measure to discriminate, control and retaliate against them. Yet generally they agreed that the family separation issue could not realistically be resolved without achieving some form of national reunification.

Many subjects and interviewees indicated that while the crucial key to the separation issue is still in the hands of both governments, they have little trust on either side in their sincerity or seriousness. They generally believe that both governments use or abuse the issue for their own political gain and thus they generally agree that non-political civilian organizations should take up the initiative and leadership in resolving the issues.

Finally, they were asked where and how they would live both at the present time and after the national reunification. The result is shown in Table 20.3. This table indicates that under the current situation the maintenance of status quo in residence is preferred. But when and if the country is reunited, more subjects wish to return and resettle with their separated families in North Korea (7; 16.3%) and in South Korea (5; 11.6%). Interestingly more male subjects than female subjects expressed a desire to resettle in North Korea.

Table 20.3
Subjects' Wishes for Living Arrangement at Present Time and After Reunification

	Female Subjects				Male Subjects			
	Present		After Reunion		Present		After Reunion	
	N	%	N	%	N	%	N	%
Each in own place	26	59.1	12	27.3	84	51.2	25	15.2
Together abroad	12	27.3	7	15.9	51	31.1	41	25.0
Together in South	1	2.3	5	11.4	2	1.2	2	1.2
Together in North	0	0.0	7	15.9	2	1.2	46	28.0
Unsure (Missing)	5	11.4	13	29.5	25	15.2	50	30.4
Total	40	100.0	44	100.0	164	100.0	164	100.0

IMPLICATIONS

The Korean division is the only and the last vestige of the ideological cold and hot wars and those ten million Koreans are the only remaining major victims of the conflict who are politically forced to remain dispersed and divided even today. Their hope and prospect for family reunions have reached a critical momentum at the present time. What it is like to meet their family members again after almost a half century of separation and uncertainty is historic and it dramatic, and calls for a careful assessment. This study as the first exploratory-descriptive study presents a preliminary picture of their experiences and expressions as lost and found family members.

Their untold lifelong stories may defy any precise analytical assessment, and their legendary human drama may depict a heroic saga beyond any statistical characterization. In a sense each subject is a profound source of insight into family life and human development at the crossroads. What emerges from this preliminary study is, however, an implicit theoretical and practical perspective on family lives as they are detrimentally affected by external forces.

According to the study subjects, the three most difficult and painful experiences they endured, especially during the initial period of separation, are (1) uncertainty about the life or death of family members; (2) homesickness and loneliness, particularly on special occasions such as birthdays, weddings, deaths, and so on; and (3) economic hardship and social discrimination as refugees. These problems are closely related to an indeterminate loss of love object. They had to suffer from these on a long-term basis and yet they felt helpless and powerless, since this pain and agony was inflicted by powerful external forces over which they had no control whatsoever. When someone is locked in such a constantly painful fate, he or she is regarded as being tied by what Koreans commonly call Han (pronounced hahn). Han is an affective state characterized by chronic depressive mood or melancholia without psychotic features or an organic base. Many interviewees expressed in different terms that they suffered from the unresolved Han that accompanies mild yet deep-seated depressive moods. Because of the typical lack of severity of the depressive syndrome, coupled by the typical Oriental disguise of face-saving modesty, they may not be diagnosed for any affective or mood disorder.

Clinically, however, their chronicity of the depressive syndrome seems to suggest the essential feature of dysthymic disorder (DSM III-R 300.40). Diagnostic criteria for dysthymic disorder indicate that the manifestations of the depressive syndrome may be persistent or interrupted by variant periods of normal mood and that there is either prominent depressed mood or a marked loss of interest in usual activities or pastimes (DSM III-R 222f).

Fortunately or unfortunately, this possible mood disorder might have been significantly repressed or curtailed by the practical necessity for hard work and survival in a highly competitive society. In fact, immigration of a large number of these subjects into the United States and Canada may be one such maneuver, with the countering and healing effect on their sufferings in terms of environmental manipulation. Once finding and visiting their separated families, individuals might have experienced a tremendous sense of triumph over their locked or unresolved Han feelings. They were in a sense reconnected to the lost past, reestablishing the destroyed part of their life, and reclaiming their denied identity. Family reunion after such a long separation is not just to achieve a physical proximity but is basically empowering—overcoming all external hostile forces and barriers and all internal depressive fears and resignation. Almost all women who visited North Korea suggested to other people who are considering their visit that they should visit as soon as possible without fear and hesitance. Thus revisioning family reunion is to support and to empower the afflicted parties by means of advocacy, mediation, and education. By teaching them of their rights, promoting their cause, and by arranging actual contacts and visits, human service practitioners can empower them and help overcome their passive enslavement by the Han. In the final analysis, revisioning family reunions is revisioning for humanization.

NOTES

1. An earlier version of this chapter was presented at the 36th Annual Program Meeting of Council on Social Work Education (Kansas City, MO, February 29–March 3, 1992). The authors acknowledge the fine cooperation of Mr. Choong-Lim Chun of the Organization for the Reunification of Separated Korean Families in Toronto, Canada, and of Rev. Hyun Hwan Kim of the One Korea Movement Committee for Separated Korean Families in Los Angeles.

2. For example, the 19th (New Delhi, 1957); 20th (Vienna, 1965); 31st (Mexico, 1971); IRC Conferences, European Security Council on Humanitarian Contacts (Helsinki, 1975), etc.

3. Technically Korean residents or citizens of the United States and Canada are free from Korean government bans and clear with American or Canadian laws for fam-

ily visits in the North, although they may be discouraged from doing so. Taking advantage of this freedom, many residing in the United States and Canada have managed to find and eventually visit their lost families in North Korea. Their visits have not been easy. Many of them, especially in 1970s and early 1980s, were subject to delays and red tape, horrendous harassment, intimidation, and open persecution as pro-communist by the Korean community and some Korean government agents.

4. According to a staff of the committee for Aid to Koreans Abroad, "a little more than 4000 persons" visited from North America as of July 1991. This figure includes (1) a significant number of participants in political, cultural, athletic, and academic events; (2) multiple family visitors and those with multiple visits; (3) privately arranged visitors; and (4) those who travelled for commercial and sightseeing purposes as well as family visits. For this study, only those who at least once have paid "registration fees" for family visits to either organization were selected, counting only one member per family for all visits. It is a guesstimate of all concerned that the sample will cover about 80 to 90% of all separated families in North America who have visited North Korea.

5. About three-quarters of the Toronto sample are citizens or residents of the United States. The low response rate of the Toronto group may be due to the slow triple transcountry postal services before reaching the researchers.

6. Two respondents indicated that while they did not visit yet, they are waiting for the visit soon. Their responses are not included in the study.

7. Various attempts to discern response patterns, if any, between organizations and between immigrant status of respondents produced no difference except that the Canadian group (1) sought family reunions about one year earlier than the American group; (2) found their families about two years earlier; (3) made their first visit about two years earlier; and (4) had an education level about one-half a step lower. But the group size is too small in comparison with the American group. Therefore all subgroups are combined in most analyses. In order to assess non-response bias, if any, the returning time of the Los Angeles group was carefully monitored and was correlated to various response patterns. It was found that their years of immigrant life and educational level were inversely correlated to their response proneness. That is, the longer they lived as an immigrant and the more they were educated, the sooner or the more likely they responded ($r = -.313$, $p = .004$; and $r = -.294$, $p = .007$, respectively). Also U.S. citizens tend to be more prone to respond than residents ($r = .390$, $p = .001$). No other response patterns were discernible. Therefore it appears that those non-respondents may be relatively recent immigrants with no citizenship and with less education than the respondents.

8. According to the custom in the 1950s, it can be assumed that about one half of the subjects, those above 21 years of age, might have married and some might have brought wives along. But most of those married men fled alone and eventually remarried in the South or in the immigration places. Men in general tend to sever psychological ties to marital relationship after so many years of separation. These remarried men might have psychologically less anxiety to meet their former legal wives. Thus they did not or could not actively seek the reunion, and they might be underrepresented in this study. Even if they searched and visited, they might have, because of their awkward situation, indicated other family members, not wives, as their closest and primary search targets. It is a not-so-funny yet common joke among them that their young wives should have been married to Chinese "Voluntary Army" soldiers during the war. Also in the Oriental culture, the blood relationship is much more important than the marital relationship. This was clearly demonstrated in the live broadcast campaign for family reunions within South Korea by the Korean Broadcasting Station in 1983: about 10% of 8,400 separated persons sought parents;

about 50% for brothers and sisters; about 40% for other relatives; and only 0.08% for spouses (*Joong-Ang Daily*, July 6, 1983).

REFERENCES

Chung, Dong Kyu. (1990). *The Three Day Promise*. Seoul: Do Shu Chul Pan Chung Am.

Gilligan, Carol. (1982). *In a Different Voice*. Cambridge, MA: Harvard University Press.

Joong-Ang Daily newspaper. (1983). Seoul, Korea, July 6.

Kaplan, A. G. (1984). "The 'Self-in-Relation': Implications for Depression in Women." *Work in Progress*, No. 14. Wellesley, MA: Stone Center Working Papers Series.

Korea Red Cross. (1976). *White Paper on the Separated Families*, Vol. 1. Seoul: Korea Red Cross.

_____. (1986). *White Paper on the Separated Families*, Vol. 2. Seoul: Korea Red Cross.

_____. (1991). *Progress of South-North Red Cross Talks*. Seoul: Korea Red Cross.

The Korea Times. (1992). Seoul, May 8.

Lee, Hyejo. (1985). *Sociology in the Divided Era*. Seoul: Han Gil Sa.

Miller, J. B. (1984). "The Development of Women's Sense of Self." *Work in Progress*, No. 12. Wellesley, MA: Stone Center Working Papers Series.

"Oh! You're Alive." (1983). Seoul: Dong-a Daily, p. 283.

Protocol Concerning Supplement to the Geneva Agreement and Protection of Victims of International Conflicts. (1977). Protocol 1. June 10.

"The Reconciliation Agreement of North and South Korea." (1992). *Korean Diaspora*, No. 82 (February). Great Neck, NY: Korean Community Council in America.

Stiver, I. P. (1985). "The Meaning of Care: Reframing Treatment Models." *Work in Progress*. Wellesley, MA: Stone Center Working Papers Series.

Surrey, J. (1984). " 'Self-in-Relation': A Theory of Women's Development." *Work in Progress*, No. 13. Wellesley, MA: Stone Center Working Papers Series.

21

Modern Feminist Issues Facing Korean American Women: A Global Perspective

Young I. Song

SEX DISCRIMINATION IN MODERN KOREAN SOCIETY, INSIDE AND OUTSIDE OF KOREA

There is a widespread assumption that a majority of people today, including Koreans in the United States, seem to be expressing more accepting attitudes toward women. Some are fairly confident that modern Korean women, especially Korean American women, are increasingly getting equal treatment in all areas. And thus, a majority of people in modern Korean society are convinced that sexual inequality is no longer a high-priority issue. This belief clearly reflects a severe lack of information and of careful observation.

Most Koreans, in addition to some Korean American people, rarely pay attention to statistics that indicate sex discrimination practices. Even when observations and results of studies are provided, the initial reaction is one of denial or skepticism. In addition, some Korean people tend to point to exceptional cases they know about, pointing out that "my Korean [woman] friend found a job which pays as much as a white man's." The pervasive ignorance of facts and an emphasis on exceptions is furthered by both intentional and unintentional denials. Another probable reason for societal complacency is that the majority of recent Korean immigrants brought sexist traditions with them from Korea. Prior to their immigration, they have suffered from explosive political and economical domestic issues and serious social problems during the Park, Noh, Chun, and Kim regimes that turned the attention of Korean people away from sexual inequality issues. In fact, such issues were, for the most part, regarded as some of the least important issues among the other urgent political issues and human rights concerns. Needless to say, this ignorance was also due to the neglect of former political leaders whose concerns about the retention and exercise of their political power overruled any reasonable attempts to tend to the needs of the people of Korea—especially women—who had very little or no political influence.

Therefore, as pervasive as it is, sex discrimination has never received adequate attention from legal and academic inquiries in Korean society. It has not been regarded as a politically correct topic within the male-dominated structure of

Korean society where the idea of male superiority and the right of men to dominate prevails and is the accepted norm. This attitude is true even of the highly educated social elite, and especially among the politicians who have severely limited any progress toward a clearer understanding about the definition of feminism by the continued manipulation and administration of unequal regulations and laws in Korea. A recognition of the patriarchal nature of the institutions in Korea and the consequence of sexism for the lives of Korean women and men is not new. The history of our past is truly a product of Korean men, and does not in any part include the role of women in the making of history. Making women visible also will require a greater understanding of the discrepancies women experience, and of the demands placed upon them. This greater understanding of women will not be achieved without challenging currently held ideas about all aspects of society and the problems encountered in daily living by Korean women, not only compared to Korean men but also to people around the world.

In fact, the ignorance of Koreans in America is increased by their false perception that the United States has achieved sexual equality. But in reality, the patterns of discrimination against women have changed instead of disappearing during the past several decades. It now includes less openly discriminatory behavior and practices compared to earlier days. Women now face more hidden discrimination that is difficult to overcome in addition to the previously even more common blatant discrimination. Although this chapter will discuss some insightful subtle and covert obstacles, most of the discussion will be focused on blatant sexual prejudices that are still alive but often hidden from the public eye. The shift from blatant to covert sexual prejudice is a typical form of modern sexism in Korean immigrant society that is very difficult to ignore. It is not easy to document this covert sexual discrimination because it is complicated to define and measure the incidences.

The silence of women in earlier generations and general invisibility in public history has resulted in gaps in our knowledge; as Shirley Ardener (1977) has noted, women's voices in many cultures have been typically muted. The inequality between men and women has emerged as one of the principal disputes occupying the attention of feminist scholars and the conscious public inside and outside of Korea in the 1990s. The controversy has spread throughout the world. Indeed, numerous international conferences, including ones in Mexico and Beijing sponsored by the United Nations, have drawn together delegates from all aspects of life to question existing beliefs of social and political equality, and even of the natural order of human experiences. Women are subservient to men in many societies, as in traditional Korean culture. Even in recent Korean immigrant society men are considered to be more important than women, and this is widely practiced in every respect.

It is important to determine the conditions and different ways that male dominance and modern sexism are assessed, to understand and discover ways to provide clear evaluation of equality or inequality between men and women in Korean American society, and to clarify our understanding of the changes taking place in Korean society and the impact sexism has on Korean American society.

Men control the Korean political and economic structure. Regardless of how Korean American women actively participate in raising economic standards of individual homes compared to Korean women in Korea and conduct domestic affairs in their households, Korean men are at the center of all political and economic decisions. Modern Korean women, both in Korea and in the United States, seem to have more power in their home than ever before, but as long as men control and hold the important positions of power and prestige of society, Korean American women continue to be subservient to men with regard to broader societal concerns. If male dominance depends on controlling the political and economic resources in society, then the degree of male dominance in Korean society should vary with the amount of resources available and supplied by the men to women in Korean society. In this case the extent of male dominance increases directly with the proportion of power and resource Korean men have withheld. In any society, status goes to those who control the distribution of valued goods and services outside the family (Friedl, 1978). But when women make very little or no contribution to the political decision making process, as in the case of the modern Korean society, women are completely subordinate as long as their services and authority are limited to domestic distribution. Korean women have little power relative to their husbands and none with respect to the outside world, although modern Korean women appear to have gained more power in their families. Thus, what contemporary Korean people want is what has always been possible—full human experiences and status including sexual equality.

This chapter will describe how and why sex discrimination practices have changed during the past several decades and will also examine the consequences of sexual inequality and suggest remedies for diminishing and eradicating sex discrimination. Particular emphasis will be placed on critical aspects of women's experiences, highlighting those social circumstances and sanctions that reinforce the acquiring of gender-appropriate behavior and those that enhance within-gender differences. This paper is concerned with discerning the life conditions that are systematically related by Korean cultural prescription and regulation, and the variations in these conditions during different periods of women's lives. Emphasis will be placed on a global perspective in analyzing the conditions that contribute to the sex discrimination that will be identified and comparatively examined across different women throughout the world.

GLOBALIZATION WITH SEXISM?

In world history, a common set of influences in the social changes of industrialization affected and challenged traditional sex role stereotyping in various societies. Even typical male-dominated societies have been reported to be changing as a result of these forces, although at different rates. These alterations seem to be the only direct opposition to traditional gender inequality. The development and expansion of feminist consciousness and values that we are witnessing among much of the world's population is an unavoidable yet remarkable phenomenon. In the last half century, Korean immigrants came to the United States to better their economic and educational opportunities. But with an unflinching spirit and less than three decades' time, Korea managed to reconstruct its economy and build itself up from the war's rubble, and become the world's twelfth largest trading partner. Now, Koreans are faced with yet another kind of social battle. This time, the struggle is to cast off its image as people of an introverted developing country and to make a run for globalization.

Korean Americans have begun to take pride in seeing their country develop what has become a strong export economy, but until a mere three decades ago Korea was one of the poorest countries in the world. Despite a rich cultural tradition, Korea was a relative latecomer to the world of industrialization, and it remained mostly a poor, feudalistic country until recently. The modernization of Korea began in the 1960s, and resulted in a radical economic turnaround. On the other hand, and despite a great eagerness, Korea was not yet mentally or intellectually ready to assume a greater role on the international stage, or to take on the responsibility that comes with maintaining a global sense of stability and prosperity in the world economy.

The majority of Korean Americans who moved to the United States after 1965 have retained their old mentality, and although the people of Korea are enjoying sudden economic success, they have not yet developed the ability to place the same level of importance and concern for growth in other equally important issues, such as human rights, a clearer and more mature understanding of democracy and political activities, despite a worldwide upward trend toward a higher global standard in terms of the sexual equality issue. The relation between a man and a woman can be considered to be the first unfair human relation, since it produced self-worship and power abuse, and has been the psychological basis of all other forms of suppression and rule (Miller, 1976). Firestone (1971) contends that today's modern civilization was established on the sacrifice of woman's sensuality-culture.

Globalization is a daunting and almost impossible task without an active participation of the promotion in sexual equality. An awareness is necessary, since the approaches toward sexual equality in diverse areas of the world are all moving in similar patterns, and toward similar directions, although they may begin from very different points and trends. We need to begin by looking at the lives of women, and then move out in expanding circles to bring in the social, political, and historical context of the present-day status of Korean and Korean American women from a global perspective.

THEORETICAL FRAMEWORK

The discussion in this paper is primarily that of a behaviorist social psychological orientation. This approach focuses on what people do in particular situations, and assumes that all human behavior is learned and can be explained by a common set of interrelated principles. This approach is combined with women-centered analysis. Explanation involves relating social behavior of women and men in modern Korea to its antecedents and consequences. Behavior is largely interpreted to include all that Korean people do and say about their attitudes, beliefs, feelings, perceptions, goals, and memories. Within this framework, the learning-oriented theoretical model has been used in the analyses of social behavior of Korean women and men in comparison to the rest of the world. The social psychological perspective approach reflects the view that people and environment are in a mutually dependent and interactive relationship. While the environment includes the immediate physical and social situation, the person may be said to include motives, habits, memories, physiological conditions, and structural characteristics, reflecting both past and future objectives and expectations. Viewing the situational variables as important determinants of behavior, it is assumed that what Korean women and men do is in relation to their own direct experiences, to the consequences that follow their behavior, and to observations of the behavior of other Korean people. This behaviorist cognitive approach is optimistic about the possibilities of future change since the situational variables are considered important determinants of the behaviors of women and men.

DISCUSSION

Superficial Changes: Attitudes Rather than Behaviors

One may assert that the general attitude toward Korean American women has changed and improved drastically from narrow and restricted to a more open and liberated. This assumption reflects attitudes rather than behaviors. Most people equate attitudes with behaviors, and then conclude that behaviors toward women in modern Korea have changed. Many adults have a great deal of difficulty in differentiating wishes and deeds, since it is not easy to separate illogical and unconscious wishes from conscious parts of the reality. Actual occurrences and displays of behaviors are not always dependent upon attitudes, and therefore, the two can occur independently of each other.

No one seems to be able to pinpoint the differentiation between actual and expected values and behaviors. Most Korean American people assume that how things should be is synonymous with how things really are. This confusion continues to emphasize and legitimate superficial changes in terms of equal sex roles. This has led many people to conclude that sex discrimination is only a minor problem. On the national level, for example, the Korean American media have played up women's "firsts"—the first female Korean American prosecutor, the first full professor of an American university, the first West Point graduate, the first female executive of a bank, or the first elected higher official. Emphasizing such firsts gives the impression that Korean American women have indeed made great improvement and even that they are really sharing equal privileges and rights with Korean men and others. At worst, many people confuse the fact that such success is only true in a few exceptional cases and is not in fact common, widespread or representative across all institutional structures. Not many people seem to realize that our ability to reveal these cases as exceptional reflects the exclusion of women from most other areas. In reality, only a few women have been upwardly mobile, and these few are often touted as being evidence of gender equality. People insist that "things have really changed." What is so often ignored, however, is the fact that such changes are highly skewed, and that they represent an extremely tiny fraction of working women.

However, many of us rely exclusively on our personal attitudes, observations, and experiences to generalize about the world at large. We assume that such generalizations are valid. However, we would be appalled at such illogical reasoning on other issues. Imagine denying the existence of poverty or suicide because we have never experienced them, or because our own families and friends have never experienced these problems. We may not recognize such inconsistencies in our understanding in relation to sexism, because compared to other problems, sex discrimination is more acceptable and is not always blatant or immediately visible. Many of today's Korean American people are not aware of discrepancies between changed attitudes and unchanged behaviors, and the scope and severity of the effects of both intentional and unintentional sex discrimination. There has been almost a complete absence of awareness of the importance of addressing non-overt and subtle sex discrimination because there were not even enough voices to speak out against overt and blatant sex discrimination in Korea during the past few decades of Korean American history. However, covert biases are equally as detrimental to accomplishing equality as overt discriminatory practices are.

Whether intentional or unintentional, the values, attitudes, and behaviors generated by covert and subtle discrimination are equally as harmful as blatant discrimination not only to men and women as individuals but also to such basic institutions as the family, economy, education, and the political system. The essential element to evaluating change in conditions for women is to see whether there are any systematic or fundamental changes in most major institutional sectors as consistent outcomes of their changed attitudes.

This change is clearly reaching into Korean American society today, which for thousands of years has had a male-dominated history while some of the modern prescriptions for ideal feminine character still exert powerful influences over Korean American women. Despite revolutionary changes that have altered almost every aspect of the lives of Korean American people, they still feel a deep and abiding sense of loyalty to their cultural past and actively seek to maintain and perpetuate their sexist ideology in the name of maintaining their cultural heritage and their sense of identity with the mother country.

We are living through an important transitional period now in which the traditional notions of Korean womanhood are rapidly becoming obsolete, so that women can no longer rely on these prescribed models of thought and attitudes. By the time they attain young adulthood, today's Korean American women realize that the attitudes of the virtuous traditional woman they have been taught to honor and emulate throughout their socialization process do not fit with reality. The more that young women have developed a clear sense of personal identity, and the higher the degree to which they begin to learn more about the pervasiveness of sexism, the more stark the disjunction between traditional ideal and modern reality becomes for them (Song, 1991, 1996).

WOMAN'S PLACE IN KOREAN AMERICAN SOCIETY AS REFLECTED IN ATTITUDE

How Sexism Affects Our Attitude

Many Korean Americans assume that the mass media reflect actual social changes and reality. Korean television viewers point to the occasional anchorwomen and to the token "powerful" women executives or attorneys on soap operas as evidence of societal gender equality. However, such shows mirror the media's perception of women as tokens or ornaments. Many Korean American people believe that the greater display of women's plays and women's drama are proof of women's liberation. There is very little recognition of the fact that many of these still present Korean women who despite having intelligent bases and beginnings, end up in the socially acceptable and traditional sex-stereotypical roles—as ignorant housewives, sex symbols, enduring women who absorb insults and mistreatment, or domestic martyrs. These women are portrayed as succeeding only with the help of a man, and as totally dependent on men for basic survival and happiness.

There are also widely publicized occasional conferences or workshops on women's issues and numerous women's magazines that advise individual women on so-called How To Do's. Most of the magazine covers show happy, smiling, and outgoing women. People see these pictures as real changes in the roles of women and assume that all women have come a long way. This is also heightened by the greater exposure of female nudity or newly acquired behaviors of young women—behaviors that used to be the male prerogative—such as smoking cigarettes.

Even among successful women who are supposedly fighters for the liberation of women from male dominance, many consider as their highest goal and dream the establishing of an ideal husband-centered family. This ideal family image entails a picture of a woman at home with her children, waiting for her husband who acts as sole provider for the family. The momentum that picked up speed during the 1960s, 1970s, and 1980s was directed toward expanding educational and career opportunities for women. While there are major differences between then and now, we also note some significant trends in a reactionary direction in the overall attitude shifted significantly in favor of expanded opportunities for women in Korean society.

Beyond active economic activity there is a broad trend in the direction of reemphasizing the traditional aspects of woman's place in the process of rapid industrialization. Korean American women are encouraged to "do the right thing" and maintain their ethnic identity so their husbands can devote themselves to building the miracle "model minority" image of success in this land of opportunity. In the last decade, along with fairly abundant material resources, we have seen a renewed emphasis on femininity, especially among many women who are well-off. For example, since the mid-1980s, there has been great deal of renewed emphasis on women looking "beautiful." Overall attitudes of modern Korean men and women reflect that the women are still not judged primarily in terms of their achievements. Korea became a society where more money is spent on women's looks than on social service programs. Plastic surgery is becoming increasingly popular, especially to young single women. Mothers of marriageable women are, in fact, encouraging their daughters to undergo plastic surgery because being attractive to men is still a major goal of most Korean women because a woman's looks are treated as her primary asset. This view and new practice of cosmetic surgery is found to be consistent in Korean American society as well.

The failure of women to get good jobs outside the home and the resurgence of femininity in the last decade have created intensified competition among Korean young women for the best available elite man. In the competition for men, women undergo expensive, painful, unnecessary, and sometimes unsuccessful surgery to improve physical characteristics that appeal to men. It is not uncommon for young women to have cosmetic surgery for such things as eye tucks, face-lifts, nose reconstruction, and fat removal. The physical characteristics of women have a major impact in modern Korean society, even though many Koreans may admit that talent, intelligence, achievements, and effort should be accorded more importance in assessing the contribution and worth of a woman.

At the individual level, the attitudes of Korean American women and men cause continuing problems. Today many Korean American women and men continue to be less informed about sex inequality, and many seem to be more conservative about sex role expectations than in the recent past. In recent years popular ideas have emphasized a variety of individualistic themes: views that take the blame off the patriarchal social condition. Today among Koreans, social Darwinism persists in individual values about the subordinate place of women in the Korean American society and also in the view that women who fail have only themselves to blame for their lack of luck. Modern Korean American women and men have been told to seek equal opportunity, but women cannot expect to share in equal rewards. Therefore, men of Korean descent can embrace the egalitarian attitude without the commitment to a significant sharing of the basic resources and rewards.

Psychological Conflict Between Achievement and Feminine Responsibility

There are two sets of expectations for women. There is the one made possible by modernization and is the product of today's world perspective—individuality, successful accomplishment, equality. On the other hand, there are those born of the Korean tradition in which the public domain belongs to men, wives and their services belong to their husbands, and family life is the responsibility of women. And often these expectations conflict. In recent years, a majority of Korean American girls eventually learned to compartmentalize, to keep separate the feelings associated with achievement from those associated with the rigid female role prescribed in their ethnicity. These two conflicting expectations are required to be handled as mutually exclusive. Separation is one strategy for coping with essentially contradictory expectations (Horner, 1971; Gray, 1983)

Indeed, the very structure of life for Korean Americans makes this distinction appear natural. Girls succeed in school, and then at home they are expected to learn the feminine pursuits. Girls are encouraged to prepare to work, but they are also expected to become mothers later. Through the years of schooling and experience on jobs and in marriage, modern Korean women frequently and continuously confront contradictions. They feel angry about sex discrimination at work or about unequal responsibility for housework at home, or feel guilty about their shortcomings for not being able to capably handle both, but to a large extent they have to manage to fulfill both sets of expectations. This frustrating situation is commonly experienced by well-educated American-born Korean women.

As women select a career path, they clearly experience the consequences of this contradiction. For men, career is the central choice. In contrast, women often find that their choices are not so concrete. The way they accomplish the resolution of this conflict is by remaining flexible in their career choices. Women often choose an occupation that is not their first choice because the majority of women desire marriage and children, which is also a central traditional feminine goal. An internal conflict confronts the contemporary Korean

American women who opts for the traditional role, who finds the independence/achievement alternative relatively unattractive, and who anticipates personal happiness and fulfillment from the role Korean ethnic society considers more appropriate for her. She can anticipate approval and love, a home, a husband-companion, children, financial security, possessions, and perhaps luxurious leisure activities, and the pleasure of being fulfilled through the success of her husband and children. But at the same time the modern Korean American girl can also anticipate negative consequences. She knows that, as a homemaker, her status, power, and influence will be limited to and dependent upon her future husband; and her ability to cope with many situations will also be limited. For whatever reason, if she should lose her husband, she may one day become discontent with homemaking, or be faced with severe economic hardship.

This is a complicated conflict, one that is difficult to resolve. Resolution is most difficult for those young women who have become competent in non-domestic areas and who have been encouraged to be independent by their parents or others, but who have also been strongly influenced by the dominant ethnic ideology through peer expectations, education and media models. Girls experience more frequent feelings of tension and psychosomatic symptoms than boys do, since although they want to be active, they also want to be popular with boys at the same time. In other words, they are growing up with an awareness of the inconsistency between competency and conflicting social expectations. When this conflict cannot be resolved, the person may turn her back on both alternatives and withdraw, unable or unwilling to make a decision. This conflict requires an adaptive, evolutionary view and strong self identity of women while constantly balancing and shifting the demands of the two conflicting sources.

Most women say they want both the alternatives of doing personally fulfilling work and having a satisfying family life in the constant struggle between love with autonomy, connectedness with independence and adventure.

Attitude Reflected in the Double Standard: Age

There is such a thing in Korean American society as the prime age for young women when their worth is considered to be the highest. Women are shy about their age because society views them as old, ten or fifteen years sooner than men. Women must endure the specter of aging much sooner than men, and this cultural attitude toward aging gives men a decided psychological, sexual, and economic advantage over women.

A man's wrinkles, while in his fifties, sixties, and so on, will not define him as sexually undesirable as much it does for women. For men, sexual value is perceived much more in terms of personality, intelligence, and earning power than physical appearance. Society places a heavy weight on women's physical appearance. The young girl may well believe that her position in society is equal to, or even higher in her relationship with men. However, women begin to notice a change in the way people treat her as she approaches middle age. A majority of Korean American women see and measure the decline of their worth, their status in the world, as they approach middle age.

There exists an institutionalization of different age definitions for men and women. For example, the age at which one can marry is a part of the cultural rules. It is perfectly acceptable for a man to marry a woman as much as fifteen or twenty years younger than he, but it is generally unacceptable for him to marry women more than four of five years older. These age gap differentials put the Korean woman at a disadvantage in several ways. Since Korean ethnic culture defines that younger age is more desirable, the customary age gap means that the man gets the more desirable partner; the women must settle for the less desirable. In the case of a divorced or widowed woman, they are severely handicapped when it comes to finding another marital partner due to the difference in the supply of future marriage partners for the men and for the women. The man can choose among all women his own age or younger. The woman, by contrast, is limited by custom to older men. She is reduced to the supply of men from those age brackets in which most men are married, and the man will likely look for younger women by virtue of his success and wealth. Yet, the difference in life expectancy between the two sexes of five to six years also works to a woman's disadvantage in another way. It means that more women will be widowed a longer period of time.

Confidence/Self-Esteem

Many studies on gender differences in self-reported personal worth or self-confidence suggest that women generally manifest lower self-esteem than men (Lott, 1985; Lenney, 1981; Heilman & Kram, 1984). Women find that they have less control over their own lives and those of men. Women generally underestimate their abilities compared to men and set lower educational and vocational goals that are unrelated to objective measures of their abilities. Women also tend to report lower self-confidence on tasks for which feedback is minimal or ambiguous, and in situations in which their work will be compared with that of a man. Women's self-evaluations are more influenced by situation variables than are men's. The attitudes toward women are also seen as typically ambivalent. This ambivalence appears to be related to a division of women into two categories distinguished by their level of assertiveness or independence. If she is passive, sacrificing her needs, then she is described as giving, fruitful, and a inspiration to men. If active and independent, then woman are often being viewed as a distracter of a man from his worldly pursuits.

The failure to provide infants with opportunities for full development is not only a function of the social and economic factors but also of the judgments about the differential nature of the two sexes. The female infant begins a life-long process of becoming a culturally defined woman. It is not surprising that the average girl, as she grows older, becomes more and more distinguishable from the average boy in her consciousness in terms of constructing and defining goals, interests, and responses. The environments in which children grow are filled with information about gender differences. Girls and boys observe, organize, relate themselves to their appropriate category, try out various alternatives, experience feedback from others, and acquire a gender identity that matches the ideology of Korean culture, and this soon becomes a core part of their conscious self.

A persistent message to the girl is that she should be flexible and not define her conscious self too rigidly and sharply, because the ultimate understanding and acceptance of herself will be related and defined by the man with whom she becomes associated. Erik Erikson (1968) viewed adolescence for women not as a time for active searching and exploring, but as a time of fluidity; the young woman's sense of identity will come primarily from the man she marries and for whom she makes a home. It is clear that in Korean culture, a woman's final self-definition of conscious being is powerfully shaped by the consciousness, attitudes, needs, ambitions, goals, and interests of her man.

The majority of Korean American women grow up expecting and assuming that they will be taken care of. Some seek independence but may be dissuaded by thinking that this is a less desirable and more difficult path for a woman. As a result, many women fear independence because they have limited possibilities in practicing it, or because they have learned that happier and culturally reinforced Korean American women should be protected, defended, sheltered, and guided by men. Such a cultural assumption, challenged by many modern Korean American women, is still part of the dominant gender ideology of today's Korean American society.

WOMAN'S PLACE IN KOREAN AMERICAN SOCIETY: AS OBSERVED IN BEHAVIOR

How Sexism Affects Behavior

Women, like men, learn continuously from birth the behavior appropriate to gender status. Gender influences motivation and social behavior. Gender, in other words, organizes social life and thus much of individual experience. The traditionalist view looks at the many ways in which women differ from men and assumes this must accord with some natural order as women have always had less power and fewer resources than men. There are many similarities between the sexes and women and men have equal potential for individual development. Differences in the relation of that potential, therefore, must result from externally imposed restraints, from the influence of social institutions and Korean values.

Our culture defines womanhood differently from manhood. Korean American women are expected to behave in ways defined as appropriate feminine behavior. Women and men can acquire the same habits, attitudes, aspirations, and motives under the same learning conditions, but acquire different behavioral propensities where their experiences and the way their responses are reinforced systematically differ. Thus, predictable personality and role consequences for women growing up in Korean American homes are not inevitable but are related to cultural emphases and training for girls directed toward assuring gender differences. Being a woman requires certain behaviors, and those behaviors are important if a women is to fulfill cultural expectations. As presented by Susan Brownmiller (1984), "Biological femaleness is not enough. Femininity always demands more."

As Korean history has clearly indicated to us, equality between the sexes is rare. In most known societies women are subordinate. Male dominance is so widespread that it is virtually a human universal; social conditions in which women are consistently dominant do not exist and have never existed (Friedl, 1978).

Parental gender-role socialization has a more global impact than does the communication of a particular set of gender-appropriate behaviors. Parents give male infants more stimulation than they give to girls, give more contingent responses to boys than to girls, and allow boys more freedom to explore than they do girls. Jeanne Block suggested the result of differing socialization for girls and boys is that boys develop "wings"—which permit leaving the nest, exploring far reaches, flying alone, while girls develop "roots"—roots that anchor, stabilize, and support growth, but allow fewer chances to master the environment (Block, 1984)

Korean American women, like women in other parts of the world, experience culturally imposed limitations on their access to resources, to positions of power, and to opportunity for personal growth in the Korean ethnic community.

Cultural Significance of Rape and Wife Abuse

It has been more acceptable in Korean American culture for a man to hit a woman in an argument, compared to non-Koreans. When a husband hits his wife, it is commonly assumed that it is for a valid reason and that the woman must have "asked for it." That such an assumption is often made is a conclusion supported from a number of sources, including the widespread prevalence of wife beating in Korean American society (Song, 1996). Family violence in Korean American society cuts across socioeconomic classes as well as occupational categories.

In the Korean American community, women have been and continue to be the victims of physical and psychological abuse. Women have been treated as second-class citizens. Violence against women finds its basis in women's second class status and their historically subordinate position in society. An abused group is one that is socially, politically, and economically subordinate; its members are excluded from various opportunities, which limits their freedom of choice and self-development. They tend to have lower self-esteem and often become the objects of contempt, ridicule, and violence; generally, they are socially isolated (Feldman, 1983).

Wife beating is an expression of patriarchal domination, the origin of which lies in the subordination of women and in their subjection to male authority and control. This relationship between Korean women and men has been institutionalized in the structure of the patriarchal family and is supported by the economic and political institutions and by the cultural belief system of Korean Americans (Song, 1996).

Battered women have learned to adjust to the lifestyle prescribed by Korean culture by taking it as the part of their marriage that their very entry into this world as women imposed upon them. The battering of women, like other crimes of violence against women, has been justified in the context of the Korean culture. It perpetuates the notion that a man should beat a woman when she does something that makes him angry.

Korean American women have developed an ability to absorb insults and injuries without protest and to assume responsibilities for others' faults; in contrast, Korean men have been incapable of bearing responsibility for their own actions, always seeking to blame others. Since this is also reflected in the societal attitudes, it is important to remember the existence of the victim's precipitation ideology, and thus blame the abuse on it. Battered women in Korean society are silent victims who have been continuously hidden by closed boundaries made by their own culture and customs.

The Effect of Sexism on Women and Relationships

Women often discover that their expectations of a love relationship are not the same as men's. Meanings of love, as well as what each looks for in the other, are often found to be distinguishably different for a woman and a man. For a woman to find satisfaction in a relationship with a man is difficult if she has been taught to lose herself in devotion to, in caring for, and in identification with him.

Korean culture, like the majority of patriarchal societies, tells women that is through the love of a man that women will achieve completeness and mature identity. Woman's whole identity hangs in the balance of her love life. She is allowed to love herself only if a man finds her worthy of love (Firestone, 1971). Not surprisingly, then, when women have written about relationships with men, they have typically described both passion and pain—an ambivalent experience, sought eagerly but with the anticipation of disillusionment and hurt. Our culture promises women fulfillment and happiness from sacrificial love between a woman and a man, but often the promise is too great and is disconfirmed by the realities of experience. The happiness to be found in relationships is often undermined when the partners are unequal in power and resources. Korean culture has made relationships difficult for women by encouraging them to find individual worth and security in relationships instead of in the totality of their lives, and by encouraging women to confuse romance with submission, and love with sacrifice, and to juxtapose man's strength against woman's weakness. Many of the behaviors acquired by women as they are socialized to be good daughters, sisters, wives, and mothers provide women with strengths in the interpersonal domain. Women are expected to be agreeable and to reduce conflict. The Korean American woman has been taught to compromise and to consider the needs and feelings of others. Women's experiences promote a communal, qualitative, and person-oriented mode of living and that women's morality rests upon consideration for other's needs, whereas men's morality is concerned with abstract rules and rights.

Girls and women are encouraged to look to other persons for evidence of their effectiveness. Then women learn to be sensitive to the needs of others, to interpret subtle cues, and to behave sympathetically. Interpersonal relationships thus become highly important contributors to women's feelings of self-esteem, and women devote considerable time and energy to talking about and taking part in person-oriented activities.

Considerable numbers of people in the Korean American community still wait for the marriage arrangement or face the hatred of their parents. Thus marriage does not involve only the personal choice of the couple, but instead it involves the consideration of parents, property, and educational compatibility. Even in a marriage of love, the bride is expected to bring a dowry to each member of her husband's side of family and relatives. It is not uncommon to hear a comment of harsh criticism toward a newlywed bride when her dowry is far less than expected or less money is spent. Even with Korean Americans today, the husband and his family have more rights and privileges, while the wife has obligations.

Perhaps the single most important lesson to be conveyed to women is that when they enter their husbands' household, they cannot, in fact, have equal rights, to demand a reciprocal role of conformity from others, including their husbands and in-laws. Furthermore, inadequacies or even absence of such recip-rocal role conformity do not entitle them to neglect their own role.   In other words, women have to learn that their individuality or personal demands intrude upon their roles, often at the risk of self-disclosure and the vulnerability result-ing from it.

Even for those who are highly educated, a woman typically expects to per-form services when she marries, and her husband typically expects to receive them. Her husband's life will tend to diverge from hers. The wife will spend more time with her home than with her husband. Being a wife means house-work for most women ranging from cooking to cleaning, from washing dishes to mending. Housewives spend long hours doing household tasks and chores despite appliances and other modern conveniences and changes in the specific nature of the tasks done. Being a wife means housework even when you are also employed outside the home in full-time work. Employed wives do less house-work than full-time homemakers but far more than their employed husbands. Although some Korean American wives do share the provider role with their husbands, husbands far less frequently share the household chores with her. No real change seems to have occurred during the past few decades in women's re-sponsibilities for household tasks among Korean couples.

Despite hardships, disappointments, arguments, and unrealized dreams, di-vorce is not more common among full time homemakers than among more financially independent women. The greater the women's earnings, the higher were the marital "disruption probabilities." Educated women have articulated their disappointments, disillusionment, boredom, and frustrations, and have talked about the isolation and lack of personal fulfillment inherent in the role of wife. The growing aspirations of financially independent and college-educated women for egalitarian marriages and expressive, sensitive, caring husbands are in sharp contrast to the traditional marriage role. Although today's Korean Ameri-can women expect more egalitarian attitudes more than their mothers did, women's aspirations are not being fulfilled.

Extensive gender differentiation produces males and females who inhabit radically different worlds (Bernard 1981), share few common experiences, care most about different things, and may not share a common language or mode of communicating (Lakoff, 1975; Song & Kim, 1992) Unequal status in any type of relationship does not foster honest and open communication and intimacy. Marital inequality does foster relatively low levels of conflict and marital disso-lution. One reason is that the bases of marital inequality lie outside the family and in the public domain of law, custom, religion, and the economy.   Where women cannot earn a decent livelihood, they are forced to remain in marriage almost regardless of the quality of the marital relationship (Lee, 1977). Friends, relatives, and others are likely to give little sympathy to a wife in marital dis-cord with her husband because she is likely to be told to try harder. Marital fail-ure becomes her failure. In most cases like this, marital problems tend to re-main covert or submerged, at least while the husband fulfills his responsibility as provider. Therefore, there is a positive relationship between stability in mari-tal status and gender inequality among marital couples due to the processes by which problems that do surface are resolved. When there is extensive inequality, marital problem resolution processes are well defined and simple, as the husband may simply exercise his authority or power where the wife has only limited options. Where women are more equal to their spouses, they may also have less motive to conceal differences of opinion, resulting in more frequent overt disagreement.

The disadvantaged Korean American women had to challenge their very self-definition as well as their objective disadvantages. Such a task required an inner strength, a struggle against powerlessness that taught and reinforced Korean women to be strong in their family. Admitting the fact that the husband is the provider of the house, the Korean woman's feeling of economic dependence was mitigated by the fact that she shared in the financial decision making around the house, managed the family budget, invested in an apartment, or felt free to spend money on the house and the family as she saw fit.

Beyond the stigma toward divorced women, the most clearly established aftermath of divorce is the economic hardship suffered by women. Despite the fact that the wives have invested heavily in time and human capital in their husband's occupational advancement, divorced women may find themselves suffering the consequences of being displaced homemakers. Such women lose their sole source of income and social status while husbands are allowed to retain their occupational assets. There is more to their dilemma than these structurally imposed societal obstacles. Most of the women also feel powerless about their own ability to do something worthwhile after their marriages have ended. They suffer tremendous feelings of self-doubt, lack of self-confidence, and low self-esteem. Their feelings of powerlessness seem to go deeper than the feelings people generally experience when they face a life crisis such as death of a spouse. Such a traditional social restriction of the institution of marriage is notably prevalent in Korean American women's status in terms of social structure.

Job and Social Status

The image of Korean American women that has been fostered in the school system and home does not fit with having a respected job or with high status of women in modern society. In an "ideal woman," supplementary roles are more emphasized and reinforced, rather than intelligence or creativity. The idea of "the wise mother and good wife" has defined the virtues of women as understanding enduring wife, self-sacrificing mother, and submissive women. The restricted role of an ideal Korean woman has led to a lack of social consciousness and narrow maternal views. These traditional pictures will no longer be supported by young Korean American people in Korea because even if men want to continue this belief, they cannot find women who fit into this image.

Married women are also forced to leave their jobs because of spinster preferentialism. A few exceptional women have taken the difficult road of education and a career. In order to succeed in society, many women have had to become like men, thus once again running against their own nature and becoming alienated from the rest of the female community. It has still not been possible for a woman to live and act as an autonomous human being without disqualifying herself as a woman.

The conflict between individual achievement and feminine responsibility is not just internal. It places constraints on women's commitments to employment. It pushes women to limit the careers they consider possible to lower paid female occupations, to give up what they have accomplished for feminine responsibility, or to spread themselves very thin.

Occupation is a man's major role, and unemployment or failure in his occupational life the worst disaster that can befall him. While men draw their self-esteem and establish their connections to others very largely through their jobs, retirement is a difficult time for most men. The woman faces a similar status loss much earlier. Korean women's status in life is that of mother; her secondary role is that of wife and homemaker. Loss of perceived sexual attractiveness and the maternal role come at a time when the husband is likely to be at the peak of his career and deeply involved in satisfying social status.

By fulfilling primary responsibility for care of the home and children, women enable their husbands to put time and energy into the pursuit of occupational success. It is the husband's work outside the home that typically has top priority in the family and that provides the family with its social standing in the community. Since it is the husband's occupation that matters in the community's evaluation of the family, it is not surprising to find that women make career sacrifices for the men. Modern employed professional Korean American wives acknowledge that their social status is derived from their husband's in the Korean community and is determined by their socioeconomic position, just as was true for their mother and grandmother. The status given to the wives is rarely influenced by their own occupations but is instead significantly influenced by that of their husbands. In the eyes of the Korean American society, a married woman takes on the status of her husband and the generally lower status of married women relative to married men. Husbands and wives are not equal in status or power. In today's Korean American society this is a source of discomfort, disillusionment, distress, and real disadvantage to large numbers of well educated women. Even when the inequality is tolerated by the wife, her husband, possessing the social advantages of worldliness, may grow dissatisfied with his wife's contributions to his ego, physical comfort, and/or will seek to find the channel to be associated with a woman who is younger, better looking, or more adoring. As unmarried women get older there are fewer available men to choose from. Those men who are available prefer younger women who are not as highly successful. Modern Korean American women who lead independent lives and do not marry tend to be well educated, well employed, financially secure, and to manifest fewer signs of psychological distress than single men.

Mass Media

Another sign of non-progressive behavior at the societal level is the treatment of women in the mass media. Modern industrialization has fostered sexist advertisements, and such advertisements cannot be avoided. Television programs have reinforced stereotypical behaviors of women and men. Overall, more men than women appear on television screens. Women are often portrayed in traditional roles. On the screen, more men than women are portrayed engaging in behaviors that show competence, skill, and intelligence. Women are much more likely to be seen in home rather than outside settings, and are more likely to be associated with food, beauty, and clothing ads. Both men and women are very likely to be portrayed in traditional roles.

Hostile behaviors, actions, and inflictions of violence on the part of men toward women are observable in a variety of contexts. For example, it is acceptable in Korean television programs or movie feature programs to have scenes where a woman gets slapped, roughed-up, or insulted. Even today, in comparison to shows and films produced and viewed during the late 1970s and the 1980s, it can be said that there have been very few changes in the ways in which Korean women are presented in Korean television programs. In fact, even since the 1960s, little progress has been made in terms of the high frequency with which women are depicted as victims. However, the late 1980s and the 1990s seem to have brought a new kind of independent women image into television. These television women have brought with them to the screen a newer image of women as behaving more assertively, and the image of the "independent/capable woman" is no longer highly unusual. Nevertheless, clear societal indications exist proving that such an image is mere fiction and not yet the norm.

Sexual inequality has created widespread negative detrimental psychological, emotional, and career consequences on women and men as individuals and on society as a whole. These negative consequences cross age, national, religious, and occupational boundaries.

Since we emphasize the importance of individual responsibility and success, women who experience sex discrimination blame themselves rather than institutionalized sexism. Although both men and women can be targets of sex discrimination, being a woman is frequently a better predictor of inequality than are other variables in Korean American society.

Being different from men in Korean American culture, women are taught and expected to be passive and to accept being ignored or ridiculed, and to take the blame when things go wrong. This is how the consequences of sexism are emotionally more harmful to women than to men. Korean culture is more accepting of psychological emotional dysfunction in women, and the socialization of women makes certain manifestations of dysfunction in women more probable than in men. Furthermore, it is widely known that married women have higher rates of mental disorders than married men. Also, married women are more likely than any other group to experience depression and psychosomatic symptoms. Middle-aged women are actually less happy or more maladjusted than middle-aged men. Among the patterns of dysfunctional behavior manifested by women, depression is the most common. The symptoms are passivity, feelings of hopelessness and helplessness, lowered self-esteem, crying, suicidal feelings, self-accusation, slowed movement, and disturbed sleep. Women are taught to look inside for the cause of problems. Women are encouraged to view the problems as originating within their own incompetence, inferiority, weakness, and so on. Marriage seems to have relatively fewer negative effects on men (Feagin, 1982).

A woman typically asks what she has done wrong, worrying, feeling guilty and punishing herself. Women are likely to turn the anger of frustration inward when they do not meet objective, or overcome barriers. Women tend to view themselves as failures and at fault if others have not been loving, attentive, approving, or rewarding to them. This is what causes the high rate of depression for women and it is centered around its relationship to how women are expected to behave. A study of a group of middle-aged Korean American women (Song, 1991) found that those most likely to experience psychological distress were women whose attitudes were most traditionally Korean, who had been traditional mothers and wives, and who had sacrificed and done the right thing, who later found out after their children left home and in an absence of a meaningful relationship with husband or job, felt deserted, abandoned, and useless. These women felt disappointed and helpless.

Some women enter as only a small proportion into institutions that have been designed exclusively by and for men. In this situation, these women face tokenism, and as members of an underrepresented group, they also experience external pressures and marginality. In such situations of under-representation, women obviously stand out. Being in the spotlight has more disadvantages than advantages, and when it s constant it can be a liability. This is what has happened to the highly visible token group of women in highly professional careers. There are several negative consequences. The first one is pressure to perform well at all times. In this situation, women are experiencing greater pressures both psychologically and physiologically. The other negative consequence is that the woman may be viewed as a person with marginal ability who has been selected to fulfill the token roll. As such, her capability may well be misinterpreted and often negatively perceived.

Unlike men who can have both a job and a family with the help of a wife, many women are finding that they cannot have both and must choose between the two if they are to be successful in either role. So, increasing numbers of women with high educational backgrounds are postponing marriage, remaining single, not having children, or getting divorced because it is becoming impossible to be a double role performer.

Sexual inequality has also created negative consequences at the societal and national level, which include a waste of talent, lowered productivity, and reduced creativity. The systematic oppression and discouragement of women results in an exclusion of invaluable societal and human resources, especially when such resources encompass those who could contribute significantly and who could creatively enrich goals in terms of higher productivity, better service, and quality.

CONCLUSION AND RECOMMENDATIONS

Despite traditionally rooted sex inequalities in Korean American culture, a number of projections indicate that prosperity and further advancement of Korean economy and politics are closely dependent on the future direction of sex equality. In the future, the highest quality work will come from the detailed application of knowledge. We are entering into a post-bureaucratic era, in which women could be only one of many alternatives to bureaucracy. Trends of formal and male oriented egotistical management are shifting out and those with natural authority based on knowledge and certain psychological skills are filtering in (Toffler, 1990). This may mean that future ground-breaking scientific discoveries, technological advances, and intellectual and humanitarian contributions of the future will be dependent on the resources and talents of women.

So long as Korean American society prescribes sexist ideology as the social norm and sets social sanctions for those who deviate from them, no meaningful choices exist for either women or men. Such restraints and discrimination due to sexism are examined and challenged throughout this chapter, in the belief that only by first understanding their manifestations can we gain the wisdom to dismantle them and create a more just society. Everywhere we see clear indications that women's lives will not return to earlier generations. Korean American men will gain from greater gender flexibility and equality, and although men as a group have profited from their poison of power, individual men are not the enemy. All of Korean culture compels men as well as women who were denied aspects of our common humanity by sex discrimination.

Women will not be equal until work in the home and the society is redistributed more equitably between the sexes. This will require a significant restructuring of institutions to allow both men and women time to do both. A society that truly values the family and also develops a genuine commitment to equal opportunity for women must find the means for both women and men to participate in child rearing and its related responsibilities, so that women do not carry the primary responsibility. Only when men are as responsible as women for the care of children will women have the possibility of independence, will children have the opportunity to develop healthy sex roles, and will home and economic, political cultural values no longer be segregated. A genuine commitment to equality of the sexes ultimately implies a restructuring of Korean society so that women and men have equal access to the responsibilities and privileges of both worlds.

Korean American society at the present time is undergoing a stage of transition in which Korean sexist social structures and norms are being challenged and broken down. However, those structures still have not been replaced by clearly discernible new norms. We are living through an important transitional period now in which the traditional notions of Korean society are rapidly becoming obsolete, so that women can no longer rely on these prescribed models of thought and attitudes. By the time they attain young adulthood, today's Korean women realize that the attitudes of the virtuous Korean American woman they have been taught to honor and emulate throughout their socialization process do not fit with reality. The more that young women have developed a clear sense of personal identity, and to the degree that they begin to learn more about the pervasiveness of sexism, the more stark the disjunction between traditional ideal and modern reality becomes for them (Song, 1991, 1996). Such Korean women inside and outside of Korea are already open to new visions of what a woman is and can be. They are being confronted by all the social and personal complexities and ambiguities that movements toward great social change generate. Korean American women and men cannot assume that someone else will fight the battle for sex equality. Related to this, they cannot assume that, over time, there will be sex equality. Each of these assumptions is wrong.

The first step to remedy blatant types of sex discrimination is for the women to identify and recognize the discrimination. And then to stand up for their rights and no longer place the burden of sex inequality on women's shoulders by reinforcing the blaming-the-victim notion. Both women and men in modern Korea should actively challenge blatant sex discrimination. People with political power can be especially instrumental in sending loud, clear, and public messages supporting sex equality. Korean women should initiate collective action for legal protection toward sex equality. Friends, family, co-workers, and supervisors should actively support women who are challenging sex discrimination through the networks.

It is critical to educate the Korean American community of women and men about the existence of sexist attitudes, of the processes of behavior manifestations, and of the harmful consequences of subtle and blatant sex discrimination by raising people's consciousness. Instruction needs to be refocused so that sex discrimination is taught to be viewed as environmental rather than natural, and a reevaluation of the definitions of stereotypical sex-role behavior of various groups is necessary.

We must endeavor toward the point where sex equality can exist in Korean American society. It is important to be inclusive of men, and not exclusively of women. Women must solicit their support, and try to communicate more openly and be willing to work together on projects.

Dehumanization of women brings on dehumanization of men, and therefore, misery for the entire Korean society. Although the number of educated women has gradually increased lately, Korean women are still under social restrictions of gender and race. They are still being discriminated against in various spheres of society and are victims of oppression. As Simone de Beauvoir indicated, the status of the woman has improved, but has not basically changed (1974).

REFERENCES

Ardener, Shirley. (1977). *Perceiving Women.* New York: Halsted.

Bernard, J. (1981). *The Female World.* New York: Free Press.

Biaggio, Mary Kay, Philip J. Mohan, & Cynthia Baldwin. (1985). "Relationships Among Attitudes Toward Children, Women's Liberation, and Personality Characteristics." *Sex Roles.* 12: 47-62.

Block, Jeanne H. (1984). "Psychological Development of Female Children and Adolescents." In Jeanne H. Block, *Sex Role Identity and Ego Development* (pp. 126-142). San Francisco: Jossey-Bass.

Brownmiller, Susan. (1984). *Femininity.* New York: Linden Press.

de Beauvior, Simone. (1974). *The Second Sex.* New York: Vintage Books.

Erikson, Erik H. (1968). *Identity: Youth and Crisis.* New York: W.W. Norton

Feagin, Joe R. (1982). *Social Problems: A Critical Power-Conflict Perspective.* Englewood Cliffs, NJ: Prentice-Hall.

Feldman, S. E. (1983). "Battered Women: Psychological Correlates of the Victimization Process." Ph.D. dissertation, Ohio State University.

Firestone, Shulamith. (1971). *The Dialectic of Sex: The Case for Feminist Revolution.* New York: William Morrow.

Friedl, Ernestine. (1978). "Society and Sex Roles." *Human Nature,* April.

Gray, Janet Dryfus. (1983). "The Married Professional Woman: An Examination of Her Role Conflicts and Coping Strategies." *Psychology of Women Quarterly,* 7(3): 235-243.

Heilman, Madeline E., & Kathy E. Kram. (1984). "Male And Female Assumptions About Colleagues' Views of Their Competence." *Psychology of Women Quarterly,* 7: 329-337.

Horner, Matina. (1971). "Femininity and Successful Achievement: A Basic Inconsistency." In Michele Hoffnung Garskof, ed., *Roles Women Play*. Monterey, CA: Brooks/Cole.

Lakoff, R. (1975). *Language and Woman's Place*. New York: Harper & Row.

Lee, G. R. (1977). *Family Structure and Interaction*. Philadelphia: Lippincott.

Lenney, Ellen. (1981). "What's Fine for the Gander Isn't Always Good for the Goose: Sex Differences in Self-Confidence as a Function of Ability Area and Comparison with Others." *Sex Roles*, 7: 905-924.

Lott, Bernice. (1985). "The Devaluation of Women's Competence." *Journal of Social Issues*, 41(4): 43-60

Miller, Jean. (1976) *Toward a New Psychology of Women*. Boston: Beacon Press.

Song, Young I. (1991). "Single Asian American Women as a Result of Divorce: Depressive Affect and Changes in Social Support." In Sandra S. Volgy, ed., *Women and Divorce/Men and Divorce: Gender Differences in Separation, Divorce and Remarriage* (Chapter 12). New York: Haworth Press.

———. (1996). *Battered Women in Korean Immigrant Families: The Silent Scream*. New York: Garland.

Song, Young, and E. Kim, eds. (1992). *American Mosaic: Selected Readings on America's Multicultural Heritage*. Englewood Cliffs, NJ: Prentice-Hall.

Toffler, Alvin. (1990). *Power Shift*. New York: Bantam Books.

Index

About the Editors and Contributors

ALICE YUN CHAI, Ph.D., is a retired associate professor of the Women's Studies Program at the University of Hawaii-Manoa. As a member of the faculty of the University of Hawaii-Manoa since 1975, she taught courses and conducted research on feminist anthropology and the history of Asian and Asian American women, women of color, and Third World women. A community activist, Chai is a founding member of the Women's Political Caucus, Gabriela-Hawaii Chapter, and has coordinated a bilingual domestic violence hotline for Korean immigrant women in Hawaii. She is also a founding member of the Women of Color Caucus in 1981 and the Sisters of Color International/Third World Women's Studies in 1991.

HYE KYUNG CHANG, Ph.D., is a senior researcher at the Korean Women's Development Institute, a government-affiliated research branch located in Seoul, Korea, whose primary research and policy development activities focus on women's issues. She received her B.A. and M.A. in political science at Ewha Womens' University in Korea, and earned her Ph.D. in sociology from the University of California at Los Angeles.

DONG SOO KIM, Ph.D., A.C.S.W., is professor of social work at Norfolk State University and is actively involved in the Association of Korean Christian Scholars (AKCS). He is an activist as well as a pioneer on the study of Korean women.

EL-HANNAH KIM, formerly MINZA KIM BOO, is a doctoral candidate at Trinity Theological Seminary, Indiana. She received both her M.A. and Ed.D. at West Virginia University, and her M.S.W. from Howard University in Washington, DC. She served on the Board of Directors of the Association of Korean Christian Scholars (AKCS) and is the Director of the Council of International Program for Youth Leaders and Social Workers at West Virginia University. Formerly a social work professor at Concord College, West Virginia, she is currently an adjunct faculty member of Trinity Theological Seminary, Indiana, and practices as a Christian consultant/scriptural counselor.

GRACE S. KIM, M.A., is a teacher and counselor at Davis Senior High School in Davis, California. Also a Korean newspaper columnist, she writes a "Dear Abby"–like column that gives advice to parents of second-generation children. She holds numerous workshops and seminars with her husband, Luke Kim, on handling intergenerational issues. She also works as an educational consultant.

KWANG CHUNG KIM, Ph.D., is a professor in the Department of Sociology and Anthropology at Western Illinois University. He received his Ph.D. from Indiana University. He is also the co-author (with Won Moo Hurh) of *Korean Immigrants in America: A Structural Analysis of Ethnic Confinement and Adhesive Adaptation* and has contributed numerous articles to academic journals.

LUKE I. KIM, M.D., Ph.D., is clinical associate professor of psychiatry at the University of California, Davis School of Medicine. While his wife, Grace Kim, focuses more on counseling for intergenerational issues/problems, Mr. Kim is an active and well-recognized clinician specializing in cross-cultural mental health issues.

SHIN KIM was professor of economics at Chicago State University. Currently, she is pursuing a doctoral degree in social welfare. She is also co-editor of *The Emerging Generation of Korean-Americans*, 1993.

MIKYONG KIM-GOH, Ph.D., is assistant professor in the Department of Human Services at California State University, Fullerton. She received a B.A. from Pomona College in Claremont, California and her M.S.W. and Ph.D. in social welfare from the University of California, Berkeley. She worked as a psychiatric social worker at the Asian Pacific Counseling and Treatment Center in Los Angeles for several years prior to joining the University. Her teaching areas include social work practice, counseling theories and techniques, and human services for immigrants and refugees. She has also written several scholarly articles on mental health service delivery in Asian American communities, and the psychological impact of community violence on victims.

PYONG GAP MIN, Ph.D., is associate professor of sociology at Queens College of the City University of New York. He has done much research on Korean immigrant entrepreneurship, Korean immigrant families, and ethnic attachment on the part of Korean and other Asian ethnic groups. He teaches race and ethnic relations and Asian American studies, as well as marriage and the family. He is currently conducting a comparative study of three overseas Korean groups (the Koreans in China, Japan, and the United States) in ethnic attachment.

AILEE MOON, Ph.D., is assistant professor in the Department of Social Welfare at the University of California, Los Angeles. She received a B.A. in economics and social welfare, and M.A. and Ph.D. in social welfare, all from the University of California, Berkeley. Her areas of research interest include social welfare finance and policy, program evaluation, and gerontology. She is a highly sought-after expert in the Korean American community on issues dealing with social policy, community services, and gerontology. She has served on the boards of several local social service agencies, including the Korean Youth and Community Center (KYCC) and the Center for the Pacific-Asian Family.

SOOK JA PAIK, Ph.D., A.C.S.W., is professor of social work at Norfolk State University. She is also active in the Association of Korean Christian Scholars. Paik and her husband, Dong Soo Kim, conducted a longitudinal study on Korean adoptees.

GIN YONG PANG, Ph.D., is teaching in the Asian American Studies Department at San Francisco State University. She received her Ph.D. in ethnic studies from the University of California at Berkeley. She is currently working on a book about Asian American intermarriage.

SIYON RHEE, Ph.D., is assistant professor in the Department of Social Work at the California State University, Los Angeles, where she teaches social work practice and human behavior. She received her B.A. in sociology from Seoul National University in South Korea, and her M.A. and Ph.D. in social welfare from the University of California, Los Angeles. Her research activities focus on cross-cultural research with Asian American populations in mental health, family, and aging.

EUNAI KIM SHRAKE received her B.A. and M.A. in Christian education from Presbyterian College and Seminary in Seoul. She was a high school teacher for three years and a teaching instructor at her alma mater before she came to the United States to further her studies. She received her Th.M. in theology at Austin Presbyterian Theological Seminary in Austin, Texas, and is currently an advanced Ph.D. candidate in the Graduate School of Education at the University of California, Los Angeles.

SUNG SIL LEE SOHNG is associate professor at the School of Social Work, University of Washington, Seattle. She teaches cultural diversity and social justice as well as social work practice and participatory research. Her research focuses on the Korean American community—community partnership, minority health issues, and community-based services. She has published numerous articles. Her recent publication topics include the oral history of the early Korean American immigrants and participatory research in community organizing.

YOUNG I. SONG, Ph.D., is professor of sociology and social services and Director of Social Services at California State University, Hayward, where she is affiliated with the women's studies program. She has taught courses on subjects such as sociology of minority groups, minority women, and contemporary women and has also carried out a variety of social work research and practices among Asian American communities. As well as being the former president of the Asian American Social Work Educators Association, she is also the founder of the Korean American Women's Association (KAWA). Her books include *Silent Victims*, 1987; *American Mosaic*, 1993 (with Eugene Kim); *Battered Women in Korean Immigrant Families: The Silent Scream*, 1996; and *Korean*

American Women Living in Two Cultures (with Ailee Moon), 1997. She has also published a number of articles in professional journals.

ISBN 0-275-95977-5

HARDCOVER BAR CODE